THE ENGLISH CIVIL WAR

THE ENGLISH CIVIL WAR

A MILITARY HISTORY OF THE
THREE CIVIL WARS 1642 – 1651

Brigadier Peter Young
D.S.O., M.C., M.A., F.S.A.

AND

Richard Holmes
M.A.

WORDSWORTH EDITIONS

First published in Great Britain in 1974
by Eyre Methuen Limited

This edition published 2000
by Wordsworth Editions Limited
Cumberland House, Crib Street, Ware,
Hertfordshire SG12 9ET

ISBN 1 84022 222 0

Printed and bound in Great Britain
by Mackays of Chatham plc, Chatham, Kent.

CONTENTS

LIST OF MAPS

PREFACE

WELLINGTON ONCE REMARKED that one might as well try to write the history of a ball as that of a battle. Writing the history of the Civil War is, to borrow the duke's metaphor, not unlike describing several different balls, occurring simultaneously in widely separated locations, with a fair proportion of the participants moving back and forth between the ballrooms. The Civil War seems, at first sight, to be a confused and disjointed series of battles, sieges and skirmishes taking place over most of England. It is no easy task to combine these events into a form which makes some sort of sense, without employing a rigid framework relying on lavish use of hindsight, which gives the war an unrealistically well-ordered appearance.

In an effort to obtain coherence without oversimplification, the authors have treated the war regionally, and have in some instances departed from the chronological sequence to do so. The other alternative, to adhere strictly to the chronological sequence, would produce an unduly fragmented picture of widely dispersed events of varying importance. The regional divisions are quite deliberately broad. There are numerous histories, of varying value, which examine the war in particular counties. While recognising the intense local feeling of the period, this is, from the military point of view, an unsatisfactory approach. The war was much more than a disconnected series of local conflicts, and campaigns were not confined within the borders of a single county.

No war, least of all a civil war, is fought in a vacuum. The English Civil War has far-reaching political, economic, social and religious significance. It originated in a complex series of interlocking crises, many of which were only temporarily submerged beneath armed conflict. This history concentrates, however, upon the military aspects of the Civil War. The struggle is placed in its context with regard to political events and social developments, but the reader who seeks a detailed examination of monopolies under Charles I, or a dissertation upon the iron industry of the Weald of Kent, would be well advised to look elsewhere.

A further deliberate limitation of scope is the exclusion of events in Ireland and, to a lesser extent, Scotland, unless they impinge directly upon the situation in England. There was intermittent fighting in Ireland throughout the period in question, and a weighty volume could easily be devoted to this alone.

When examining the armies and commanders of the Civil War one must avoid applying modern standards. Firstly, the art of war in the seventeenth century embodied doctrine and practice which succeeding centuries have transformed almost beyond recognition. Secondly, most of the participants in the Civil War were, in the early stages at least, amateurs, who often had few means at hand for aquiring professional skill. The modern officer, however small his aptitude, and however lacking in originality he may be, has but to turn to manuals and drill books, learned journals and official histories dealing with every aspect of war. In the Civil War it was different. Regimental officers could consult one of the numerous drill books to master the rudiments of infantry or cavalry drill, but there was little to guide more senior officers in the perilous realms of strategy or logistics. Brigades, and even armies, were sometimes commanded by men with no military experience, and without even the doubtful solace of a staff manual. Such men were fortunate indeed if they had a professional officer at their elbow, and more fortunate still if they allowed themselves to heed his advice.

Although the conflicts of the 1640s and 1650s are usually merged under the enveloping title of Civil War, an apter description would be Civil Wars, for there were three separate and clearly divided contests. The First Civil War, which is undoubtedly the most significant, and to which the major part of this work is devoted, stretched from the summer of 1642 to the surrender of the   last Royalist fortress in March 1647. It ended with Charles I a prisoner in the hands of the Scots, and the New Model Army the dominant power in the land. The Second Civil War, combining Royalist revolts in England with a Scottish invasion, began in March 1648 and ended with the battle of Preston and the fall of Colchester in late August the same year. The beheading of the King followed in January 1649, but in June 1650 Charles II raised an army in Scotland, only to be defeated at Dunbar and Worcester, fleeing the country in October 1651. Major military operations ceased with Worcester, but a constitutional crisis and continual Royalist plotting produced an atmosphere of unrest which was dispelled only by the Restoration of Charles II in May 1660.

The authors have adopted a system of sub-headings for events of major importance. These are not designed as summaries of the material that follows them, but rather as a series of signposts for the reader.

For their material on the First Civil War the authors have drawn heavily upon the work of the late Lieutenant-Colonel Alfred H. Burne, D.S.O., F.R. Hist. Soc., a military historian of note whose knowledge of the period was tempered with sound military judgement. In 1959, Peter Young was co-author with Lieutenant-Colonel Burne of *The Great Civil War: A Military History of the First Civil War 1642–1646*. This new book uses the earlier as a starting point for an entirely fresh, considerably enlarged, assessment of the whole conflict.

The author's thanks are due to Zoë Longridge, Marilyn Patrick and Andy Peal, who were faced with the unenviable task of typing from a manuscript which stretched legibility beyond all reasonable limits. Finally, the authors owe a debt of gratitude to Arthur Banks, who designed and produced the maps.

NOVEMBER 1973

P.Y.

E.R.H.

PART ONE

THE ROAD TO WAR
FEBRUARY 1625–AUGUST 1642

Chronology

1625		Death of James I: Accession of Charles I.
		Count Mansfeld's expedition.
1627		Île de Rhé expedition.
		Darnell's case.
1628		Petition of Right.
		Assassination of Buckingham.
March 1629– April 1640		Eleven years' personal rule.
1631		Battle of BREITENFELD.
1632		Thomas, Viscount Wentworth, appointed Lord-Deputy of Ireland.
		Battle of LÜTZEN.
1633		William Laud becomes Archbishop of Canterbury.
1634–7		The Laudian visitation.
1634		First writs for Ship Money issued.
1637		John Hampden tried for refusing to pay Ship Money.
1638		National Covenant signed in Scotland.
1639		First Bishops' War against the Scots, ended by the Treaty of Berwick.
1640	January	Wentworth created Earl of Strafford.
	April	The Short Parliament.
	June	Second Bishops' War; English defeated at Newburn.
	October	Treaty of Ripon ends Bishops' War.
	November	The Long Parliament meets. Impeachment of Strafford.
	December	Impeachment of Laud.
1641	May	Strafford beheaded on Tower Hill.
		Oliver Cromwell and Sir Henry Vane bring in a bill for the abolition of the Episcopacy.
	June	Ship Money declared illegal.
	July	Court of the Star Chamber, Councils of Wales and the North abolished.

	October	Rebellion in Ireland.
	November	The Grand Remonstrance carried by 159 votes to 148.
1642	4 January	The King fails in his attempt to arrest the five members.
	10	The King leaves Whitehall.
	31	Sir John Hotham secures Hull, by direction of Parliament.
1642	23 February	The Queen departs for Holland, taking the Crown Jewels.
	2 March	The King sets out for the North, despite the remonstrances of Parliament. Both Houses resolve that the 'kingdom should be put in a posture of defence', and appoint the Lords Lieutenant as commanders of the militia.
	5	The Militia Ordinance passed.
	19	The King enters York.
	23 April	Sir John Hotham refuses to admit the King to Hull.
	14 May	The King issues a warrant summoning the Horse of the county of York to attend him in arms.
	2 June	The Nineteen Propositions sent to the King.
	9	Parliament passes an ordinance appealing for plate, money and horses.
	12	The King resolves to put into execution the Commissions of Array.
	2 July	The fleet declares for Parliament, and accepts the Earl of Warwick as its admiral.
	15	Parliament appoints the Earl of Essex as captain-general. Skirmish at Manchester between Lord Strange and the townsmen.
		The Queen, at the Hague, gives Prince Rupert his commission as general of the Horse.

One

THE CAUSES OF THE WAR

On Monday 22 August 1642, the Royal Standard of King Charles I was hoisted into the gusty air above Castle Hill at Nottingham. Although this action was not in any way decisive, it did mark a significant turning in the long downward path that led to the English Civil War. The roots of conflict between Monarch and Parliament were firmly earthed in the history of the preceding century. In examining them, the historian must inch his way along a knife edge. A multiplicity of factors contributed to the conflict which drifted into war in the autumn of 1642. To give overwhelming weight to any single factor is to impose a coherence which was certainly lacking at the time, while, on the other hand, simply to catalogue the events which led up to the war is to shirk the evaluation which must, after all, be one of the prime duties of the historian.

The explosive situation of 1642 was brought about by a combination of constitutional, religious and economic pressures. Each of these would, on its own, have been serious but not necessarily fatal. A subtly interlocking combination of all three, superimposed on a background of general European crisis, was to produce the final breakdown.

Each of these three broad crises impinges on the others to a remarkable degree. Certainly, to contemporaries, the lines between politics, economics and religion were thinly drawn; witness, for example, the frequency with which monopolies, an economic irritant to the King's opponents, were branded with the term 'Popish'. The kernels of conflict were deep-seated. King James I, who had succeeded to the throne on the death of Queen Elizabeth in 1603, had been faced with a number of problems, which Puritan intrigue and Stuart mismanagement combined to worsen. James, brought up by Scots Presbyterians, was welcomed by the English Puritans, who hoped that the new monarch would accede to their initially moderate requests for Church reform. James, realising the extent to which the monarchy depended upon the episcopacy, typically summed up the situation in the aphorism 'No Bishop, No King', and unhelpfully warned the Puritans that he would 'harry them out of the land' if they failed to conform with his religious policy. His first meeting with

Parliament proved inauspicious, with the Commons maintaining that they held their privileges as of right rather than by the King's grace.

James had inherited a deficit of £400,000 from Elizabeth, and, as the royal finances worsened, so the King's efforts to recoup himself brought him into renewed conflict with Parliament. It was, indeed, only natural that Parliament should look upon James's money-raising efforts with alarm. As Christopher Hill has pointed out, 'Parliament in the seventeenth century represented exclusively the propertied classes'.[1] In an age of galloping inflation, it became increasingly impossible for the King to 'live of his own' even under normal circumstances. The cost of government was rising alarmingly, and James added to it by the personal extravagance which his predecessor had shunned. The monarch, it is true, had several means at hand by which to raise money, yet most of these served either to alienate a proportion of the propertied classes, to diminish the King's assets, or both. One reliable means of producing ready cash was to sell Crown land. But, as the shrewd Lionel Cranfield, Earl of Middlesex, observed, 'in selling land he [the King] did not only sell his rent, as other men did, but sold his sovereignty, for it was a greater tie of obedience to be a tenant to the King than to be his subject'.[2]

Land was not the only commodity at the monarch's disposal. James also sold patents of nobility; this increased the power of the financial aristocracy, and by increasing its numbers tended to diminish the prestige of the House of Lords. The other various sources of royal finance were the 'ordinary' revenues originating, in the main, from residual feudal dues, ranging from Tunnage and Poundage to the bitterly unpopular Rights of Wardship and Purveyance. There were also 'extraordinary' revenues originally demanded in the time of war, usually taking the form of a subsidy granted by Parliament. It was a sign of the times that James's efforts to increase customs duties – largely justifiable in an age of expanding trade and mounting inflation – were sharply contested. Parliament also endeavoured to destroy the more obnoxious of the lingering feudal dues; the Great Contract of 1610 proposed the abolition of Wardship and Purveyance, in return for a regular income of £200,000 a year. The Great Contract, however, was never implemented, largely because its provisions satisfied neither King nor Parliament. James's own extravagance increased the problems faced by his financial advisers. Robert Cecil, later Earl of Salisbury, and the capable Cranfield, both strove to put the King's finances on a sounder footing by increasing revenue and cutting down the pensions and sinecures of courtiers. This, predictably, failed to appeal to the latter, who combined with the Commons – an unlikely alliance – to thwart these attempts at financial reform.

If relationships between King and Parliament were hardly improved by the monarch's efforts to increase his ordinary revenue, they were positively imperilled by royal appeals for extraordinary revenue. The King's growing

[1] Christopher Hill, *The Century of Revolution* (London 1961), p. 43.
[2] Quoted ibid., p. 47.

dependence on subsidies necessitated the frequent summoning of Parliament, and at the same time provided that body with a means of applying pressure on the Crown. The King could only avoid this by impositions levied by means of the royal prerogative, itself the focal point of the constitutional conflict. King James's exercise of the prerogative was, however, supported by law. In 1606 a city merchant, Bates, was tried for refusing to pay an imposition levied on currants; the judges found for the Crown, and one went on to declare that 'the King's power is double, ordinary and absolute'.[1]

The existence of absolute power could not, logically, be denied. An absolute right, to take action in instances not covered by law, and particularly in the case of national emergency, had to exist. On this supporters both of King and of Parliament were agreed. The question was where this power lay. Did it lie with the King alone, as James or his successor would have claimed? If not, where indeed did it lie? Certainly, no Parliament of James's reign, or even of the early years of Charles's, would have claimed this ultimate power for itself. Parliamentary inability to provide a valid constitutional theory was self-evident. Sir Edward Coke's reliance on legal antiquarianism was one response to this question, and the theory of 'joint sovereignty' of King, Lords and Commons, was another. Neither approach was totally convincing, but both combined to bridge the gap between Parliamentary opposition to the royal prerogative for practical reasons and the final formulation of the doctrine of parliamentary sovereignty.

James I is often condemned for extreme use of the prerogative. In fact, his error lay more in wanton use of power: in tactlessness on a grand scale. He complained to Parliament about the disastrous state of his finances, but at the same time lavished money on a succession of detested favourites. More serious was his failure – or, rather, the failure of his ministers – to manage the House of Commons. Between 1604 and 1629 the 'opposition' seized control, the Speaker ceased to be compliant with royal commands and the King's ministers lost their grip on the House.[2]

When, in February 1625, James died, his son Charles inherited not only his father's problems, but also the cause of many of them – George Villiers, Duke of Buckingham, James's last favourite. With cynical disregard for national sentiment, Buckingham arranged a marriage between Charles and the French Catholic princess, Henrietta Maria. He also promised to help Richelieu in the reduction of the Huguenot stronghold of La Rochelle. It is scarcely surprising that Charles's first Parliament, which met in 1625, began a fierce attack on Buckingham, and was dissolved without granting supply. Even Tunnage and Poundage, traditionally voted to each monarch for life, were withheld. The Parliament of 1626 proved equally intractable. To meet the cost of the war

[1] J. R. Tanner, *Constitutional Documents of the reign of James I* (Cambridge 1960), p. 340.
[2] *See* W. Notestein, *The Winning of the Initiative by the House of Commons* (Ralegh Lecture 1924).

with Spain, begun in the last year of James's reign, as well as the projected campaign against La Rochelle, Charles was compelled to resort to desperate measures. A hopeful appeal for a 'free gift' in July 1626 met with a poor response. Charles then levied Tunnage and Poundage by prerogative, and went on, in September, to demand a forced loan, which was about as unpopular then as a capital levy would be today. Several of those who refused to pay were imprisoned. Five of these unfortunates applied for a writ of habeas corpus, but in Darnell's[1] case (sometimes known as the Case of the Five Knights) in November 1627, the judges maintained that they were imprisoned '*per speciale mandatum domini regis*', a valid exercise of the royal prerogative.

The proceeds from the forced loan were all the more necessary because Buckingham, by a remarkable reversal of policy, had mounted an expedition to relieve La Rochelle. This proved totally fruitless. It was ruinously expensive, and the soldiers, before and after the brief campaign, were billeted on householders in the Southern Counties, giving rise to protests which were soon to be echoed in Parliament. Charles's third Parliament met in 1628, and, in the Petition of Right, declared that both the collecting of taxes without Parliamentary consent, and arbitrary imprisonment, were illegal. The billeting of soldiers in private houses, and the application of martial law to civilians, were likewise prohibited. Significantly, no mention was made of impositions, nor was any action taken against Buckingham. Parliament endeavoured to consolidate its position by granting the King Tunnage and Poundage for a single year only. Charles had been levying this without Parliamentary sanction for three years, and naturally resented any suggestion that it might be subject to control. In the ensuing dispute Parliament was prorogued on 26 June.

Buckingham was assassinated the following month, stabbed by John Felton, a discharged naval officer of Puritan leanings. His death removed the Commons' principal *bête noire*, but the underlying causes of conflict remained. When Parliament reassembled in 1629 the Commons became embroiled in an attack on the ceremonialism of the court clergy, as well as a renewed dispute over existing questions; it was speedily dissolved. Charles now embarked upon a period of eleven years of personal government, during which the religious problem combined with the constitutional crisis to alienate the King from many of his subjects. William Laud, Bishop of London and, from 1633, Archbishop of Canterbury, rose rapidly into royal favour. Laud's many opponents maintained erroneously that he was tainted with Popery. He was, in doctrinal terms, very moderate, but was steadfastly opposed to Calvinism. He therefore endeavoured to enforce religious uniformity and to remove the Puritan threat to the established Church. Laud and his adherents were dependent for their authority upon royal goodwill; thus they naturally supported the King on constitutional questions. The Puritans saw the Arminians, the high-Church followers of Laud,

[1] Sir Thomas Darnell, Bart, was released in 1628. He died in about 1640.

backed by the royal prerogative, as a threat to their very existence, and, conversely, sought safety in the power of Parliament.

Among both the King's supporters and his antagonists, religious and political considerations were closely linked. Laud's rigid insistence on obedience to the letter of the law won him much unpopularity, not only among Puritans but also among the great mass of English Protestants. Laud's opponents were dealt with severely. In 1637, William Prynne,[1] a lawyer, the Reverend Henry Burton and Dr John Bastwick were publically mutilated, heavily fined, and imprisoned by order of the Star Chamber, one of the prerogative courts. The uproar which accompanied this affair stemmed not from the severity of the sentences, for such grisly occurrences were sufficiently commonplace in the seventeenth century, but from the fact that those punished were gentlemen, members of a class traditionally free from the savagery of corporal punishment.

Queen Henrietta Maria was a Roman Catholic, and in 1637 a papal agent was received at Whitehall. Catholicism was bitterly unpopular among the vast majority of the population, who still remembered the Spanish Armada of 1588 and the Gunpowder Plot of King James's time (1605). Any of Laud's measures which made, or seemed to make, life easier for the Catholics, was the object of public condemnation.

Laud was also attacked for his sinister influence on foreign policy. The Elector Palatine, Protestant husband of the Princess Elizabeth, Charles's own sister, had been exiled from his principality by Spanish troops. Shortly before his death, James had sent out a dismally unsuccessful expedition, under Count Mansfeld, to restore him. Charles soon made peace and thereafter maintained excellent relations with Spain. Spanish bullion was landed in England and minted before being used for the payment of the very troops who were harrying Protestants in the Low Countries. Finally, Spanish soldiers – seen, since the days of Elizabeth, as the traditional enemy of Englishmen – were allowed to use English ports in transit from Spain to the fighting in Holland.

Charles's disastrous foreign policy was, in many respects, symptomatic of the two great flaws which were ultimately to bring down his régime. Firstly, lack of money prevented the pursuit of a vigorous foreign policy. The cost of war was rising alarmingly and the necessary finance could be obtained only by recourse to Parliament, which, as had been shown by bitter experience, was likely to make its grant of subsidies subject to unacceptable conditions. It was difficult enough to make ends meet in times of peace. The Court of Wards continued its depredations, and the King's antiquarian lawyers dredged up archaic statutes which permitted the fining of alleged offenders.

In 1634, the King added to his existing exactions by levying Ship Money. This was an extension of the established practice of demanding ships, or money to provide ships, from coastal towns. It could well be argued that, with the

[1] Prynne (1600–69) had lost his ears in the pillory in 1634. He was now branded on both cheeks as well as being deprived of what remained of his ears.

growing strength of the French and Dutch navies, English naval power should be increased. Ship Money was also a technical improvement on other forms of taxation; its collection was centrally controlled, and it was based on a new assessment of income. Charles's attempts to raise Ship Money were, however, hotly contested. The monarch's opponents saw the continued levying of the tax as contrary to the Petition of Right. Moreover, it was apparent that if the King was successful in levying Ship Money year after year, he would not be compelled to summon Parliament at all, and so would be subject to no constraint in his ecclesiastical policy.

These constitutional and religious considerations allied with more mundane economic motives in promoting resistance to Ship Money. In 1637 the question came to a head with the refusal of John Hampden, a wealthy Buckinghamshire landowner, to pay. The resultant case went against Hampden by a narrow margin, seven judges finding for the King and five for Hampden. It was, nevertheless, a moral victory for Charles's opponents. Even the Royalist Clarendon admitted that the case 'left no man anything which he might call his own', and consequently men 'thought themselves bound in conscience to the public justice not to submit. . . .'[1]

The second royal failing, so amply illustrated in foreign policy, was one of administration and, to a degree, of public relations. Charles's foreign policy was clearly out of concert with the wishes of the majority of his subjects, yet the King, unwilling to put his finger on the national pulse, paid no attention to this. He also seemed unaware of the consequences, both for the conduct of his government and for the stature of the monarch in the eyes of his people, of the composition, behaviour and attitude of his court. James I had surrounded himself with a selection of worthless spendthrifts, and failed to support his more capable advisers who endeavoured to contest governmental inefficiency and court extravagance. Charles, while not sharing his father's liking for 'gaudy young men', was surrounded by individuals bent on power, privilege and financial gain. Against this unedifying backcloth, Charles appeared before his nation. Like his father he lacked the fine mixture of easy familiarity and regal aloofness which had so characterised the Tudors. Instead, he created Divine Right into a way of life, living in pallid elegance in a court whose extravagances offended those who resented paying taxes for its upkeep, as well as those who had tried and failed to gain entrance to its privileged circle. The King's support of Arminianism, together with his admiration for the Catholic monarchies of France and Spain, and his failure to aid the Continental Protestants during the Thirty Years War, superimposed new strains on the existing tension between court and country, and between Arminian and Puritan.

Charles's victory in the Ship Money case seemed to indicate that, for the time at least, personal rule remained secure. It was not destined to remain so

[1] Edward Hyde, Earl of Clarendon, *The History of the Rebellion* . . . (Oxford 1826, 8 vols), Vol. 1, p. 123.

for long. Events in Scotland were to bring about the upheaval that led to its downfall. James, with rash disregard for the heavy opposition which greeted him, had reintroduced bishops into Scotland. Charles compounded this miscalculation with an attempt to recover Church lands from the nobles into whose hands they had fallen. The final blunder was the attempt, in 1637, to introduce a new liturgy into Scotland. This provoked a fierce outburst of organised resistance, which the weak royal governmental machinery in Scotland could do little to contain. Early in 1638 the National Covenant, a strongly worded statement of belief, was signed throughout the country. An assembly, meeting at Glasgow, declared episcopacy abolished. Charles made efforts to coerce the Scots into submission. They responded to royal threats of force by raising an army under Alexander Leslie, a veteran of the Thirty Years War. Charles's attempt at invasion failed to get under way, and he was forced to conclude the Treaty of Berwick. The King, however, regarded this as little better than a truce and summoned Thomas Wentworth, Earl of Strafford, from Ireland. Strafford had been involved in the Parliamentary opposition to Charles in the 1620s; the *volte-face* by which he accepted a peerage and later the Lord Lieutenancy of Ireland, earned him the undying hatred of his erstwhile Parliamentary colleagues. Strafford's ability made him all the more unpopular; Charles's opponents were plagued by the nightmare of Strafford's return to England with an Irish army at his back.

When, however, he arrived in England in the autumn of 1639, Strafford brought no assistance but his energetic personality. He advised Charles to call a Parliament and procure from it sufficient money to raise an army for the invasion of Scotland. The King complied, and on 13 April 1640 Charles's personal rule ended when the Short Parliament met at Westminster. It refused to grant supply unless its grievances were redressed, and it was speedily dissolved. In these unpropitious circumstances Charles embarked upon the disastrous Second Bishops' War. The sullen, unwilling and hastily levied forces which shambled north in the early summer of 1640 deserted in droves, mutinied, and showed their religious sympathies by setting fire to the new communion rails in churches. A Devonshire contingent murdered one of its officers who was suspected of Catholicism.[1] The Scots met this rabble at Newburn on Tyne, and routed it with little difficulty. With Northumberland and Durham occupied, and the Scots before Newcastle, Charles had little option but to sue for peace. The Scots demanded compensation at the rate of £850 a day until the signing of a treaty, and Charles was forced to turn to Parliament for support.

The Long Parliament met in early November. This time the King's opponents held the whip hand, for his urgent need for money prevented Charles from dissolving Parliament. Pym, the leader of the 'Opposition', was in contact with the Scots, and exploited the royal weakness to the full. Strafford was sent to the

[1] *See* C. H. Firth, *Cromwell's Army* (London 1962), pp. 13–14.

Tower, where he was later joined by Laud. The Commons' first stroke against Strafford, impeachment before the Lords, failed, but was rapidly followed by an Act of Attainder which brought Charles's ablest servant to the block. Charles consented to Strafford's death with the greatest reluctance, hoping that it would act as a safety valve for the turbulent emotions raging in Parliament and the City. He was wrong. Even before Strafford died, Parliament had opened a determined attack upon royal authority.

The Triennial Act laid down that Parliament should meet at least once every three years, and provided a mechanism whereby Parliament could be summoned should the Crown neglect to do so. The prerogative courts, including the hated Star Chamber, were abolished and all non-Parliamentary taxes were declared illegal. A further Act decreed that this Parliament should not be dissolved without its own consent; it has become known to history as the Long Parliament. Ironically enough Charles approved this measure on the same day that he gave the royal assent to Strafford's attainder. Had the constitutional question been the only issue at stake between King and Parliament, it is possible that the conflict might have ended there – at least for a time.

The religious problem, however, remained. While there had been a great degree of unanimity within Parliament over the constitutional issue, such agreement was lacking in matters of religion. There was, it is true, a general wish to subordinate Church as well as State to Parliamentary, rather than Royal, authority. But beneath this broad agreement lurked two divergent views. The Root and Branch Petition of 1640 and the so-called Root and Branch Bill epitomised the views of religious extremists, seeking a total abolition of Episcopacy and the Book of Common Prayer. A more moderate view found expression in the Bill on Church Reform, read twice in the Lords in early July 1641. This Bill sought not to abolish the bishops, but to compel them to preach regularly and to deprive them of temporal authority.

Events in Scotland, then, had necessitated the calling of the Long Parliament, thus ending Charles's personal rule. The Treaty of Ripon concluded the Second Bishops' War. The Scots withdrew in September 1641, while efforts were made to pay off the English forces as quickly as possible. If Scotland had kindled the fires of conflict between King and Parliament, Ulster fanned the flames to an unprecedented ferocity. With the removal of the 'Thorough' Strafford, power in Ireland had passed into the hands of the Puritan Lords Justices. In October, latent discontent broke into rebellion. There was a general rising in Ulster; the native Irish, who had lost their estates to English and Scots colonists, and whose religion made them subject to restrictive legislation, fell upon the interlopers. Although an attempt on Dublin Castle failed, English possessions were in danger of being overrun. Hundreds of Protestants were butchered, or died of ill-treatment, and in England rumour magnified and distorted these atrocities. There was widespread suspicion of royal complicity in the rebellion – suspicion which was fostered by forged royal commissions in the hands of the rebels.

Parliament at once determined to raise an army for the suppression of the rebellion, but, not unnaturally, was disinclined to entrust its command to a royal nominee.

The crisis in Ireland thus impinged directly upon the constitutional conflict. While the majority of the Lords and a substantial minority of the Commons were satisfied with the measures of constitutional reform already enacted, the extremists considered that more radical legislation was necessary. The issue was one of trust. Pym and his colleagues lacked confidence in Charles's desire to conform with the Parliamentary restrictions recently imposed upon him. On 8 November Pym pushed through the Commons a request for the King 'to employ such counsellors and ministers as shall be approved by his Parliament ... that so his people may with courage and confidence undergo the charge and hazard of this war. ...'[1] But the extremists' control over the Commons was diminishing, reduced both by the religious split and by the increasing unwillingness of many members to embark upon what seemed a revolutionary course of action, unbuttressed by 'fundamental law'. The Grand Remonstrance, an outspoken criticism of Charles's eleven years of personal rule, was carried by the narrow margin of eleven votes after a long and tumultuous debate. Charles returned to London from Scotland on 25 November, and six days later was presented with the Remonstrance. Armed conflict might yet have been averted despite the roarings of the London mob. Parliament still had firm control over royal finances, and by withholding Tunnage and Poundage could threaten the King with bankruptcy. Charles, however, counting on the conservatism which he was convinced prevailed in both Houses, overplayed his hand. Alarmed by a rumour, probably spread by Pym's agents, that the Commons intended to impeach the Queen, Charles ordered his Attorney-General to impeach six of his main opponents: Lord Mandeville and the 'five members' – John Pym, John Hampden, Sir Arthur Hesilrige, Denzil Holles and William Strode. Charles hoped that, with the troublemakers removed, the conservative element in Parliament would assume control. On the following day, 4 January, Charles made his greatest tactical blunder. He appeared at the House of Commons, escorted by some 300 well-armed followers, and demanded the five members.[2] But, warned by Lady Carlisle, to whom the Queen had foolishly disclosed the plan, his 'birds had flown' and found shelter in the City, which was still at fever pitch. On 6 January a royalist descent on London was believed imminent; the gates of the City were shut, and a host of the citizens turned out in arms. The sight of the City's armed readiness was too much for Charles, and on

[1] Gardiner, *Constitutional Documents of the Puritan Revolution* (Oxford 1962), p. 200.

[2] Opinions vary on the amount of force used or implied on this celebrated occasion. Although Clarendon maintains that the King was attended 'only by his usual guard' (op. cit., Vol. II, p. 126), the Commons debate on the subject tells of 'a great multitude of men, armed in warlike manner with halberds, swords and pistols. ...' These worthies allegedly brandished their weapons in a threatening manner, and gave vent to such cries as 'A pox take the House of Commons, let them come and be hanged'. (Gardiner, op. cit., pp. 238–9.)

10 January he left his capital to the mercy of the mob and the extremists in Parliament. He was never to return as a free man.

Once away from London, the King was beset by conflicting advice. One militant clique, supported by the Queen, backed any measures, however violent, which would end the incipient rebellion. More reasonable advice came from the group which had included Edward Hyde and Lord Falkland, men who had supported the early reforms of 1640–1, and had only joined the King's party when the Grand Remonstrance seemed to them to carry matters too far. Charles chose, characteristically, the worst of compromises. He paid lip service to the aims of the latter group, thereby retaining its support, without which his cause would have been hopeless. At the same time, he cherished the ambition of crushing the 'rebellion' by force. Negotiations with Parliament were soon resumed, but were impeded by Charles's insincerity and Pym's intransigence. Charles endeavoured to secure Portsmouth and Hull, sent the Queen abroad with instructions to raise money, arms and troops on the Continent, and then made his way to York, in an attempt to concentrate his northern adherents. The question of the Irish army remained a focal point of conflict. Neither side dared let the other have control of this force. Parliament failed to gain royal approval of its Militia Bill, giving command to the Lords Lieutenant of the counties, but nevertheless passed the measure as an ordinance, and although, without the royal assent, it lacked the force of law, Parliament treated this and its other ordinances as legally valid, and won de facto recognition for its authority, at least in London and the adjoining counties.

The passing of the Militia Ordinance brought war one step nearer. Many members of both Houses, alarmed both by the increasingly radical nature of Parliamentary measures, which sought to seize rather than modify sovereignty, and by the violence of the London mob,[1] journeyed north to join the King. With the departure of many of the moderates, the Puritan extremists gained a firmer control at Westminster. On 1 June both Houses approved the Nineteen Propositions, which were sent to the King at York. These laid down revolutionary changes. They would, in practical terms, have taken sovereignty from the King and placed it in the hands of Parliament. To the King, the propositions were anathema, and other sections of the political nation, too, found them unacceptable. They threatened to replace royal tyranny by Parliamentary despotism.

Growing extremism within Parliament in the first half of 1642, together with the continuing social disorder, considerably strengthened the King's party. On 12 June, Charles issued Commissions of Array, summoning the county militias. Exactly a month later, both Houses of Parliament voted to raise an army, and placed it under command of the Earl of Essex. Both sides set about raising troops, faced with the difficult task of subjecting a pacific populace to the stresses of civil war.

[1] It should be noted that unrest was not confined only to volatile London. There were serious outbreaks of violence in many other parts of the country.

Two

THE NATION DIVIDED

Just as the war itself originated in a multiplicity of causes, so the nation was divided along a series of irregular, jagged lines which defy simple interpretation in clear-cut social, religious, geographical or economic terms. It was in no sense a class war, a conflict between the nobility and commoners or even between Court and Parliament. Both Houses of Parliament – and indeed, the 'ruling class' at all levels, from great nobles to country gentlemen – were split. They were, it is true, not split evenly. A majority of peers supported the King; yet divisions here, as in other legal or social groups, often seem strangely illogical. It would appear natural for the most recently created peers to adhere to the monarchy – but this was far from being universally true. Charles found to his cost that gratitude was at the best an uncertain motive. Of the holders of more ancient titles, some opposed the King because of his recent actions in cheapening the nobility, or because they had been denied lucrative office at court. Many endeavoured to hedge the decision altogether, attempting an uneasy neutrality, while others changed sides during the course of the war.[1] In the early stages of the conflict, peers played an important part on the Parliamentarian side; Essex, Manchester, Saye and Sele, Stamford, and Warwick being among the most notable. As the war went on, however, it became apparent that even the most steadfastly Parliamentarian among the peers had retained a high degree of social conservatism, and tended to oppose both parliamentary radicalism and military decisiveness.

A great deal of research has been conducted on the alignment of members of the House of Commons.[2] It would seem that the eventual division of members between King and Parliament cannot be directly associated with social position or economic background. Two factors which may be significant are that Parliamentarian members were, on the whole, ten years older than their

[1] The Earls of Holland, Bedford and Clare were but three of the prominent men who changed sides.
[2] See particularly D. Brunton and D. H. Pennington, *Members of the Long Parliament* (London 1954).

Royalist colleagues and tended to have been more active in the committees of the pre-war House.

As hostilities gained momentum, it became increasingly difficult for prominent men in the provinces to avoid direct involvement. In many areas, the existing pattern of local alliances and animosities decided alliance to King or Parliament. Local magnates with a tradition of mutual hostility or rivalry would be unlikely to join the same side; the adherence of one to Parliament could be the signal for the other to join the King. Self-interest in its more basic forms also played its part. If a locality was occupied by troops, there was a strong and not unreasonable incentive for local gentlemen to declare themselves in favour of whichever cause those forces chanced to represent.

In general, in most areas there were two parties – one supporting the King and the other Parliament. The relative strength of the groups was dependent upon a mixture of local and national factors. The more economically advanced areas, including rural clothing areas, tended to be strongly anti-Royalist – though even these men were never universally pro-Parliament. It can be argued that the economic policy of the Stuarts had worked in opposition to the manufacturing and trading interests of the nation; but some merchants had undoubtedly profited by royal economic policy. London, and the other principal ports, with the possible exception of Bristol and Newcastle, were strongly Parliamentarian. This was of considerable significance. The main arsenals of the country were speedily seized by the King's enemies, and Parliamentarian possession of the major ports made the task of importing munitions both costly and hazardous for the Royalists.

If economics did not provide the political nation with a clear line of cleavage, neither did religion. Oliver Cromwell himself admitted that religion 'was not the thing at first contested for'. There was, it is true, an inclination among moderate Anglicans to support the King, while those whose beliefs fell within the broadening bracket of Puritanism tended to support Parliament. Yet a man's religion in no sense guaranteed his political allegiance to one side or the other. Many Catholics, for example, preferred to lie low rather than support Charles, whose toleration deserved their loyalty. But at least none of them fought for the Parliament. Religion, perhaps more than any other issue, became clouded by propaganda; the Parliamentarians branded their enemies as loose-living Papists to a man, while the King's adherents reviled their opponents as crop-headed, psalm-singing Puritans. There was little more than a grain of truth in either of these vituperative generalisations. The life-style and mode of dress, certainly amongst the officers, on either side was not notably different. Both tended to wear long hair, and flamboyance was a common feature in the military dress of the day. Until the formation of the New Model Army both armies raped and plundered, especially when lack of pay compelled them to live by marauding. Yet there were commanders on either side who strove to impose good discipline. Nor did England witness horrors to equal the worst excesses of the Thirty Years War; Leicester and Bolton cannot justly be compared with the sack of Magdeburg.

There was little enthusiasm for the war, save among a small minority on either side. Sir Edmund Verney, a Puritan, was faced with a dilemma that must have confronted many men in the hectic months of 1642; he hated the prospect of civil war, and hoped that the King would yield to the demands made by Parliament. Yet, after much heart-searching, he wrote: 'I have eaten his bread and served him near thirty years, and will not do so base a thing as to forsake him; and choose rather to lose my life (which I am sure to do) to preserve and defend these things which are against my conscience to preserve and defend.'[1] Verney spoke prophetically; he was killed two months later at Edgehill. The motives of others were less clear. Sir John Gell of Derbyshire joined Parliament, although, as the Puritan Mrs Hutchinson wrote, 'no man knew for what reason... for he had not understanding enough to judge the equity of the cause, or piety or holiness, being a foul adulterer all the time he served the Parliament, and so unjust that without remorse he suffered his men indifferently to plunder both honest men and cavaliers ...'.[2]

Whatever the political complexion of the England of 1642, militarily the country was pale indeed. Sir Charles Firth described the history of the Civil War as 'the evolution of an army out of chaos',[3] going on to point out that the military system of the Stuarts was lamentably inefficient, and illustrating the military impotence of the nation under James I. However, though peace had prevailed in England for well over a century, Europe had for some time echoed to the sounds of gunfire, and many Englishmen had had a chance to learn their trade abroad. The States of Holland employed four English and four Scots regiments of Foot, and there were also English regiments in the service of Spain and France. Numerous Englishmen and more Scots had served in the Swedish army of Gustav Adolf, and profited by their close acquaintance with the military innovations made by that remarkable commander. Mansfeld's abortive expedition, and Buckingham's equally fruitless descent upon La Rochelle, also served to provide officers and men with military experience of a sort. So did the disastrous Bishops' Wars. After the rout at Newburn in August 1640, a degree of discipline was instilled into at least some of the English levies. On 10 September the King reviewed 2,000 Horse and 1,000 Foot at York, and 'they looked very well to the eyes of civilian observers. Secretary Vane ventured the opinion that Gustav Adolf had never had better. With these, and Strafford's boasted army from Ireland, the Scots were as good as dead men.'[4]

[1] *Verney Memoirs* (London 1892, 4 vols), Vol. I, p. 277. Sir Edmund was a monopolist, and was in receipt of a court pension, which no doubt influenced his decision. His eldest son espoused the cause of Parliament, while the other two fought for the King.
[2] Lucy Hutchinson, *Memoirs of the life of Colonel Hutchinson* (London 1885, 2 vols), Vol. I, p. 180.
[3] Firth, op. cit., p. 1.
[4] C. V. Wedgwood, *The King's Peace* (London 1958), p. 352.

There was, naturally, a scramble for the services of such professional officers as were available. Parliament even went so far as to give half pay to unemployed officers on the pretext that they would be given commands in Ireland. In July 1642, a broadsheet was published in London, entitled *A List of the Names of Such Persons who are Thought to be Fit for Their Accommodation and the Furtherance of the Service in Ireland, to be Entertained as Reformadoes.* . . . This list included 30 officers of Horse and 138 of Foot. Sixty-three of these officers served in the Earl of Essex's army, while more than 30 were to hold Royalist commissions.

But what of trained rank and file? There was no standing army, but local defence was in the hands of the Trained Bands. These were militia units raised by each county, and not bound to serve beyond their boundaries. They were, in the main, of indifferent quality. They drilled for only a few days each year; Colonel Ward, in his *Animadversions of Warre*, described these sessions as 'matters of disport and things of no moment'.[1] Ward goes on to describe how 'after a little careless hurrying over their postures, with which the companies are nothing bettered, they make them charge their muskets, and so prepare to give their captain a brave volley of shot at his entrance into his inn: where after having solaced themselves for a while after this brave service every man repairs home, and that which is not so well-taught then is easily forgotten before the next training'.

Yet the London Trained Bands presented a different picture. In the autumn of 1642 they numbered 6,000 men organised in six regiments.[2] All the colonels were aldermen, and the force as a whole was commanded by Major-General Phillip Skippon, an experienced soldier and a veteran of the Dutch service. Clarendon describes him as 'a man of good order and sobriety, and untainted with any of those vices which the officers of that army were exercised in'. He was, though, 'altogether illiterate'.[3] Many of these citizen soldiers took their military art seriously. Small groups of them met at the Artillery Garden in Bishopsgate, and the Military Garden in St Martin's Field, where they received training from professional officers.

The lameness of Charles I's military system had been demonstrated with embarrassing clarity in the Bishops' Wars. The problem posed to both sides at the outbreak of the Civil War was, then, immense; they were faced with the task of raising, training and equipping armies, at a time when weapons were becoming increasingly sophisticated and costly, and military innovations made up-to-date training the *sine qua non* of success. All this had to be accomplished in a nation which lacked any sizeable cadre of trained men.

[1] Robert Ward, *Animadversions of Warre* . . . (London 1639), p. 30. Bad though the Trained Bands were, Ward's scathing comments are not true of all of them. It was the Cornish *posse comitatus* that drove the Roundheads from the county at the battle of Braddock Down; some northern units, too, proved pugnacious and effective.

[2] Originally the Red, White, Yellow, Blue, Green and Orange Regiments. These were reinforced by several regiments of auxiliaries, and by a small number of dragoons.

[3] Clarendon, op. cit., Vol. II, p. 165.

Both sides were confronted by the problem of providing equipment for their newly raised armies. Here the Roundheads had the advantage, for they held London, and with it the Tower, England's principal armoury. Soon the armouries at Hull and Portsmouth were also in Parliamentarian hands. The possession of London was an asset to the Roundheads in other respects. The 6,000 men of the Trained Bands gave the Earl of Essex a nucleus of trained infantry, a sort of strategic reserve; moreover, the London Bands, unlike those of other counties, would, on occasion, consent to serve away from home.[1] The Cornish *posse comitatus*, though formidable at home, would not go abroad into Devon.

'Moneys,' as Charles himself observed, 'are the nerves of war.' The City of London provided Parliament with weighty financial backing which was, in the long run, bound to outweigh the voluntary contributions of the King's supporters. Many of the magnates who rallied to the King were, it is true, very rich men, but their assets were often tied up in land, timber and mines, and they could not be realised speedily or at a fair valuation. Nevertheless, particularly during the early stages of the war, personal fortunes were lavished on paying and equipping troops.

Parliament's possession of the main government arsenals gave the Roundheads an early advantage in matters of equipment. The Royalists relied upon six main sources for the provision of arms and equipment; foreign purchase, capture, improvisation, the magazines of the Trained Bands, the resources of cities, towns and universities, and, finally, private armouries and stables.

Foreign purchase was vital. Large quantities of arms came in from Holland, avoiding the blockade imposed by the fleet which, in July 1642, had declared for Parliament. The Stadtholder Frederick Henry of Orange backed Charles beyond the limits of diplomacy; on several occasions Dutch men-of-war intervened to protect Royalist merchantmen from the attentions of Parliamentarian warships.[2] Capture was another fruitful source of equipment. Early victories gave the Cavaliers a rich haul of horses, arms, ammunition and ordnance. The western army profited most from this and, indeed, perhaps could not have kept the field at all without such windfalls.

The magazines of the county Trained Bands were useful to both sides. They were, though, much more important to the Royalists, as the Parliamentarians already had control of the much better stocked arsenals of the Tower and of Hull. Charles mustered the Trained Bands on his advance south from York, enlisted those who were prepared to fight for him, and used the arms of the remainder to equip his levies.

Private arsenals were an equally useful source of supply. Such armouries were by no means rare. Noblemen, like Lord Paulet or Lord Mohun, could

[1] They could not be relied upon to do so for any length of time; witness Sir William Waller's repeated trouble with his Trained Band contingent.
[2] Prince Rupert narrowly escaped capture off Flamborough Head in early August 1642, thanks to a Dutch vessel which ran out its guns to deter a Parliamentarian man-of-war.

even provide small pieces of artillery. Nor were private arsenals confined to magnates. Captain Richard Atkyns of Tuffley, Gloucestershire, who raised a troop of Horse early in 1643, mustered sixty men in one month, 'almost all of them well armed; Master [John] Dutton giving me thirty steel backs, breasts and head pieces, and two men and horses completely armed. . . .'[1] Captain Robert Millington, who commanded a company of Foot at Edgehill, brought with him eighty muskets which were his own property.[2]

Cities, towns, and the universities also provided the Royalists with an assortment of arms. Although the main centres of arms production – London, Birmingham and the Weald of Kent – were in the hands of the Roundheads, the Cavaliers made serious attempts to remedy the deficiencies. Oxford, the Royalist capital, became the scene of frenzied activity. A powder-mill was set up in the ruins of Osney Abbey, and a sword factory at Wolvercote. Uniforms for the Foot were manufactured in the schools from cloth seized in Gloucestershire. York, Newark and Exeter also witnessed similar, though less diverse, activity.

Despite these various sources of supply, the Royalist army never was fully equipped, though it took only a short time for Parliamentarian forces to attain a satisfactory level of equipment. Clarendon gives a depressing picture of the Royalist armament for the Edgehill campaign. Some arms had been received from Holland and still more borrowed from the Trained Bands. Thanks to these expedients 'the Foot (all but 300 or 400 who marched without any weapon but a cudgel) were armed with muskets, and bags for their powder, and pikes; but in the whole body there was not one pikeman had a corselet, and very few musketeers who had swords'.[3] Things were little better with the mounted arm. 'Amongst the Horse, the officers had their full desire if they were able to procure old backs and breasts and pots, with pistols for their two or three first ranks, and swords for the rest; themselves (and some soldiers by their examples) having gotten, besides their pistols and swords, a short pole-axe.'[4]

It was, then, a country short of both military equipment and martial skill that, in the summer of 1642, witnessed the raising of two armies. Both, of necessity, consisted of amateurs of varying degrees of aptitude and enthusiasm, with a leaven of professionals. The war cut unevenly across social, economic and religious groupings. Men followed the dictates of conscience, the habit of obedience, or often the simple instinct of self-preservation. The Parliamentarians had the advantage in terms of material resources, with the fleet, the City, and the country's main arsenals under their control, while the Royalists, under-equipped, strove to make up their deficiencies in armaments from numerous

[1] *Military Memoirs; Richard Atkyns and John Gwyn*, edited by Brigadier Peter Young and Norman Tucker (London 1967), p. 7.
[2] Petition, Bod. Lib. Rawl. MS. D. 18, f. 27.
[3] Clarendon, op. cit., Vol. III, pp. 265–6.
[4] Loc. cit.

sources. The detailed organisation of each army differed slightly, but both forces were organised along similar lines. Tactics, too, would vary only to a very limited extent. This similarity is scarcely surprising, for both armies based their organisation on the standard form prevailing in pre-Civil War England, and their tactics on the numerous drill books available, tempered with innovations tried in the crucible of Continental warfare.

Three

ORGANISATION AND TACTICS

The English Civil War occurred when the military art was undergoing rapid change. This 'military revolution' was to have far-reaching impact, not only on the conduct of war itself but also upon the attitude, orientation and political priority of European nations. The heavy, armoured horsemen had been the dominant force in medieval warfare; the mass of untrained feudal infantry all too often had no other function than to fall in despairing huddles before the swords of the victorious cavalry. The supremacy of the feudal chivalry was challenged by three very different forces. The English longbowmen of Crécy, Poitiers and Agincourt gave an early demonstration of the effectiveness of missile weapons. The gradual replacement of the longbow by the hand gun, however, led to a decrease in the effectiveness of these arms. In the words of Michael Roberts, 'the period of military history which extends from Charles the Bold to Tilly is marked above all by a catastrophic diminution in the fire-power of the infantry arm'.[1] Nevertheless, infantry firepower continued to limit the value of cavalry.

The second, more potent, check to the dominance of the horseman came from the rise of disciplined infantry employing shock tactics in tightly massed formations. The steady hedgehogs of Swiss pikes disposed effectively of the Burgundian cavalry at Grandson and Morat (1476). The Swiss, though, suffered from manifold weaknesses; they failed to pay attention to tactical innovations, lacked any means of planning a strategy to match their tactics, and were extremely vulnerable to gunfire. Notwithstanding these defects, until their great defeat at Marignano in 1515, the Swiss infantry struck terror into the hearts of all who heard their heavy tread and saw their mobile forests of pikes and halberds. The third influence on the decline of cavalry was the Hussite *Wagenburg*, using war-wagons mounting light guns, but this was a tactic of very limited application.

By the close of the sixteenth century one of the crucial questions facing military theorists was the correct composition of infantry formations, that is, the proportion of missile to pole arms, pikes, halberds and the like. Conversely,

[1] Michael Roberts, *Essays in Swedish History* (London 1967), p. 57.

34

the rôle of cavalry provided these theorists with another problem. The development of trained infantry, equipped with bows, muskets and pikes, made life unpleasant for the horseman. Hitherto his rôle had lain primarily in shock action, but it was becoming increasingly inadvisable to charge hedgehogs of pikes interlaced with musketeers. The cavalry's response was a complex manoeuvre known as the caracole. Horsemen, in deep formation, approached the opposing infantry at a trot. The front rank discharged its pistols at the Foot and trotted to the rear, allowing the second and successive ranks to repeat the process. The difficulty was that the wheel-lock pistol was outranged by the musket and, on occasion, even by the pike. Furthermore, as generations of horsemen have found to their discomfort, a horse does not make the steadiest of weapon platforms.

The Spanish *tercio* was one solution to the infantry dilemma. In its basic form, the *tercio* was a 3,000-strong mass of pikemen surrounded by musketeers, with extra sleeves of shot at the corners. It thus combined firepower with shock action, but did so in a manner which tended to be wasteful and inflexible. This factor, coupled with the prevalence of mercenaries with a vested dislike of bloody or conclusive engagements, and the growing difficulty of bringing a battle to a decisive end, by shock action, led to stagnation, from which the art of war was rescued only by the reforms of the Dutch Prince Maurice of Orange. Maurice devised a novel infantry unit, the battalion, which was drawn up in shallow formation, thus making better use of the available manpower. Maurice's small battalions were certainly not the whole answer to the military problem, and new, smaller *tercios*, wooden though they were, proved their worth on countless battlefields until Rocroi (1643).

It was left to Gustav Adolf to complete the process which Maurice had begun. The Swedish King drew up his infantry in units even shallower than the Dutch battalions, with only six ranks to Maurice's ten. Firing was originally conducted by the process of the countermarch, in which each rank fired, then marched to the rear of the formation to reload. Gustav soon replaced this with the salvo, in which the musketeers formed up only three deep, and all fired at once. The pikemen then clinched the decision by pressing forward into the disordered enemy ranks.

A logical development from the flexible, aggressive Swedish battalion was the celebrated Swedish brigade. Here, three or four battalions were combined, often into a wedge-shaped formation, with one battalion in reserve. Added firepower was provided by the light 'regimental piece', anything up to a three-pounder, firing roundshot or grape, which had a devastating anti-personnel effect at close range.

Gustav's reform of cavalry tactics was no less startling than his innovations in infantry and artillery. His most significant contribution to the mounted arm was the reintroduction of shock action. The wheeling trot of the caracole was abandoned, and the depth of formations consequently reduced to six ranks – on some occasions, to three.[1] Horsemen were trained to reserve their fire as long as possible, and then fire only once before going in with the sword. Colonel Robert Munro describes how at Breitenfeld, 'the resolution of our horsemen ... was praiseworthy, seeing that they never loosed a pistol at the enemy till they first discharged theirs'.[2] Gustav appreciated, though, that cavalry had little chance of breaking steady Foot unless the infantry were first shaken by fire. The Swedish King accomplished this by the use of 'commanded' musketeers attached to the cavalry. This was far from an ideal solution, for the musketeers, encumbered with musket, bandolier and musket rest, had little chance of keeping pace even with trotting cavalry. Nevertheless, the technique of employing musketeers in this fashion provided the Horse with a degree of firepower, without sacrificing their potential for the cavalryman's primary rôle of shock action.

On Wednesday 17 September 1631, Gustav met the Imperialist generals Pappenheim and Tilly at Breitenfeld, near Leipzig. Gustav had already demonstrated his own brilliance and the determination of his Swedes on several battlefields, but it was Breitenfeld which proved the worth of his military reforms. The Imperialist generals drew up in the traditional formation, with infantry in the centre, and cavalry hovering on the wings. The Swedes formed up checkerwise, with cavalry on each flank, interlaced with bodies of musketeers. If this came as a surprise to Tilly, so too did the staccato rapidity of Swedish musketry, the result of careful training and long practice. A determined thrust by Pappenheim against the Swedish right was briskly repulsed. Tilly seized this opportunity to attack the already shaken troops on the Swedish left; Gustav's unlucky Saxon allies broke in disorder, leaving the Swedes exposed to the onslaught of Tilly's Horse. An army drawn up on conventional formation could not have withstood this shock, but the flexibility of the Swedish brigade enabled Gustav's harassed troops to face the assault. Gustav then committed his fresh reserve of cavalry, cut off the enemy's Horse from his Foot, and pushed the exhausted Imperialists in rout down the Leipzig road.

The tactics which had won Breitenfeld were adopted in due course by most of the contending armies in the Thirty Years War. Changes occurred only gradually and often in a very diluted form. In England, the impact of the military developments of the Thirty Years War was lessened both by geographical isolation and by the lack of any military machine upon which reforms could take effect.

TERRAIN

Tactics are determined largely by the characteristics of the weapons in use at the time, and the ground over which conflict takes place. Towns in the England of

[1] This appears to have been done first at Breitenfeld. *See The Swedish Intelligencer* (London 1632–5), I, p. 124.
[2] *Monro his Expedition with the Worthy Scots Regiment* (1637), Pt II, p. 69.

the 1640s were pitifully small, and industry primitive, by today's standards. The nature of the countryside was rural/agricultural rather than urban/industrial. Communications were poor. Before the days of Macadam, even main roads were badly surfaced, rutted and potholed by the effects of weather and transport. Small loads were carried on pack-horses, while heavier burdens made the jolting journey in heavy wagons, bucketing from rut to rut along the uneven surface. Most travellers rode, and the going could be rough even for a single mounted man. Rain turned the road-surface into a quagmire; wagons sank into the mud, and horses splashed dangerously among the potholes. Such roads imposed enormous limitations upon military movement, in particular that of artillery and supplies.

John Ogilby's monumental *Britannia* of 1675 illustrates the road system of the late seventeenth century. Roads followed, in most cases, their present routes. There were, however, some significant deviations,[1] often where modern engineering has enabled a road to overcome a gradient or land surface. Where possible, heavy equipment, in particular siege artillery, was sent along rivers, or even by sea, though the latter method was of more use to the Parliamentarians, who held command of the sea, though not everywhere in great strength.

Seventeenth-century England was predominantly rural, yet its country districts looked very different from today's. Of course, a few areas were much more enclosed in the seventeenth century than they are now – the ground over which the first Battle of Newbury was fought is a good example – and such enclosed areas were often a network of small hedges criss-crossing the surface of the land. But the enclosing of the countryside took place, generally speaking, during the eighteenth century. Woods were more common, and of greater extent, in the seventeenth century than in the England of the twentieth century. The great forests of medieval times, such as Windsor and Epping, were still substantial.

With the exception of the woods and enclosed land the face of England was remarkably open. Arable land was often cultivated in strips, divided only by large furrows. A large amount of common land remained; this too was open. Ownership boundaries were marked by fences, hedges and sometimes ditches. Obvious though it is, it should be remembered that barbed-wire – scourge of the twentieth-century battlefield – had not been invented, and many hedges were thus perfectly jumpable for cavalry.[2]

A final factor influencing terrain was the large number of fortresses, of various types, that studded the country. Most of these were medieval, obsolete in terms of seventeenth-century siegecraft, but nevertheless very valuable to their holders.

---

[1] The Marlborough–Devizes road is a case in point. *See* Ogilby, *Britannia*, p. 11.
[2] And not for cavalry only; at First Newbury, Captain John Gwyn 'jumped over hedge and ditch' while carrying the colours of Sir Thomas Saluisbury's regiment of Foot. He seems to have used the colour-staff to pole-vault the obstacle! *See* Atkyns and Gwyn, op. cit., pp. 40, 53.

For although the growing power of artillery and the increasing use of high-angled fire made stone walls an increasingly less viable form of defence, the marshalling of siege equipment required great effort and the reduction of even the most archaic fortresses was likely to take a considerable time.[1] Moreover, in the early stages of the war, neither side possessed a really adequate battering train. The best equipped of the Parliamentarian armies, under the Earl of Essex, took a fortnight to reduce Reading, and the Royalists failed completely in their attempt on Gloucester, which was neither strongly held nor well fortified. Besides these older fortresses, defences were improvised at the outset of the Civil War; these consisted, in the main, of earthworks, often sited so as to keep the besieger out of battering range of an older stone fortification.[2]

WEAPONS AND EQUIPMENT

If the terrain over which the English Civil War was fought would have seemed unfamiliar to modern eyes, the weapons used in the conflict would have appeared extremely primitive. Infantry were equipped with the musket and the pike. The musket was a muzzle-loading weapon, employing matchlock ignition. Its use entailed a degree of skill and a good deal of cumbersome equipment. The musketeer carried, in addition, a forked rest to steady the barrel when firing,[3] a bandolier, from which hung small cylindrical powder containers, a priming flask and a bullet pouch. The match – a length of cord soaked in saltpetre – completed the musketeer's equipment. The match was normally hung from the belt; when the musket was to be fired, a length roughly two feet long was cut off, lit at both ends, and held in the left hand. To load, the powder from one of the containers on the bandolier was poured down the barrel, and a bullet dropped down on top of the powder. In battlefield conditions the experienced musketeer would hold one or more bullets in his mouth, as this speeded up the process. A piece of wadding, which might be tow, rag or paper, completed the act of loading, and the weapon was now ready for priming. Here the musketeer pushed back the cover of the flash pan, filled the pan with fine powder from his flask, closed the cover and blew away the excess powder. The short length of match then had one of its ends inserted in the cock, and adjusted so as to descend into the flash pan when the trigger was pulled.

The disadvantages of the matchlock were numerous. The weapon and its impedimenta were heavy. It was inaccurate and slow-firing; a skilled musketeer

---

[1] Witness the sieges of Basing House and Donnington Castle.

[2] The Royal Commission on Historical Monuments (England) has produced a particularly interesting study of Civil War fortification, *Newark On Trent; The Civil War Siegeworks* (London 1964).

[3] The rest was falling into disuse by the time of the Civil War, but was never entirely abandoned during that conflict.

might get off two or even three rounds a minute, but he would be lucky, taking deliberate aim, to hit a man sixty yards away. Worse, the musket was unreliable. The match might go out, or splutter and ignite the firing powder prematurely; it might even ignite one of the charges in the bandolier. Windy or rainy conditions turned the act of loading into a nightmare and made ignition more doubtful even than usual. To be effective, a musketeer had to have his match alight; yet it was obviously impossible to keep it alight continuously. Furthermore, at night lighted matches betrayed movement and provided the enemy with an aiming-mark. It is scarcely remarkable that musketeers were the least prestigious element of the infantry; gentlemen in the ranks still preferred, as in Shakespeare's day, to 'trail the puissant pike'.[1]

What the pike lacked in finesse it made up for in simplicity. At the time of the Civil War, pikes varied in length between twelve and eighteen feet. This difference is partially explained by the habit of the pikemen, when on service, of cutting a foot or two off their pikes to make them more manageable.[2] The shaft of the weapon was usually made of ash, and the head of steel, with languets stretching some way down the shaft to prevent a sword cut lopping off the head. It was customary to select the tallest, strongest recruits as pikemen, not only because the use of the pike required considerable strength and agility, but also owing to the weight of the pikeman's defensive armour. This comprised the 'pot', a steel helmet, often with a ridge along the top, a back and breastplate, known as the corselet, a gorget covering the throat, and long tassets protecting the thighs. In addition, the fully equipped pikeman carried, as did the musketeer, a short sword.[3] Infantry officers wore swords, but also carried a partisan, a short spear. Sergeants carried the halberd, a staff weapon with an axe blade.

The mounted arm had undergone a considerable change in the years immediately prior to the Civil War. In the sixteenth century a variety of cavalry – cuirassiers, lancers, pistoleers 'shot on horseback', and light Horse – had served in English forces. By the outbreak of the Civil War, however, the cuirassier, clad in full armour, was obsolescent. This was partly because of the difficulty of finding horses strong enough to bear his weight. Monk, a professional soldier who, as commander-in-chief in 1660 was instrumental in bringing about the

---

[1] The advantages of pike over musket were much debated amongst seventeenth-century military theorists. See Firth, op. cit., pp. 76–8, 385–90. The invention of the bayonet eventually rendered the pike obsolete, though Marshal Saxe, in *Mes Rêveries*, somewhat eccentrically recommended its re-adoption – it had vanished from French service in 1703, and disappeared from the British army two years later.

[2] *See* Firth, op. cit., p. 73.

[3] General George Monck, in *Observations upon military and political Affairs* (London 1796, but written over a century earlier), emphasised that a pikeman should carry 'a good stiff tuck'. (Tuck is a corruption of *estoc*, a short thrusting sword.) Speaking, no doubt, from bitter experience, he points out (p. 42) that 'if you arm your men with [long] swords, half the swords will, upon the first march you make, be broken with cutting of boughs'.

Restoration, pointed out that 'there are not many countries that do afford horses fit for the service of cuirassiers'.[1] Secondly, the weight of armour was an encumbrance to the wearer as well as to his horse. Sir Edmund Verney, summoned to serve in full armour against the Scots in 1638, remarked: 'It will kill a man to serve in a whole cuirass.'[2] A few cuirassiers appeared in the Civil War. Sir Arthur Hesilrige raised a regiment which did good service in the west and south in 1643 and 1644. Hesilrige's 'Lobsters' were, according to Clarendon, 'the first seen so armed on either side, and the first that had any impression on the King's Horse, who, being unarmed [unarmoured] were not able to bear a shock with them. . . .'[3] The 'Lobsters' were badly cut up at Roundway Down (13 July 1643) but fought well at Cheriton (29 March 1644). It seems probable that some of the senior Royalist officers fought in cuirassier armour; the Earl of Northampton was certainly equipped in this fashion when he was killed at Hopton Heath (19 March 1643).

The lancer, too, had almost disappeared from the armies of the Civil War. The Scots cavalry certainly used the lance; Lord Balgony's regiment made good use of it at Marston Moor, as did the Scottish lancers in the retreat from Preston. There were, though, no lancers in either the Royalist or the Parliamentarian armies.

The majority of cavalry on either side were known as harquebusiers, a term which fell into disuse during the war. They were armed, ideally, with a carbine, a pair of pistols, and a sword. Obviously, the matchlock was most inconvenient for the mounted man; the difficulty of managing gun, match and powder on horseback may easily be imagined. Consequently, cavalry firearms usually employed either wheel-locks or flintlocks. The former ignition system consisted of a steel wheel with a serrated edge, against which a piece of pyrites was held in a pair of jaws. The wheel was wound up – 'spanned' against a powerful spring. Pressure on the trigger released the spring, rotating the wheel and causing a stream of sparks to pour onto the touch-hole. Unfortunately, pyrites tended to fragment; furthermore, if a wheel-lock weapon was left spanned for some time it might fail to operate.[4] The wheel-lock's expense also tended to limit its use as a military weapon.

The snaphaunce, and its subsequent development, the flintlock, were less expensive, and more reliable, than the wheel-lock. Both snaphaunce and flintlock employed a piece of flint, held in the jaws of the cock, striking against a steel plate, to produce a spark.

Yet, despite the comparative efficiency of flint ignition, the matchlock

[1] Ibid., p. 40.
[2] Firth, op. cit., pp. 112–13.
[3] Clarendon, op. cit., Vol. IV, p. 120.
[4] At the siege of Wardour Castle in March 1644, Ludlow's room was breached by a mine, and 'my pistols being wheel-locks, and wound up all night, I could not get to fire, so that I was forced to my sword for the keeping down of the enemy. . . .' *The Memoirs of Edmund Ludlow* . . ., edited by C. H. Firth (Oxford 1894, 2 vols), Vol. I, p. 72.

remained the main infantry firearm throughout the Civil War and, indeed, for some years afterwards. Some infantrymen were fortunate enough to be armed with flintlock weapons. To use matchlocks in close proximity to large quantities of gunpowder was obviously dangerous, so the 'firelock guard' for the artillery and ammunition carried weapons with flint ignition.[1]

Military unpreparedness meant heavy reliance upon weapons obtained from private sources, conforming little with any regulation pattern.[2] Many of the best firearms used in the Civil War were of a sporting rather than a military design. Some of these were undoubtedly rifled;[3] at the siege of Sherborne Castle in 1642 a marksman equipped with a 'birding piece' picked off several Parliamentarian officers. Monck suggested that six fowling pieces should be issued to each company, especially for the purpose of sniping at the enemy's officers.

The general scarcity of weapons had its effect upon the mounted arm. There seems to have been a shortage of firearms among Parliamentarian cavalry, while the Royalist Horse were worse equipped. A variety of swords was used. Since a sword was an ordinary part of the everyday dress of a gentleman, many horsemen simply carried their 'civilian' sword. This might well be a rapier, with either a swept- or cup-hilt. The military version of the rapier, the 'Pappenheimer', a slightly stouter, swept-hilt weapon, was also popular. These were essentially thrusting weapons, useful for the first impact of a charge, but less easy to manage in a hand-to-hand mêlée. More effective cut-and-thrust weapons were the Walloon sword, a businesslike sidearm with a stiff blade and wide guard, and the 'mortuary' sword. The latter had a cut-and-thrust blade and a basket hilt. The term 'mortuary' postdates the Civil War, and was based on the erroneous belief that the heads embossed on the hilt of these weapons represented the head of the executed Charles I.

The defensive equipment of a cavalryman comprised breast- and back-plates, and helmet. The latter was of two main types: the three-barred helmet of English origin, or the so-called 'Dutch pot' with a single sliding noseguard. Royalist Horse were usually less well equipped in this respect than their Parliamentarian opponents. As the war progressed, though, armour fell out of favour with even the Roundhead Horse. Many troopers preferred to trust to a buff-coat, which permitted easier movement but none the less gave a good degree of

[1] It is interesting to note that, after the war, these troops were equipped with a light flintlock called a fusil, and thus became known as fusiliers.
[2] It may be argued that 'regulation pattern' is a misnomer. *The King's Instructions for Musters* laid down explicit specifications of arms and equipment, but these seem to have been more honoured in the breach than the observance. *See* Lord Orrery, *Art of War*, p. 29, quoted in Firth, op. cit., p. 80.
[3] Rifled weapons, though uncommon, were by no means new. They existed in Europe in the sixteenth century, and on 24 June 1635 A. Rotispen was granted an English patent 'to rifle, cut out and screw barrels'. *See* W. Y. Carman, *A History of Firearms* (London 1955), pp. 105-6.

protection. It was an important item of equipment; made of thick·buff-leather, full-skirted and often sleeved, it would turn a sword cut and often deflect a thrust.[1] Gorgets and steel gauntlets for the bridle arm were also worn on occasion.

Also mounted, but always counted separately from cavalry proper, were the dragoons. They were essentially mounted infantry, and originally owed their name to their weapon, the 'dragon', a musket-bored carbine. Dragoons were used for a variety of tasks; providing outposts and vedettes, holding defiles or bridges in the front or rear of an army, and, on the battlefield, lining hedges or holding enclosures. They might also be used to provide musketeers to cooperate with the cavalry. They usually fought dismounted; their horses, cobs and the like, were not the most fiery of steeds, costing only half the price of a cavalry trooper's horse.[2] Their arms, too, were cheap, consisting only of a musket and sword, though the officers might also carry pistols.[3] The dragoons wore no defensive armour, and usually neither buff-coat nor helmet. Like cavalry proper, their muskets hung on a wide belt, hooked on to a swivel on the side of the weapon.

DRESS

One of the hoarier myths about the Civil War is that its soldiers did not wear uniform. Another is that the traditional British red coat came in with the New Model Army. At Edgehill, the first battle of the war, the King's lifeguard wore red coats, as did the Roundhead regiments of Lord Robartes and Denzil Holles. There was certainly a degree of uniformity, always within companies and usually within regiments. Records of the issue of uniform to the armies of both sides abound. Thomas Bushell, 'Warden of our Mint and Mr. Worker of our Mines Royal', was responsible for 'clothing our life Guard and three regiments more, with suits, stockings, shoes and monteros when we were ready to march in [to] the field. . . .'[4] The army of the Eastern Association and the New Model went as far as to issue coats with linings of a different colour, the origin of regimental facings.[5] Officers and sergeants were, by reason of their rank, not provided with uniforms of a general issue, but were permitted to wear more or less what

[1] A good buff-coat was an essential, but extremely expensive, item of equipment. In 1640, a good one would cost £10 or more, while £5 or £6 would buy only a poor one. *See* Firth, op. cit., p. 118.

[2] Ibid., p. 124.

[3] Where possible, dragoons were provided with snaphaunce weapons to give them the chance of firing from horseback – a perilous task with a matchlock! Monck (*Observations*, p. 43) recommends that dragoons should be equipped with a musket barrel and snaphaunce lock; this would enable them to use the same ammunition as musketeers. He makes no mention of pistols for dragoons, and the accounts of the New Model Army have no reference to the supply of pistols to dragoons.

[4] Sir Henry Ellis, *Original Letters*, 2nd series, Vol. III, p. 309.

[5] *See* Brigadier Peter Young, *Edgehill* (Kineton 1967), pp. 23–5.

they liked. Their ranks could be identified, in the case of the infantry, by their partisans and halberds. The formation, in 1645, of the New Model Army completed the tendency towards growing uniformity, as far, at least, as the Parliamentarians were concerned. *Perfect Passages* of 7 May 1645 states that 'the men are Redcoats all, the whole army only are distinguished by the several facings of their coats'. In the Royalist armies the trend was reversed as regiments became smaller and were sometimes amalgamated. At Naseby, for example, several Royalist regiments, the residue of small red-, blue- and green-clad units, presented a rather multicoloured appearance.

There was considerable uniformity in headgear as well as in doublets. Pikemen usually wore a steel helmet and musketeers a broad-brimmed felt hat, often decorated with plumes. The cavalry on both sides favoured helmets while in action; it is a common error to regard the lobster-tailed helmet as a purely Parliamentarian issue. On the line of march, however, the felt hat was popular with horsemen; it was lighter than the helmet, and offered better protection from sun and rain. The infantry had caps as well as hats. These were, in the main, Monmouth Caps, produced at Bewdley. Symonds describes their manufacture: 'First they are knit, then they mill them, then block them, then work them with tassels, then sheer them.'[1] He fails to point out, alas, what the finished product looked like. Somewhat more luxurious was the montero cap: at Naseby a cavalier 'who we have since heard was Rupert' led a party of horse to attack Fairfax's baggage train. A Roundhead described him as 'being a person somewhat in habit like our general, in a red montero as the General had. ...'[2] Corporal Trim in *Tristram Shandy* describes his montero as '... scarlet, of a superfine Spanish cloth, dyed in grain, and mounted all round with fur, except for about four inches in the front, which was faced with a light blue, slightly embroidered. ...'

As with all armies, footwear was an important part of the equipment of the contending forces. Infantry wore low shoes, which cost, in 1649, half a crown.[3] Cavalry boots were longer, reaching up to the thighs, while dragoons seem to have had a shorter, lighter variety. Boots were usually waterproofed by waxing with a tallow–beehive mixture. As a further protection against inclement conditions, cavalrymen were provided with cloaks. There are indications that infantry also had some form of outer garment for cold or wet weather.[4]

Although there was uniformity within regiments, and later, to an extent, within armies, the danger of mistaken identity on the battlefield remained great. Identification was achieved in three ways. Firstly, by scarves or sashes,

---

[1] *The Diary of Richard Symonds* (London 1889), p. 14.
[2] Quoted in Firth, op. cit., p. 240.
[3] Ibid., p. 235.
[4] Ibid., p. 234. In 1642 Parliament ordered 7,500 suits for the army in Ulster. Each was to consist of a cap, doublet, cassock, breeches, two pairs of shoes, and two shirts for each man. The cassock was a long, cloaklike garment, forerunner of the modern greatcoat.

those of the Parliamentarians being orange-tawny, and those of the Royalists red. Secondly, by field-signs: at Marston Moor, for example, Parliamentarians all wore a white handkerchief or piece of paper in their hats. Sir Thomas Fairfax, by removing his field-sign, succeeded in making his way from one wing of the hostile army to the other. The third means of identification was the field-word, a slogan shouted by the combatants. At Marston Moor the Parliamentarians shouted 'God with us', while the Royalist word was 'God and King'. At Naseby, the corresponding field-words were 'God our strength' and 'Queen Mary'. These devices all made recognition more positive, but misunderstandings occurred and ruses were frequent. For example, when at Edgehill Sir Faithfull Fortescue's troops deserted as a body to the King, several were killed in error, as they failed to discard their orange scarves.[1] On at least two occasions Royalist senior officers were captured through mistaking an enemy regiment for one of their own.

CAVALRY

The regiment was the standard unit of both Horse and Foot in Roundhead and Royalist forces. The size and composition of the regiment varied, however, in each army. Royalist regiments of Horse usually had three field officers – colonel, lieutenant-colonel and major – and six troops, three of them commanded by captains and the other three by the field officers, though in practice the colonel's troop was led by his captain-lieutenant. Each troop had, besides its commander, three more commissioned officers, a lieutenant, a cornet and a quartermaster. There were also at least two corporals and a trumpeter. The theoretical strength of a royalist cavalry regiment was 500, though usually the regiment would rarely exceed six troops of about 70 officers and men, a total of 420. On active service, particularly towards the end of the war, this number fell alarmingly. When Lord Wilmot's brigade, consisting of some of the best regiments, mustered at Aldbourne Chase on 10 April 1644, its component units varied greatly in strength. The four strongest each numbered 300, while the two weakest were only 100 strong.

Most Roundhead regiments of Horse had only two field officers – a colonel and a major – who, like their Royalist counterparts, were also troop commanders. Parliamentarian troops numbered, in theory, 71 officers and men, and this total was very often exceeded. The cavalry of the Earl of Essex's army, mustered at Tiverton in the summer of 1644, numbered 3,205 officers and men organised in thirty-nine troops, including one of dragoons – an average of over 84 per troop.

Many of the country gentry followed the King. They and their adherents were often accomplished horsemen, brought up in the hunting field. This gave the royalist Horse a valuable advantage in the early days of the war: at Edgehill,

[1] See also Orrery's cautionary tale, op. cit., p. 186.

for example, they charged uphill, taking hedges and ditches in their stride, routing the Horse on the Parliamentarian left. Cromwell pointed out to his cousin John Hampden the reasons for the initial inferiority of Roundhead Horse. 'Your troopers . . .' he remarked, 'are most of them old decayed serving-men and tapsters, and such kind of fellows. Their troopers are gentlemen's sons, younger sons and persons of quality. . . . You must get men of a spirit that is likely to go on as far as gentlemen will go, or else I am sure you will be beaten still.'[1]

Cavalry in the Civil War normally fought three deep, though on occasion they took the field double-ranked, that is to say six deep. At Roundway Down, for example, Captain Richard Atkyns describes how 'we advanced at a full trot, three deep, and kept in order: the enemy kept their station, and their right wing of Horse, being cuirassiers,[2] were I am sure five if not six deep, in so close order that Punchinello himself, had he been there, could not have got in to them'.[3] Nevertheless, the cuirassiers, though presenting an unbreakable front, were out-flanked and badly cut up. In the early stages of the war the Roundhead Horse followed the Dutch practice and fired before charging, while the Royalist Horse, coached by the capable Prince Rupert, generally reserved their fire until after the initial impact of the charge. By the closing stages of the conflict, however, the Horse on both sides as a rule charged at speed, and used their pistols in the mêlée.

While many of the troopers on both sides were experienced horsemen, only a small proportion were trained and disciplined soldiers. This latter point, natur-ally, applies less to the cavalry of the New Model Army. Nevertheless, the mounted troops on both sides exhibited, in the words of Leonard Cooper,

> the virtues and faults which were evident in so many later battles, notably in the Peninsula and at Waterloo, at Balaclava and in the Sikh Wars. In the charge they were admirable. They could ride and use their weapons; and their courage and dash were unshakeable. But they lacked discipline in battle, and were led by officers who had learned more from the hunting field than from war. After a successful charge they were headstrong in the pursuit and quite incapable of rallying until they were exhausted and, usually, until they were too far from the battle to influence its further course. As Wellington said, they always galloped too fast and too far.[4]

Yet there were Royalist regiments that learned to rally, and could charge two or three times in the same day, as at Hopton Heath and Chalgrove Field.

Cromwell's troopers of the New Model Army were altogether better –

---

[1] Quoted in C. V. Wedgwood, *The King's War* (London 1958), p. 139.
[2] Hesilrige's 'Lobsters' in this case.
[3] Atkyns and Gwyn, op. cit., p. 23. Atkyns and his cornet, Robert Holmes, the future admiral, became engaged in a fruitless combat with the iron-clad Sir Arthur.
[4] Leonard Cooper, *British Regular Cavalry 1644–1914* (London 1965), p. 13.

partly because they charged at a 'pretty round trot' instead of the gallop of Rupert's Horse. At the only other time in English military history when cavalry have been tightly controlled – under Marlborough – they also charged at the trot. In the Civil War, however, cavalry charges were disorganised affairs. It was difficult for officers to keep control unless they personally headed the charge – in which case they were likely to become casualties at an early stage. The better-mounted troopers, or those with easier ground to cross, tended to get ahead. The natural excitement and fear of the horses completed the picture; once the charge started it was extremely difficult to halt.

INFANTRY

Infantry, like their mounted colleagues, were organised in regiments. These consisted, in theory at least, of ten companies, three commanded by the field officers and the remainder by captains. The colonel's company contained 200 men, the lieutenant-colonel's 160, the major's 140, while those of the captains consisted of only 100 men. Company commanders were assisted by a lieutenant and an ensign, two sergeants, three corporals and two drummers. In the Royalist army there was an extra appointment, that of gentleman of the arms, whose task it was to look after the company's weapons. The Foot regiments of both armies also possessed a surgeon and a surgeon's mate. Medical arrangements were rudimentary in the extreme, and few soldiers could expect to survive major surgery. The wounded from a large action soon swamped the available doctors, and often all that could be done was to billet these unfortunates on nearby villages. Most senior officers had their own personal surgeons, but even so were lucky if they could be extracted from the stricken field in time to receive attention. In almost all cases a serious wound meant death.

The infantry company contained, again in theory, two-thirds musketeers and one-third pikemen. This balance was far from universal: at Edgehill, for example, the Royalist army seems to have contained more or less equal numbers of pikemen and musketeers. The company would normally fall in in six ranks, with the pikemen in the centre of the formation. Each file of six was headed by its leader, whose second-in-command brought up the rear of the file – doubtless to encourage the faint-hearted. Thus assembled, the company could be put through the labyrinth of the seventeenth-century drill book. Space does not permit detailed discussion of infantry drill. It should, though, be noted that most of the officers on both sides were amateurs, and must therefore have taken some time to master the drill themselves. Furthermore, it seems unlikely that all the manoeuvres described by the military theorists of the time could be carried out by what were, after all, hastily levied troops. Infantry regiments on both sides would have been schooled in the technique of 'fire by introduction', in which the front rank fired, the rear rank marched forward between the files and fired, followed by the next rear rank, and so on. In 'fire by extraduction' the process was reversed, the front rank moving to the rear after firing. On occasion only three ranks were formed, and a single salvo replaced the rolling fire of the other two methods.[1]

A regiment drawn up for action would resemble a company, in having all its pikemen in the centre, and its musketeers on the flanks. These bodies of pikemen and musketeers were known as 'divisions'. Another possibility was for the regiment to form 'grand divisions', with two wings, each consisting of pikemen with musketeers on each flank. An army would normally deploy with its infantry regiments thus formed up, in two or three lines, with their front screened by a 'forlorn hope' of musketeers. Following an exchange of fire between these parties, the first line of infantry moved forward and opened fire. After a number of volleys, the pikemen brought their pikes up into the 'charge' and moved forward to 'push of pike'. They were often assisted by the musketeers, who pressed in wielding their muskets by the barrel, 'clubbing them down' as Major-General Sir Thomas Morgan put it.[2] This might decide the battle; on the other hand, both sides sometimes recoiled a short distance and fell to firing once more.[3]

If attacked by cavalry, infantry formed a circle, with the pikemen inside and the musketeers outside. The latter crouched under the pikes, and were thus able to fire, while the pikes, stretching over their heads, kept off the cavalry. Musketeers were sometimes equipped with 'swine-feathers' (or 'Swedish Feathers'), stakes sharpened at either end, which they planted in the ground, facing outwards, so as to provide extra protection. These useful accessories were, though, a further encumbrance for the already heavily laden musketeer, and were not often carried. With the invention of the bayonet, some years after the Civil War, the celebrated square replaced the cumbersome circle of pikemen and musketeers, every musketeer being, in fact, his own pikeman.

COLOURS

The similarity of the military heritage of both sides is illustrated by the fact that each used the same system for their colours of Horse and Foot. Throughout the Civil Wars, and at least as late as the reign of James II, every company and troop had its own colour, guidon or standard.

The system in vogue in 1642 is described by Captain Thomas Venn, whose military experience, though his book was published in 1672, went back to 1641 and 1642.[4] Venn tells us that, in the Foot,

[1] The salvo, or salvee as it was sometimes known, was used with shattering effect by the Swedes at Leipzig in 1631. It was certainly employed by the Parliamentarian Foot; see Major Richard Elton, *The Compleat Body of the Art Military* (London 1650), ch. lix.

[2] Quoted in Firth, op. cit., p. 104.

[3] As happened, for example, at Edgehill.

[4] Captain Thomas Venn, *Military Observations or the Tacticks put into practice* (London 1672), p. 186.

The Colonel's colour is in the first place of a pure and clean colour, without any mixture. The Lieutenant-Colonel's only with Saint George's Arms in the upper corner next the staff, the Major's the same, but in the lower and outmost corner a little stream blazant, and every Captain with Saint George's Arms alone, but with so many spots or several Devices as pertain to the dignity of their respective places.

These devices displayed on the captains' colours were often taken from the colonel's armorial bearings. Sir Edward Stradling's colours bore the *cinquefoil* of his house, and a Colonel Talbot had dogs for his devices. The first captain of the regiment in question would display one of these devices, the second captain two, and so on. It was thus possible for soldiers to locate their company by the position of its colours, and the difficult task of rallying was made easier. The colours of a company were carried by its ensign.

The guidons of the dragoons followed the same pattern as infantry colours, but were considerably smaller. The infantry size of 6½ feet by 6½ feet was obviously unmanageable on horseback, so dragoon guidons were the same size as the standards of cavalry proper, 2 feet by 2 feet.

Cavalry standards followed much less of a set pattern than those of the Foot. The field was generally the same colour for each troop in a regiment, but the devices or mottoes borne on the standards were usually of a religious or political nature, and often differed from troop to troop.[1]

ARTILLERY

Artillery displayed, then as now, no colours. At the time of the Civil War, artillery was still regarded by some as a branch of science bordering on the occult, though the excellent use made of it during the Thirty Years War[2] had illustrated the growing importance of the arm. Indeed, as early as Marignano it had proved very effective. The guns used in the Civil War were divided into ten classes,[3] but standardisation was far from complete and even contemporary authorities often confuse the type and calibre of the ordnance they describe.

[1] *See* Young, op. cit., p. 36, plate 4.
[2] At Leipzig the Imperialist infantry were severely galled by the fire of the Swedish light guns. Monro attributed the successful passage of the Lech in April 1632 to the 'great force of artillery, for this victory was obtained by our cannon alone'. Monro, op. cit., Pt II, pp. 68, 118. *See also* C. V. Wedgwood, *The Thirty Years War* (London 1962), p. 315.

[3]

	Calibre of Piece (*ins*)	Weight of Piece (*lbs*)	Length of Piece (*ft*)	Weight of Shot (*lbs*)
Cannon royal	8	8000	8	63
Cannon	7	7000	10	47
Demi-cannon	6	6000	12	27
Culverin	5	4000	11	15

The guns most widely used in the Civil War were the lighter field-pieces; larger pieces of artillery were cumbersome to transport and difficult to site. The sort of proposition that might be achieved can be seen from the court paper, *Mercurius Aulicus*, describing how at Cropredy Bridge the Royalists 'took all their [Parliamentarian] 14 pieces of ordnance, whereof 11 brass viz . . ., 5 sakers, 1 twelve-pound piece, 1 demi-culverin, 2 minions, 2 three-pound pieces. . . .'[1] At Marston Moor Prince Rupert lost all his artillery: Firth maintains that the largest were demi-culverins and the smallest drakes.[2] On the field of battle, cannon were normally positioned in the intervals between the regiments of Foot in the first, and sometimes the second, line. Larger pieces might be placed upon high ground to fire over the heads of the infantry, but this was a difficult and potentially dangerous manoeuvre. If a position was held for any length of time, emplacements might be constructed to provide the guns with a better firing platform.[3] The Swedish practice of attaching two light field-pieces to each regiment of Foot seems to have been followed in both Royalist and Parliamentarian armies.[4]

The artillery of the seventeenth century was, by modern standards, crude and inaccurate.[5] Roundshot was the normal type of ammunition used, though case shot – a canister of musket balls which spread in a wide arc leaving the muzzle – was deadly against massed formations at close range. Each piece was normally served by a gunner, his mate, and one or more labourers or matrosses. The powder charge was sometimes pre-packed into cartridges, but more often simply carried in a barrel and transferred to the gun by means of a metal scoop.

[1] The Royalists also captured 'two barricadoes of wood, which were drawn upon wheels, and in each seven small brass and leather guns, charged with case shot . . .' (Clarendon, op. cit., Vol. IV, p. 503). This type of weapon was best suited to the defence of streets, bridges, breaches and the like; it was obsolete by the time of the Civil War. However, multi-barrelled guns continue to attract interest, and several early machine guns – for example the Gatling and the *Mitrailleuse* – were multi-barrelled.

[2] Firth, op. cit., p. 154.

[3] The picture-map of Naseby in Joshua Sprigge, *Anglia Rediviva* (London 1647); there is a good facsimile reprint available (Gainesville, Florida, 1960), showing typical artillery deployment. At Lansdown, Waller's guns were emplaced; traces of the gun positions can still be seen.

[4] See Elton, op. cit., p. 145.

[5] Prussian gunners of a later century were to have a saying, 'The first shot is for the Devil, the second for God, and only the third for the King'. Prince Kraft von Höhenlohe-Ingelfingen, *Letters on Artillery* (translated, London 1888), p. 56.

	Calibre of Piece (*ins*)	Weight of Piece (*lbs*)	Length of Piece (*ft*)	Weight of Shot (*lbs*)
Demi-culverin	4½	3600	10	9
Saker	3½	2500	9½	5¼
Minion	3	1500	8	4
Falcon	2¾	700	6	2¼
Falconet	2	210	4	1¼
Robinet	1¼	120	3	¾

From William Eldred, *The Gunner's Glasse* (London 1646).

Not unnaturally, artillery drill books emphasised the importance. of covering the powder barrel to prevent accidents![1]

SUPPLY AND TRANSPORT

Transport and commissariat were, like the artillery, primitive by modern standards. Sir James Turner, who served with the Swedish, Scots and Royalist armies, affirmed that 'the ordinary allowance for a soldier in the field is daily two pounds of bread, one pound of flesh, or in lieu of it, one pound of cheese, one bottle of wine, or in lieu of it, two bottles of beer. . . .'[2] When, as was often the case, it proved impossible to supply the troops with any food at all, they were allowed to live 'at free quarter'. Turner pointed out the obvious defects of this system, which

> proves oft the destruction of a country: for though no exorbitancy be committed, and that every man both officer and soldier demand no other entertainment than what is allowed by the Prince or State where they serve; yet when an army cannot be quartered but close and near together, to prevent infalls, onslaughts and the surprise of an enemy, it is an easy matter to imagine what a heavy burden these places bear . . . and withal it is very hard to get soldiers and horsemen kept within the limits of their duty in these quarters after they have hunger, thirst and other hardships in the field. It is true, all Princes who for preservation of their armies from extreme ruin, and for want of treasure, are necessitated too often to make use of this free quarter, do not only make strict laws and ordinances, how many times a day officers and soldiers are to eat, and how many dishes every one according to his quality is to call for, but likewise set down the precise rates, and values of these dishes, that the host be not obliged to do beyond those limitations, yet the grievance continues heavy and great.[3]

The Horse, often operating some distance from the main body of their army, frequently took advantage of free quarter. Lord Hopton relates how, during the Royalist advance into Somerset in the summer of 1643,

> there began the disorder of the horse visibly to break in upon all the prosperity of the public proceedings. The Town agreeing willingly to raise and pay 8,000 li composition (which would have sufficed for some weeks necessary pay for the whole Army). The country being then full, and not relucting at free quarter soberly taken, and the Generals being very full advertised of the opportunity to begin a discipline in the army, and being themselves very

---

[1] Mishaps were, nevertheless, not infrequent. At the siege of Reading in 1643 an officer, firing a cannon, 'by chance fired the [powder] barrels . . .' killing and wounding several men. *See* Firth, op. cit., p. 151.
[2] Sir James Turner, *Pallas Armata* (London 1683), p. 201.
[3] Loc. cit.

desirous of it were yet never able to repress the extravagant disorder of the horse to the ruin and discomposure of all.[1]

Both sides recognised that free quarter eroded discipline and alienated the civilian population, and tried, where possible, to supply themselves. The Royalists, using Oxford as their base, set up magazines and stores there. Bread and biscuit were baked under the supervision of the wagon-master-general, and sent forward to the army in commandeered country carts. Parliamentarian forces under the Earl of Essex were little better off. Essex's commissariat was supervised by a 'commisary for the provisions', and the train of some forty wagons by the 'carriage-master-general'.[2]

However, even when sufficient food was stored centrally, the means for its distribution were so slender as to make free quarter all too common. Those providing the troops with quarters were reimbursed by tickets, redeemable at a later date. It cannot have been easy, in a fluid civil-war situation, for householders to turn these tickets into cash, and there are but few instances of this happening, though Prince Rupert seems to have managed it at Shrewsbury.

PAY

The question of soldiers' pay in the Civil War is complicated by the fact that scales of pay changed several times during the course of the conflict; furthermore, the soldier who actually received the sum to which he was entitled could count himself lucky. In December 1642 the Royalists were offering six shillings a week to musketeers, twelve shillings and tenpence to dragoons, and seventeen and sixpence to cavalry troopers. It was expected, however, that these individuals would provide their own arms and equipment.[3] When, in 1649, the New Model Army was formed, infantrymen were paid eightpence a day, dragoons one shilling and sixpence and troopers two shillings. As food prices rose, so the pay of the New Model Army was increased. By 1659 soldiers were being paid ninepence, dragoons one shilling and eightpence and cavalrymen two shillings and threepence. While mounted men were quite well paid, the unfortunate infantryman earned about the same as an agricultural labourer – scarcely an inducement to voluntary enlistment.

The officers of both armies received much higher rates of pay than the men they commanded. In 1644 a Royalist captain of Foot received £2 12s 6d a week, his lieutenant £1 8s 0d and his ensign £1 1s 0d. Their counterparts in the Earl of Essex's army earned, in a month, £7 0s 0d, £5 12s 0d and £4 4s 0d

[1] Ralph, Lord Hopton, *Bellum Civile* (Somerset Record Society, 1902), p. 47. This useful edition also contains accounts by Colonel Walter Slingsby.
[2] Firth, op. cit., p. 213.
[3] Proclamation of 3 December 1642. R. Steele, *Tudor and Stuart Proclamations 1485–1714* (Oxford 1910, 2 vols), Vol. I, p. 2316.

respectively.[1] Senior officers did even better, with some Royalist generals receiving about £10 a day, and Parliamentarian colonels £63 monthly.[2]

Impressive though these scales were, it appears that, in the Royalist army at least, they were more honoured in the breach than in the observance. Captain Richard Atkyns tells us how 'my troop I paid twice out of mine own purse'[3] in early 1643. After the action at Chewton Mendip on 10 June 1643, Atkyns received 20s a man 'for the wounded of my troop, and also of my division . . . of Sir Robert Long, then Treasurer of the Army; which was all the money I ever received for myself, or troops, during the war'.[4] In January 1644 Sir John Mennes, who had been general of the ordnance under Lord Capel, wrote to Prince Rupert that 'I must crave your Highness's pardon if I quit the place, for I have not wherewithal to subsist any longer, having received but £22 now in eleven months, and lived upon my own, without free quarters for horse or man. The fortune I have is all in the rebels' hands, or in such tenants as have forgot to pay.'[5]

Nor were the Parliamentarian forces much better off. 'Constant pay' was one of the inducements to enlist in the New Model Army. In 1644 Parliament attempted the expedient of placing all officers above the rank of captain on half pay, promising to pay them the remaining half after the conclusion of hostilities. This policy was in fact implemented in the New Model Army from its formation, offers of 'constant pay' notwithstanding. When, in 1647, the disbandment of the New Model Army was begun, soldiers were given 'debentures', which commuted the pay owed them into land. This proved an unsatisfactory solution, as many soldiers, for whom ready cash was more attractive than the distant prospect of land ownership, sold their debentures at well below their face value.

Pay was not the only source of financial gain to the Civil War soldier. The arms, equipment, and horse of a prisoner were regarded as 'lawful plunder'.[6] When a town was taken by storm, it was customary for it to be given up to pillage for a specified period. Sometimes, a besieged town would offer a cash payment, as part of its surrender terms, to avoid the attentions of the soldiery. Also common was the practice of giving 'storm money' in lieu of plunder to troops engaged in an assault. This helped preserve discipline and prevented the unnecessary destruction that inevitably ensued when a town or fortress was thrown open to plunder.[7]

The inhabitants of a town of strategic importance, such as Bristol, Gloucester

[1] Uncalendared State Papers, SP 28.
[2] Ibid.
[3] Atkyns and Gwyn, op. cit., p. 8.
[4] Ibid., p. 15.
[5] Eliot Warburton, *Memoirs of Prince Rupert and the Cavaliers* (London 1849), Vol. II, p. 372.
[6] Firth, op. cit., p. 191.
[7] When Reading surrendered in April 1643, Essex's men were promised twelve shillings per man in lieu of plunder. The cash was not, alas, forthcoming, and they promptly mutinied.

or York, had little chance of escaping involvement in the war. For the remainder of the population, direct contact with the war depended upon such factors as geographical location, occupation, political involvement and, of course, luck. It was quite possible for inhabitants of remote areas to be practically unaware of the war's existence. There is a story that on the morning of Marston Moor, a ploughman working there was advised to move off to avoid the battle. He inquired who the fighting was between, and, upon being told that the King and Parliament were the contenders, remarked in astonishment, 'what, has them two fallen out then?' Such total ignorance was by no means typical, though. Indeed, the gentry on both sides showed increasing alarm at the dangerous unrest which the war encouraged among the lower orders.

Recruitment was, initially at least, by voluntary enlistment, and much depended upon the prestige of the officer who sought to raise troops. Local magnates recruited from retainers and tenantry, and were often able to raise homogeneous and well-equipped units fairly rapidly.[1] Certain areas provided fruitful recruiting-grounds. Many of the best Royalist Foot were raised in Wales and Cornwall, and the scholars of Oxford showed little reluctance to exchange gown for buff-coat. The Parliamentarians recruited particularly well in East Anglia and the Home Counties.

Although both armies ostensibly maintained the policy of enlisting only volunteers, impressment was widely used. Prisoners of war were, on occasion, drafted *en masse* into their captor's forces. For the common soldier without clearly defined loyalties such service was infinitely preferable to the discomfort and tedium of prison life. As the war went on, it became increasingly common for able-bodied civilians to be conscripted; even the New Model Army was compelled to rely upon a proportion of pressed men, many of whom could only be brought to the colours by force.

Such methods of recruitment, combined with irregular pay and hard service, resulted in widespread desertion. Even in the first months of the war, before enthusiasm had had much chance to wane, soldiers deserted in considerable numbers. When two of Essex's regiments marched from Oxford for Worcester on 2 and 3 October 1642, many of the men were missing, 'the captains and constables going up and down the town to seek them: many of them having flung away their arms, and run away'.[2] Royalist and Roundhead provost-marshal-generals, aided by the regimental provost-marshals, struggled hard against the problem of desertion, and, as the war progressed, treatment of

[1] Newcastle's celebrated Whitecoats are a prime case in point. At the other end of the social scale is Richard Shuckburgh of Shuckburgh, who was out hunting near Edgecote on 22 October 1642, when he was summoned before the King, passing on his way to Edgehill. Shuckburgh was graciously received, and immediately went home, armed his tenantry, and appeared on the field of battle next day. After the capture of Banbury, he is said to have gone home and fortified himself on top of Shuckburgh Hill, where he was attacked and defended himself till he fell wounded, with most of his tenants about him.

[2] Quoted in Young, op. cit., p. 10.

deserters became increasingly harsh. Even so, those deserters who were appre-hended and hanged were comparatively few. The great majority returned to their homes, and stayed there.

Those who were fortunate enough to avoid the attentions of the recruiting-sergeant could still suffer from the war. Pillage was not uncommon, and free quarter all too frequent. Even areas which were not scenes of major conflict had to sustain the depredations of those local gentlemen who held out for King or Parliament in their fortified houses, and, unconfined by regular discip-line, raided almost as they chose.

Although a large proportion of the nation was, from time to time, indirectly involved in the war, the percentage of adult males who actually fought was not high. At Marston Moor, the largest battle of the Civil Wars, about 46,000 men were engaged on both sides, while less than half this number fought at Naseby. The population of England and Wales was probably in excess of 5 million. Even reducing this to exclude women and men above or below military age, or unfit for service, to a figure of 1½ million, the proportion of men under arms remains fairly small.

The command and staff system used by both sides must also be considered. Again, as both armies shared a common background, and were based largely on the military establishment of pre-Civil War England, there was a great degree of similarity between Royalist and Parliamentarian headquarters.

COMMAND AND STAFF

The theoretical command structure of an army in the 1640s consisted of a captain-general in supreme command assisted by a staff which might include his second-in-command, the lieutenant-general, and a field marshal, whose duties were precisely those indicated by his title. Each of the three main arms – Horse, Foot and Artillery – had its own general, with a lieutenant-general as his second-in-command. In addition the Foot had a sergeant-major-general – a rank from which the first word was soon omitted – who was usually a pro-fessional soldier, giving specialist advice to his general and lieutenant-general, who might well lack military experience, owing their rank to their social posi-tion rather than to their martial qualities. In the cavalry, the commissary-general performed the same function as the sergeant-major-general of Foot. The artillery was commanded by the general of the ordnance, though it was customary for his lieutenant-general to do most of the work.

This, in outline, was the structure employed by both armies. But in practice the system failed to exhibit the logic and relative clarity which it did in theory. Certain posts, for example, might be unfilled, while, on the other hand, one individual might hold more than one appointment. A further complication was the use of the Council of War. This was composed of senior officers, and met to consider the course of action to be adopted by a commander. In the

Civil War the composition of the Council on each side varied from time to time; the Royalist Council certainly included several relatively junior officers and colonels, as well as the King's ministers.[1] Furthermore, the degree of obedience shown by different commanders to the decisions of their Council of War differed sharply.

The Royalist army was under the personal command of the King, as captain-general. He was assisted by a Council of War, comprising military and civil officers. Lord General (or, in modern parlance, Chief of Staff), was the Earl of Lindsey. He was mortally wounded at Edgehill, and was replaced by Patrick Ruthven, Lord Forth, a somewhat bibulous veteran, who had learned his trade in the Swedish army. The Royalist Horse was led by Charles's nephew, Prince Rupert, general of the Horse. Rupert was undoubtedly one of the most vivid personalities to emerge from the war. He is all too often written off as a *beau sabreur*, a good cavalry leader and little else. In fact, though only twenty-two at the outbreak of war, he had considerable military experience, and had employed three years' imprisonment, following his capture at Lemgo in Westphalia, to improve his knowledge of military theory. A superb horseman, skilled swords-man, and excellent shot, Rupert provided the Royalist Horse with the positive leadership they required. Yet his knowledge of engineering and gunnery was also useful, as were his talents for siege warfare. Rupert's second-in-command, initially commissary-general, and later lieutenant-general of Horse, was Henry Wilmot, a fair disciplinarian, a man of considerable personal bravery and some military experience but too much of the politician.[2] The infantry were in the capable hands of their sergeant-major-general, Sir Jacob Astley, a small, taciturn man, whose wide experience was backed with sound theoretical knowledge. A less attractive character was the sergeant-major-general of dragoons, the testy and imperious Sir Arthur Aston. His unlikely military record included service in Russia, Poland and Germany. Sir John Heydon, a competent and zealous officer, served as lieutenant-general of ordnance. Several offices – that of general of the Foot, for example – were initially untenanted.

If the Royalist chain of command seems complex on paper and confused in action, the Parliamentarian command structure was even worse, lacking a generally accepted source of authority which the Royalists, at least, had in the King. Robert Devereux, third Earl of Essex, was captain-general of the Forces of Parliament. He had commanded a Foot regiment in the Dutch service, and was well liked by both officers and men. Clarendon called him, at the time of the Second Bishops' War, 'the most popular man of the kingdom, the darling

---

[1] For example, on 14 December 1642 the Royalist Council of War which met at Reading included Lieutenant-Colonel William Legge of Prince Rupert's regiment of Horse. Legge was junior to several officers not present at the Council.

[2] He had been captain of Horse in the Dutch service, and had served as commissary-general of the Horse in the Second Bishops' War. He was captured at Newburn after charging the Scots with a handful of followers.

of the sword-men'.[1] He was, however, sadly limited as a strategist, and could on occasion be both dilatory and obstructive. The Horse had the misfortune to be commanded by the Earl of Bedford, a congenial nobleman with a total absence of military experience. His lieutenant-general, Sir William Balfour, was, however, an experienced and thoroughly able officer. There is some doubt as to the command of the Foot. The office of sergeant-major-general was initially held, it seems, by Colonel Thomas Ballard, and later by Philip Skippon and Sir John Merrick. The Earl of Peterborough, general of the ordnance, lacked, like Bedford, military experience. Unfortunately, Peterborough's second-in-command was not of the high calibre of Bedford's, for the lieutenant-general of the ordnance, Philibert Emanuel Du Bois, was distinguished only by his general lack of competence. He did not survive the first campaign.

Both armies included a host of other staff officers. Some of these were in a strange position, holding 'general' appointments but lacking exalted rank. Two examples will suffice: Captain William Smith was the Royalist provost-marshal-general, while Captain Thomas Richardson served as carriage-master-general to Essex's army. Similar appointments were those of scoutmaster-general, whose duties were the collection and processing of intelligence, and muster-master-general, who was responsible for the listing and enumerating of the army. Other officers served as adjutants, aides-de-camp, and gallopers, providing headquarters with a rudimentary administrative and communications system.

Command in the field lacked precision. There were no permanent formations larger than a regiment. Brigades or 'tertios' were formed, but usually on a flexible, almost *ad hoc* basis.[2] A brigade was commanded, as a rule, by the senior colonel of the regiments comprising it. The rank of colonel-general existed in the Royalist army but it was attached to a particular arm (e.g. colonel-general of dragoons) or a geographical area (e.g. colonel-general of Shropshire and Cheshire). A general would command from his carriage or, more probably, from his horse's back. The maps at the commander's disposal were scarce and inaccurate. Telescopes, or 'perspective glasses' as they were called, would have been available to very few officers. Watches existed, but were so uncommon as to make the synchronisation of manoeuvres impossible; hence the frequent use of signals by gunfire. More detailed communication was achieved by giving a verbal or written message to a staff officer, who would then deliver it in person – a time-consuming, dangerous and insecure procedure.

The armies which moved into battle in the autumn of 1642 presented a strange paradox. They were infinitely better organised and equipped than the Royal army which had fought the Scots, yet they were, by Continental standards, poorly armed and alarmingly inexperienced. Some of their commanders were, it is true, professional soldiers, but the overwhelming majority of officers,

---

[1] Clarendon, op. cit., Vol. I, p. 202.
[2] Though the Royalist garrison drawn out of Reading in early 1644 seems to have remained a tertio, and was even called the Reading brigade later that year.

as well as rank and file, were innocent of the military art. At the head of the Royalist army stood the shy, aloof, obstinate, almost chilly figure of King Charles I, whose own mismanagement had contributed materially towards the worsening of the pre-war crisis, and who was, it might be argued, largely responsible for the escalation of that crisis into armed conflict. Personally brave, though isolated by his Court from real personal contact with the men who made up his army, Charles epitomised the paradoxes of 1642. His only qualification for command was his own royal position, itself one of the major issues at stake in the conflict. The best of his adherents, men like Hyde, Culpepper and Falkland, advocated reform and shuddered at the prospect of war, but became embroiled in the struggle by the same process of inescapable logic which was to drive so many reluctant Englishmen into the vortex of Civil War.

PART TWO

THE FIRST CIVIL WAR
AUGUST 1642–AUGUST 1646

Chronology

1642	2 August	Colonel George Goring, Governor of Portsmouth, declares for the King.
	4	Action at Marshall's Elm, Somerset.
	10	*Oliver Cromwell* defeats an attempt to remove the plate of the Cambridge colleges.
	15	*Cromwell* seizes the magazine at Cambridge.
	17	The Cornish Cavaliers muster on Bodmin race-course.
	21	Dover Castle surprised by the Parliamentarians.
		Prince Rupert joins the King.
	22	The King raises his standard at Nottingham.
	2 September	*The Earl of Bedford* besieges Sherborne Castle.
	7	Goring surrenders Portsmouth to Sir William Waller.
		Action at Babylon Hill, near Yeovil.
	10	*Essex* at Northampton with 20,000 men.
	13	The King marches from Nottingham to Derby.
	18	The King reaches Stafford.
	19	The King marches to Wellington.
		Essex leaves Northampton.
		Hertford retreats from Sherborne Castle.
	20	The King reaches Shrewsbury.
	23	Action at Powick Bridge.
		Hertford sails from Minehead for South Wales.
		Hopton marches into Cornwall.
	24	*Essex* occupies Worcester.
	25	Hopton joins Sir Bevil Grenvile in Cornwall.
	12 October	The King marches from Shrewsbury and advances on London.
	19	*Essex* leaves Worcester.
		The King arrives at Kenilworth Castle.
	23	Battle of EDGEHILL.
	25	*Essex* retires to Warwick.

	27	The King takes Banbury.
	29	The King occupies Oxford.
	3 November	The King marches from Oxford to advance on London.
	12	Prince Rupert storms Brentford.
	13	*Essex*, reinforced by the London Trained Bands, faces the King at Turnham Green.
	29	The King retires from Reading to Oxford.
	1 December	Newcastle forces the crossing of the Tees at Piercebridge.
		Waller takes Farnham Castle.
	3	Newcastle enters York.
	5	Wilmot takes Marlborough.
	7	Newcastle takes Tadcaster.
	9	The Royalists settle upon their winter quarters around Oxford.
	13	*Waller* takes Winchester.
	27	*Waller* takes Chichester.
1643	19 January	Battle of BRADDOCK DOWN.
	23	*Sir Thomas Fairfax* takes Leeds and Wakefield.
		Newcastle retires to York.
	2 February	Rupert takes Cirencester.
	22	The Queen lands at Bridlington Bay.
	15 March	*Waller* secures Bristol.
	18	The Earl of Derby storms Lancaster.
	19	Battle of HOPTON HEATH.
		Derby takes Preston.
	24	*Massey* defeats Lord Herbert's Welsh at Highnam.
	30	Battle of SEACROFT MOOR.
	13 April	Battle of RIPPLE FIELD.
	21	Rupert takes Lichfield.
	25	*Waller* takes Hereford.
		Royalists fail to relieve Reading – action at Caversham Bridge.
		Battle of SOURTON DOWN.
	27	*Essex* takes Reading.
	13 May	Action at Grantham.
	16	Battle of STRATTON.
	21	*Sir Thomas Fairfax* storms Wakefield.
	18 June	Action at Chalgrove Field.
	30	Battle of ADWALTON MOOR.
	5 July	Battle of LANSDOWN.
	13	Battle of ROUNDWAY DOWN.
	26	Rupert storms Bristol.
	28	Action at Gainsborough.

	10 August–5 September	Siege of Gloucester.
	4 September	Prince Maurice takes Exeter.
	18	Action at Aldbourne Chase.
	20	First Battle of NEWBURY.
	25	Solemn League and Covenant signed.
	6 October	Maurice takes Dartmouth.
	11	Action at Winceby.
		Newcastle raises the siege of Hull.
	9 December	Hopton takes Arundel Castle.
	13	*Waller* storms Alton.
1644	6 January	*Waller* recaptures Arundel Castle.
	19	The Scots army begins to cross the Tweed.
	25	Battle of NANTWICH.
	5 February	Action at Corbridge.
	21 March	Prince Rupert relieves Newark.
	29	Battle of CHERITON.
	6 May	Manchester storms Lincoln.
	25	Rupert storms Stockport.
	27	Rupert storms Bolton.
	11 June	Rupert takes Liverpool.
	29	Battle of CROPREDY BRIDGE.
	2 July	Battle of MARSTON MOOR.
		Alasdair MacDonald arrives in Scotland.
	16	Surrender of York.
	21 August	Battle of BEACON HILL.
	31	Battle of CASTLE DORE.
	1 September	Battle of TIPPERMUIR; Montrose defeats *Lord Elgin's* Covenanters.
	13	Battle of ABERDEEN; Montrose defeats *Lord Balfour of Burleigh.*
	20 October	The town of Newcastle falls to the Scots.
	27	Second Battle of NEWBURY.
	6 November	Rupert appointed lieutenant-general of all the King's armies.
	9	Relief of Donnington Castle.
	19 December	Self-Denying Ordinance passed by Commons – revised version passed by Lords 3 April 1645.
1645	2 February	Montrose defeats *Argyll* at Inverlochy.
	19	Maurice relieves Chester.
	22	*Mytton* takes Shrewsbury.
	4 April	Formation of the New Model Army.
		Montrose takes Dundee.
	22	Rupert surprises *Massey* at Ledbury.

	24	*Cromwell* defeats Northampton near Islip. Surrender of Bletchingdon House.
	29	*Cromwell* repulsed at Faringdon Castle.
	9 May	Battle of AULDEARN; Montrose defeats *Urry*.
	30	Rupert storms Leicester.
	14 June	Battle of NASEBY.
	18	*Fairfax* takes Leicester.
	2 July	Battle of ALFORD; *Baillie* defeated by Montrose.
	10	Battle of LANGPORT.
	23	Fall of Bridgewater.
	1 August	*Laugharne* beats Stradley on Colby Moor.
	15	Battle of KILSYTH; Montrose defeats Baillie.
	10 September	Rupert surrenders Bristol.
	13	Battle of PHILIPHAUGH; Montrose defeated by David Leslie.
	24	Battle of ROWTON HEATH.
	14 October	Storm of Basing House.
1646	3 February	Surrender of Chester.
	16	Battle of TORRINGTON.
	12 March	Hopton surrenders to *Sir Thomas Fairfax*.
	21	Last Royalist army dispersed at Stow-on-the-Wold.
	5 May	Charles surrenders to the Scots at Southwell.
	24 June	Surrender of Oxford.
	19 August	*Fairfax*'s troops enter Raglan Castle.
1647	16 March	Surrender of Harlech Castle, the last remaining Royalist fortress.

Four

THE EDGEHILL CAMPAIGN

The war opened with a Royalist reverse which was to have important long-term effects. The town of Hull had served as arsenal for the Scots war, and the weapons and ammunition it contained were desperately needed by Charles, who, in the early months of 1642, was preparing to raise an army at York. The King was to lose these valuable munitions through a combination of ill-luck and political shortsightedness. If Parliament held command of the sea, it would be difficult for the Royalists to seize Hull; moreover, the contents of the arsenal could be conveyed by sea to London if Hull seemed in danger.

The attitude of the navy was thus of vital importance. Its command lay in the hands of the Lord High Admiral, the Earl of Northumberland, who, trying to avoid involvement, declined to go to sea, pleading ill-health. The King then nominated Sir John Pennington as vice-admiral, to command the fleet in place of Northumberland. The latter, however, was entitled to appoint his own vice-admiral, and, prompted by Parliament, selected Robert Rich, Earl of Warwick. Warwick was an experienced soldier, a capable seaman and administrator, but, unfortunately for the King, a rigid Parliamentarian. Parliament went on to appoint Sir George Carteret rear-admiral. This was a strange decision, as Carteret was well-known to be a Royalist. Charles, claiming Parliament's action to be illegal, ordered Carteret not to serve.

Parliament capitalised on its newly acquired hold on the navy by ordering 'that two ships, of those in pay under the command of Earl of Warwick, be sent to the river of Humber, to clear the passage to the Town of Kingston upon Hull. . . .'[1] Sir John Hotham, Governor of Hull, was ordered not to admit the King or his followers and when, on 29 April, Charles appeared before the city, Hotham denied him entry. To make matters worse, the armaments at Hull, except for those needed to defend the town, were shipped to London; and a Royalist vessel, the *Providence*, bringing arms from Holland, was driven into the Humber by Parliamentarian warships and captured, though not before she had unloaded her cargo. Understandably piqued by this opposition from what

[1] *Lords Journals*, V, 20, quoted in *Documents relating to the Civil War*, edited by J. R. Powell and E. K. Timings (London 1963).

he regarded as his own navy, Charles sent Northumberland an order revoking his commission as Lord High Admiral, thereby also nullifying the commission of Warwick. Pennington, with a letter to the captains, was sent to the Downs, but was outmanoeuvred by Warwick, who, on 2 July, summoned a Council of War, which all but five captains attended. Warwick's position was speedily confirmed by Parliament, and the intransigent captains were subdued. With this, the King lost control of the fleet. He retained some of the vessels which brought, though at increasing peril, arms and ammunition from Holland, and commissioned a number of privateers. Nevertheless, the consequences of Parliament's command of the sea were momentous. The Royalists were heavily dependent upon munitions from abroad, and Warwick's fleet, though small, interdicted this flow with increasing effectiveness. Foreign intervention, too, was rendered improbable by Parliamentarian naval supremacy; not only did Charles's loss of the navy reduce his prestige in diplomatic circles, but it also turned military assistance to the King into a hazardous venture which no European power would contemplate.

In the first week of July, the Earl of Lindsey, using the Yorkshire Trained Bands, who seem to have been largely loyal to the King, and who had already covered the unloading of munitions from the *Providence*, blockaded Hull, and built three forts commanding the Humber. Warwick despatched several ships to Hull under his rear-admiral, Thomas Trenchfield. Sir John Meldrum, a competent professional soldier, had already arrived by sea with troops to strengthen Hotham's garrison. Trenchfield disembarked a further 1,500 men, and battered Lindsey's forts with his ships' guns. An assault by Meldrum then drove off the Royalists; the importance of Parliamentarian sea-power was emphasised for the second time in three months.

King Charles set about raising his army while still at York. A troop of Horse, commanded by the Prince of Wales, was raised for the protection of the King's person.[1] In June, Charles set about issuing commissions of array to his supporters in all counties, ordering them to muster troops and survey arms. In July, he began to issue commissions in earnest. Suitably commissioned, an officer would raise volunteers by beat of drum.[2] By the time Charles raised his standard, on 22 August, recruiting was well under way, though so few troops were actually assembled at Nottingham that Sir Jacob Astley warned the King 'that he could not give any assurance against his majesty being taken out of his bed, if the rebels should make a brisk attempt to that purpose'.[3]

Nevertheless, as August wore into September, the Royalist army grew steadily. Sir William Pennyman, Colonel John Belasyse, one of Lord Faucon-

---

[1] It became the nucleus of Prince Charles's regiment of Horse.
[2] Some officers were unlucky. Lieutenant John Roane, Yeoman Pricker to the King, tried to recruit in Walsall, but the Mayor 'refused to let him beat up his drum and apprehended him'. Historical Manuscripts Commission, Portland MSS., Vol. I, p. 63.
[3] Clarendon, op. cit., Vol. III, p. 194.

berg's sons, and Sir Ralph Dutton, all produced well-recruited regiments at Nottingham. Prince Rupert, too, joined the army at Nottingham, bringing with him the engineer Bernard de Gomme and the fireworker Bartholomew La Roche, as well as other officers. Lord Forth also arrived with a score of experienced Scots officers. Recruiting for the cavalry went less rapidly, doubtless because of the expensive arms and equipment needed. The Marquis of Worcester lent Sir John Byron £5,000 for 'mounting money'[1] for his regiment; even so, Byron's Horse were still under strength at Edgehill. The Royalist Horse were initially kept in the field by voluntary subscription, as the Royalist peers and ministers had undertaken to pay the Horse for three months at two shillings and sixpence a day.

Nottingham was too close to the growing Parliamentarian forces to serve as a secure concentration area, and on 13 September Charles marched west to Derby, recruiting as he went. Derbyshire miners joined in some strength, enlisting mainly in the lifeguard, commanded by Lord Willoughby d'Eresby, which had been raised, as had the Lord General's regiment, in Lincolnshire. At Derby the King was faced with the problem of selecting a line of march. Two regiments, those of Sir Thomas Salusbury and Sir Edward Stradling, had been raised in North and South Wales respectively,[2] so the King eventually decided to make for Shrewsbury, which was well-placed to ensure communications with Wales. The Royalists arrived there on 20 September and were joined by the regiments of Earl Rivers, Sir Edward Fitton and Sir Thomas Aston, all raised in Cheshire. Sir Lewis Dyve's regiment took the opportunity to add local volunteers to its nucleus of Lincolnshire and Bedfordshire men. The Somersetshire regiment of Sir Thomas Lunsford, Stradling's Welshmen and Sir John Beaumont's Staffordshire Foot joined the army towards the middle of October, after successfully eluding Essex's army in the Worcester area. By the time they reached the King, however, the Royalist advance on London was already under way.

Parliament started to raise troops in early June, though Essex himself was not commissioned as captain-general until 13 July.[3] The cavalry was originally raised in troops, each numbering sixty men. There were soon at least seventy-seven of these troops, which were, rather belatedly, organised into regiments.[4] There appear to have been two regiments of dragoons, under Colonel John Brown and Colonel James Wardlawe, each regiment comprising six troops of

---

[1] Mounting Money was the exception rather than the rule in the Royalist army. In the Parliamentarian army, though, each captain who undertook to raise a troop of Horse received £1,100 to provide his troops with arms and horses. See Firth, op. cit., p. 18.

[2] Two more regiments, those of Herbert and Owen, were, in fact, also being raised in Wales, but were not ready in time for Edgehill.

[3] Godfrey Davies, 'The Parliamentary Army under the Earl of Essex', English Historical Review, 1934, p. 33.

[4] This reorganisation seems to have been only partially completed by the time of Edgehill. See Peter Young, Edgehill, pp. 99–100.

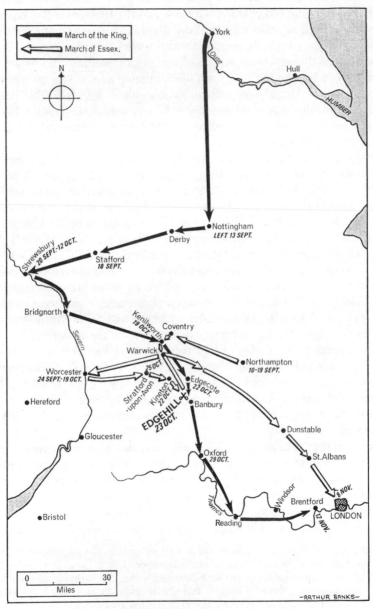

March of the King.

March of Essex.

York

Hull

HUMBER

Ouse

Nottingham
LEFT 13 SEPT.

Derby

Shrewsbury
20 SEPT.-12 OCT.

Stafford
18 SEPT.

Bridgnorth

Kenilworth
19 OCT.

Coventry

Warwick

Severn

Worcester
24 SEPT.-19 OCT.

Northampton
10-19 SEPT.

Hereford

Stratford
-upon-Avon

25 OCT.

Edgecote
22 OCT.

Kineton
22 OCT.

EDGEHILL
23 OCT.

Banbury

Gloucester

Dunstable

Oxford
29 OCT.

St.Albans

Bristol

Thames

Windsor

Brentford

8 NOV.

LONDON

Reading

12 NOV.

N

0   30
Miles

~ARTHUR BANKS~

I   THE CAMPAIGN OF EDGEHILL, 1642

between sixty and one hundred men. No fewer than twenty regiments of Foot were raised, mainly from London, the Home Counties, and the South Midlands. Recruitment was no doubt improved by the fact that Parliamentarian colonels, unlike their Royalist counterparts, were liberally provided with levy money. This sufficiency of cash did not last long, however, for, as Essex's army concentrated around Northampton in early September, there were increasing complaints about that omnipresent problem, lack of pay. Essex reviewed his troops on 14 September, and to his experienced eye the sight cannot have been altogether encouraging. Shortage of pay combined with absence of training to make many regiments sullen and uncooperative. Nevertheless, the raw material had potential, and there were some experienced officers to leaven the untrained masses.

Though the Royalist army exhibited higher morale, it was numerically smaller, and the situation at the outset of the campaign favoured Essex, whose army at first lay between that of the King and his most probable objective, London. Soon, however, Essex marched on Worcester, where the Royalist Sir John Byron, with his regiment of Horse, had arrived on 19 September with the plate of the University of Oxford. Although the town's defences proved to be in derelict condition, Charles hoped that it might be held, and sent Prince Rupert, with eight troops of Horse and ten companies of dragoons, to reinforce Byron.

Rupert arrived at Worcester on 23 September, correctly appreciated that the town was untenable, and ordered a withdrawal. To cover this manoeuvre, he rode to Powick Bridge, a mile and a half south of the city, and took up a covering position. The cavalry were dismounted, and posted in a slight depression just north of the River Teme while the dragoons lined the hedges between them and the bridge. Rupert then let his men get some sleep. Unknown to the Prince, a Parliamentarian force was close at hand. Colonel John Brown, a professional soldier and commander of one of Parliament's dragoon regiments, had left Essex at Allerton on 22 September and marched, via Upton-on-Severn, in an effort to make contact with a force of Gloucestershire Roundheads who were advancing on Worcester by way of Tewkesbury. Brown had at his disposal ten troops of Horse and five companies of dragoons, roughly 1,000 men in all – about the same number as Rupert commanded.

THE ACTION AT POWICK BRIDGE, 23 SEPTEMBER

After a gruelling night march, Brown's detachment reached Powick Ham, the meadow south of the bridge, before dawn on 23 September. There had already been some disagreement between Brown and his troop commanders, three of whom, Captains Edward Wingate, Nathaniel and John Fiennes, were Members of Parliament. These officers advocated caution, but Brown was supported by Colonel Edwin Sandys, the next senior officer. Brown kept his troops mounted for the rest of the night, tiring horses and men, and singing a Psalm or two. After it became light, he lined the low ridge running from Ham Hill to Powick Church with dragoons, but, it seems, failed to post an observer in the church tower, or to push a reconnaissance forward across the bridge. Either of these basic precautions could have resulted in early warning of the Royalist advance. Nothing more was done until about 4 p.m. when a messenger arrived from Sir William Balfour, lieutenant-general of the Horse, informing Brown that Essex's main body was now nearing Worcester, although the artillery had not managed to keep up. Brown and Sandys decided to march at once, but first had to override their troop commanders, who suggested that a little more care should be taken. While Brown was bringing down his dragoons, Nathaniel Fiennes managed to persuade Sandys to send a small party ahead to gain intelligence. Sandys crossed the bridge, where only four could go abreast, and moved on up the lane; there he halted, almost within musket shot of Rupert's dragoons, ordered forward the commanded men of the advanced guard, and pressed on.

Rupert's dragoons opened fire on the Roundhead Horse at point-blank range, and, although they failed to stop the impetuous Sandys, the dragoons' musketry gave the Royalist cavalry time to mount. Rupert, who with his principal officers, including his younger brother Maurice, had been resting under a hawthorn tree, decided to charge the enemy as soon as they came in sight. Prince Maurice, Lord Digby, Wilmot and Byron and other officers and gentlemen fell in about the Prince while their troops came on in order behind them.

Sandys was moving so fast that the troops in the rear had to gallop to keep closed up. Once clear of the lane, the Roundhead commanders made all possible speed to deploy, but before the first five troops were through the gates. and before those already in the field were properly drawn up, Rupert's men charged.

The impact of the Prince's charge was considerable. Sandys's troop lost their leader and fled. Nathaniel Fiennes's men fought better, receiving the charge of Sir Lewis Dyve's troop. Sir Lewis's men fired their pistols as they came on, in the Continental style, but were received with a volley of carbine fire and were quite badly cut up in the ensuing mêlée. However, Fiennes's success was isolated; his troop was split up, some being driven into his brother's troop, on his left. Nathaniel himself managed to hack his way to the gate, and with his cornet and four or five men rode for the bridge and got across. As the victorious Cavalier Horse drove the broken Roundheads towards the Teme, Brown held the bridge with his dragoons and checked the pursuit. Nathaniel Fiennes tried in vain to make some of the cavalry stand, but many of the officers had fallen, and the troopers would stop for nobody. The fugitives from Powick Bridge crossed the Severn at Upton and galloped towards Pershore, meeting Essex's lifeguard, who became infected with the panic and, imagining the Cavaliers to be hot on their heels, rode, loose rein and bloody spur, back to the main body of the Earl's army.

The Cavaliers, meanwhile, had rounded up between fifty and eighty prisoners and retreated into Worcester, marching that night to Tenbury. The wounded Roundhead officers were left in the city, Prince Rupert giving orders that they should be carefully looked after. Richard Crane, the commander of the Prince's lifeguard, an officer who had fought under him at Breda and Lemgo, took the despatch and six or seven captured cornets to the King, whom he found at Chester. Charles knighted Crane, whose news no doubt came as a good omen to the Cheshire Cavaliers, then actively engaged in levying soldiers. The casualties in this action were few in number: twenty-eight men were buried, some of them Cavaliers; in addition, a number of the Roundheads were drowned. In all, Brown's casualties may have been totalled between 100 and 150, including at least fifteen out of some sixty commissioned officers. The Cavaliers lost few, and none of name, though Prince Maurice, Wilmot, Dyve, Lucas and one of the Byrons were among the wounded.

The results of the first action of any campaign are moral rather than physical. An engagement where not more than 2,000 men were involved would warrant little attention in the later stages of the war. There were many such, and some must pass altogether unnoticed in these pages. But at Powick Bridge, the first serious clash between the main armies of Charles and Essex, the Cavaliers drew first blood, setting the tone of much that was to follow. This action proved, in Clarendon's words, of 'great advantage and benefit to the King. . . . For it being the first action his Horse had been brought to, and that party of the enemy being the most picked and choice men, it gave his troops great courage, and rendered the name of Prince Rupert very terrible indeed . . . [for many of the Roundhead fugitives] . . . in all places, talked loud of the incredible and irresistible courage of Prince Rupert and the King's Horse.'[1]

On 12 October, the King set out from Shrewsbury to march on London. With him were thirteen regiments of Foot, ten of Horse and three of dragoons, together with the twenty cannon of the train of artillery. Other units were in the process of being raised, or were already marching to join the Royalist army. Essex had twenty regiments of Foot, sixty-one troops of Horse and forty-six guns.[2] Much of this force was spread around in garrisons – Hereford, Worcester, Coventry, Northampton and Banbury were all strongly held – and a detachment in Warwick Castle covered Essex's lateral communications. This dispersion was questionable, since it prevented Essex acting with any decisiveness against the Royalist main body. It might, however, be argued that Essex was unable, for political reasons, to take the offensive; negotiations between King

[1] Clarendon, op. cit., Vol. III, pp. 236–7. Clarendon also mentions that none of Rupert's men were wearing their armour; they would, no doubt, have removed it before snatching some sleep. The fact that the Roundheads were upon them before they had time to buckle on back and breast illustrates the impetuous haste of Sandys's advance.
[2] According to the news-sheet *Speciall Passages*, whose numbers, making no mention of dragoons, are questionable.

and Parliament had only recently been broken off, and were to be intermittently resumed later.

The Royalist advance was delayed by atrocious weather, and by the lumbering column of impedimenta: artillery, senior officers' coaches, spare saddle horses, pack animals, victuallers, and, inevitably, women, clogged the muddy Midland roads as the King moved south. The rate of advance was consequently slow, and a sally by the garrison of Warwick Castle carried off some of the baggage, which had become isolated from the main body. Some degree of dispersion was, indeed, essential. There were few tents available, and the sharp October nights made it necessary for the army to spend each night quartered in a wide circle of villages.

The Earl of Essex left Worcester on 19 October, endeavouring to interpose his army between Charles and London. He was, though, encumbered by his train, which 'was so very great that he could move but in slow marches'. A further impediment to operations was, as Clarendon so trenchantly points out, that 'neither army knew where the other was'.[1] This was owing to poor intelligence[2] and insufficient cavalry reconnaissance. The cavalry of both sides were what later centuries would term heavy. Their commanders were preoccupied with their primary rôle, shock action on the battlefield, as cavalry officers have all too often tended to be. Forward reconnaissance was sadly neglected.[3]

On Saturday 22 October the Royalist army arrived at Edgecote, near Banbury. A reconnaissance in force, under Lord Digby, an amateur soldier if ever there was one, had found no traces of the Roundheads, who marched into Kineton after dark. On arrival at Edgecote, the Royalists held a Council of War, where it was decided that the army would spend the following day resting in quarters, with the exception of Sir Nicholas Byron's Brigade, which, reinforced with two brass demi-cannon and two brass culverins, was to assault the Parliamentarian garrison of Banbury.[4]

The Royalists spent the night, as was their custom, widely dispersed in the area between Cropredy and Edgecote. The King himself was at Edgecote, and Lindsey was at Culworth. Rupert was quartered at Wormleighton, and as his quartermasters rode into the village, they met their Roundhead counterparts,

---

[1] Partially due to the fact that Essex had no scoutmaster-general. The exceptionally able Sir Samuel Luke was not commissioned as such until 14 January 1643. See *Commonwealth Exchequer Papers*, SP 28, 127.

[2] Clarendon, op. cit., Vol. III, p. 272.

[3] Reconnaissance and pursuit are, traditionally, the rôle of the light cavalry, which did not really exist in the Royalist or Parliamentarian armies. The *chasseur* and hussar of succeeding centuries were trained and, in theory, equipped to carry out these essential tasks, but even so they very often failed to do so. The French cavalry in 1859 and 1870, the Union cavalry in the Chancellorsville campaign and their Confederate opponents at Gettysburg all proved lamentably bad at reconnaissance.

[4] Banbury was held by the Earl of Peterborough's regiment of Foot and a troop of Horse. The guns allotted to Byron were the heaviest with the army at the time. See p. 77, n. 1 below.

apparently also searching for billets. The Parliamentarians were taken prisoner, and Rupert promptly followed up by sending twenty-four troopers of his own regiment, under Lieutenant Clement Martin, to Kineton. Martin returned with the news that the Roundheads were present in strength. Rupert was all for attacking without delay, but this bold and hazardous plan was not carried out. The King, who heard Rupert's news at around midnight, seems to have taken some of the advice which his nephew offered, and issued orders for a concentration, early on the 23rd, on Edgehill.[1] Essex seems to have been less well informed. He appears to have thought that the King was still intending to attack Banbury, and decided to march at once to its relief.

THE BATTLE OF EDGEHILL, 23 OCTOBER

The main road from Kineton to Banbury is crossed squarely by the ridge of Edgehill. This rises 300 feet from the surrounding plain, and faces north-west, curling eastwards at its northern end. It is some three miles long; its slope is steep, reaching a gradient of one in four. Although now wooded, in 1642 Edgehill was bare, apart from one small clump of trees. The plain between the hill and Kineton was fairly open in the centre, though there was some scrub and furze, and a single hedge ran between what are now Thistle and Battle Farms. This hedge still exists, with a track running alongside it. On the Royalist right wing there were five or six hedges which were to lie between the two armies, while the other wing was very enclosed on the Kineton side with a number of small fields and orchards. What makes the battlefield difficult to locate with precision nowadays is that some copses that were present at the time of the battle have been cut down, and others have been planted since that time. The greater part of the battlefield is covered by an ordnance depot which makes it difficult to visit the scenes of the fiercest fighting.

Prince Rupert arrived at the rendezvous upon Edgehill by daybreak. The rest of the Horse arrived between 10 and 11 a.m., and were followed by the Foot, whose vanguard came up at about noon, though the rearguard did not appear till more than two hours later. Looking towards Kineton, the Royalists could see 'the Rebels' Army drawing out, and setting themselves in Battalion . . .'.[2] Essex had an opportunity of placing himself between the King and London by rising early and moving rapidly south-east, but had failed to do so, probably because his quarters were widely dispersed, and his concentration, like that of the Royalists, required time. As it was, the Cavalier army lay between the Roundhead general and his base.

The Parliamentarian army, if not already on the move, must have been

[1] Warburton, op. cit., Vol. II, p. 12.
[2] Sir William Dugdale (?), *A Relation of the Battel fought between Keynton and Edgehill* . . . (Oxford 1642). This, the Royalist official account, is reprinted in Peter Young's *Edgehill*, pp. 261–4.

assembled in and around Kineton, when at about 8 a.m. the alarm was given of the Royalist concentration. Adoniram Bifield, Chaplain to Cholmley's regiment, rode out and claimed that 'it pleased God' to make him 'the first Instrument of giving a certain discovery of it, by the help of a prospective glass from the top of a Hill . . .'.[1] Essex could see little of the Royalist dispositions, for the hill was so steep that only men on the very edge were visible. He was, moreover, preoccupied by several considerations. There had, as yet, been no major clash between the main armies on either side, and Essex was reluctant, for political as well as tactical reasons, to attack. Furthermore, the concentration of his army was incomplete, and if the Cavaliers declined to attack him, he could expect to be stronger next day by three regiments of Foot, eleven troops of Horse and not less than seven guns. Although the King lay between the Earl and London, he had Warwick Castle at his back, and, with the Royalists concentrating against him, the danger to Banbury was averted.

The strength of Essex's army lay between the Kineton–Knowle End road and the Little Kineton–Radway road, between 1¼ and 1½ miles from the centre of Kineton. Essex's right, Lord Feilding's regiment of Horse, with two regiments of dragoons covering its flank, was posted where the wood known as the Oaks now stands. Sir William Fairfax's regiment of Foot lay on Feilding's left, but still south-west of the road. The Parliamentarian centre was drawn up in two lines. In the first line were the Foot brigades of Sir John Meldrum[2] and Colonel Charles Essex.[3] The latter formation was supported by Colonel Thomas Ballard's[4] brigade, while the cavalry regiments of Sir Philip Stapleton and Sir William Balfour supported Charles Essex. Sir James Ramsey, with 24 troops of Horse and 600 musketeers (the latter taken from Ballard's brigade), composed the left wing. Ramsey placed bodies of musketeers between the squadrons in the first of his two lines and posted the remaining 300 to line hedges on his left, with a proportion at right-angles to the rest of his line, so as to be able to take any assault in enfilade. Those of the Parliamentarian guns that could be brought up were probably placed in pairs between the bodies of infantry in the front line.

The somewhat disjointed concentration of the Royalists, whose arrival at Edgehill was spread over six hours or more, gave their generals ample time to observe the disposition of the enemy and to quarrel about their own. The Earl of Lindsey, as Lord General, was senior to all other Royalist officers, with the

---

[1] Adoniram Bifield, *Letter*, British Museum, Thomason Tracts E.124 (21). Also reprinted in Peter Young, op. cit., pp. 317–19.

[2] Three regiments – Robartes's, Constable's and Meldrum's (previously Lord Saye and Sele's) in the first line, with one, Fairfax's, drawn back slightly so as to cover the right flank.

[3] Four regiments – Essex's, Wharton's, Mandeville's and Cholmley's – in line. These were probably drawn up, as were the remainder of the Parliamentarian infantry, in eight ranks, as was customary in the Dutch service, whence Essex drew most of his tactics.

[4] The regiments of the Earl of Essex, Ballard, Brooke and Holles. The three brigades of Foot were each about 4,000 strong.

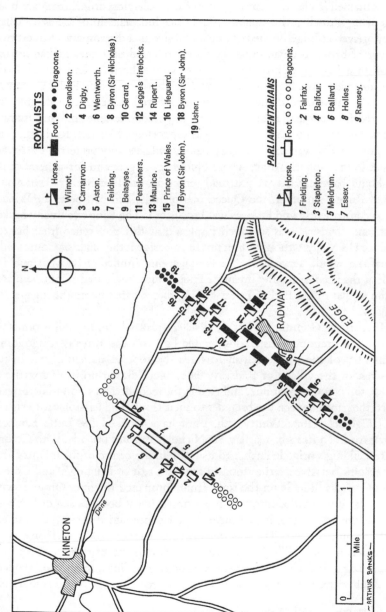

ROYALISTS

▲ Horse. ■ Foot. ●●● Dragoons.

1 Wilmot.
3 Carnarvon.
5 Aston.
7 Feilding.
9 Belasyse.
11 Pensioners.
13 Maurice.
15 Prince of Wales.
17 Byron (Sir John).
19 Usher.

2 Grandison.
4 Digby.
6 Wentworth.
8 Byron (Sir Nicholas).
10 Gerard.
12 Legge's firelocks.
14 Rupert.
16 Lifeguard.
18 Byron (Sir John).

PARLIAMENTARIANS

▨ Horse. ▢ Foot. ○○○ Dragoons.

1 Fielding.
3 Stapleton.
5 Meldrum.
7 Essex.

2 Fairfax.
4 Balfour.
6 Ballard.
8 Holles.
9 Ramsey.

KINETON

Dene

EDGE HILL

RADWAY

N

0   Mile   1

—ARTHUR BANKS—

2 EDGEHILL

obvious exception of the King, but Rupert's commission as general of the Horse contained 'a clause exempting him from receiving orders from anybody but the King himself',[1] thus making the Prince independent of Lindsey. When Lindsey arrived at Edgehill, he became embroiled in a dispute with Rupert over the order of battle to be adopted. Lindsey 'preferred the order he had learned under Prince Maurice, and Prince Henry, with whom he had served at the same time, when the Earl of Essex and he, both of them, had regiments'.[2] Rupert advocated instead the more complex Swedish brigade, a flexible and battle-tried formation, but one which required considerable skill and training amongst officers and soldiers. Rupert was supported by Patrick Ruthven, Lord Forth. Forth had served under Gustav Adolf, and naturally preferred the Swedish order to the Dutch. Astley, whose opinion as sergeant-major-general of the Foot should have carried weight, had served in the Dutch army, but was a friend of Rupert's mother, the Queen of Bohemia, and had been the Prince's tutor, so consequently said little, as was his custom. The King eventually backed Rupert, and Lindsey 'was so much displeas'd at this preference [that he] ... said, Since His Majesty thought him not fit to perform the office of Commander in Chief, he would serve him as a Colonel, and immediately went and put himself at the head of his Regiment of Foot, which he desired might be placed opposite to that of the Earl of Essex, hoping thereby that he might engage him personally'.[3]

Sir Bernard de Gomme has left an excellent plan which, though it omits the guns and the dragoons, casts considerable light on the Royalist dispositions. The infantry of the centre fell in towards the foot of Edgehill, that is, just north-west of the village of Radway. They were drawn up in five tertias or brigades, three in the front line, and two in the second. The second-line brigade covered the gaps between the brigades to their front. The left-forward brigade, that of Colonel Henry Wentworth, must have blocked the Little Kineton–Radway road. To its right rear lay Sir Nicholas Byron's brigade, with Colonel Richard Feilding's brigade farther to its right, in the centre of the infantry line. Colonel John Belasyse's tertia stood to the right rear of Feilding's, and Colonel Charles Gerard's brigade on the right front completed the line. On each wing were the cavalry, divided into two more or less equal bodies, each of five regiments, drawn up in two lines. Prince Rupert commanded the right wing and Henry Wilmot the left. The Gentlemen Pensioners, a troop of Horse under their lieutenant, Sir William Howard, K.B., lay to the rear of the Foot, near 'Colonel Leg's firelocks', who were no doubt guarding the train of artillery. Some doubt exists as to the location of the three regiments of Royalist dragoons,

[1] Clarendon, op. cit., Vol. III, p. 270.
[2] Ibid., p. 271.
[3] James II, *Life of James II ... collected out of memoirs writ of his hand ...*, edited by J. S. Clarke (London 1816). James was present at Edgehill as a boy; his valuable account is reproduced in Peter Young, op. cit., pp. 274–80.

who numbered, in all, about 1,000. It seems likely that two regiments were under Sir Arthur Aston on the left, while Colonel James Usher's regiment was on the right. The dragoons would probably have dismounted to line hedges on the flanks of the wings of Horse.

The Royalist artillery, although it had not half as many cannon as the Parliamentarian train, had an infinitely more able lieutenant-general, Sir John Heydon, who had managed to organise a train of twenty guns. The lighter pieces were placed either in front of, or between, the bodies of Foot in the first line.[1] The heavy guns were placed in battery on the lower slopes of Edgehill, probably to the rear of the right brigade, for that is where the firelocks appear in de Gomme's plan, and one would expect them to be in a position to guard the train.

The battle began with a somewhat ineffective artillery duel. The Parliamentarian guns, profiting by the nature of the ground which gave them a ricochet while denying it to their opponents, seem to have made the better practice, though casualties were light on both sides. Usher's dragoons were then sent to clear the musketeers from the edges on the Roundhead left, 'which they very well performed'.[2] Sir Arthur Aston carried out a similar service on the Royalist left. Rupert then ordered his wing to advance. He trotted forward in good order, breaking into the canter and finally the gallop when close to the hostile cavalry. Ramsey's Horse awaited the impact while stationary – a dubious tactic. They fired their carbines at the approaching Royalists when they were still out of range,[3] and, shaken by the ineffectiveness of this fire, and the wholesale defection of Sir Faithful Fortescue's troop, turned and fled. Rupert's men pursued the Roundheads into Kineton, doing considerable damage amongst the fleeing troopers and the small bodies of musketeers who had interlarded the Parliamentarian squadrons. Sir John Byron's men, forming the second line of Rupert's wing, seeing the opposing cavalry driven from the field, 'thought there was nothing more to be done but to pursue those that fled, and could not be contained by their commander, but with spurs and loose reins followed the chase . . .'.[4] Much the same happened on the Royalist left; Wilmot's charge swept away Lord Feilding's regiment, and Lord Digby, commanding Wilmot's second line, joined in the pursuit. With this, the greater part of the Royalist Horse poured off north-westwards. Prince Rupert managed to halt three troops

---

[1] Joshua Moone, Colonel John Belasyse's secretary, states that two cannon were placed 'before every body of Foot . . .'. This seems an unusual procedure, but the evidence of an eye-witness cannot be lightly overruled. *See* HMC New Series, Vol. III, 1903. Also Peter Young, op. cit., pp. 288–91. The Royalist artillery mustered twenty guns, viz.: Demicannons, 2; Culverins, 2; Demi-culverins, 2; Falcons, 6; Falconets, 6; Robinets, 2. *See* Dr Ian Roy, *The Royalist Ordnance Papers, 1642–6*, Part I (Oxfordshire Record Society, 1964). Peter Young, 'The Royalist Artillery at Edgehill, 23 October 1642', *Journal of the Society for Army Historical Research*, 1953.
[2] Dugdale, op. cit.
[3] *The Vindication . . . of Sir James Ramsey*, TT 669, f. 6,184.
[4] Clarendon, op. cit., Vol. III, p. 278–9.

from his wing, while Lieutenant-Colonel Sir Charles Lucas, Lord Grandison and a few other level-headed officers rallied 200 troopers on the left.

While the Royalist cavalry spurred forward on the flanks, the Royalist Foot began their advance. They were led by the veteran Sir Jacob Astley. 'Oh Lord!', he prayed, 'Thou knowest how busy I must be this day. If I forget Thee, do not Thou forget me.' With this, he rose to his feet, shouted 'March on Boys', and moved off with his infantry at a steady pace, the two rear brigades closing up into the gaps, and the whole body thus 'came on very gallantly to the Charge'.[1] The sight of the oncoming Royalists, together with the rout of the Parliamentarian wings, proved too much for Charles Essex's brigade, which broke in disorder, despite the efforts of Essex himself and a few stout-hearted officers. Disaster was averted by Ballard, who marched his brigade forward into the gap left by the fugitives, covering the left of Meldrum's brigade.

Ballard moved up in time to sustain the impact of the 10,500 Royalist Foot. A bitter struggle raged as the infantry came to push of pike. Both sides stood their ground with great determination. As James II observed, 'it were reasonable to imagine that one side should run and be disordered; but it happened otherwise, for each as if by mutual consent retired some few paces, they struck down their colours, continuing to fire at one another even till night'.[2]

Although the cavalry on the Parliamentarian wing had left the field in flight, two regiments, those of Sir William Balfour and Sir Philip Stapleton, in the rear of Meldrum's brigade, were as yet unengaged. Balfour led them forward, through the gaps in Meldrum's front, against the Royalist Foot. Stapleton's attack was briskly received by Sir Nicholas Byron's brigade, but Balfour's men crashed into Feilding's brigade and broke it, capturing its commander and two of his colonels, Stradling and Lunsford. The cavalry surged forward into the Royalist heavy guns and cut down some of the gunners, but no means were at hand for spiking the cannon. Balfour eagerly called for 'nails, nails', but had to content himself with cutting the drag-ropes to prevent the guns being moved. With this, he prudently fell back to his original position. Stapleton, meanwhile, had taken up a position guarding the Parliamentarian guns, whose escort had taken to their heels, and succeeded in firing one of the pieces at some oncoming cavalry, who turned out to be Balfour's victorious troops making their way back.

Essex now ordered an attack on Sir Nicholas Byron's brigade. Lord Robartes's and Sir William Constable's regiments of Foot, supported by the cavalry of Balfour and Stapleton, charged Byron, and, aided by Ballard with the regiments

---

[1] *An Exact and True Relation of the Dangerous and Bloody Fight . . . neere Kyneton . . .* (London, 28 October 1642), in John Rushworth, *Historical Collections . . . 1618–1649* (London 1659–1701, 7 volumes), Part III, Vol. II, pp. 35–9. Also in Peter Young, op. cit., pp. 306–11. This letter to Pym is signed by six Parliamentarian officers, and may be deemed the official Parliamentarian account of Edgehill.

[2] James II, op. cit.

of the Lord General and Lord Brooke, broke into the Royalist brigade and drove it back some way. The Earl of Lindsey, fighting on foot at the head of his regiment, had his thigh broken by a musket shot, and fell, mortally wounded. His son, Lord Willoughby d'Eresby, commanding the redcoats of the lifeguard, bestrode the fallen Earl, plying his half-pike with resolution until he was captured. The lifeguard itself was locked in combat with Constable's regiment. Sir Edmund Verney, Knight Marshal of England, who bore the banner royal in the ranks of the lifeguard, was attacked, and 'killed two with his own hands, whereof one had killed poor Jason (his servant) and broke the point of his standard at push of pike before he fell. . . .'[1] The standard was captured, and sent to the rear in the hands of Robert Chambers, the Earl of Essex's secretary. Byron's brigade suffered fairly heavily; Sir Nicholas himself was wounded, Lieutenant-Colonel Monro of the Lord General's regiment killed, and Lieutenant-Colonel Sir William Vavasour of the lifeguard captured.

Meanwhile, Sir Charles Lucas had launched his 200 Horse in a charge against Essex's rear. Fortunately for Meldrum and Ballard they ran into a mob of runaways, probably from Charles Essex's brigade, cut them about, and pressed on pell-mell, taking colours and killing fugitives. Captain John Smith, of Lord Grandison's regiment of Horse, took a colour of Lord Wharton's regiment, but, on looking round, found he had only one man left with him. As he trotted back to the King's army he noticed six horsemen, escorting a man on foot who was bearing what appeared to be one of the company colours of the lifeguard. At this moment a boy called to him 'Captain Smith! Captain Smith, they are carrying away the standard!' Smith was eventually persuaded that it was indeed the banner royal, and saying 'they shall have me with it, if they carry it away!' dashed forward, with a cry of 'Traitor, deliver the standard!' He killed one Roundhead, wounded another, and, though himself hurt, drove off the others and recaptured the banner. Smith further distinguished himself by freeing Colonel Richard Feilding, and was, on the following day, knighted for his exploits.

Prince Rupert's Horse were still engaged in pursuing fugitives, and reaping a rich booty in colours and equipment – including the Earl of Essex's coach – in and around Kineton. It is unreasonable to blame Rupert, as many historians have, for the recklessness of his cavalry. Controlling cavalry has always been extremely difficult, and the relative inexperience of Rupert's men, most of whom had at most only a few months' military service, further worsened the Prince's task. Blame might, more reasonably, be laid on Sir John Byron, who should have prevented the second line of cavalry becoming involved in the pursuit, and instead used it against the flank of the enemy infantry. The Royalist cavalry were eventually checked by the arrival of the Parliamentarian forces

[1] Letter of Sir Edward Sydenham to Ralph Verney, 28 October 1642, quoted by Major Peter Verney in *The Standard Bearer* (London 1964), p. 202. Also in Peter Young, op. cit., pp. 291–2.

who had been quartered too far away to intervene in the battle proper. Several troops of Horse converged on Kineton, where they joined the leading elements of Colonel John Hampden's brigade, on its way to join Essex. With this, Rupert's cavalry drifted back towards their own lines, their horses for the most part blown, and their riders tired. Five Royalist troops were charged by Stapleton and escaped only with loss, but with the return of much of the Royalist cavalry their harassed Foot 'made up a kind of Body again'.[1] The infantry of the Royalist right 'retired orderly, and at last made a stand; and having assistance of cannon, and a ditch before them, held us play very handsomely . . .'.[2]

Lord Falkland urged that the cavalry should renew the attack. Rupert, usually ready for any desperate venture, could not agree; his horsemen were exhausted and disorganised, and darkness was falling rapidly over the stricken field. There was even a proposal that the Royalists should abandon the position under cover of darkness, but Charles, his natural obstinacy strengthened by Sir John Culpeper's forthright arguments, decided against this, and spent the night himself at the foot of the hill, at what is now called King's Leys Barn. His troops slept where they could, still within cannon shot of their equally tired and famished opponents. Both armies had been fought to a standstill, and, though each side claimed victory, the battle ended in the stalemate of mutual exhaustion.

During the night Essex was reinforced by Hampden's brigade, consisting of two regiments of Foot, with Lord Willoughby of Parham's regiment of Horse, several troops that had rallied on the brigade at the close of the previous day, and some cannon. Hampden and his officers were eager to fight, but Essex did not share their confidence. His cavalry had suffered severely, and the infantry of Charles Essex's brigade had ceased to exist as a formed body.[3] Nor were the Royalists in much better order. Clarendon tells us that 'a third part of the Foot were not upon the place, and of the Horse many missing'.[4] A large proportion of those absent had disappeared in search of more comfortable lodgings, and reappeared during the course of the morning, but the general air of confusion that prevailed made any renewal of the Royalist attack impossible.

At about noon the King sent Sir William le Neve, Clarenceux King of Arms, to offer pardon to all of Essex's army who would lay down their arms. Sir William was brusquely received by the Earl, and his mission proved predictably fruitless. Neither side was eager to renew the action, and the King ordered his men back to the quarters they had occupied before the battle, while Essex retreated on Warwick.

Edgehill is usually reckoned a drawn battle. Certainly, the losses on both sides were about equal – perhaps 1,500 in all. On the Royalist side, the old Earl of

---

[1] John Rushworth, op. cit.
[2] Ibid.
[3] Colonel Sir Henry Cholmley's regiment of Foot, for example, had 1,200 men on 1 October, and only 552 on 23 November. Most of those missing were Edgehill casualties or deserters.
[4] Clarendon, op. cit., Vol. III, p. 283.

Lindsey died of his wound, reproaching his captors for their disloyalty, and Lord Forth was appointed Lord General in his place. Sir Edmund Verney and Lord d'Aubigny were among the dead, while numerous senior officers were wounded or captured. The Parliamentarians had lost Colonel Lord Saint John, Essex's old page and comrade-in-arms, and Colonel Charles Essex who, after his own brigade had taken to its heels, joined Ballard's and died fighting. Although Edgehill was indecisive in tactical terms, it represented a strategic victory for the King, who had cleared the road to London, and captured seven guns to add to his needy train of artillery. While Essex licked his wounds at Warwick, the King prepared to resume his march on his disaffected capital.

Both armies, their rudimentary administration strained to the uttermost, were remarkably slow in getting on the move again. The Royalists, whose primary consideration should have been a rapid descent on London, were somewhat quicker off the mark than their opponents, but even so did not take Banbury until 27 October. It capitulated as soon as the Royalist guns opened fire; the garrison was allowed to depart without its arms, and a large number joined the Royalists. Shortly after this, Rupert proposed to the Council of War that a flying column of 3,000 Horse and Foot should march on Westminster. This suggestion, though rather rash, might have produced useful results, particularly if the column had arrived hard on the heels of those of the Edgehill fugitives who had fled to London and announced dismally that all was up with Essex's army. Rupert's proposal was overruled, and the King marched to Oxford, 'which was the only city of England that he could say was entirely at his devotion; where he was received by the university to whom the integrity and fidelity of that place is to be imputed, with all joy and acclamation'.[1] The occupation of Oxford was of major importance to the Royalists, for it was to be their capital and chief fortress for nearly four years.

From Oxford, the King moved to Reading, which he entered on 4 November. In London, meanwhile, the atmosphere of gloom was slowly replaced by one of growing resolution. The Commons authorised the enlistment of apprentices, and sent a request for aid from the Scots to 'put an end to this unnatural war and combustion in the Kingdom'.[2] London's determination was increased by the news of the depredations of the Cavaliers on their march southwards. Londoners were convinced that a good deal of looting would accompany a Royalist entry into the City, and were eager to avert this. Morale was further raised by the arrival, on 8 November, of Essex's army, which had entered London from the north.

The Royalists moved slowly on the capital. Rupert summoned Windsor Castle on 7 November, but met with defiance from John Venn, M.P., and his garrison. On 11 November Charles entered Colnbrook, where he was met by the Earls of Northumberland and Pembroke, together with three members of

[1] Ibid., p. 298.
[2] Ibid., pp. 307–8.

the House of Commons. This delegation presented a petition offering to treat with the King; Charles made a temporising reply, but ordered Rupert to attack Brentford the following day.

Brentford was held by two of the steadiest regiments in Essex's army, those of Lord Brooke and Denzil Holles, and when Rupert swept into the town, out of the mist on the dawn of 12 November, the Roundhead infantry made a stout defence, but were eventually thrust back into the Thames. Many were slain or drowned, though some managed to swim the river to safety. The Royalists, according to Clarendon, took over 500 prisoners, 11 colours and 15 cannon.[1]

The storming of Brentford, with the virtual destruction of its garrison, was an important tactical success. It was soon followed by another when some barges, loaded with troops, guns and ammunition, were engaged by Royalist artillery firing from Sion House. One barge blew up in mid-stream, several more were sunk, and the remainder captured.

The Parliamentarian response to these rebuffs was impressive. The London Trained Bands mustered in Chelsea Fields on 12 November: 6,000 strong, well-armed and enthusiastic, their bright arms touched by the sinking sun, they marched out to face their King. At their head was Major-General Philip Skippon, a veteran of the Dutch service in which he had risen from the ranks by sheer merit; few generals on either side were to earn higher reputation for skill, courage and leadership. By the morning of 13 November an army of some 24,000 men was drawn up on the Common at Turnham Green. Three thousand more under Sir James Ramsey held the passage of the Thames at Kingston, the first bridge above the old London Bridge. In order to be able to operate on either side of the river, Essex sensibly used his pontoon train to throw a bridge of boats across the Thames at Putney. This done, he withdrew Ramsey's force to London Bridge so as to cover the City from the south. Essex's cautious decision to abandon Kingston before the place was even threatened was possibly prompted by the disaster suffered by his forces on the previous day.

Throughout 13 November the two armies faced each other at Turnham Green. Charles was heavily outnumbered; his men were tired, cold, and poorly equipped in comparison with their opponents, who were backed with the resources of London and the Tower. Turnham Green was, in the words of S. R. Gardiner, 'the Valmy of the English Civil War'.[2] No battle took place, the King wisely withdrawing to Hounslow during the night, while Astley and Rupert sustained the rearguard. There was still the possibility that Charles might have swung south-east, linked up with his supporters in Kent, and threatened London from the south, profiting by his superior mobility. Unhappily for the Royalist cause, Charles decided to adopt the safest course of

[1] Ibid., pp. 327-8.
[2] Samuel Rawson Gardiner, *History of the Great Civil War 1642–9* (London 1903, 4 volumes), Vol. I, p. 56.

action, and fell back to Reading, which he entered on 19 November, and thence to Oxford.

Both sides now sent their main armies into winter quarters. Essex, with his advanced post at Windsor, disposed his forces to cover the western approaches to the capital, while on 9 December the King's Council of War at Oxford settled their winter quarters over a wide area in Oxfordshire, Buckinghamshire and Berkshire. Sir Arthur Aston, colonel-general of dragoons, a testy and imperious veteran who had served in the Russian and Swedish armies, was fortifying Reading. He had six regiments of Foot and two of Horse. His communications with Oxford were secured by strong garrisons at Wallingford and Abingdon. Oxford itself was held by four regiments of Foot. A circle of garrisons girdled the King's temporary capital, with Banbury, Brill, Wallingford, Abingdon, Faringdon and Burford forming an outer ring. Oxford was entirely covered by rivers – Thames and Cherwell – except on the north side, which was doubly protected, for in that direction there was a second line of regiments quartered at Enstone, Woodstock and Islip. Fortifications, the plan of which has been carefully preserved for us by de Gomme, were put in hand, and eventually cost over £30,000. The medieval walls of Oxford were not used. On the north side the line ran east and west through the sites now occupied by the University Museum and Keble College, St Giles Church being just inside the line.[1]

The campaign ended, Essex was quite prepared to hibernate. Many of his followers, including Cromwell and Ireton, returned to their districts to defend their homes and levy new forces. On the King's side the same process occurred. Richard Bagot, who had fought the campaign as a captain in Bolles's regiment, returned to Staffordshire and rose to be Governor of Lichfield; Gervase Holles, the antiquarian who had been major to Sir Lewis Dyve, returned as a colonel to his native Grimsby. Both the main armies were seriously weakened by this process.

But if Essex was only too happy to live a quiet life, the Cavaliers were more active, and during the winter they began to clear their communications with the west. Wilmot stormed Marlborough on 5 December and on 2 February 1643 Rupert assaulted Cirencester. On the Parliamentary side only Sir William Waller displayed any activity. He destroyed two regiments at Winchester on 12 December, adding to the reputation he had already begun to make by his capture of Portsmouth.

[1] MS. Add D.114 in the Bodleian Library throws some interesting light on the problems of fortifying the city. Some houses had to be demolished to clear the glacis (f. 14). Citizens were ordered to work on the fortifications, or to pay 12d for each day's default (f. 22). This seems to have applied to soldiers as well as civilians. A Lieutenant Godwin retorted that 'when colonels and other soldiers of his rank payed he would also'. Quartermaster Stone similarly replied he would 'not pay till the King pay him' (f. 24).

Five

THE WAR IN THE WEST–I

Fighting broke out in the west even before the events described in the preceding chapter.

The early phases of the war there saw three distinct campaigns: one in Somerset and two in Devon and Cornwall. In the first, despite some tactical successes, the Cavaliers were driven out of Somerset and split up. The Marquis of Hertford crossed into Wales with his infantry, who joined the King in time for Edgehill, while Sir Ralph Hopton joined the Cornish Cavaliers and became their general in the two campaigns during which they cleared their own county and twice invaded Devon. A forty-day truce divided these last two campaigns.

William Seymour, first Marquis of Hertford, was fifty-four; he loved his ease and his books, and had become mentally and physically lazy. He was entirely without military experience, yet he had been made lieutenant-general of the six western counties, an astonishing choice from a military point of view. In his youth he had loved and secretly married the ill-starred Arabella Stuart, and for this James I had lodged him in the Tower. Yet, though few men had less reason to love the Court, he had shown himself a notably loyal and steady supporter of the King. He was besides a man of great wealth and vast estates, and generally liked for his civil and affable manners, though he could be haughty enough when he thought himself ill-used.

Hertford, though he was confident of being able to execute the Commission of Array, was accompanied only by the Earl of Bath, Lord Seymour, Sir Ralph Hopton, and a few other good officers, attended by their normal retinue. Of these the man who was destined to play the most notable part in the western war was Hopton, one of the best generals produced by the First Civil War.

Sir Ralph Hopton, K.B., was at this time forty-four years old. He was no longer a professional soldier, though he had served on the Continent during the early years of the Thirty Years War, fighting for the Elector Palatine and reaching, in 1642, the rank of lieutenant-colonel in the army under Count Mansfeld. Clarendon has much good to say of Hopton, who 'had a good understanding, a clear courage, an industry not to be tired, and a generosity that was not to be exhausted'. He was, moreover, 'a man of great honour, integrity and piety'. Nevertheless, Clarendon tells us that in debates on the conduct of the war he was too long in making up his mind, and too apt to change it afterwards, 'which rendered him rather fit for the second than the supreme command in an army'.[1] However, Clarendon was not with the western army at the time of Hopton's greatest successes, and though he had known him previously, for both were Members of Parliament, he did not meet him during the war until after he had been seriously wounded. At the beginning of the war Hopton owed his position as one of the Cavalier leaders to his wealth and social position, for his previous military experience, though valuable, was by no means remarkable. His reputation was yet to be made.

Hertford had joined the King at York in early April, taking with him the young Duke of York. Appointed lieutenant-general of Hampshire, Wiltshire, Dorset, Somerset, Devon and Cornwall, equipped with Commissions of Array, and accompanied by his brother Lord Seymour and Sir Ralph Hopton, Hertford left Beverley in mid-July, and reached Bath by the end of the month. When he arrived there, Hertford consulted his supporters as to whether to begin his work at Bristol or at Wells, choosing the latter place, in the centre of Somerset, because the gentry of that county were for the most part well disposed to the King. Had he chosen instead to have secured Bristol, the second city in the Kingdom, he would probably have done the Royalist cause a far better service. From Wells the Marquis sent his orders to Sir Edward Rodney,[2] colonel of the nearest Trained Bands, to draw in his regiment, which duly appeared, well-armed, but, for the most part, unwilling to fight.

In Somerset, Hertford found a number of officers already engaged in levying troops for the King's own army. Lieutenant-Colonel Henry Lunsford soon raised 240 Foot for his brother's regiment,[3] armed from the magazine at Wincanton; Captain John Digby[4] and Sir Francis Hawley each raised troops for Lord Grandison's regiment of Horse.[5] A third troop was raised by Hopton at his own expense, and some ammunition was obtained from the magazine at Wells. It was proposed that Lord Paulet and the gentry should guarantee to levy and lead enough Horse and dragoons to disperse any opposition, but nothing came of this project. Hopton, not unnaturally, was disgusted: 'The error of uneffective and unfinished consultations began betimes,' he wrote, 'and hath too constantly attended the business throughout.'[6]

Meanwhile the Roundhead leaders, Sir John Horner and Colonel Alexander

---

[1] Clarendon, op. cit., Vol. IV, p. 473.
[2] Member of Parliament for Wells.
[3] This became Prince Rupert's Bluecoats in the summer of 1643.
[4] There were three colonels of this name in the Royalist army. This one was the brother of Lord Digby, and fought throughout the war in the west, notably at Torrington. He was Member of Parliament for Milborne Port.
[5] They never joined their regiment, for after serving at Edgehill it was destroyed at Winchester in December.
[6] Hopton, op. cit., p. 3.

Popham,[1] had summoned their supporters to come armed to a general meeting which was held at Shepton Mallet on 1 August, promising to send several fat bucks for them to feast on. Early on the morning in question, the Marquis sent Hopton with his own troop and a number of volunteers, well appointed, to prevent this meeting. The Roundheads, some 1,200 strong, appeared and faced Hopton's force for some hours, but they did not come to blows. 'Thus innocently,' says Hopton, 'began this cursed war in those parts. . . .'[2] Throughout England similar scenes were enacted that summer, each party striving to act legally and to put off the evil day when they must imitate their half-forgotten ancestors of Barnet and Bosworth.

Hertford's next move was to issue warrants summoning the western Trained Band regiments, and in addition to collect volunteers, horses and arms. Ames Paulet, youngest son of Lord Paulet, and Edward Stawell were so diligent in this latter task that within three days they brought in forty horses, twenty dragoons and a wagon-load of arms to Wells. On 3 August some constables gave the Marquis notice that Sir John Stawell's[3] regiment of Trained Bands were ready to march, and asked that some Horse and dragoons might be sent to secure 'Borrough Bridge', the passage over the River Parret above Bridgwater.

The Powick Bridge of the western war took place at Marshall's Elm, between Wells and Somerton, on 4 August 1642, where 80 Cavaliers under Sir John Stawell routed 600 Roundheads under John Pyne, the M.P. for Poole. The Royalists owed their victory to the skilful tactics of Lieutenant-Colonel Lunsford, who drew up their Horse on Walton Hill in a single rank in such a way that only their heads showed. The Roundheads naturally believed that there were two more ranks in rear. Lunsford placed two small parties of dragoons in gravel pits – which can still be seen – in front of the main body. When the Roundheads eventually advanced, a very small volume of fire – about forty rounds – was sufficient to make them 'stagger'. A sharp charge at this critical moment put an end to the business.

Despite this minor disaster, the local Roundheads were still formidable. On the next day, while Hertford was holding a review near Wells, great bodies of Foot with flying colours, some Horse and some iron guns appeared on the top of the Mendip Hills. Horner, Popham, Strode, Pyne and others had drawn together a force from south and east Somersetshire and from Bristol, which the Cavaliers estimated at 10,000 or 12,000 men. Hertford had no alternative but to retreat. He reached Sherborne two nights later. Here a Council of War decided to put the old Castle into a state of defence, and to try to recruit more men.

The rest of August passed peacefully enough, and the Cavaliers used the lull

[1] Popham was Member of Parliament for Bath.
[2] Hopton, op. cit., p. 5.
[3] Member of Parliament for Somerset.

to good effect. A number of good officers joined, including Colonel Sir Thomas Lunsford, whose brother by this time had raised him 400 men.

Parliament, alarmed, no doubt, by the action at Marshall's Elm, sent down the Earl of Bedford who, towards the end of the month, concentrated 7,000 men at Wells. Besides the Somersetshire Roundheads, he had a contingent from Dorset under Denzil Holles, another of the five members,[1] and Sir Walter Earle,[2] an old soldier. From Devonshire came Sir John Northcote[3] and Sir George Chudleigh with their followers. This host appeared before Sherborne on 2 September, whereupon the Marquis with all the Foot and volunteers betook himself to the Castle, and Hopton, who was now lieutenant-general of the Horse, advanced with the mounted men and took several prisoners 'in the very face of their army'.[4] Instead of quartering in the town, the Roundheads camped in a field about three-quarters of a mile north of the Castle. Seeing them so cautious, the Cavaliers threw 300 Foot into the town.

During the night the Roundheads made a battery, too far off as it proved, and in the morning (3 September) they opened fire on the town 'with as much fury as they could'.[5] All that day they tried to force their way in but Hopton had placed many small parties of musketeers in the little gardens that flanked their lines of advance, and, keeping the Horse in reserve, beat them off with loss. At about 4 p.m. the Roundheads gave up, and retired to camp.

About midnight, Hopton and Sir John Berkeley, his major-general of Horse, were going the rounds, when it occurred to them that it would be interesting to see how the Roundheads would receive an alarm. With the small body of Horse and dragoons which escorted them they beat in their enemies' horse guards, ordering the dragoons to fire upon their Court of Guard. The results were all that could be desired, for this put the Roundheads into confusion and they remained under arms 'shivering, and blowing their nails till morning'. Seeing their tactics so successful the Cavaliers repeated the dose every night while the siege – if such it can be called – lasted.

On Sunday the Cavaliers observed a new work about a musket shot nearer the Castle than the original battery. That evening Sir Thomas Lunsford laid his artillery, two small drakes from Lord Paulet's house and a great fowling piece of Sir John Stawell's,[6] so as to command the new battery. Then in the dead of night he fired a salvo, which did some execution, and alarmed the Roundheads so much that, according to a Cavalier source, 800 of them deserted. However that may be, Bedford now proposed a treaty by which the Roundheads were to be permitted to march off quietly. To this the Marquis merely replied that

---

[1] Member of Parliament for Dorchester.
[2] Member of Parliament for Weymouth and Melcombe Regis.
[3] Member of Parliament for Ashburton.
[4] Hopton, op. cit., p. 12.
[5] Loc. cit.
[6] This weapon probably resembled the modern punt-gun.

'as they came thither upon their own counsels, so they might get off as they could'.[1] On 6 September they pulled down their tents and marched to Yeovil, fetching a compass to avoid Sherborne town. The Cavaliers marched out and 'attended their rear with a warm skirmish'.[2] An army barely 600 strong had compelled one of 7,000 to retreat discomfited.

On 7 September Hertford sent Hopton towards Yeovil to carry out a reconnaissance in force. Sir Ralph, with about 100 Horse, 60 dragoons and 200 Foot, marched off at 2 p.m. and drew up his men on Babylon Hill, which looks down on Yeovil Bridge. After about an hour, Hopton was preparing to withdraw when a brisk Roundhead attack nearly took him by surprise. After a confused skirmish, the Royalists fell back in some disorder. The Roundhead commanders claimed that 'if the night had not come on and a very dark one, we had made a great execution amongst them'. 'This rough medley,' wrote Hopton, 'gave apprehension to both parts', but although the Roundheads had rather the better of the occasion they 'liked their bargain so ill'[3] that they left Yeovil and marched south to Dorchester.

Hertford, who had been reinforced by a thousand men of the Dorsetshire Trained Bands, remained stationary at Sherborne until he heard that Colonel George Goring had lost Portsmouth to Sir William Waller and that Byron had quitted Oxford. On 18 September the Council of War agreed to retreat across Somersetshire and quarter near Bristol 'whereby any advantage that might be offered, might be taken upon that City'. Unfortunately, that night the Marquis was persuaded to march to Minehead, where every Thursday he would, so he was told, find enough Welsh barques to transport all his force into Wales.

Hopton pointed out the disadvantages of this course, but Hertford persisted in it although Taunton, Wellington and Dunster Castle were all held by the Roundheads. After four days' march the Royalists reached Minehead on 22 September, to find only two coal boats at the quay. That afternoon Bedford's advanced guard reached Watchett.

On Hopton's advice the Marquis now divided his force. He, with the volunteers, the Foot, the drakes and the baggage, took passage to Wales, marching in due course to join Charles's main army. Hopton, Berkeley, Digby and Hawley with 110 Horse and 50 dragoons marched through north Devon into Cornwall, reaching Sir Bevil Grenvile's house at Stowe without opposition.

Bedford, satisfied that the Parliamentarians of Devon and Cornwall could easily deal with so small a body, rejoined Essex with most of the forces he had led into the west, and fought, as we have seen, at Edgehill. But he was leaving his work half done.

[1] Hopton, op. cit., p. 13.
[2] Ibid., p. 14.
[3] Ibid., pp. 15–16.

Hopton reached Stowe on 25 September. His arrival tipped the balance in favour of the Cornish Cavaliers, who up to that time had succeeded in levying but few soldiers. In Cornwall men doubted the legality alike of the Parliament's Militia Ordinance and of the King's Commission of Array. Both sides were anxious for a truce until the harvest was gathered in, and when, on 17 August, the Royalists had called for a general muster on Bodmin race-course, no more than 180 men had appeared, the majority of these being Sir Bevil Grenvile's servants and tenants.

Hopton played his hand well, standing his trial at Truro Assizes for bringing armed forces into Cornwall. The jury not only acquitted him, but thanked him for coming to their aid. The Trained Bands came out for the King, and the mayor agreed to let them have the town arms. When on 4 October Hopton reviewed the *posse comitatus* on Moilesbarrow Down, he found himself at the head of 3,000 well-armed men, besides clubmen.

If they were for the most part ill-trained peasantry, Sir Richard Buller, the Roundhead leader, had but 700 of the same sort at Launceston, with which to resist them. Advancing, Hopton was able to occupy the town unopposed, and to secure the line of the Tamar. Buller fled into Devonshire.

Recognising the difficulty of persuading the Trained Bands to leave their own county, Hopton and the Cornish Cavaliers now began to raise an army of volunteers. Sir Bevil Grenvile, Sir Nicholas Slanning, Colonel John Trevanion, Colonel William Godolphin, and Lord Mohun soon raised considerable regiments of Foot, and Captain Edward Cosoworth levied a troop of dragoons. The men were armed partly from the private armouries of the gentry, partly with arms belonging to the Cornish Trained Bands, and partly with weapons imported from the Continent. The men were paid and often maintained by their officers out of their own resources. The royal fortresses of Pendennis and St Mawes were secured by their Cavalier governors, Slanning and Lieutenant Hannibal Bonython. The former organised a fleet of privateers which, despite Warwick's warships, preyed upon the merchant shipping in the Channel, and brought munitions into Falmouth, St Ives and Penzance.

The Committee of Public Safety, despite its preoccupation with the defence of London, now spared another thought for Plymouth and the west. On 11 October it authorised the Deputy-Lieutenant of Cornwall to raise 1,000 men and ordered two troops of Horse to join this army. It also commanded the Committee of Devon to provide 500 dragoons. Later in the month it again sent the Earl of Bedford with seven more troops of Horse and 1,000 Foot. All this was not sufficient to prevent Hopton's cavalry raiding across the Tamar, and early in December he cut off Plymouth's water supply. The Committee now gave Lord Robartes command, and ordered that three regiments of volunteers and 1,000 dragoons should be raised for the relief of the town. Arms and money were forwarded by sea.

The Royalists now decided to close in on Plymouth. Their first move was to occupy Mount Edgcumbe House and Millbrook to secure the Cornish side of the Sound. Their second was to cross into Devonshire and drive the Roundhead General Ruthin, a Scots officer, from his quarters at Plympton.

The first move provoked the Roundheads to attempt two amphibious raids on Millbrook. On the first occasion Sir Alexander Carew, Governor of St Nicholas Island, landed and captured some of Cosoworth's dragoons, but Major Walter Slingsby, of Mohun's regiment, managed to hold out until relieved by Hopton in person. The next time the Roundheads landed by night, evidently in some force for it took thirty-six boats to carry them. Slingsby beat them from his half-completed works, forcing them to a disorderly retreat.

The five regiments of Cornish volunteers were insufficient to blockade Plymouth and so the Cavaliers attempted to raise the *posse comitatus* at Modbury on 6 December. The Devonshire men were not as warlike as their neighbours and Hopton was disappointed to find the gathering 'rather like a great fair than a posse'.[1] He could scarcely find enough armed men to guard the town and send out a cavalry patrol. His colleagues at Plympton, warned how things stood, ordered half of Grenvile's regiment to join him at Modbury early next morning, and sent two troops to patrol the roads from Plymouth. Despite these precautions, Ruthin sallied out that night with 800 Horse and dragoons and got to Modbury unopposed. The High Sheriff and many Devonshire gentry were taken and the posse dispersed, while Hopton and Slanning had a narrow escape. Ruthin had more sense than to fall back on Plymouth. Quickly securing his prisoners he rode for Dartmouth, thus avoiding Hopton's efforts to intercept him.

This was a great setback to the Royalists. With time they could easily have doubled their army from their Devonshire friends, and raised a force sufficient for a close siege of Plymouth. This scheme Ruthin had nipped in the bud, leaving them with scarcely enough men even to observe the place. The Cavaliers, however, were not content with a deadlock. They now determined to try their luck at Exeter, summoning the city on 30 December, and storming Topsham so as to cut its communications with the sea. Once more Ruthin foiled them for, 'advancing nimbly with a good party of Horse and musketeers mounted and being well guided off from the Cornish quarters', he flung himself into Exeter.

The Cavaliers had over-extended themselves, as Hopton tacitly admits: 'Their expectation of ammunition, subsistance and increase [of numbers] from the County utterly failed, so as the army was enforced in that bitter season of the year (encumbered with all sorts of wants, and with the disorder and general mutiny of the Foot) to retreat towards Cornwall.'[2] These administrative difficulties may be traced directly to Ruthin's successes.

The Cavaliers fell back by Crediton and Okehampton. Ruthin, who knew

[1] Ibid., p. 25.
[2] Ibid., p. 27.

the state they were in, pursued and clashed with them at Bridestowe but was beaten off, for the temperamental Cornish Foot no sooner heard of his approach than they 'put themselves into a very excellent order of obedience beyond expectation'.[1] Ruthin now attempted to force the passage of the Tamar at Saltash. Planting his artillery on the Devon side, he brought three warships into the river, and battered the town for about a week, with not less than eighty guns, attempting under cover of this supporting fire to land his infantry from boats. But his bombardment had done little damage and he was everywhere repulsed. The element of surprise was lacking and without it his river crossing operation had little chance of success.

This check was not serious to the Parliamentarians, for reinforcements from Somerset and Dorset now managed to cross the Tamar at Newbridge. The Cavaliers were compelled to abandon the line of the river, but they had foreseen this and some days previously had summoned the posse to join them at Bodmin. Ruthin concentrated at Liskeard, eager to add to his successes before the Earl of Stamford, who was approaching with yet another Roundhead contingent, should supersede him.

Meanwhile the Cavaliers had literally had a windfall. On 17 January a fierce storm drove three Parliamentarian warships, well furnished with arms and money, into the Royalist port of Falmouth. It was a reorganised Cornish army that met once more on Moilesbarrow Down, rearmed, and with a fortnight's advance of pay in its pockets. Morale was high when, without cannon or baggage, they advanced and quartered in Lord Mohun's park at Boconnoc. There they held a Council of War and decided to attack next day whether they found Ruthin in the field or at Liskeard. By the King's commission the western army was commanded jointly by Lord Mohun, Hopton, Berkeley and Colonel William Ashburnham, or by any two of them. This strange arrangement they now set aside, inviting Hopton to act as commander-in-chief, proof that they already recognised him as their ablest soldier. From this time onwards his leadership in the Cornish army was virtually unquestioned.

THE BATTLE OF BRADDOCK DOWN, 19 JANUARY

Next morning the Cavaliers marched out and about noon came in full view of Ruthin's army drawn up upon a fair heath between Boconnoc and Braddock Church. Information about the positions adopted is rather scanty. The Roundheads, according to Colonel Sir Bevil Grenvile, 'were possessed of a pretty rising ground which was in the way towards Liskeard, and we [Cavaliers] planted ourselves upon such another against them within musket shot'. Hopton himself merely says that he drew up the Foot in the best order he could on the west side of Braddock Down. In front of the army he placed an advanced

[1] Ibid., p. 28. The attitude of the Cornish compares interestingly with that of Sir John Moore's men on the retreat to Corunna.

guard – a 'forlorn'[1] he calls it – in little enclosures. The few Horse and dragoons he placed on the wings in the customary manner. The artillery had been left at Bodmin, but Hopton had two small iron minion-drakes brought up secretly from Lord Mohun's house and planted 'upon a little Borough within random shot of the Enemy's bodies'.[2] These he concealed from the Roundheads by placing small parties of Horse in front of them.

The Parliamentarians had more Horse than the Royalists, but the Cornish Foot outnumbered the opposing infantry. For about two hours the two armies were content to skirmish: 'we saluted each other with bullets,' says Grenvile. Both sides wished to 'keep their ground of advantage and to have the other to come over to his prejudice'. Hopton soon decided to attack, only waiting to hold prayers at the head of each unit, 'mass', as the Roundheads styled it.

This done, Hopton suddenly unmasked his two drakes and ordered a salvo. Whether this little stratagem served to unnerve the Roundheads we cannot tell. Leaving the reserve of Foot in position, Hopton now advanced with the rest of his army. Both wings of Horse charged, but it was the Cornish infantry that won the day. Grenvile, well seconded by the other regiments, led the van, his men following him so gallantly down one hill and up the other that they struck terror into the Roundheads, who did not even stand the shock of the first charge, but fled in great disorder. They stayed only long enough, it seems, to kill two men. They probably fired one ill-aimed volley before their opponents were well within range and then took to their heels. All the way to Liskeard they ran, and there the townsmen rose against them. The Cavaliers pursued, and entered the town unopposed. 1,250 prisoners, one account says 1,500, fell into their hands, with all the baggage and ammunition and many arms. Better still, five guns were among the spoils. One was only a saker, but the rest were brass and included one piece fourteen feet long with the Rose and Crown of the Tudors engraved upon it.[3] Two twelve-pounders taken here were to be the mainstay of Hopton's artillery for several years.

Cornwall was now firmly in the hands of the Cavaliers once more. But the moral results of Braddock Down were even more important than the physical. The Roundheads, including Captain Alexander Pym, son of a more celebrated

[1] Short for 'forlorn hope', a corruption of the Dutch *verlorener oppen*. This term could be applied to an advanced guard, a screen of skirmishers, or the troops spearheading the assault on a town or fortress.

[2] Hopton, op. cit., p. 30.

[3] This piece is somewhat puzzling. No standard gun of the Civil War period, whatever its calibre, exceeded twelve feet in length. Henry VIII adopted the Tudor rose with a crown and his initial as an ordnance mark towards the end of his reign; the gun in question is more likely to have been Elizabethan. It would probably have been an unusually long culverin, weighing about 5,500 lbs and requiring twenty horses to draw it. It is unlikely that it was either a cannon or a basiliske, for these weapons required at least fourteen yoke of oxen or thirty horses to drag them over rough ground, and were thus quite unmanageable in the field. The authors are grateful to the late Brigadier O. F. G. Hogg, author of *English Artillery 1326–1716* (London 1963), for this information.

father, had 'tried the goodness of their horses in this chase'. Ruthin had only himself to thank for this abrupt conclusion to his series of triumphs, for 'this attempt was not only without but against the order of my Lord General [Stamford]'.[1] Hopton, on the other hand, now emerged as a general of real merit. He, a Somersetshire foreigner, had won the trust of the Cornish.

On the 20th the Cavaliers rested and gave thanks for their victory, but they were not content to rest on their laurels. The time had come for a second invasion of Devon. Dividing their force, they directed one column against Stamford, who had reached Launceston before he heard of the disaster, but now beat a hasty retreat to Tavistock.

A second column under Hopton and Lord Mohun stormed Saltash on 22 January, capturing 140 more prisoners, 4 guns and a ship of nearly 400 tons mounting 16 cannon. Ruthin, who had been working hard to fortify the place, escaped in a small boat to Plymouth. Some of his followers, less fortunate than he, crowded into such craft as they could find, swamped them, and were drowned.

The threat to Plymouth was grave, but its garrison was still not much weaker than the Cornish army, weakened once it crossed the Tamar by the refusal of the Trained Bands to leave their own county. The Cavaliers now endeavoured to blockade Plymouth, for a proper siege was still beyond their resources.

Sir John Berkeley, after successfully beating up Major General James Chudleigh's quarters at Kingsbridge, tried the same at Okehampton on 8 February. The Roundheads dispersed on hearing of his approach but rallied at Chagford. There, in a confused dawn skirmish, the Cavaliers lost one of the noblest of their number, Sidney Godolphin, the poet, who, as a volunteer, had been serving throughout the campaign. He was, in Sir Bevil Grenvile's words, 'as gallant a gent. as the world had'.

Despite this setback, the Cavaliers continued to blockade Plymouth, but it was at best a deadlock and a relief force was gathering at Kingsbridge. Its task was none too difficult, for the Cavaliers were scattered. Slanning and Trevanion were at Modbury; Ashburnham and Grenvile at Plympton; Lord Mohun and Hopton north of Plymouth, probably at Ham.

At 1 p.m. on 21 February, the Parliamentarian force fell upon Modbury. The fight raged all through the afternoon and on into the night. After a stubborn resistance the Cavaliers fell back to Plympton, leaving 100 dead, 150 prisoners, 1,100 muskets and 5 guns. Next morning the Cornish army, having sent their heavy carriages and guns across the river to Saltash, concentrated on Roborough Down before falling back on Tavistock. Thus ignominiously ended their second invasion of Devon. Stamford and Ruthin, happy to be rid of them, agreed on 28 February to a local cessation of hostilities. Hopton was merely playing for time. The Cornish were tired after the strain and hardship of their winter campaign and ammunition was short. Astonishingly enough the armistice was

[1] Letter of Thomas Wrote to John Pym.

spun out for forty days, during which both sides prepared for the further struggle which they recognised as inevitable.

THE BATTLE OF SOURTON DOWN, 25 APRIL

Stamford reorganised his army so that by 15 April he had 3,500 well-armed Foot and 8 troops of Horse.[1] The truce expired at midnight on 22 April. Stamford, suffering from gout, was lying at Exeter, and James Chudleigh, son of Sir George, a professional soldier who had fought in Ireland, and already a major-general at the age of twenty-five, led the army. He marched out of Lifton with 1,500 musketeers, 200 pikemen and 5 troops of Horse, advancing over Polston bridge to attack Launceston.

Hopton occupied Beacon Hill,[2] with half of Grenvile's regiment, and lined the hedges at its foot with musketeers. He had a magnificent observation post and a splendid position but not enough troops to man it. Fortunately for him, Godolphin's regiment now arrived. Chudleigh reached the outskirts of Launceston about 9 a.m., but it was not until an hour later that he began to assault Beacon Hill, driving Grenvile's musketeers from the hedges. At about 11 a.m. Major Slingsby appeared with Lord Mohun's regiment, and Berkeley arrived with some troops of Horse and dragoons. Thus reinforced, Hopton held his ground throughout the day, inflicting considerable losses on the Parliamentarians.

At about seven in the evening, Slanning and Trevanion joined him, but at the same time Chudleigh was reinforced by 700 of Sir John Merrick's London Greycoats, and by 100 of Sir John Northcote's regiment led jointly by their major and, oddly enough, the Earl of Stamford's chaplain. The Roundhead reinforcements defended Polston Bridge against the Royalist cavalry.

Hopton, whose whole army had now arrived, decided that the time had come for a counter-attack. Regrouping his Foot into three bodies under himself, Berkeley and Major-General Thomas Bassett, he advanced in three separate columns, which simultaneously charged Chudleigh's main body. Shaken by their previous losses and exhausted by the day-long struggle, the Roundheads were quickly disordered. A number of factors saved them from complete rout: the gathering darkness, the steadiness of the Greycoats who covered their retreat, and the gallantry of their young commander. Chudleigh himself brought up the rear, and when some of his followers, eager to be gone, told him it was impossible to save the guns, he harnessed the oxen to them with his own hands. The explosion of a powder magazine which scorched a number of the Cornish discouraged them from further pursuit.

On 25 April the Cavaliers heard from a friend in Okehampton that the Roundheads were in great disquiet, and determined to make a night march

[1] Mary Coate, *Cornwall in the Great Civil War* (Oxford 1935), p. 57.
[2] Known locally as the Windmill.

and fall upon them at dawn the next morning. The Cornish army now consisted of 3,000 Foot, and five 'voluntary' regiments, 300 Horse and 300 dragoons. They had four guns, including the two 12-pounders taken at Braddock Down. Hopton thought this army 'appear'd upon the view the handsoms't body that had been gotten together in those parts in all that war',[1] but pride came before a fall. Chudleigh, with 100 good cavalry, was on the alert, determined to waylay Hopton in the dark.

Never, as Hopton admits, had the Cavaliers felt less fear of their enemy. Lord Mohun and he, with Berkeley and Bassett were 'carelessly entertaining themselves in the head of the dragoons'[2] when they suddenly saw the Roundheads within carbine shot. Chudleigh's party fired a volley and charged, Captain Drake who led them shouting 'Fall on, Fall on, they run!' The dragoons panicked and fell back upon the Horse, and the Roundheads riding amongst them routed half the army. Mohun and Grenvile made a stand by the guns, and Hopton sent word to Slanning to bring the rearguard of the army up to the cannon. Here the Roundhead cavalry were beaten off, but they killed some sixty men. Wishing to follow up his success, Chudleigh sent to Okehampton for the rest of his men, 1,000 Foot. The Cavaliers manned an ancient trench and awaited the second charge, planting 'Swedes' feathers' in front of their guns.

The advancing Parliamentarians were given away by the lighted matches of their musketeers. As soon as they came within range the Cornish fired two cannon at them, and this time the hearts of the Roundhead infantry failed them. It seems they liked a night march as little as the Cavaliers. But their cavalry made yet another charge, this time as far as the 'Swedes' feathers'. Surprised perhaps by this unexpected obstacle, Chudleigh decided to go home, and retired to his quarters. A fierce tempest broke over the moor, drenching the combatants, and adding to their miseries.

It had been an unpleasant night for both sides, but the Cavaliers had had the worst of it, though they were not long in rounding up their runaways and restoring order. Henry Carey, the new High Sheriff of Devonshire, was reduced to making his way home in woman's apparel. Another survivor of the fiasco was Captain Christopher Wray, of Mohun's regiment, who 'being then but fifteen years of age and little of stature, but a sprightly gallant youth . . .' was taken prisoner to Okehampton. His captors, taking him for a trooper's boy, guarded him carelessly and in the night he slipped away, rejoining three days later at the head of a dozen stragglers. Wray was knighted at Bristol later in the year and at the end of the war was a colonel.

Sourton Down was a disaster to the Cavaliers both morally and materially. They fell back to Bridestowe in disorder, leaving behind many weapons and horses, five barrels of powder and Hopton's portmanteau with all his papers. In it were letters from the King, from which, though they were in cipher,

[1] Hopton, op. cit., p. 38.
[2] Loc. cit.

Stamford learned that the Cavaliers had orders to march into Somerset and join hands with Prince Maurice. This combination the Earl determined to prevent.

Stamford spared no pains to prepare for the next bout, ordering his own forces to rendezvous at Torrington, there to join with such contingents as could be spared from the garrisons of Barnstable and Bideford. Ample stores of food and ammunition were collected. Sending Lieutenant-General Sir George Chudleigh and 1,200 Horse to surprise the Cornish *posse comitatus* at Bodmin, the Earl crossed into Cornwall on 15 May and advanced to Stratton, where he took up a strong position on the hill that now bears his name. He had 5,400 Foot, 200 Horse and 13 guns. To meet this invasion Hopton could muster only 2,400 Foot and 500 Horse, for he felt compelled to leave garrisons at Saltash, Millbrook and elsewhere. Nevertheless, he was eager for battle once more. His administrative difficulties compelled him to seek a swift decision.

On the evening of 15 May, Hopton, who had advanced via North Petherwin and Week St Mary, was in touch with the Roundheads at Efford Mill near Stratton. That night the Cornish commanders held a Council of War 'where it was quickly resolv'd, notwithstanding the great visible disadvantage, that they must either force the Enemies' Camp, while the most part of their Horse and dragoons were from them, or unavoidably perish'.[1]

THE BATTLE OF STRATTON, 16 MAY

The Roundhead position was indeed a strong one. Stamford Hill runs north and south and is about 200 feet above sea level. On the east it is steep and thickly wooded, an obstacle inaccessible to cavalry and difficult for infantry. Elsewhere the slope is gentler. On the summit an ancient earthwork served as a battery.

During the night most of the Cornish army crossed the stream at Efford Hill and occupied enclosures on the east side. They stood to their arms all night, but there was no fighting until daybreak, when a fire fight began with the Round-head infantry lining hedges not more than 200 yards away. Hopton brought up the rest of his army, and divided the whole into four columns of Foot each about 600 strong, giving each two cannon. The first column under Lord Mohun and himself was to attack the south of Stamford's camp; on the west were two columns, one under Berkeley and Grenvile, the other under Slanning and Tre-vanion. Bassett and Godolphin were to assault from the north. By attacking in an arc in this way Hopton forced the enemy to fight with their backs to the precipitous slope which made their position impregnable from the east. In reserve he kept Colonel John Digby with 500 mounted men upon a sandy common, which is now Bude Golf Course.

The fight began at about five o'clock in the morning, the Cornish Foot pressing up the hill and the Roundheads, who had 5,400 Foot, 'obstinately endeavouring to keep them down. The fight continued doubtful with many

[1] Ibid., p. 42.

countenances of various events' until about 3 p.m., by which time the Cornish had little ammunition left. Major-General James Chudleigh chose this moment for a counter-attack. Advancing with a stand of pikes, he attacked Grenvile, who was at the head of a similar party. Chudleigh charged so smartly that there was some disorder, and Sir Bevil himself was knocked over, but, being immediately relieved by Berkeley, who led the musketeers of this column, and by some of his own officers, he threw in his local reserves and managed to capture Chudleigh himself.

The other three converging columns were doing equally well, and drawing nearer to one another as they pressed on up the hill, and the Roundheads began to give way, abandoning their dead and some of their guns. Between 3 p.m. and 4 p.m. the Cavalier commanders 'happened to meet all together in one ground near the top of the hill, where having joyfully embraced one another they pursued their victory, and recovered the top of the hill, which the enemy had quitted in a rout'.[1] Robert Bennett, who commanded 120 musketeers of Sir Samuel Rolles's regiment of Devonshire Roundheads, says the Cavaliers came in on his rear because the left wing failed,[2] and so one can imagine the two right-hand columns of the Cavaliers pushing along the top of the plateau, rolling up Stamford's line.

Colonel John Weare, who commanded another Devonshire regiment, gives us a glimpse of the last stage of the battle, 'where I continued all the fight, my General [Stamford] having not twenty men left with him, when he fired with our assistance divers pieces of ordnance upon the enemy. . . .' All was over. Stamford fled to Bideford, and thence to Exeter, leaving 300 dead, and 1,700 prisoners. The Cavaliers took thirteen brass guns, a mortar, seventy barrels of powder and a great magazine of provisions, a timely prize when they had not four barrels of powder left and when officers and men had lived for the last three or four days on a dry biscuit apiece.

Stamford deserves blame for sending away his cavalry while the Cornish army was still in being. This looks like over-confidence. But in the battle he and his men had fought stoutly enough, which makes the Royalist victory all the more remarkable. Hopton's attack by converging columns was a feature of this fight and of his counter-attack at Lansdown. His tactics were far from typical of his day.

Sir George Chudleigh, hearing of the disaster, beat a hasty retreat from Bodmin, many of his troopers falling into the hands of the Cornish. Hopton now occupied Launceston, where he heard that the Marquis of Hertford and Prince Maurice were marching westwards. His great victory at Stratton gave him the opportunity to join them, and although Plymouth and Exeter were still in the hands of the Roundheads, he advanced without delay and met them at Chard on 4 June.

[1] Ibid., p. 43.
[2] Coate, op. cit., p. 71.

Six

THE WAR IN THE NORTH, 1643–1

During the opening three months of the Civil War there had been little observable strategy in the plans of the high command on either side. Indeed, for all practical purposes it resolved itself into a struggle for the capital with a series of disconnected local struggles for the supremacy. But with the turn of the year and the coming of spring 1643 the Royalists showed signs of a more comprehensive strategy which may be described as a concentric movement on London from north, north-west and west – the strategy of exterior lines.

The previous chapter described the first steps in this grand plan, where in the extreme south-west Sir Ralph Hopton always had London as the ultimate goal. In the centre the King was consolidating his advanced position around Oxford, within four days' march of London. In the north a third army was gathering under the Earl of Newcastle, whose ultimate aim was also to push southwards towards London. This can be described as a 'pincer movement' by the western and northern armies, with a third army in the centre in cooperation with the other two. No written document in such specific terms is known to exist but the evidence for the plan is circumstantial and compelling, and its gradual development and unfolding through the greater part of the year of 1643 forms a fascinating study.

No such grand strategy is discernible on the Parliamentary side. Whereas the Royalists had the single command of the King, the Roundheads had a host of independent-minded leaders over whom the Earl of Essex, the captain-general, had but little influence or control. The war, in practice, was conducted by an unwieldy committee, control being in the hands of the Houses of Parliament in London.

While the King's main army was on its march to Edgehill, and Sir Ralph Hopton was raising troops in Cornwall, fighting broke out in Yorkshire. Although the Royalists of the county were divided, an issue had to be decided there before any advance on the capital from the north could be undertaken. Forces were more or less evenly balanced; Yorkshire had provided the King with numerous recruits in the summer of 1642, and this naturally detracted from the Royalist strength within the county.

William Cavendish, 1st Earl of Newcastle,[1] commanded the King's forces in the north. At the age of fifty, the Earl was completely lacking in military experience. He owed his military rank to his ability to raise and equip an army from his own financial resources. An extremely wealthy man, he had spent £20,000 entertaining Charles at Welbeck in 1633. Newcastle should neverthe-less not be written off as a dilettante; he was a skilful horseman, a good fencer, and had some grasp of administration. He relied heavily on his lieutenant-general, James King, later Lord Eythin. King was a Scots soldier of experience, who had risen to the rank of 'general-major' in the Swedish service.[2] He returned to Scotland in 1640, and succeeded the treacherous Earl of Newport as lieutenant-general early in 1643. He exercised the same functions for Newcastle that Ruthven did for Charles, performing the duties of a modern chief-of-staff.

Facing this potent combination was the Parliamentarian commander, Ferdin-ando, 2nd Baron Fairfax, who, at fifty-nine, was somewhat past his prime. He was, however, solidly supported by the clothing towns of the West Riding – Leeds, Bradford, Halifax, and Wakefield – and backed by his elder son, Thomas. Sir Thomas Fairfax has never attracted the attention that historians have lavished upon that other great Parliamentarian general, Oliver Cromwell. Although Fairfax never achieved Cromwell's political eminence, he was a soldier of immense ability. Thirty years old in 1642, he had served under Sir Horace Vere in the Netherlands, and in 1637 married Vere's daughter, Anne. He commanded a company of dragoons against the Scots, and witnessed the rout at Newburn. Sir Thomas was perhaps the only Parliamentarian commander who was Rupert's equal in dash and drive. He was tremendously popular with his soldiers, whose morale always rose when 'the Rider of the White Horse', as he was known, appeared on the field. If, in battle, he was Parliament's Rupert, the similarity ended there, for, unlike his impulsive counterpart, Fairfax was a mild man in civil life. Sincerely religious, though without the flames of fanaticism that surged through so many of his comrades, Sir Thomas was a quiet, almost retiring man, interested in animals, nature, and poetry. He was no extremist, and was to dissociate himself from the acts of the court which tried Charles I.

Working in uneasy cooperation with the Fairfaxes were the Hothams, father and son, who menaced the Cavaliers of the East Riding from behind the double walls of Hull, the strongest fortress in the Kingdom. The Hothams tended to regard themselves as Lord Fairfax's allies rather than his subordinates, even after his commission had arrived from London. In the North Riding Sir Hugh

---

[1] Later 1st Marquis and 1st Duke of Newcastle.
[2] King had served alongside Rupert in the Elector Palatine's abortive invasion of West-phalia in 1638. He attributed the disaster at Lemgo (Vlotho) to Rupert's rashness, while the latter blamed his capture on King's slowness. This tension was to have unfortunate effects when the two officers had to cooperate, for tact was no more the *forte* of King than it was of the prickly Rupert.

Cholmley, a man no less independent than the Hothams, held Scarborough Castle for Parliament. Other Roundheads were raising troops in Richmond and Cleveland.

In Yorkshire, as in so many parts of England, there were attempts to prevent the outbreak of hostilities by local negotiations. But even while the Yorkshire Cavaliers were negotiating with Lord Fairfax, they appealed to Newcastle for assistance as early as 20 September, a month before Edgehill. Newcastle, after laying down certain conditions, agreed to help, and set about recruiting.

Newcastle was none too soon, for his opponents were already on the move. On 4 October the younger Hotham took Cawood Castle, ten miles south of York, breaking the truce between Lord Fairfax and the Cavalier leader. Lord Fairfax himself took the field by 21 October, and the danger to the Yorkshire Cavaliers was real indeed. Newcastle moved south at the end of November, with an army about 8,000 strong, of whom 2,000 were Horse and dragoons. As he marched, the Earl wisely covered his lines of communication with garrisons at Newcastle, Tynemouth Castle and Hartlepool, amongst other places. In an effort to prevent Newcastle reaching York, the younger Hotham, with three troops of Horse and four companies of Foot, boldly marched out to meet him, and on 1 December vainly contested the crossing of the Tees at Piercebridge. Hotham was brushed aside and the Earl reached York, held for the King by the resolute Sir Thomas Glemham,[1] who had been appointed governor of the city. Here Newcastle was later joined by King, and by George, Lord Goring, who was to command the Horse. Goring had served as colonel of Foot in the Dutch service, and had returned to take part in the Scots wars. As governor of Portsmouth he declared for the King but was forced to surrender to Sir William Waller. Clarendon writes acidly of him,[2] but although he was undoubtedly over-fond of intrigue and the bottle, he was a brave man and an excellent cavalry commander on the day of battle.

Newcastle's arrival was welcome to the Yorkshire Cavaliers, who had been roughly handled by Sir Thomas Fairfax in several skirmishes. Encouraged by the Royalist abandonment of Leeds, Lord Fairfax advanced to Tadcaster, ten miles from York – a bold move, as he had only 1,000 men. Here he was posted along the River Wharfe, covering the West Riding from which he drew his resources. Sir Thomas was sent with 300 Foot and 40 Horse to guard the crossing at Wetherby, and successfully beat off a night attack launched by Glemham and 800 men from York.

Newcastle appeared before Tadcaster on 6 December. Lord Fairfax had by

[1] Sir Thomas Glemham (d. 1649?) served as a lieutenant-colonel of Foot in the First Bishops' War. He gained a well-merited reputation for tenacity, holding York, Carlisle and Oxford successively during the First Civil War. He was in arms in the Second Civil War, and assisted Sir Philip Musgrave in seizing Carlisle.

[2] Clarendon speaks of his 'repeated treachery' and 'incomparable dexterity and sagacity' in deceiving. (Clarendon, op. cit., Vol. III, p. 224.)

now concentrated his forces, and had about 1,500 men available. His Council of War rightly judged the town untenable, but before Fairfax could draw his men up on an advantageous piece of ground nearby, Newcastle's army was upon them. The Earl's plan was simple enough. He proposed to attack from the east with his main body, while his lieutenant-general, the Earl of Newport, with most of the Horse and dragoons, fell upon the Parliamentarians from the west. This manoeuvre failed to work because of the non-appearance of Newport's column. Newcastle, undaunted, threw his 4,000 Foot at the makeshift defences around Tadcaster. The first assault was beaten off with loss, as the Roundheads held their fire until the Cavaliers were very close, and then poured in an effective volley. After regrouping, the Earl's men came on again, and managed to break into part of the town, manning two or three houses, from which, however, they were ejected by a brisk counter-attack. The battle swayed to and fro from mid-morning to early evening, and Newcastle's men withdrew with the onset of darkness and bivouacked in the fields nearby, resolved to try again the next day.

Lord Fairfax rightly suspected that the Earl's casualties – perhaps 100 men – had been heavier than his own, but his ammunition was dangerously low. Consequently, he fell back, under cover of night, to Selby. This seems to have been a strange decision, for although Fairfax's presence at Selby permitted him to remain in contact with Hull, it left the clothing towns, the source of much of his support, uncovered. Newcastle occupied Tadcaster on the morning of 7 December, capturing a number of Parliamentarian stragglers, and driving a wedge between Fairfax and his friends in the West Riding.

Newcastle's next move was to secure Pontefract Castle, which lay directly between the Roundheads in the West Riding and the Hothams at Hull. This done, Newcastle sent Sir John Henderson, a Scots veteran, to secure Newark and the vital passage of the Trent, without which it would be impossible to send arms or men to the King. Newark was to remain in Royalist hands throughout the First Civil War; not only did it cover the Trent crossing, but it also threatened much of Nottinghamshire and Lincolnshire.[1]

By mid-December the situation facing Lord Fairfax was far from ideal. He held Selby and Cawood, but Newcastle was 'absolute master of the field'.[2] The Parliamentarian regiments forming in Richmond and Cleveland had dissolved 'of themselves' on the Earl's arrival, 'having it yet in their choice to dwell at home or to leave their houses to new comers'.[3] Sir Hugh Cholmley, with 700 men, had shut himself up in Scarborough, and Colonel Sir Matthew Boynton had withdrawn into Hull with his 800 men. No help was forthcoming from either of the neighbouring Parliamentarian leaders, Sir John Gell of Derbyshire or Sir Anthony Irby of Lincolnshire. Fairfax himself remained at Selby with the

[1] See *Newark on Trent . . . siegeworks*, RCHM, 1964.
[2] Clarendon, op. cit., Vol. III, p. 444.
[3] Ibid., p. 443.

bulk of his army, with a detachment under the younger Hotham, now his lieutenant-general, at Cawood, and, not without misgivings, awaited a renewed Royalist offensive.

Newcastle was content to follow the custom of the time and leave his army in its winter quarters, levying more men and waiting for the spring. Sir Thomas Fairfax had less regard for seasonal convention, and raised troops in the Bradford area, calling in the countrymen. Thus supported, on 23 January he marched on Leeds. The garrison rejected a formal summons to surrender, and Fairfax stormed the place. 'The business was hotly disputed for almost two hours,' he wrote, 'but after the enemy was beaten from their works, the barricades were soon forced open to the streets, where Horse and Foot resolutely entering, the soldiers cast down their arms and rendered themselves prisoners.'[1] Although the casualties in this action were relatively small – about fifty in all – the loss of Leeds caused Newcastle great concern. The Royalist garrisons of Wakefield and Pontefract withdrew on York, and Newcastle recalled his troops from Newark, leaving Henderson to hold the town as best he could with locally raised forces. The Earl soon reoccupied Pontefract, though Sir Thomas Fairfax's possession of Leeds had reopened communications between Selby and the clothing towns.

The favourable situation in Yorkshire made it a suitable landing-place for the Queen. Henrietta Maria had been in the Netherlands, raising money on the Crown Jewels, purchasing arms, and forming a nucleus of professional soldiers eager to return to England for service in the Royalist armies. Escorted by a small fleet under the Dutch Admiral Martin Van Tromp, she set sail from Holland on 9 January, but was forced to return owing to a storm which buffeted her convoy for six long days. She sailed again on 6 February, and landed at Bridlington on 22 February. Newcastle, warned of her approach, had secured Bridlington on 12 February with a party of Horse, and moved there himself with a large part of his army in time to welcome the Queen and unload the much-needed stores.

The Earl of Warwick's vice-admiral, William Batten, had failed to intercept the Queen on the high seas, but appeared off Bridlington while unloading was in progress, and opened a heavy bombardment with over 100 cannon, concentrating, it seems, upon the Queen's lodging, 'whereupon she was forced out of her bed, some of the shot making way through her own chamber; and to shelter herself under a bank in the open fields'.[2] Van Tromp eventually forced Batten to desist by threatening to fire on him, and the Queen proceeded to York, where she arrived on 7 March.

The Queen's return to England, and the arrival of her munitions convoy, was a source of comfort to the Royalists. Their opponents, meanwhile, were

---

[1] *Fairfax Correspondence* (Vols I and II, ed. G. W. Johnson, London 1848, Vols III and IV, ed. R. Bell, London 1849), p. 36. *See also* TT E.8.23, E.87.1.
[2] Clarendon, op. cit., Vol. III, p. 445.

trying to put their organisation on a firmer footing. An Eastern Association comprising Essex, Suffolk, Norfolk, Cambridge and Hertford had been established on 20 December. Five days earlier a Midland Association of Leicester, Derby, Nottingham, Northampton, Buckingham, Bedford, Rutland and Huntingdon had come to being. The one was headed by Lord Grey of Wark and the other by Lord Grey of Groby, son of the Earl of Stamford. Nevertheless, all was far from well with the supporters of Parliament. The Pamphlet War reached new intensity with the founding, in January 1643, of the Royalist newsheet *Mercurius Aulicus*, whose witty, scandalous satire 'sent up' Parliamentarian reports with riotous abandon. 'Sir Jacob Astley lately slain at Gloucester desires to know was he slain with a musket or a cannon bullet,' mocked *Aulicus*. Unfortunately, the King was less adept at public relations than some of his supporters. The storming of Brentford was seen in the City as a breach of truce, and the King's answer to the peace petition, formally read on 13 January 1643, was outspoken and aggressive. The Earl of Northumberland was sent to Oxford with commissioners from both Houses,[1] but in the meantime the war party steadily reasserted its hold over the Commons. Charles played into Pym's hands by allowing Newcastle to commission large numbers of Roman Catholics, and by opening negotiations with the Irish rebels to end the rebellion and thus free the Marquis of Ormonde's troops for service in England.

The strengthening of the war party at Westminster was paralleled by Parliamentarian successes in the field. Rupert, after storming Cirencester on 2 February, had been foiled at Bristol early in March. Waller, fresh from a series of minor triumphs, set up his headquarters there towards the end of the month, so that the Oxford Cavaliers, whose main army was still in winter quarters, now had Essex to their east and 'William the Conqueror' to their west, though the former had not yet taken the field. In Cornwall the forty-day truce was still in being, but in Cheshire, after a similar period of neutrality, Sir William Brereton had won several successes for Parliament. Lancashire, like Cheshire, had contributed generously to Charles's army in the previous autumn: with so many of their best men away with the King, the local Cavaliers were gradually losing ground at home.

In the north-east, however, events moved in favour of the Royalists. Towards the end of February, Major-General Ballard, with a hastily extemporised force from Lincolnshire, Nottinghamshire and Derbyshire, descended on Newark. Sir John Henderson received warning of the impending attack, and attempted to surprise Ballard's quarters in the Beckingham area, north-east of Newark but was unable to do so, and fell back on the town. On 27 February Ballard, with over 6,000 men, appeared before Newark itself. Henderson fought a

---

[1] Northumberland and his colleagues presented the Oxford Propositions, very much more moderate in content than the Nineteen Propositions sent to the King at York in June 1642. Although these new terms appealed to some of the King's more moderate advisers, they were unacceptable to Charles himself.

delaying action on Beacon Hill, and retired into the town where, on the following day, Ballard assailed him. One of Ballard's three brigades was sent to attack the medieval Spittal, while another, of Nottinghamshire and Derbyshire men, advanced to within pistol-shot of the works, aided by a bombardment. This brigade was supported, in mid-afternoon, by the other two, who were met by the bulk of the garrison. A hot fight ensued, until Henderson, seeing that the Roundheads 'began to wax weary of their work', led out a sortie which drove off Ballard's Foot and overran three of his six guns. The Parliamentarians lost heavily, Ballard himself being among the wounded. The Roundhead general drew off next day, his men grumbling that his treachery or incompetence had caused their defeat.[1] Thus the Parliamentarians lost their best opportunity of taking Newark, whose fall would have been a serious blow to the Royalist cause, for without it the King could not hope to receive reinforcements and ammunitions from the north. The new Eastern Association had made no attempt to assist in this operation.

Ballard's failure before Newark was followed by a month's lull, at the end of which the Royalists scored a useful diplomatic point. Sir Hugh Cholmley, governor of Scarborough, like so many others, had taken up arms with the greatest reluctance. 'I am forced to draw my sword,' he wrote, 'not only against my countrymen but many dear friends and allies some of which I know both to be well-affected in religion and lovers of their liberties.'[2] The arrival of the Queen tipped the balance in Cholmley's uneasy mind; he declared for the King, and was reappointed to the command of Scarborough, 'which he discharged with courage and singular fidelity'.[3]

Cholmley's defection did more than provide the Royalists with the useful port of Scarborough. Sir John Hotham and his son were increasingly hesitant in their allegiance to Parliament, and Cholmley's action encouraged them to cease cooperating with Lord Fairfax. This made the latter's position at Selby precarious, as supplies were no longer forthcoming from Hull. Lord Fairfax consequently decided to retreat to Leeds, and sent his son to cover this retirement by thrusting towards Tadcaster. The garrison of Tadcaster fell back on York without a fight, and Sir Thomas entered the town and began to demolish the defence works. Newcastle, who was posted with his army on Clifford Moor ready to intercept Lord Fairfax's retirement on Leeds, suspected some design against York, and sent Lord Goring with twenty troops of Horse and dragoons to retake Tadcaster.

[1] There were suggestions that Ballard's heart was not in it. An officer of some experience, he had fought well at Edgehill. He was relieved of his command following his failure at Newark, and was replaced by Sir John Meldrum. See Hutchinson, op. cit., Vol. I, pp. 205, 206, 208n.
[2] Calendar of State Papers (Venetian), 1642–3, p. 236. Clarendon maintains that Cholmley's long friendship with Sir John Hotham was the reason for his initial adherence to Parliament. (Clarendon, op. cit., Vol. III, p. 446.)
[3] Clarendon, op. cit., Vol. III, p. 446.

THE BATTLE OF SEACROFT MOOR, 30 MARCH

Goring reached the town just as Fairfax left it. Although the bridge had been destroyed, Goring got his men across the river and pursued Sir Thomas, who, with only three troops of Horse to cover his several thousand Foot, was at a grave disadvantage as he prepared to cross the open ground of Bramham Moor. Fairfax sent his Foot off across the moor, and tried to hold the narrow lanes leading to it with his cavalry. Goring pressed on with about 500 Horse, not waiting for General King, who was marching to his assistance with Foot and guns. Fairfax checked Goring for a time, and then fell back on to the moor where he found, to his chagrin, that his Foot had remained stationary. Nevertheless he formed the Foot up into two bodies and, with his Horse at the rear, marched off in good order, with Goring's troopers, in three bodies, following at a respectful distance, just out of musket range.

Goring bided his time. The Parliamentarians got safely across Bramham Moor on to the smaller Seacroft Moor, and began to get careless. It was a hot day and the officers had great trouble getting the men out of the houses where they had gone in search of drink. Seeing the increasingly ragged Roundhead formation, Goring struck. His trumpets blared out, and the Cavaliers came on at the gallop, crashing into the flank and rear of Fairfax's sweating soldiery. The hastily raised Bradford countrymen fled, and the rest of the infantry soon followed. Fairfax had too few pikemen to form a hedgehog and stave off the exultant troopers. Rallying a few officers he retreated with much difficulty, losing his cornet in the rout. Two hundred men fell, and eight hundred were taken. Fairfax ruefully admitted that it was one of the greatest losses he ever sustained, but was somewhat consoled by the fact that his father's forces had reached Leeds unmolested.

Goring was not the only distinguished cavalry officer in Newcastle's army. The Earl had another in the twenty-two-year-old Charles Cavendish, second son of the Earl of Devonshire, a natural soldier, who had served in the 1641 campaign under the Prince of Orange and had fought as a volunteer in the lifeguards at Edgehill. Appointed lieutenant-general to Goring, he soon made his name in a series of hack-and-thrust affairs. In the spring Newcastle sent him south with a small column to join hands with Colonel-General Hastings's forces in the Midlands and with the Lincolnshire Royalists. With the help of Henderson and the Newark garrison he stormed Grantham on 23 March. His next success was the action on Ancaster Heath on 11 April, when he defeated a combined force of 1,500 Roundheads under Lord Willoughby of Parham and the younger Hotham.

Newcastle's gradual advance southwards was beginning to cause grave concern in the Eastern Association, the real core of the Roundhead resistance. Oliver Cromwell, who had raised a troop of Horse in August 1642, and was now a colonel, was already at Huntingdon by 10 April with six or seven troops of Horse. Early in April he had summoned 12,000 men from Cambridge, Norfolk and Suffolk. Of these, 5,500 under Lord Grey of Wark marched on 10 April to join Essex at Reading. The others were intended to make head against Newcastle, whose army now amounted to about 16,000 well-armed men, of whom nearly 3,000 were Horse and dragoons. This number must have included garrisons as well as the forces of the Queen and General Cavendish, but it was nevertheless a formidable host. If Newcastle moved south with this great army the Eastern Association would be hard put to bar his path. That he was unable to do so was largely due to the continued activities of Lord Fairfax and his diminutive army.

Cromwell now posted his forces across the path of the northern Cavaliers On 22 April he established his headquarters at Peterborough, where his trooper. amused themselves by burning the books in the Cathedral and by acts of iconoclasm. Cromwell had come to the fore rapidly since his return from the Edgehill campaign. His swift rise is somewhat surprising, for he was totally lacking in military experience, and had no great personal fortune or lofty social position to compensate for this. The son of a stolid Huntingdonshire country gentleman, in 1616 Cromwell went up to Sidney Sussex College, Cambridge, which William Laud was later to describe as 'a hotbed of Puritanism'. In February 1639 he was elected to represent Huntingdon in Charles's third Parliament, and it is significant that his only reported speech before this assembly was on a religious topic, for by this time Cromwell had become a zealous Puritan. Rough and rugged in appearance, he dressed simply, favouring dark colours. His character was complex, and much of it remains puzzling. At times he was sharp, abrupt and decisive, while at others he was capable of indecision and vacillation. Despite his Puritanism, Oliver 'loved an innocent jest', and though his sense of humour was not very subtle, it was of a kind to appeal to his soldiers. On the outbreak of war he was commissioned as a captain of Horse, and on 10 August 1642 he defeated an attempt to send the plate from Cambridge colleges to the King, and went on to seize the town magazine. His troop's role at Edgehill is not known for certain, though it seems to have been insignificant. Already in February 1643 he was referred to as colonel – there is no evidence that he ever held the rank of major or lieutenant-colonel – and besides being a Member of Parliament he was also a member of both the Eastern and the Midland Counties Associations. His name now begins to figure in contemporary newspapers: he is already as important in his sphere as Hampden and Hesilrige, more so than Strode and Stapleton. And already he was recruiting his troopers among the 'godly', according to Whitelocke 'most of them freeholders and freeholders' sons, who upon a matter of conscience engaged in this quarrel'.[1] In a well-known letter of 29 August 1643, Cromwell tells much of how he selected his officers:

[1] Bulstrode Whitelocke, *Memorials of the English Affairs* . . . (London 1682), p. 68.

I would rather have a plain russet-coated captain that knows what he fights for, and loves what he knows, than that which you call a gentleman and is nothing else. I honour a gentleman that is so indeed.

I understand Mr Margery hath honest men will follow him: if so, be pleased to make use of him. It much concerns you to have conscientious men.[1]

It was not only the Cavaliers that looked askance at such officers. The Earl of Manchester, Cromwell's immediate superior, speaking over a year later, complained, doubtless with a measure of exaggeration born of the malice between them,

Colonel Cromwell raising of his regiment makes choice of his officers not such as were soldiers or men of estate, but such as were common men, poor and of mean parentage, only he would give them the title of godly, precious men. ... I have heard him oftentimes say that it must not be soldiers nor Scots that must do this work, but it must be the godly to this purpose. ... If you look upon his own regiment of Horse, see what a swarm there is of those that call themselves godly; some of them profess that they have seen visions and had revelations.[2]

It is evident that the Ironsides, as Cromwell's men were known, were far from typical of the men who served the Parliament. Quantity rather than quality was sufficient for most commanders; countrymen armed with clubs, Royalist prisoners and deserters, pressed men of every description, were to be found in the ranks of Essex, Fairfax and Waller. The Cavaliers too raised men where they could. Cromwell, though, placed great emphasis upon 'personnel selection'.

On 25 April he joined forces with Sir Miles Hobart, a Norfolk colonel, and Sir Anthony Irby in besieging a Royalist cousin, Captain Cromwell, who had made a garrison at Crowland. The place surrendered after a three-day siege, which is only remarkable as being Cromwell's first. Indeed, it seems that it was the first time he had been in action since Edgehill. Thus well had Fairfax kept the Royalist wolf from the Eastern Association's door.

At the end of April the Roundheads were holding their own in the west, while in the Thames Valley, Essex was actually advancing. It was only in the north that things looked black for Parliament. The Cavaliers were concentrating at Newark and an invasion of the Eastern Counties seemed imminent. On 2 May the Commons ordered Cromwell, Irby and seven others to secure Lincolnshire. Accordingly, Lord Grey of Groby and Cromwell received orders from Essex

[1] Thomas Carlyle, *The Letters and Speeches of Oliver Cromwell* (London 1904, ed. S. C. Lomas, 3 volumes), Vol. I, p. 154.

[2] *Manchester's Quarrel: Documents relating to the quarrel between the Earl of Manchester and Oliver Cromwell* (London, Camden Society, 1875, ed. J. B. Bruce and D. Masson), p. 72.

to rendezvous at Stamford with Sir John Gell, and with the Nottingham forces, and then to join the Lincolnshire Roundheads. But this ambitious combination broke down largely because Grey was afraid Hastings might attack Leicester.

A Parliamentarian force under Lord Willoughby of Parham, Sir John Hotham and Cromwell eventually concentrated at Sleaford on 9 May. Their intention was to make another attack on Newark, so long a thorn in their side. They made little haste; although they reached Grantham on 11 May they were still quartered there and in the neighbouring villages two days later. This delay gave the Royalists time for a counter-stroke. They concerted their plans with great secrecy, Cavendish bringing his men from Gainsborough and meeting Henderson with the Newark Horse near Grantham in the dead of night. Their combined force amounted to twenty-one troops of Horse and three or four of dragoons, perhaps 1,200 men in all.

THE ACTION AT GRANTHAM, 13 MAY

In the early hours of the morning of 13 May, Cavendish descended on three of Lord Willoughby's troops quartered at Belton, and cut them to ribbons, killing seventy men and taking forty prisoners with only trifling loss to his own side. Late in the evening of the 13th the Royalists advanced again and faced the Roundheads within two miles of Grantham. The ensuing action has received great, indeed disproportionate, attention from military historians, who see it as a vital part of Cromwell's military education. It was doubtless a formative influence on Cromwell, but the only good account of the fight is his own, and the action's significance in general terms is somewhat limited.

The two bodies of cavalry drew up facing each other just out of musket range, while the dragoons of either side skirmished for an hour or more. Then, in Cromwell's words, 'they not advancing towards us, we agreed to charge them', and did so at 'a pretty round trot, they standing firm to receive us'.[1] After a brief mêlée, the Royalists were driven from the field with 100 casualties and 45 prisoners. Cromwell claimed, rather questionably, to have lost 'two men at the most'. Cavalry battles are not won by standing and waiting; the Parliamentarian victory was due to their eventual decision to charge – though it took them long enough to make up their minds. Cromwell certainly gained self-confidence – and confidence in his men – from Grantham; he was also taught an elementary lesson in the art of war. Nevertheless, despite this success, the Parliamentarians abandoned their attempt on Newark, suggesting that, perhaps, their casualties had not been as light as Cromwell maintained.

This minor success was followed by a more important Parliamentarian victory in the north. Sir Thomas Fairfax planned a night attack on Wakefield, with the object of taking prisoners who could be exchanged for the Roundheads taken by Goring at Seacroft Moor. Believing that the Royalist garrison

[1] Carlyle, op. cit., p. 135.

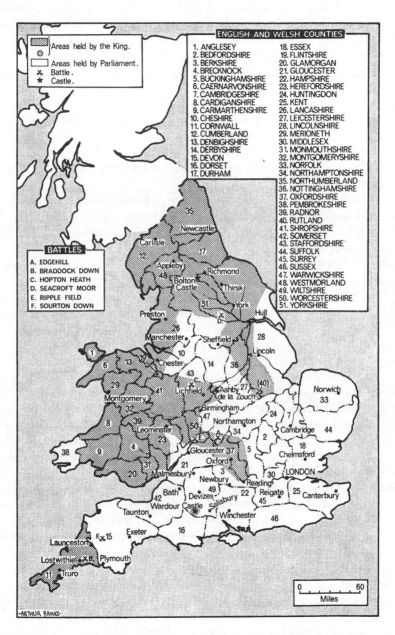

ENGLISH AND WELSH COUNTIES

Areas held by the King.
Areas held by Parliament.
✗ Battle.
★ Castle.

1. ANGLESEY
2. BEDFORDSHIRE
3. BERKSHIRE
4. BRECKNOCK
5. BUCKINGHAMSHIRE
6. CAERNARVONSHIRE
7. CAMBRIDGESHIRE
8. CARDIGANSHIRE
9. CARMARTHENSHIRE
10. CHESHIRE
11. CORNWALL
12. CUMBERLAND
13. DENBIGHSHIRE
14. DERBYSHIRE
15. DEVON
16. DORSET
17. DURHAM

18. ESSEX
19. FLINTSHIRE
20. GLAMORGAN
21. GLOUCESTER
22. HAMPSHIRE
23. HEREFORDSHIRE
24. HUNTINGDON
25. KENT
26. LANCASHIRE
27. LEICESTERSHIRE
28. LINCOLNSHIRE
29. MERIONETH
30. MIDDLESEX
31. MONMOUTHSHIRE
32. MONTGOMERYSHIRE
33. NORFOLK
34. NORTHAMPTONSHIRE
35. NORTHUMBERLAND
36. NOTTINGHAMSHIRE
37. OXFORDSHIRE
38. PEMBROKESHIRE
39. RADNOR
40. RUTLAND
41. SHROPSHIRE
42. SOMERSET
43. STAFFORDSHIRE
44. SUFFOLK
45. SURREY
46. SUSSEX
47. WARWICKSHIRE
48. WESTMORLAND
49. WILTSHIRE
50. WORCESTERSHIRE
51. YORKSHIRE

BATTLES

A. EDGEHILL
B. BRADDOCK DOWN
C. HOPTON HEATH
D. SEACROFT MOOR
E. RIPPLE FIELD
F. SOURTON DOWN

0 _____ 60
Miles

-ARTHUR BANKS-

3   ENGLAND AND WALES, MAY 1643

was only 800 or 900 strong, Sir Thomas set out with about 1,500 Horse and Foot collected from Leeds, Bradford, Halifax and Howley House, between Pontefract and Bradford. The Roundheads met at Howley House at midnight and reached Wakefield about four o'clock in the morning, only to find the Cavaliers on the alert, their works manned and 500 musketeers lining the hedges around the town. Fairfax and his officers held a brief consultation and decided to attack none the less. The Parliamentary Foot under Major-General John Gifford and Colonel William Fairfax stormed the works in three places and after two hours of fighting some of the Foot carried one of the Royalist barricades and tore it down. Sir Thomas charged through the gap at the head of his own troop, followed by two others. The street was full of Royalist Foot, but Fairfax charged right through them, leaving them to be mopped up by his infantry.

The two Royalist commanders were Goring and Sir Francis Mackworth, the sergeant-major-general of Newcastle's Foot. Goring was sick of a fever, but with the presence of mind which seldom failed him in an emergency, rose from his couch, and, swiftly mounting, led a counter-attack. 'And presently,' wrote Fairfax, 'we were charged again with Horse led by General Goring, where, after a hot encounter, some were slain, and himself taken prisoner. . . .' The Royalists, meanwhile, had been reinforced by Sir William Lambton's regiment, which had come to the aid of the garrison while the fight was in progress. Pushing on single-handed, Fairfax found himself in the market-place, face to face with this fresh unit and three troops of Horse. Luckily for him he was well mounted, and putting his horse at once at one of the Royalist barricades he got clear away. Meanwhile, Major-General Gifford had brought a captured gun into action from the churchyard and a second charge by the Roundhead Horse drove the Cavaliers out of town. Most of their Horse got away, but about 1,500 prisoners and much ammunition fell into the hands of the victors. The Roundheads were astonished to discover that they had attacked a garrison of not less than 3,000 infantry and seven troops of Horse. Four guns were taken. Mackworth was among those who had managed to escape.

With the capture of the impetuous commander of his cavalry, Newcastle was compelled to lean more than ever on the methodical General King. Once more Fairfax had made his presence felt, at a moment when things elsewhere were beginning to go badly for the Roundhead armies, for in the west, Hopton had won his victory at Stratton and in the centre the first convoy of munitions had just reached Oxford.

By the end of May, Lord Grey of Groby had concentrated an army of between 5,000 and 6,000 men at Nottingham. There were troops from Derbyshire and Lincolnshire besides Cromwell and the younger Hotham, but the commanders quarrelled and their army did little or nothing to prevent the Queen's army marching south. Henrietta Maria, who had left York with some 4,500 men on 4 June, set out from Newark on 21 June. Cavendish stormed

Burton-on-Trent on 2 July and the Queen was able to join forces with the King on 13 July. Not only did she bring reinforcements sufficient to tip the balance in the South Midlands, but her absence left Newcastle free to concentrate on his main objective – Lord Fairfax. Relieved of responsibility for the Queen's safety, the Earl advanced rapidly and on 22 June he took the Parliamentarian stronghold of Howley House.

THE BATTLE OF ADWALTON MOOR, 30 JUNE

Following this, Newcastle prepared to move on the Fairfaxes, who still held Bradford. A moorland ridge (now partly built over) runs east from Bradford, reaching its highest point near the little village of Adwalton, five miles away. On the morning of 30 June Newcastle arrived there and, warned of the approach of Fairfax, halted and occupied a position astride the ridge, about 1,500 yards wide at that point. His position ran some 700 yards west of Adwalton, with its right embracing the road to Bradford and its left a short way down the southern slope. His army was about 10,000 strong, and his artillery included two demi-cannon, nicknamed Gog and Magog.[1] The Parliamentarian army consisted of about 4,000 trained troops and an unspecified number of country folk armed mainly with agricultural implements and totally devoid of discipline.

Despite this disparity in numbers Lord Fairfax had moved off at about seven or eight o'clock in the morning and advanced straight up the Adwalton road. One and a half miles short of that village he drove in the Cavalier Forlorn Hope posted on a small hillock called Westgate Hill. He pushed on, and coming in sight of his opponents' position he deployed his army on a line some 500 yards short of them. He himself commanded the centre and the reserve, General Gifford the left and Sir Thomas Fairfax the right. The latter's division was posted on the southern slope of the hill, where it was entirely out of sight of the remainder of the army.

The battles that ensued consisted for the most part of a series of cavalry charges on the part of the Royalists and of counter-charges by the Parliamentarians. Those counter-charges were delivered with great spirit, especially on the southern flank. Sir Thomas Fairfax was holding an enclosure, with his musketeers, about 1,000 strong, lining the hedges next to the moor, 'which,' he writes, 'was good advantage to us who had so few Horse'. His dragoons were dismounted and he kept his five troops of cavalry in support. Ten or twelve troops of Horse charged in, striving to get through a gate from the moor where only five or six could enter abreast. The few that broke in 'found sharp entertainment'[2] from Fairfax's cavalry, while those that stayed in the road got

---

[1] A cannon ball from one of the guns, and several smaller ones, are now kept in the village school. There were possibly some drakes (light field-pieces) present, for there is a Drake Lane near the village.
[2] HMC Portland MSS., I, pp. 717–19.

as hot welcome from the musketeers that flanked them in the hedges. In the end the Cavaliers, who had lost their commander, Colonel Thomas Howard, were forced to retreat and the Roundheads 'gained ground on them'.

The Cavaliers, thirteen or fourteen troops, led this time by Colonel George Heron, came down again and charged. Fairfax's men defended themselves as before, but this time with much more difficulty, for many of the Cavaliers got in among them. But in the end the Royalists were beaten off and their leader slain. After a second charge Sir Thomas Fairfax led an impetuous pursuit along a convenient ledge of fairly level ground that led up to a hedged lane named Warren Lane, leading down the hill to the south, 600 yards from the Roundhead position. The charge came to a halt at this lane and Sir Thomas prudently recalled his troops to their original position. As he withdrew, the Royalists fired one of their guns and by a strange chance hit four men of Captain Copley's troop, who while their comrades were fighting about them had been stripping Colonel Heron's body. Sir Thomas, a strictly religious man, regarded this as an Act of Divine Justice.

Meanwhile, on the left wing, where Gifford with a similar force was engaged with the Royalist Foot, things were also going well for the Roundheads, whose resolute bearing made Newcastle think of retreating. Indeed, he had already given his orders, and some of the Cavaliers had actually marched off the field. Now came one of those sudden and unexpected changes of fortune which so often decide the fate of battle. Colonel Skirton,[1] 'a wild and desperate man', Fairfax calls him, desired his general to let him charge once more. This initiative was rewarded. Advancing with a stand of pikes – most of Fairfax's Foot were musketeers – he broke in upon Gifford's wing, which, being unsupported by the reserve, lost ground. Perhaps the Royalists struck a portion of the line held by the country levies. Sir Thomas Fairfax blames Gifford, 'who did not his part as he ought to have done', and also some disaffected officers. He does not explain how it was that his father did not throw in his reserve.

The Cavaliers were not slow to see their advantage and pursue it, bringing up fresh troops. The Roundheads lost heart, and, beginning to flee, were soon broken. Newcastle's Horse charged again, and the Royalists turned their guns upon the main body of Lord Fairfax's Horse, killing many and routing the remainder.

Once the rot was started the whole of the Roundhead left, followed by the reserve, gave way and fled down the road to Bradford. Incredible though it may sound, Lord Fairfax had not warned his son that he was falling back – or perhaps his messenger failed to get through – and Sir Thomas, as we have seen, was out of sight of the rest of the army. He maintained his ground, and when at long last someone got through with orders to retreat he found himself practic-

[1] There seems to have been no colonel of this name in the Royalist army. Fairfax is probably referring to Colonel Posthumous Kirton, a veteran of the Dutch service, who was to fall with the Whitecoats at Marston Moor.

ally surrounded, the Cavaliers having cut the Bradford road. Accordingly, he withdrew to the south down the main road to Halifax, eight miles away. Having arrived there, he found that Bradford was still holding out, and he turned sharp to his right, reaching the town despite the fact that his Foot had marched fifteen miles that day and fought a battle. Only a general who had a tight hold of his troops and an iron will could have accomplished this. Next morning he took command of the town, his father having made off for Leeds. Sir Thomas's conduct that day was the brightest spot on the Parliamentary side, but he may be censured for failing to keep in touch with the troops on his left during the battle. The Roundheads lost three guns, 500 killed, and 1,400 prisoners. The Royalist losses, though they included several senior officers, were relatively light.

Newcastle could move fast when he chose. He arrived before Bradford that night, and his batteries opened fire from close range the following day. The Roundheads had two drakes on top of the tower, which was lined with woolpacks, but the Cavaliers battered it so that it was impossible to stay on it. By Sunday night the attackers had gained both ends of the town, and the Parliamentarians were down to their last barrel of powder. Sir Thomas Fairfax and Major-General Gifford broke out that night with a party of fifty Horse, but the Foot were less successful and the garrison, 300 strong, surrendered next day.

Lord Fairfax tried to secure Leeds, but 700 Royalist captives broke out of the prison and seized the magazine with 1,500 arms and 12 cannon, holding the town until Newcastle relieved them. Lord Fairfax, his army now reduced to three or four troops, beat a hasty retreat to Selby. Hotham had chosen this moment to declare for the King, but when things seemed most desperate the citizens of Hull secured him, and the defeated Roundhead commanders made their way there, a hazardous journey of sixty miles through a host of enemies. To Sir Thomas things must have seemed black indeed. His wife had been captured in the flight from Bradford and he himself was wounded. But things might have been worse. Fairfax's wound healed well, and the courtly Earl of Newcastle, who disdained to make war on women, sent Lady Fairfax to Hull in his own coach. Secure behind the walls of Hull, the Fairfaxes began to raise new forces and soon mustered about 2,500 Foot and 700 Horse, but the initiative in Yorkshire lay firmly with the victorious Newcastle.

Events had taken a different course, however, across the Pennines in Lancashire. James Stanley, formerly Lord Strange and now Earl of Derby, had achieved some success in that county, but his heavy-handed methods had alienated much of the population. He had failed to take Manchester early in the war; he had more luck at Lancaster, but burnt the town after its capture. He was eventually challenged by Ralph Ashton, Member of Parliament for the county, who scattered Derby's disorderly forces at Whalley Abbey. Although Derby managed to get some of his troops away, he slunk off to the Isle of Man, and only returned to Lancashire in early 1644 when Rupert swept into the county and temporarily reasserted Royalist control. His countess held out in Lathom House, defying repeated Parliamentarian summons to surrender, and this tied down numerous Lancashire Roundheads who might have been employed elsewhere.

Seven

THE WAR IN THE CENTRE

While in the west the Cornish Cavaliers were carrying all before them, and Newcastle was gradually gaining control in Yorkshire, operations in the centre were of a more episodic and disconnected nature, making it more than usually difficult to follow the swirling sequence of events. At first the initiative lay with the Parliamentarians, who outnumbered the King's Oxford army considerably. Essex faced the King in the Thames Valley while another Roundhead army, under Sir William Waller, was operating farther south. Charles was, as we have seen, too weak to attack London without help from his forces in the north or west, which were as yet fully occupied in their own territories. During the winter, therefore, the King was content to improve his central position by enlarging the territory he held around Oxford. On 5 December Wilmot and Digby, temporarily submerging their growing mutual dislike, stormed Marlborough. This useful success was overshadowed when, on 13 December, Waller performed a similar feat at Winchester, cutting up Lord Grandison's small but promising regiment of Horse in the process.[1]

It was Rupert who swung the situation once more in the Royalist favour, storming Cirencester on 2 February 1643, and herding its garrison off to Oxford, where the captives arrived in time to shamble into prison before the horrified gaze of the Parliamentarian commissioners. Waller, meanwhile, continued his career of conquest in the south, taking Farnham Castle, Arundel Castle and Chichester. Although they were only victories over ill-armed levies, they won Waller great popularity with the citizens of London and the nickname 'William the Conqueror'. Much more important, they won him command of the Western Association, which was formed on 11 February 1643, and included Gloucestershire, Wiltshire, Somersetshire, Worcestershire, Shropshire and the City of Bristol, where he set up his headquarters in March.

Sir William Waller was forty-five years old in 1643. As a young man he had been in the Venetian service, and had later fought the Imperialists in Bohemia and the Palatinate. In the Long Parliament he was Member for Andover, and was commissioned to raise a regiment of Horse in 1642. He gained an early

[1] *See* the Rev. G. N. Godwin, *The Civil War in Hampshire, 1642–5* (London 1904), p. 44.

success by forcing Goring to surrender Portsmouth, but did less well at Edgehill where his regiment galloped from the field with the rest of the Parliamentarian left wing. Waller was a tactician of considerable ability, and speedily gained a reputation for skilful use of ground. The Royalist Colonel Walter Slingsby maintained that he 'was the best shifter and chooser of ground when he was not master of the field, that I ever saw; which are great abilities in a soldier'.[1] *Mercurius Aulicus* in 1644 derived some humour from Waller's careful use of terrain; 'you know his condition of old; hills, bogs, hedges, these you must grant him, he'll not fight else'.

By February, the King's Oxford army was in an unenviable position. Essex, with his headquarters at Windsor, threatened Oxford from the south-east – though the only sign of life from the Earl's army had been an abortive attempt on the Royalist outpost of Brill on 27 January, where Colonel Arthur Goodwin's attack was repulsed with loss by Sir Gilbert Gerard and two Lancashire regiments of Foot. Waller barred the road to South Wales, one of the best Royalist recruiting areas. Lord Herbert, son of the Roman Catholic Marquis of Worcester, a man who spent altogether nearly a million pounds in the Royalist cause, had already raised a small army of about 1,500 Welsh Foot and 500 Horse, well armed and equipped. Unfortunately, Herbert lacked experienced officers. His brother, Lord John Somerset, 'a maiden soldier', commanded the Horse; the Foot were entrusted to Colonel Richard Lawdy, a professional soldier. Lawdy was killed in a skirmish in the Forest of Dean, leaving Herbert's army 'destitute of persons of experience to command them'.[2] Waller moved quickly against Herbert's Welshmen. While the latter threatened Gloucester from the north, Waller marched rapidly through Wiltshire with about 2,000 Horse and dragoons, took Malmesbury, crossed the Severn in boats, and surprised Herbert's army at Highnam on 24 March. The inexperienced Welshmen soon capitulated, and Waller sent nearly 1,000 prisoners to Gloucester. So passed what Clarendon unkindly terms 'that mushroom army, which grew up and perished so soon'.[3]

This unhappy episode worried the King but little, and was soon followed by numerous Royalist successes. Lichfield Close was seized and held by some local Royalists; Lord Brooke, Parliament's commander in Warwickshire and Staffordshire, was killed by a musket-ball while watching the progress at the siege. Nevertheless, Sir John Gell maintained pressure on the Close, and eventually compelled its surrender. Stafford, too, was garrisoned by some local gentlemen, who were spared the fate of their friends in Lichfield by the arrival of the Earl of Northampton, who relieved them and prepared to march on Lichfield.

Spencer Compton, second Earl of Northampton, was forty-one years of age, and had served in Breda and Lemgo. He had with him his own and Prince

[1] Hopton, op. cit., p. 91.
[2] Clarendon, op. cit., Vol. III, p. 465.
[3] Ibid., p. 467.

Charles's regiments of Horse and a handful of Foot. He was joined near Stafford by Colonel-General Henry Hastings and several of his mounted regiments, bringing his total force to some 1,200 men. To oppose them, Gell cooperated with Sir William Brereton, the leader of the Cheshire Roundheads. Although Brereton had no military experience, he was a sound man who exercised his command 'with notable sobriety, and indefatigable industry (virtues not so well practised in the King's quarters)'.[1] Gell and Brereton planned to rendezvous on Hopton Heath, about three miles north-east of Stafford, and launch a combined attack on the town.

THE BATTLE OF HOPTON HEATH, 19 MARCH

At about noon on Sunday 19 March Gell's little army of Horse and Foot, about 750 strong, ascended the hill out of Weston on the Stafford road, whilst Brereton in similar strength was approaching from Stoke along the Salt road. On hearing of Gell's approach, Northampton hurriedly collected his men from their scattered quarters and marched out up the long gradual slope to meet his opponent.

The roads from Sandon and from Weston to Stafford cross the ridge on the south side of the Trent valley, 2,000 yards apart. This ridge runs due east–west and from its summit the church towers of Stafford may be seen. Gell was the first to ascend it, and he at once realised that it would form an excellent locality for the junction of the two columns and a good defensive position in case of attack. He therefore deployed his troops along it without waiting for the arrival of Brereton. Running along the east side of the Stafford road was the stone wall bounding Ingestre Park, on which Gell rested his left flank. On the right of the road a carriage road 300 yards in length ran along the ridge top, leading up to a country seat called Heathyards.[2] The house was in the centre of a small park or enclosure 500 yards in diameter, and bounded by a stone wall. On the south side the wall was about 200 yards down the gentle slope and provided an excellent line for Gell's Foot and dragoons. The three heavy field guns were placed on the top of the ridge near the house, while the eight drakes were pushed forward into the front line. Farther to the west there were some hedges for a few hundred yards, opening on to rough moorish ground, pitted with rabbit holes. Here Gell placed his main body, with his small force of cavalry on his extreme right, where they were shortly joined by Brereton's Horse, while the Cheshire Foot plodded along some distance in the rear. When eventually they arrived, they prolonged the line to the west, though 1,500 yards, the distance usually cited, seems an impossibly long front for so small an army.

As the Cavalier Horse approached they could see the Roundhead guns in the

[1] Ibid., p. 451.
[2] The house has since been replaced by a farmhouse, but vestiges of the boundary wall remain on the north side.

enclosure on the ridge with the wall of Ingestre Park on their right hand, and consequently they deployed to their left. There was a halt for thirty minutes within a few hundred yards of the enemy, during which dragoons were sent out to silence the opposing dragoons, which they succeeded in doing. A sharp fight ensued. The Cavaliers now dragged up a heavy 29-pounder, or demi-cannon, named Roaring Meg. The Dunrobin MS.[1] gives a graphic account of the havoc she caused. 'We drew up our cannon, which was one very good piece and did great execution, for the first shot killed six of their men and hurt four and the next made such a lane through them that they had little mind to close again.' Gell's stand of pikes drawn up on the rabbit warren must have offered a magnificent target.

The Cavaliers now decided to make a general onslaught against the hostile centre. The first furious charge, led by the gallant Northampton in person, was completely successful, both Gell's and Brereton's Horse being put to flight in less than a quarter of an hour. All but a few were driven from the field. North-ampton now rallied his Horse for a second charge – 'a most desperate attempt' Brereton called it – against the remnants of the Roundhead Horse who were sheltered by their infantry. The Cavaliers were met with a volley which did some damage, but rode over some of the hostile Foot, and almost routed Gell's main body. However, they were then so pelted by musketry that they were driven back, though not before they had taken eight pieces of ordnance, including two carts of drakes, in the hedges. The going over the rabbit warrens made things doubly difficult for the cavalry, but even so they overran the main battery.

But a disaster had befallen the Cavaliers, for Northampton was himself un-horsed – quite possibly owing to a rabbit hole – and was temporarily separated from his men. Surrounded by enemies he killed a colonel and several others with his sword. His armour was so good that he held his own until someone struck off his helmet with the butt of a musket. Summoned to surrender, he answered, 'I scorn to take quarter from such base rogues and rebels as you are',[2] and was killed by a blow on the head with a halberd.

Undeterred by this, Sir Thomas Byron, commanding Prince Charles's regi-ment of Horse, launched a third charge, recapturing the guns, killing more of Gell's Foot and driving the last remnants of his Horse from the field; but now he also fell wounded with a shot in the thigh. Hastings essayed a fourth charge but this time the horsemen were so scattered and disorganised and their horses so blown, that he found it quite impracticable. Dusk was now falling. Gell's men were also feeling the strain, and had reached the end of their tether. Three of their guns had been taken, retaken, and taken again. Their Horse had long

---

[1] Lieutenant-Colonel A. H. Burne (ed.), 'The Battle of Hopton Heath, 1643'. Transcribed from the Sutherland Papers, Vol. 2, f. 69, preserved in Dunrobin Castle Library. (The Staffordshire Record Society, 1936.)

[2] Clarendon, op. cit., Vol. III, p. 458.

since departed, and under cover of the darkness the Roundhead Foot of both Gell and Brereton slipped silently away, leaving the Royalists in possession of the field. In addition to the guns they had lost about 500 casualties, while their opponents' loss was under 50, though many were officers.

The action of Hopton Heath illustrates the danger of attempting to unite forces on the battlefield. Brereton was late at the rendezvous; had his infantry been in position in time, things would have gone hard with the Royalists. As it was, Northampton's quick and bold initiative completely foiled the Parliamentarian plan. The Roundhead commanders retreated in widely divergent directions – Brereton to the north-west back to Stone and ultimately into Cheshire; Gell to the north-east to Chartly, where his errant Horse rejoined him, and then to Uttoxeter. Their project of capturing Stafford by a swift *coup de main* had ended in disaster.

Northampton's death, and the inevitable confusion which it produced, prevented effective exploitation of the Royalist victory. Lichfield remained in Parliamentarian hands, and continued to threaten communications between Oxford and the north. To remedy this, Rupert was sent into the Midlands. On 3 April he took the intensely Puritan town of Birmingham, and a week later he burst into the town of Lichfield, and laid siege to the strongly held cathedral close, which surrendered on 21 April after the explosion of a mine, the first time gunpowder had been used for this purpose in England. Rupert garrisoned the place, an essential link in the tenuous chain of communication between Oxford and Yorkshire, and then fell back to Oxford to aid the King, who was threatened by the activities of Essex in the Thames Valley. At Oxford, Rupert was joined by Maurice, fresh from his exploits in the west.

Following his victory over Lord Herbert's Welshmen on 24 March, Waller had advanced into Monmouthshire, taking Monmouth, Chepstow and Ross-on-Wye. Prince Maurice was despatched from Oxford to aid Lord Herbert, who had luckily escaped the fate of his troops at Highnam, and was threatening Waller from the west with an army extemporised from garrisons. Maurice rendezvoused with Grandison at Tewkesbury, crossed the Severn, possibly on a bridge of boats above the town or by the bridge at Upton, seven miles to the north, and marched south to cut Waller's communications with Gloucester. The wily Parliamentarian sent his infantry, guns and baggage across the Severn at Aust, opposite Chepstow, and led his force against Maurice, whose 2,000 Horse and Foot were deployed in the Forest of Dean to meet just such a manoeuvre. There was a confused skirmish at the village of Little Dean, but Waller broke through safely, and made contact with Lieutenant-Colonel Massey, the Governor of Gloucester. Waller directed Massey, with his troops from Gloucester, to seize Tewkesbury, while his own men rested. In this Massey succeeded on the morning of 12 April, and was joined by Waller that evening.

THE BATTLE OF RIPPLE FIELD, 13 APRIL

Maurice, meanwhile, had seized the bridge at Upton, and pushed his troops across it early on the morning of 13 April. Waller correctly anticipated this move, but did not attempt to reach the Upton area before Maurice's army was safely on the east bank of the Severn. The Parliamentarians marched north out of Tewkesbury over King John's bridge, which spans the River Avon, up the steep slope of Mythe Hill, and, with the Severn on their left, followed the old road[1] towards Worcester. This highway is marked by crosses set up by King John, the first being at Ripple, three and a half miles north of Tewkesbury. Beyond the village the ground slopes up gradually for about 400 yards to the crest of The Bank, *alias* 'Old Nan's Hill',[2] a ridge running east and west between the point where Ripple School (now a private house) stands, and the village of Uckinghall near the river. The ridge is not long, and curves gradually south at its western end. To the north it falls sharply to the flat plain – Ripple Field. This area was divided by hedges into a number of enclosures: the first, north of 'Old Nan's Hill', is known as Deadland Field, and it is joined by another, Scarlet Close.

As Waller reached the ridge, he could see Prince Maurice's army, probably drawn up in three bodies, with its right flank resting on the Severn. Maurice had about 2,000 men, and although his musketeers were deployed in hedges on his flanks, it cannot have been difficult for Waller to make an accurate estimate of his strength. Waller himself had something like 1,500 men, but, apart from Massey's own company of bluecoats, his troops were all mounted. His artillery had 'neither shot prepared nor cannoneers that understood the business'.[3]

Maurice was extremely wary of Waller (who was already known as an able tactician), and suspected that the latter would try to draw his men into an ambuscade. When some troops of Parliamentarian cavalry advanced, Maurice repulsed them, but pursued only across the open ground towards the foot of 'Old Nan's Hill'. This preliminary skirmish would account for the bodies buried in the Deadland Field. Some of the Parliamentary officers were eager for a battle, but Waller, disconcerted perhaps by his failure to forestall Maurice at Upton (if, indeed, that had been his intention), was in two minds about it. His subordinates – evidently without orders – opened fire with their artillery, but they did little or no damage. There is a flat ledge near the top of the hill, where several guns could have been planted, though elsewhere the hillside seems too steep. From this ledge or from the crest their fire would plunge, and the cannon balls instead of ricocheting would bury themselves in the ground.

---

[1] Not the modern A38, but a road running slightly west of it.

[2] A corruption of Ordnance Hill.

[3] John Corbet, Massey's chaplain, probably an eye-witness, in J. Washbourne, *Bibliotheca Gloucestrensis: a collection of ... tracts relating to the county and city of Gloucester during the civil war* (London 1823).

Discouraged by the repulse of his cavalry, and finding his position too extensive for a single company of Foot, Waller now decided to withdraw. His route lay down the lane, from the rear of his right flank to Ripple village. To cover this movement Waller sent out his dragoons to face the Royalists in Ripple Field, and placed Massey's musketeers in the bushes at the mouth of the lane, while he drew off his cavalry – these last somewhat shaken perhaps by their earlier repulse. By this time it seems likely that Maurice had advanced to within about half a mile of Waller's position. At any rate the Parliamentary gunners had opened fire, which they would hardly have done at longer range, and it is evident that the Prince could see what was going on. He could also see that 'Old Nan's Hill' had a much gentler gradient to the west than to the north. He decided therefore to make his main attack from the west, in other words, a right hook.

Maurice's attack was well timed. It struck Waller's army just as it was entering the lane, and caused great confusion. The Roundhead dragoons were broken – perhaps by a frontal holding attack – and disordered their own musketeers. Hot on their heels came the Royalists. The Roundheads were struck almost simultaneously by the right-hand Royalist column, which had dashed into Uckinghall, swung left, and now came galloping along the ridge from the west. Massey at once sent to Tewkesbury for reinforcements, and Sir Arthur Hesilrige persuaded his own troop to charge, leading them on gallantly. His Lobsters and some of Massey's bluecoats fought hard to give the rest time to rally,[1] but after standing for a while 'in a maze' they suddenly faced about and ran like a flock of sheep. The last stand was made near a big barn which can still be seen in the middle of Ripple. Some of the bewildered Parliamentary troops seem to have made for the ford over the Severn at Uckinghall, but the road to it was already cut: in trying to swim the river a number were drowned. Most of the fugitives made off to the south, by the way they had come.

The Royalists pursued Waller's broken men for nearly three miles towards Tewkesbury, but when the runaways reached the narrow track that ran down the Mythe Hill, near the old house known as King John's Castle, they met Massey's reinforcements who had hastened across the Avon. The fresh troops, undismayed by the scene of confusion that met their gaze, checked the Royalist cavalry with a galling fire, and Massey himself fought hand-to-hand with their leader, Major Thomas Sheldon of Prince Maurice's regiment of Horse. Most of the Roundhead cavalry had fled by this time but Massey was rescued by a handful of his officers. The remnants of Waller's force were able to fall back into Tewkesbury, and Maurice pursued no farther because he could not force the bottleneck of King John's Bridge.

This sharp reverse cost the Roundheads eighty killed; few of their infantry

---

[1] One of Massey's men succeeded in shutting a gate in the faces of the Royalist pursuers. It is curious that its exact location on the road just north of Ripple can be told from a map of 1775.

can have escaped from Ripple. The Royalists admitted no more than two men killed, but must have had a number wounded. Prince Maurice, though a stout fighter, is not usually credited with much military skill, but he was the first Cavalier general to get the better of 'William the Conqueror'. Of the Parliamentarians, only Massey and Hesilrige emerged with credit from the rout of Ripple Field. Waller's usually excellent eye for the ground seems to have failed him. Sir William could have drawn up his men on top of 'Old Nan's Hill' in such a way as to make Maurice wonder whether he had a greater force in rear,[1] but instead he ordered his men on to the forward slope of the hill 'and discovered their weakness in full view'.

Maurice now retired to Evesham, whence he was soon recalled to assist in the attempt to relieve Reading. Waller soon recovered from his shock, and on 25 April he captured Hereford after a feeble resistance. There he lingered for about a fortnight, before leaving for Gloucester. He had not enough men to leave a garrison behind him. It seems likely that, since Ripple, he and Massey were not cooperating wholeheartedly, he was somewhat short-handed.

Maurice, like his brother, returned to Oxford in time to move against Essex, who lay before Reading. An attempt at relief was thwarted on 25 April at Caversham Bridge, and the town fell two days later.[2] This was a severe blow for the King, since Reading was a useful stepping-stone for Essex's advance on Oxford, and had a similar importance for any Royalist move on London.

Fortunately for the King, Essex moved with painful slowness. Hampered by sickness in his army, and a shortage of pay for his troops, the Earl did not leave Reading until 10 June. By this time the Royalist position had greatly improved. On 15 May the Queen's first great convoy, forty wagon-loads of arms and munitions, including 300 barrels of powder, reached Oxford. From that time forward the King's own army was not noticeably worse armed than Essex's, and, with reinforcements from the north, and with the addition of the Reading garrison, who had been allowed to march out with their arms, it was numerically at least as strong. Another factor was Hopton's victory far away at Stratton on 16 May. The King, knowing that the Cornish Royalists were short of cavalry, had already determined to send some, and on 19 May Hertford and Maurice marched west to join them. From now on Waller's attention was focused on the western army; he was no longer in a position to cooperate with Essex even if he had so desired, though he still threatened the road to South Wales. Royalist reinforcements would have to come thence via Upton on Severn and Evesham to Oxford.

---

[1] As Lunsford did at Marshall's Elm, for example.

[2] The irascible Sir Arthur Aston, governor of the town, had been struck by a falling tile and rendered literally speechless. His place was taken by Colonel Richard Feilding, who was court-martialled for surrendering the town, and narrowly escaped death. He lost his regiment, but fought bravely at Cheriton the following year. Aston, whose injury was, one suspects, more diplomatic than physical, soon recovered.

THE CHALGROVE RAID, 17–18 JUNE

Essex remained immobile in Thame for a week. On 17 June he sent a substantial detachment to occupy Islip and hold the passage of the Cherwell above Oxford, a manoeuvre which came to nought. Rupert was not slow to riposte. Colonel John Urry, a Scots professional, had deserted to the Royalists a few days earlier. This officer, who was to change sides twice more during his career, was able to supply accurate information as to Essex's quarters. Moreover, he reported the approach of a convoy bringing £21,000 to pay the Earl's army. Rupert accordingly set out across Magdalen Bridge on the afternoon of 17 June. With him were three regiments of Horse, numbering 1,000 in all, 350 dragoons under Lord Wentworth, and 500 'commanded' Foot without colours, led by Colonel Henry Lunsford. Major William Legge commanded the forlorn hope of 100 Horse and 50 dragoons.

Rupert's small force crossed the River Thame at Chislehampton Bridge, brushed past a Parliamentarian quarter at Tetsworth, and reached Postcombe in the early hours of the morning, destroying a troop of Horse. Rupert pushed rapidly on to Chinnor, where he caught Sir Samuel Luke's newly raised Bedfordshire dragoons in their quarters. About 50 of the dragoons were killed and 120 captured, with three of their guidons, 'buff bibles on a black background'.

Leaving Chinnor in flames behind him, the Prince then hurried on, hoping to surprise the convoy. However, a countryman had warned the escort of Rupert's approach, and the convoy was safely hidden in the woods that fringe the Chilterns. Thwarted in his main aim, though with some reason for self-congratulation, Rupert ordered a withdrawal. The Parliamentarians tried hard to intercept him, rousing their men out of quarters and marching to cut off the Prince's retreat. Rupert was not seriously threatened until he neared the Thame. He sent Lunsford and his musketeers to secure Chislehampton Bridge, and drew up his Horse in Chalgrove Field, about a mile and a half east of it, to face his pursuers until his Foot could get into position. He placed his dragoons in ambush on either side of a lane leading to the bridge in his rear.

The pursuing Parliamentarians came in sight, riding down Gilton Hill; a party of dragoons cantered ahead, dismounted, lined the hedge that separated the two sides, and opened fire, while the cavalry trotted up behind them in line, trying to delay Rupert until more substantial forces could come up. The Prince sat his horse calmly at the head of his lifeguard, but when the carbines of the hostile dragoons emptied a saddle or two, his patience was exhausted. 'This insolency,' he said, 'is not to be endured,' and, clapping spurs to his charger, dashed forward and cleared the hedge, followed as best they could by Sir Richard Crane and the rest of his own troop. As soon as about fifteen men had joined him, the Prince drew them up in a single rank until the rest could come up, and charged. There ensued a brisk mêlée; the Parliamentarian dragoons fled, but the Roundhead Horse stood their ground well for a time, until Rupert's lieutenant-colonel, Daniel O'Neale, and Lord Percy, general of the artillery, led their regiments against the Parliamentarian flanks and completed the rout. John Hampden, who had made frantic efforts to get some troops together to oppose Rupert, and who, as a colonel of Foot, had no reason but his arden spirit to bring him into a cavalry skirmish, received two bullets in the shoulder.[1] Mortally wounded, he rode painfully across country to Thame, where, on 24 June, he died. Hampden's death was a serious loss to the Parliamentarians. He had contributed greatly to preventing a breakdown between Essex and Parliament; his tact, diplomacy and boundless energy were to be sadly missed.

Rupert returned safely to Oxford, and, a week after Chalgrove, Urry led a party of Horse as far as West Wycombe, producing considerable alarm in London, and thereby increasing the Capital's discontent with Essex. John Pym did what he could to support the harassed Earl, and played a vital part in the formation of strategy in these dark days. This strategy was, it is true, little more than an effort to cope with each successive emergency as it occurred, but Pym's contribution was, none the less, vital. On 19 July, for example, orders were given to the Earl of Rutland, Sir Henry Vane the younger, and three other members of the Commons to go to Edinburgh and arrange for the intervention of a Scots army. Three days later, on 23 July, the Excise Ordinance was issued, increasing customs duties and thereby placing the Parliamentarian finances on a sounder footing.

Pym's influence on Parliamentarian morale was perhaps more important than the material effects of his tireless energy. There were, indeed, several reasons for spirits to be low. The death of Hampden, and the defeat of Gell and Brereton at Hopton Heath were followed by further reinforcements for the King's Oxford army,[2] and, disastrously, by the almost complete destruction of the Parliamentarian armies in the west.

[1] There is some evidence that his hand was blown off by the bursting of his pistol, and this is perhaps the likelier story.
[2] On 13 July the Queen met her husband on the field of Edgehill. She brought an army of about 3,000 men, 8 or 9 guns and 100 wagons of supplies. With this reinforcement, the King at last outnumbered Essex.

Eight

THE WAR IN THE WEST–2

By the midsummer of 1643 the tide seemed to be running steadily in favour of the King. In Yorkshire, Newcastle had roundly beaten the Fairfaxes at Adwalton Moor. Brereton and Gell had been sharply handled at Hopton Heath, and Maurice had mauled Massey at Ripple Field. Essex was firmly checked by the fortresses round Oxford, and his army was dispirited by the Chalgrove Raid and the death of John Hampden. In the west, the Royalists concentrated for a major offensive.

Shortly after his victory at Stratton, Hopton heard that a force under Hertford and Maurice was marching west from Oxford to join him. With Devonshire as yet unsubdued – Plymouth, Exeter, Bideford and Barnstable all held Parliamentarian garrisons – it was no mean feat on the part of Hopton to persuade his Cornishmen to march into Somerset; that he succeeded is a measure of their confidence in him. Leaving a force to blockade Plymouth and Exeter he arrived at the rendezvous at Chard on 4 June.

With Maurice were three regiments of Horse; his own, the Earl of Caernarvon's and Colonel Thomas Howard's, some 1,500 in all. There were, in addition, 1,000 newly levied Foot and 10 or 11 cannon. Hopton had 3,000 seasoned Foot, 500 Horse, 300 dragoons, and 4 or 5 cannon. There was, initially, some friction between the two forces. Hopton complained of the 'disorder of the Horse',[1] while Maurice's men did not get on well with the Cornishmen. Captain Richard Atkyns remarked that 'the Cornish Foot could not well brook our Horse (especially, when we were drawn up on corn) but they would many times let fly at us: these were the very best Foot I ever saw, for marching and fighting; but so mutinous withal, that nothing but an alarm could keep them from falling foul upon their officers.'[2]

More serious was the question of command. The size of Hertford's army in no way reduced its command structure. Clarendon remarks that 'how small soever the Marquis's party was in number, it was supplied with all the general officers of a royal army, a general, a lieutenant-general, general of Horse,

[1] Hopton, op. cit., p. 47.
[2] Atkyns and Gwyn, op. cit., p. 12.

general of the ordnance, major-general of Horse, and another of Foot. . . .'[1]
Hertford was the senior officer present, but was, as we have seen, no soldier,
and seems to have been content to act as a figurehead. There was, though, grave
danger that friction might arise between Hopton and Maurice; the one had his
Cornish victories behind him, while the other had already defeated Waller at
Ripple Field, and it was with Waller that the Royalists now had to deal. It is
impossible to be certain how this difficulty was overcome, but the indications
are that Hopton, besides acting as a kind of chief-of-staff, actually commanded
the whole force in the field, while Maurice was usually content to confine his
activities to the mounted arm. As usual, operations, except when actually in
close contact with the enemy, were directed by a Council of War consisting of
the senior officers of both contingents.

With Bristol and Gloucester firmly in his hands, Waller had concentrated
his field army about Bath, where he had been reinforced by 1,200 Horse and
dragoons sent by Stamford. Besides these, he had Hesilrige's 'Lobsters' and his
own cavalry which had followed him from London. The exact strength of his
army is unknown, but it can scarcely have been less than that of his opponents,
while in cavalry it certainly outnumbered them. His infantry, however, was
not to be compared with Hopton's experienced Cornish Foot.

The Royalists did not advance against Waller at once, but secured their base
by occupying Taunton, Bridgwater, Dunster Castle and Wells, which they
did without much opposition. Colonel Thomas Howard's regiment of Horse
was sent into Devonshire, and was replaced by Sir James Hamilton's regiment,
which came from Worcester, and whose bad behaviour had been raising a
storm of protest. There was no serious engagement between the two armies
until 10 June, when there was a sharp cavalry skirmish near Chewton Mendip.
Prince Maurice was temporarily captured in this hack-and-gallop affair, but was
rescued, thanks to the initiative of Richard Atkyns.[2]

On 2 July the Royalists reached Bradford-on-Avon, six miles south-east of
Bath. Waller lay some four miles away, across the river, well placed to resist
any direct advance on the city. The Royalist commanders decided to outflank
Waller from the east, and moved north towards Monkton Farleigh. Waller,
however, kept the bulk of his army drawn up on Claverton Down, but constructed a bridge to supplement the ford near Claverton House, and pushed a
strong detachment on to Monkton Farleigh Hill, with an ambush at its foot, on
the Bradford road.

On 3 July Hopton advanced; his Cornish infantry soon rooted out Waller's
ambush party, and the detachment on Monkton Farleigh was thrust back on
Batheaston. Waller's main position at Claverton now became visible to the
Royalists, and Maurice swung the bulk of the infantry against it, taking the
bridge and compelling Waller to retreat on Bath. Hopton, meanwhile, had

[1] Clarendon, op. cit., Vol. IV, p. 109.
[2] Atkyns gives a lively account of this action. *See* Atkyns and Gwyn, op. cit., pp. 13–16.

pursued Waller's outlying detachment through Batheaston, to the southern end of Lansdown, as the Royalists were in some disorder, and open to a flank attack down the Avon Valley. Hopton accordingly determined to fall back into Batheaston, and await the return of Maurice before making any attempt on Lansdown.

Lansdown Hill is an exceptionally strong position. It runs north-westwards from Bath, forming a sharp-sided ridge, some three miles in length, with a broad, flat top. On the morning of Tuesday 4 July, the reunited Royalist army set off for Lansdown, only to discover Waller securely ensconced on top of the feature. At about one in the afternoon the Royalist Council of War decided to retreat to Marshfield, and entrusted the manoeuvre to Hopton, who covered his withdrawal by lining the hedges with 1,000 musketeers, and holding the Parliamentarians off with a strong body of Horse, 'with which at last he marched off without any loss, and drew a strong party of the Enemy's Horse within the Ambuscade of musketeers, which having tasted they quickly retired'.[1] The Royalists thus reached Marshfield in safety.

THE BATTLE OF LANSDOWN, 5 JULY

Early the next morning Waller marched to the northern end of Lansdown Hill and proceeded to construct field fortifications, sending a party of Horse out towards Marshfield, driving in the Royalist pickets.[2] With this, the Royalist army marched south-west, and the dragoons of both sides skirmished from hedge to hedge along the Royalist axis of advance over Tog and Freezing Hills. The Royalist commanders, considering that this type of fighting would do little except consume ammunition, of which they had little enough, decided to return to Marshfield.[3]

Waller decided to exploit the Royalist withdrawal, and sent Colonel Robert Burrell with some 1,000 'arm'd [armoured] Horse and dragoons' to charge them in flank and rear. The Parliamentarian dragoons, using their muskets from the hedgerows, 'made us retreat so disorderly, that they fell foul upon our Foot....'[4] The confusion in the narrow lane, with only limited room for manoeuvre on the hillside to either flank, was increased owing to Hopton's having posted Cornish musketeers in the intervals of the Horse.[5] The bold

---

[1] Hopton, op. cit., p. 53.
[2] Major George Lower of Colonel Thomas Howard's regiment of Horse commanded the Royalist forlorn hope. Atkyns (op. cit., p. 17) accuses him of negligence, though Hopton speaks well of him (Hopton, op. cit., p. 52). Lower was killed later that day.
[3] Hopton, op. cit., p. 53.
[4] Atkyns and Gwyn, op. cit., p. 18.
[5] Hopton had done this at Maurice's request (Hopton, op. cit., p. 53). It was a standard tactic in the Swedish service, and was favoured by Rupert. Although on occasion successful, it was a risky practice and often resulted in confusion and casualties. *Vide* the fate of the hapless musketeers interlarding Ramsey's Horse at Edgehill.

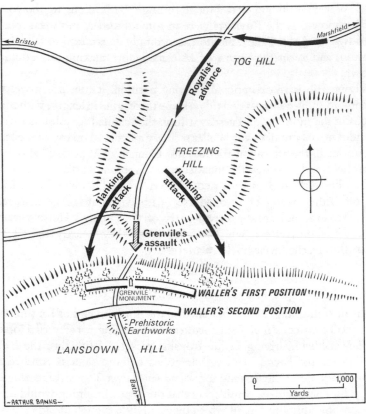

4 LANSDOWN

Cornishmen held on even though the Horse they were supporting dissolved in a rout, and were speedily aided by Hertford's lifeguard of Horse, and later by the Earl of Caernarvon's regiment, which pursued the Parliamentarians to the foot of Lansdown Hill. While Caernarvon, with his customary vigour, pushed back the Roundhead Horse, Sir Nicholas Slanning, with 250 musketeers, prised the Parliamentary dragoons away from the hedges from which they supported their cavalry. Waller threw two more regiments of Horse into the mêlée in the valley between Lansdown and Freezing Hills, but the fire of the Cornishmen drove them off with loss.

By about 2 p.m. the entire Royalist army was at the foot of Lansdown Hill facing Waller's formidable position at the top of the feature. The Roundhead general's several guns were in the centre of his position more or less covering the road as it wound up from Freezing Hill, and most of his infantry were at least partly sheltered by breastworks. The slopes of the hill were less wooded than they are now; a thin belt of trees skirted the road, but farther to the flanks the woods grew thicker, very much as they do today. The surrounding country was for the most part unenclosed, but there was a long stone wall 'half a culverin shot' in rear of Waller's gun position. There is today such a stone wall, about 400 yards from the crest, which may well be the wall in question.

As the discomfited mass of Parliamentarian Horse and dragoons struggled back up Lansdown Hill, the Cornishmen, in full cry, desired to press on, shouting 'Let us fetch those cannon'.[1] Hopton ordered an advance, 'sending out as they went strong parties of musketeers on each hand to second one another, to endeavour under the cover of the enclosed grounds to gain the flank of the enemy on the top of the Hill, which they at last did. . . .'[2] While the Royalist musketeers pushed Waller's men back through the woods on either flank of the Parliamentarian position, the main assault went in up the road. The pikemen and Horse advanced up the hill in the face of a withering fire.[3] Richard Atkyns gives a graphic description of the scene. Signs that the Parliamentarians were flying made Lieutenant-Colonel Sir Robert Welsh 'importunately desire the Prince to have a party follow the chase, which he gave him the command of and me the reserve. . . . As I went up the hill, which was very steep and hollow, I met several dead and wounded officers brought off; besides several running away, that I had much ado to get up by them.'

The situation was saved by Sir Bevil Grenvile, whose regiment was drawn up on Freezing Hill. Grenvile must have seen the repeated repulses of the Royalist Horse; he deployed his musketeers behind a wall on his left, placed some Horse on his right, where the ground was more open, and moved off down the main road at the head of his stand of pikes. Sir Bevil's pikemen ploughed up the road, littered with the debris of previous attacks, and surged forward to the crest of the hill. Here they received three charges from Waller's cavalry; in the last of these stages the gallant Sir Bevil and many of his men fell, but the remainder stood firm. As Atkyns ascended the hill, he 'saw Sir Bevill Grinvill's [sic] stand of pikes, which certainly preserved our army from a total rout, with the loss of his most precious life: they stood as upon the eaves of a house for steepness, but as unmovable as a rock; on which side of this stand of pikes our Horse were, I could not discover; for the air was so darkened by the smoke of the powder, that for a quarter of an hour together (I dare say) there was no light seen, but what the fire of the volleys of shot gave. . . .'[4]

The resolution of Grenvile's Cornishmen undoubtedly saved the Royalists from disaster. The Horse had suffered heavily, and much of it behaved badly. Hopton said that 'of 2,000 there did not stand above 600'.[5] Many officers and

---

[1] Hopton, op. cit., p. 95.
[2] Ibid., p. 54.
[3] It has been asserted that the attackers, while climbing the hill, would be immune from hostile artillery fire as the guns could not be depressed sufficiently to hit them. This is not so; see Lieutenant-Colonel A. H. Burne, *More Battlefields of England* (London 1952), pp. 169-71.
[4] Atkyns and Gwyn, op. cit., p. 19.
[5] Hopton, op. cit., p. 54.

troopers spurred off to Oxford, 'to carry tidings of our defeat before it was'.[1] A high proportion of officers had been killed and wounded; ammunition was scarce, extreme fatigue pervaded the ranks after a long day of marching, counter-marching and fighting, and deep gloom descended over the Cornishmen at the death of their leader Grenvile. Nevertheless, the Royalists had seized the line of redoubts along the crest, and the Parliamentarians had fallen back to the stone wall some 400 yards away. Waller's musketeers lined the wall, and gaps were broken in it for the Horse to charge through. These gaps were covered by cannon and pikemen. The musketeers on the Royalists' right, who had, in common with their fellows on the left, skirmished up the hill through the woods on either flank of Waller's position, worked their way forward to some pits between the woods and the wall 'from whence we galled them cruelly'.[2]

The Royalist hold on Lansdown remained, however, tenuous. 'We were then seated,' wrote Slingsby, 'like a very heavy stone upon the very brow of the hill, which with one lusty charge might well have been rolled to the bottom.'[3] As it was, the Parliamentarians were in no condition to deliver this attack. A desultory fire fight continued for some time, abating a little with nightfall. At about one in the morning firing flared up again, Horse and Foot could be heard moving in Waller's lines, and his musketeers fired a smart volley. The Royalist commanders, who had remained at the head of their troops, gave a reward to a soldier to steal silently forward to investigate. This individual found that the Roundheads had retired, leaving lighted matches on the wall, and pikes stuck in the ground along it, to delude the Royalists into thinking that they remained in position.

Waller's withdrawal left the victorious Royalists in possession of the battle-field. Had Waller held on longer his opponents may well have fallen back, for, as Slingsby remarked, 'we were glad they were gone for if they had not I know who had within an hour. . . .'[4] As it was, the Royalists were unable to proceed, for they were desperately short of ammunition and two-thirds of their Horse had decamped. They remained on the field until daylight, sent out cavalry scouts who reported that Waller was once again in Bath, and began to withdraw on Marshfield at 8 a.m.

At this juncture the Royalists suffered a piece of appallingly bad luck. Their army was drawn up on Tog Hill, and Hopton was looking at the prisoners taken the previous day. Some of these were sitting in a cart which also contained several barrels of powder. Hopton was accompanied by Major Thomas Sheldon of Prince Maurice's Horse, Captain Atkyns, and some other officers. Atkyns describes what followed:

[1] Atkyns and Gwyn, op. cit., p. 19.
[2] Hopton, op. cit., p. 96.
[3] Loc. cit.
[4] Loc. cit.

The Major desired me to go back to the regiment, while he received orders of his Lordship; I had no sooner turned my horse, and was gone three horses lengths from him, but the ammunition was blown up, and the prisoners in the cart with it; together with Lord Hopton, Major Sheldon, and Cornet Washnage [sic] who was near the cart on horseback, and several others: it made a very great noise, and darkened the air for a time, and the hurt men made lamentable screeches. . . . I found his Lordship miserably burnt, his horse singed like parched leather, and Thomas Sheldon (that was a horses length further from the blast) complaining that the fire was got within his breeches, which I tore off as soon as I could, and from as long a flaxen head of hair as ever I saw, in the twinkling of an eye, his head was like a blackamoor. . . .[1]

Hopton was temporarily blinded and paralysed, and had to travel on a bed in Hertford's coach. The able Major Sheldon died next day. With Hopton's tragic accident, morale sank. Gloom was deepened by the death or wounding of several capable officers; Grenvile, Lord Arundel of Wardour, Colonel Sir George Vaughan, and the Earl of Caernarvon had all become casualties at Lansdown.[2]

As the dispirited Royalists retraced their steps through Marshfield, Waller, hearing of Hopton's mishap and the loss of so much precious powder, drew reinforcements from the garrison of Bristol, and pursued. The Royalists halted at Chippenham for two days, but early on Sunday 9 July, on the approach of the enemy, they resumed their march and reached Devizes that night. Lieutenant-Colonel Richard Nevill, of Caernarvon's regiment of Horse, covered the withdrawal with considerable ability,[3] but Waller pressed hard upon the retreating Royalists and hustled them into the town. Prince Maurice ordered Slingsby, with Lord Mohun's regiment, to hold a ford[4] north-west of the town until he could draw up the army 'upon the hill by the Town'[5] – Roundway Hill. Slingsby's men held the line of the brook for half an hour, suffering about sixty casualties, for 'they were exposed too openly'.

On the next day, 10 July, the Parliamentarians drew up their whole army facing the Royalists on Roundway Down, but the latter, not caring to give battle, withdrew into Devizes, placing their artillery train in the castle. Waller then came down the hill, and encamped in the valley north of the town. That

---

[1] Atkyns and Gwyn, op. cit., p. 20.
[2] Grenvile was killed. Arundel had received two pistol-bullets in the thigh, Vaughan had a sword-cut, and Caernarvon had been shot in the leg. Thanks to – or, perhaps, in spite of – the ministrations of their surgeons, the latter three officers recovered.
[3] Or so say Hopton and Atkyns. Slingsby, however, maintains that 'our Horse offered to make [i.e., cover] the retreat, but after a charge or two, made too much haste to the town'. (Hopton, op. cit., p. 97.)
[4] Rowde Ford, about two miles north-west of Devizes Castle, on the Chippenham road.
[5] Hopton, op. cit., p. 97.

evening the Royalists held a Council of War in the house where Hopton lodged, Sir Ralph, in his own words, 'being then not able to move himself thence but as he was carried in a chair. . . .'[1] The Council unanimously resolved that Hertford and Maurice should break out that night with all the Horse, and march with all speed to Oxford, while Hopton with the Foot and guns would defend Devizes until relief could come. This plan was put into execution, and the cavalry got clear without loss. This was just as well for them, for on the next day Waller 'draws his whole force close to the Town and beleaguers us around, lying in many places within carbine shot; raised a battery upon a hill near the town, and then incessantly day and night pours great and small shot into us'.[2] There were no proper defence works at Devizes, so the Royalists had to make do with hedges and banks, but they barricaded every road to keep out the besieger's Horse.

The shortage of ammunition in the town was serious, for not only powder, but also match, was lacking, and Captain Pope, the comptroller of the ordnance, reported to Hopton that, having issued ammunition for the first action, he had only 150 pounds of match left. But the indomitable Hopton was not at a loss to amend this deficiency: he sent a guard from house to house to gather all the bedcords in the town, and to have them beaten and boiled in resin. This expedient produced 15 cwt of match.

Meanwhile, Maurice, skirting round to the south-east, had eluded Waller and, covering forty-four miles during the night – a remarkable achievement – clattered into Oxford, with horses exhausted and men grey with fatigue, on the morning of 11 July. The King was already aware of the straits of the western army. As early as 9 July the Earl of Crawford with 600 Horse had been sent west from Oxford with a convoy of ammunition, while on 10 July Lord Wilmot was ordered to march thither with his brigade, for it was appreciated that Waller's cavalry outnumbered that of the western Cavaliers. Sir John Byron's brigade was now added to Maurice's own Horse and on 12 July they set out to join Lord Wilmot and go to the relief of the Cornish Foot. Hertford, exhausted by his recent exertions, stayed at Oxford to recuperate.

Waller spent 10 and 11 July in continual but fruitless attempts to batter the town into submission. On 12 July he sent in a trumpeter to arrange for the free passage of Sir Bevil Grenvile's body, and took the opportunity to let it be known that his cavalry had intercepted Crawford's convoy and beaten it off.[3] He therefore offered Hopton terms of surrender. The latter, glad to give his men some rest and to spare his ammunition, spun out the negotiations for seven or eight hours. But, fortunately for the Royalists, help was at hand.

---

[1] Ibid., p. 56.
[2] Ibid., pp. 97–8.
[3] The Earl of Caernarvon's and Sir James Long's regiments of Horse were briskly attacked, between Marlborough and Devizes, by Waller's own regiment. They abandoned five of the wagons they were escorting, and lost eight colours to boot.

THE BATTLE OF ROUNDWAY DOWN, 13 JULY

Wilmot, the commander of the relief force, made his rendezvous at Marlborough. He had with him his own brigade and Byron's, besides Crawford's contingent – this latter somewhat shaken; altogether 1,500 Horse of the Oxford army. To these must be added some 300 of Maurice's Horse who, despite their tiring marches, were still fit to fight. Wilmot had no infantry at all and only two light guns – probably two 'galloping guns' with the gun detachments riding on horses, the earliest form of horse artillery. Thus, on the morning of 13 July, Wilmot, with only 1,800 men, was nearing the besieged town, marching along the old Bath road. He had arranged that when he drew near he would fire off both cannons, to notify the garrison of his approach.[1]

Waller had decided to assault the town on the evening of that day. As a preliminary, he subjected it to a heavy bombardment from the hill 600 yards to the east. Part of this bombardment was deliberately aimed at St John's church, and pretty good practice was made, the marks of which are still visible. Hopton still hoped to be able to hold out long enough to allow for the arrival of reinforcements. This, he calculated, would not be for a few days, and he was thus pleasantly surprised on the morning of 13 July to discover that his opponents had marched off to the north, apparently to meet a relieving force. Hopton at once ordered his men to stand to.

The route of Wilmot's force is somewhat difficult to retrace with certainty. The road from Marlborough to Swindon and Devizes did not take its present course (via Shepherd's Shore, four miles from Devizes) but ran on west-south-west for two miles. It crossed Wansdyke 500 yards to the north-west of Shepherd's Shore, at a spot that is still of great archaeological interest. It is marked by a tumulus, and was evidently the junction of two sections of Wansdyke. From this point the road ran on for 2,000 yards, and then swung south, near a three-sided prehistoric earthwork, and ran down Roundway Hill into Devizes.

Wilmot advanced along the old road as far as Bishop's Canning Down, and then probably turned off to Roughridge Hill, where he fired off his two cannon as a signal to the garrison. These were apparently heard, for the Earl of Marlborough, general of the ordnance, replied with his guns from Devizes Castle. Hopton's men could also, it seems, see at least part of the relieving force.

---

[1] Wilmot's exact route remains disputed. Hopton states that the signal guns were heard, and 'a very gallant party of the King's Horse appeared three miles off upon the hills'. (Hopton, op. cit., p. 57.) Sir John Byron's account, BM Add. MSS. 1103 d. 77 (5), reprinted in Peter Young, 'The Royalist Army at the Battle of Roundway Down', *Journal of the Society for Army Historical Research*, 1953, is useful, but fails to solve the controversy. Byron says that Waller drew up on 'a high hill that overlooks the town' two miles from the Royalists. He makes no mention of the Royalists swinging very wide of the road – as they would have had to do to reach Morgan's Hill, one of the positions from which it has been suggested that the signal guns were fired. It seems certain that the guns were fired from

An interesting situation was now developing. In the town were perhaps 3,000 Royalist Foot. Approaching from the north-east were 1,800 Royalist Horse. In between the two was the Roundhead army, consisting of 2,500 Foot and 2,000 Horse, with eight field guns. Waller thus outnumbered each of his opponents, whose only chance seemed to rest in a combined attack. Wilmot evidently realised this; hence the signal guns. He also despatched a messenger, who seems to have been captured. Although the signal guns were heard, and Waller's withdrawal noticed, the garrison's Council of War declined to march out against Waller, fearing 'that all that was seen might be but a stratagem of Sir William Waller's to get the forces out of the town'.[1] Hopton, seriously ill as he was, lacked the forcefulness to persuade the Council of War to move. The garrison's slowness is difficult to excuse; they were not to arrive on the field until the major part of the action had been fought.

Waller marched directly on to Roundway Down. When near the top of the slope he must have seen Wilmot advancing, on his right, in the area of the tumulus where the old Bath road crosses Wansdyke. In front of Waller lay a shallow valley, with gentle slopes to north and south. To the north, King's Play Hill and Morgan Hill edged the valley, while Roundway Hill – then known as Bagdon Hill – formed its southern limit. This valley formed, as Atkyns remarked,[2] a superb arena for a battle, and in it Waller decided to offer battle to the oncoming Royalists.

Having fired his signal guns from Roughridge Hill, Wilmot returned to the road, and continued his march. Seeing Waller halt and deploy, Wilmot did likewise; delay, rather than speed, was his policy, for the moment, for time was required for Hopton to marshal his army and march out of the town to effect a junction. Wilmot had no way of knowing that Hopton's Council of War had decided against such a plan. He spent at least half an hour forming up, and the afternoon must have been well advanced when all was ready.

Waller had formed his line in the conventional fashion, with his Foot in the centre, astride the road, his Horse on the two wings, and his guns in the intervals between the Horse and Foot. Sir Arthur Hesilrige's cuirassiers, the Lobsters, were on the right, on the north-eastern slopes of Roundway Hill. Wilmot, meanwhile, deployed his army with two brigades abreast his own on the left, Byron's on the right with the third, Crawford's, in support. After a brief skirmish, in which the Royalist forlorn hope, under Major Paul Smith, drove

[1] Hopton, op. cit., p. 57.
[2] Atkyns and Gwyn, op. cit., p. 23.

Roughridge Hill, and that Wilmot then advanced east. This would agree with the line of flight of Waller's horsemen. To suggest that Wilmot attacked south-west from Morgan's Hill implies that the Parliamentarian Horse, broken and riding *ventre à terre*, turned sharply westwards in order to fall down the steep slope on the west edge of the down. This will not do; they would certainly have fled directly away from the Royalists, who must, therefore, have attacked from the east.

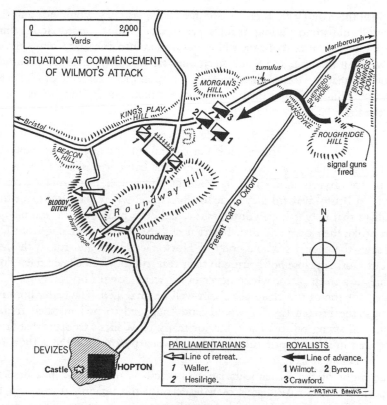

5 ROUNDWAY DOWN

their Roundhead opponents back into Waller's main body, somewhat disordering it, Wilmot advanced. His brigade moved off ahead of Byron's, three deep at full trot, and in good order. Hesilrige, his cuirassiers five or six ranks deep, moved forward to meet him.

Sir Arthur's advance seems to have masked the Parliamentarian guns, which failed to fire. As Hesilrige's men were in such close order, the Royalist charge overlapped each of their ranks. There followed a stiff mêlée, at the conclusion of which 'that impenetrable regiment' at last gave ground, and streamed off in disorder. Atkyns pursued Sir Arthur himself, but was unable to penetrate the knight's armour with sword or pistol.

As Hesilrige's broken troopers galloped off the field, Byron led his brigade forward, ineffectively engaged by two Parliamentarian guns.

By this time [he wrote] we were come very near Waller's Brigade, and the command I gave my men was, that not a man should discharge a Pistol till the enemy had spent all his shot, which was punctually observed. So that first they gave us a volley of their carbines, then of their pistols, and then we fell in with them and gave them ours in the teeth; yet they would not quit their ground, but stood pushing it for a pretty space, till it pleased God (I think) to put new spirit into our tired Horse as well as into our men, so that though it were up the Hill, and that a steep one, we overbore them, and with that violence that we forced them to fall foul upon other reserves of Horse that stood behind to second them, and so swept their whole Body of Horse out of the field. . . .[1]

With the defeat of Waller's brigade, the entire Parliamentarian cavalry was in flight. Many of the troops took the natural line of retreat due west. This proved unfortunate, for the western edge of the battlefield is formed by a steep escarpment. Byron relates that he 'pursued them near three miles[2] over the Downs in Bristol way till they came to a precipice, where their fear made them so valiant that they galloped down as if it had been plain ground, and many of them broke their own and their horses necks'. Slingsby,[3] watching from Devizes, saw 'the enemy's whole body of Horse face about and run with speed, and our Horse in close body firing in their rear, till they had chased them down the hill in a steep place, where never horse went down nor up before'.[4] The scene at the top of the 'steep place' can well be imagined. The better horsemen amongst the broken cavalry would have managed to pull up their frenzied mounts, or swing off to a flank, but for many of Waller's troopers that fateful day ended in a last frantic tumble down the sharp slope into the aptly named 'Bloody Ditch' at its base.

The flight of the Parliamentarian Horse left Waller's Foot in a desperate position. Under Sir William's own leadership, the infantry, formed in two bodies, defended themselves with some determination against isolated cavalry attacks. They also had to endure some fire from four of their own guns which were captured and turned against them. By this time, the Royalist commanders in Devizes were convinced that the action on Roundway Down was anything but a ruse, and soon the sturdy Cornish Foot were marching steadily up the road from the town. As Hopton's infantry came in sight, Wilmot increased the pressure on Waller's Foot, who had begun to move off, still in good order. Byron joined in the attack with those of his men whom he had managed to rally, and with this 'their officers thought it not fit to stand any longer, but such as had horses rode away as fast as they could, and too fast for us to overtake them, and the rest blew up their powder and threw down their arms and betook themselves to their heels'.[5] The majority surrendered; some fled, and many of the latter were cut down in the open.

Well might Sir William Waller bewail 'my dismal defeat at Roundway

[1] Byron, op. cit.
[2] About 2,500 yards would be a more accurate estimate.
[3] Byron, op. cit.
[4] Hopton, op. cit., p. 98.
[5] Byron, op. cit.

Down'.[1] His army had, for practical purposes, ceased to exist. Cavalier claims to have killed 600 and taken 800 prisoners are probably not too far from the truth. Waller had also lost eight brass guns and all his baggage and ammunition; those of his men who had not become casualties had scattered to the four points of the compass, many of them to their homes, from which they were disinclined to venture forth again.

The battle of Roundway Down is one of the most interesting of the entire war. The Royalists failed to mount a coordinated attack on Waller, and yet, largely by virtue of the tremendous morale of their Horse, succeeded in winning. Lord Wilmot showed leadership of a high order. His decision – if, indeed, it was deliberate – to avoid contact with the infantry in the early stages of the action was sound: the Parliamentarian Foot were unable to intervene in the cavalry battle with either fire or steel, and could do little but stand and gape. Wilmot's generalship at Edgehill had been less praiseworthy, and it is possible that in this battle he was urged on by Prince Maurice. It is difficult to impute any serious error to Sir William Waller. His dispositions seem sound enough, though the bulk of his Horse probably made the mistake of standing fast to receive a charge, rather than moving forward to meet it. Waller blamed Essex for his defeat, pointing out how strange it was 'that he, lying with his whole army within ten miles of Oxford, should suffer the chief strength of that place to march thirty [sic] miles to destroy him. . . .' It is interesting to speculate as to what course the battle would have taken had Sir Ralph Hopton been in the saddle. It is natural to suppose that he would have had his own way at the Council, and that his infantry would have joined in the battle simultaneously with, or very shortly after, Wilmot's attack. In this case, the result could hardly have been more decisive than it actually was, but the battle might have been of shorter duration.

The sudden destruction of Waller's field army presented the King's Council of War at Oxford with an excellent opportunity to complete the conquest of the west. On 15 July, Prince Rupert marched from Oxford to join the western army. He had with him a substantial force. Lord Grandison, Colonel Henry Wentworth and Colonel John Belasyse commanded the three brigades of Foot, while the two wings of cavalry were led by Sir Arthur Aston, now major-general of the Horse, and Colonel Charles Gerard. There were, in addition, nine troops of dragoons under Colonel Henry Washington. The train of artillery was commanded by a Frenchman, Bartholomew da la Roche, seconded by Captain Samuel Fawcett. Wilmot had returned to Oxford after Roundway Down, and the western army had occupied Bath, the garrison of which retired on Bristol. Waller himself, with the debris of his field army, had taken refuge in Gloucester, but did not remain there long; as Rupert marched towards the city he bolted to Evesham and thence to London.

[1] Sir William Waller's *Experiences*, MS. in the Library of Wadham College, Oxford.

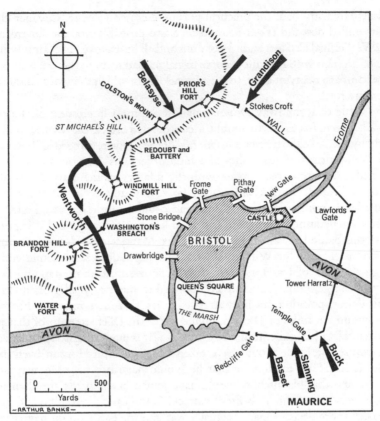

6   THE STORM OF BRISTOL

Rupert's first objective was Bristol, the second most important port in the Kingdom. Once Bristol had fallen, Rupert was to proceed against Gloucester, and thus eliminate these two Parliamentarian strongholds in the south-west. The Prince accordingly sent messengers to the western army, which lay near Bath, directing it to rendezvous south of Bristol while his own contingent moved in from the north.

The defences of Bristol were, although incomplete, quite formidable. An inner ring of fortifications, skirting the Avon and Frome Rivers, lay within a broader circle of defences. These consisted of five forts, linked by an earthwork about five feet high and three feet thick at the top. The forts themselves were self-contained, with dry ditches and palisades around them, though they lacked any artificial glacis thrown up in front of the walls to give additional protection against bombardment. South of the town, the Avon formed the outer defence line. About 800 yards from this river's confluence with the Frome, the curtain wall turned north, through Water Fort, up to Brandon Hill Fort. From there it ran downhill slightly, and then turned up again to Windmill Hill Fort, and a redoubt and battery on St Michael's Hill. North-east of St Michael's Hill stood Colston's Mount, flanked in turn by Prior's Hill Fort, at the northern point of the defences. The wall ran on from there to the low ground by the Frome, to Lawford's Gate, and on to Tower Harratz, Temple Gate, Redcliffe Gate and the Avon.

On 23 July, Rupert, accompanied by a small group of officers, rode out over Durdham Down to Clifton Church. This reconnaissance party was engaged by cannon from Brandon Hill Fort, but no casualties were suffered. Rupert left Colonel Washington with his dragoons and a small party of commanded Foot to hold Clifton Hill. Washington's men successfully repulsed a prowling attack that night. To the south of the town, Maurice's men went into quarters, and began to erect batteries and move guns forward into them.

On 24 July Rupert summoned the city. Colonel Nathaniel Fiennes, the governor, declined to capitulate. He had 300 Horse and 1,500 Foot, besides townsmen, and nearly 100 guns, to hold the broad circuit of defences. On the following day, Rupert crossed the Avon for a conference with Maurice and his colleagues. This Council of War was far from united as to how to proceed. Rupert's officers wanted to take the town by escalade, whereas the officers of the western army preferred to open a formal siege. 'They were both in the right,' maintained Slingsby, since the ground to the north was well suited for storm, while in the south it favoured a more methodical approach. Eventually, though, 'Prince Rupert prevailed with his brother, and it was then resolved upon to give a general assault'.[1]

THE STORM OF BRISTOL, 26 JULY

Rupert gave the brigade commanders a free hand as to how they should attack the fortifications. The Cornish Foot formed up in three columns to assault the wall around Temple Gate, while Rupert's three foot brigades attacked the northern curtain at more widely dispersed points. The assault was to begin at daybreak on 26 July. The field-word for the day was 'Oxford', and, for easier identification, every man was to wear something green, a sprig of leaves or suchlike, while nobody was to wear a neckerchief. The signal for the assault was to be given by the firing of two demi-cannon from Lord Grandison's battery.

Things went wrong from the start. The eager Cornishmen attacked prematurely, at about 3 a.m., forcing Rupert to fire the signal earlier than planned. On Rupert's left, Grandison's brigade made a determined attack, first on Stokes Croft, and later on Prior's Hill Fort. In the first attack Captain Fawcett fastened a petard on the gate of the work, but this device only broke two or three of the bars. The Royalists got into the very ditch of the Prior's Hill Fort,

[1] Hopton, op. cit., p. 92.

but were eventually beaten off, leaving the ditch full of their dead. Young Lord Grandison was mortally wounded. Belasyse was no more successful in his attack on Windmill Hill Fort. For lack of scaling ladders and faggots to fill the ditch his men were held up, some taking cover under a stone wall. Rupert himself met some of Belasyse's troops retreating, and led them on again, having his charger shot under him in so doing.

Wentworth's brigade attacked between Brandon Hill and Windmill Hill Forts, but the ground was so bushy and uneven that the soldiers soon fell into disorder. As they pushed up the re-entrant between the two forts they came under very heavy fire, which made them run close up to the works so as to get into the dead ground. Wentworth, Washington, and several other colonels led the way, and once they had reached the defences they found themselves practically invisible from the forts. Hurling grenades over, they stormed the line, the defenders streaming back towards the town. The Royalists now began to tear a breach with their halberds and partisans, and even with their bare hands. Lieutenant-Colonel Littleton galloped along inside the line with a blazing fire-pike, further discouraging the garrison, many of whom fled with cries of 'Wildfire'. Major Hercules Langrish had been posted to support the defending infantry at this point, but he failed to charge. Colonel Fiennes's Horse eventually put in a counter-attack, but 300 Royalists were already over the wall, and some musketeers lining a hedge soon repulsed the cavalry. Fiennes's men came on again, but several Royalist officers ran at them with fire-pikes, and this proved more than horse or man could endure.

The western army had attacked in three brigades, with Colonel Brutus Buck on the right, Sir Nicholas Slanning in the centre and Major-General Bassett on the left. Carts and wagons had been collected to roll into the ditch to serve as a bridge, but the ditch proved too deep. Fortunately, Prince Maurice had foreseen this, and had provided faggots and scaling ladders. The Cornish fell on resolutely, but after half an hour were driven back by showers of bullets and stones. Their losses were very heavy. Colonel Buck managed to reach the top of the wall but was struck off by a halberd, and perished in the ditch. Slanning and Trevanion were shot down within a few yards of each other, the former dying on the spot and the latter some time afterwards. Bassett and Colonel Sir Bernard Astley were both wounded, and Slingsby, helping to push a cart into a ditch, fell in himself in his armour, and was carried off unconscious.

It was now about 4 p.m. Wentworth's men pushed on to another strongpoint, 'Essex's Work', which they took, more by luck than judgement, for the defenders saw some Foot running towards them and fled, though their fancied assailants were in fact trying to avoid some Parliamentarian cavalry. Wentworth consolidated this position until joined by Belasyse's brigade and some Horse under Aston. He then advanced to College Green and towards the Quay, supported by Aston, who made for Frome Gate, part of the inner ring of defences. For two hours the fight raged around Frome Gate, the Parliamentarians sallying out with covering fire from the windows behind them, while 200 of the women of Bristol laboured to raise a bulwark of earth and woolsacks inside the Gate. Here fell the gallant Colonel Henry Lunsford, shot through the heart on the stairs, now known as Christmas Steps. Belasyse himself was badly wounded in the head, and his men were flagging when part of Grandison's brigade arrived and thrust the Parliamentarians into the town.

Once his men were in the suburbs, Prince Rupert posted himself at Washington's Breach, where he could best receive intelligence and send back directions. His command post was within easy range of two of the forts, but the defenders were rapidly losing heart. The Prince, determined to reinforce success, sent to Maurice for 1,000 of the Cornish Foot, but the fight was done, as Fiennes asked for terms before they could arrive. The articles of surrender permitted the defenders to march out safely; officers were to keep their arms, and cavalry troopers their horses and swords. All ranks were allowed 'bag and baggage, provided it be their own goods'.[1] However, discipline broke down when the garrison attempted to march out on the morning of 27 July, and many of the defenders of Bristol were plundered of those goods which the articles of surrender entitled them to keep.[2] Fiennes, on his return to London, was court martialled for his allegedly premature surrender, and sentenced to death, but reprieved at Essex's behest. It is difficult to agree with the verdict against the unfortunate Fiennes. He fought hard in defence of a city, most of whose wealthier inhabitants were certainly hostile to him. His force was pitifully inadequate to hold a line over three miles long. It would, indeed, have been a difficult task for a similar force equipped with more modern weapons. This in no way detracts from Rupert's achievements, for when five out of the six Royalist brigades were held up, he prosecuted his one success with relentless vigour. Tribute must also be paid to the dogged valour of the Royalist Foot. Maurice's men showed their customary determination in their assault on the southern defences, and were responsible for containing a large part of the garrison in that area. The three brigades which attacked from the north also fought well – the forcing of Frome Gate, when the troops were on the verge of exhaustion, was a splendid feat of arms.

[1] Clarendon, op. cit., Vol. IV, p. 145.
[2] Several excuses were offered for this behaviour. Rupert maintained that Fiennes had marched out at a different place and time to those specified in the articles of capitulation. The pillaging of the Royalist garrison of Newbury, after the town's surrender to Essex, together with the allegation that much of the Roundhead's 'bag and baggage' was itself loot, were likewise cited in an effort to justify this lapse.

Nine

THE WAR IN THE CENTRE, 1643

With Bristol safely in Royalist hands, King Charles and his Council of War deliberated at length as to their next move. While the Parliamentarians were still dispirited by Rupert's great victory, the Earl of Caernarvon overran Dorset, capturing Dorchester, Weymouth and Portland. Sir Walter Erle abandoned the siege of Corfe Castle and shut himself up in Poole, and in the rest of the county only Lyme held out. Maurice, meanwhile, with the old western army, went to complete the conquest of Devonshire, where Exeter and Plymouth were still in the hands of the Parliamentarians. Affairs were less satisfactory in the north, where Newcastle was strangely idle, and in Lincolnshire Cavendish had been killed at Gainsborough.

The most important decision confronting Charles's Council of War was the use to which the King's Oxford army was to be put. Eventually, the Council determined to take Gloucester, thus clearing the Severn valley and opening up Royalist communications between Oxford and South Wales. The governor of the city, Colonel Massey, was believed not to be a convinced Parliamentarian, and it was hoped that he would surrender the city when summoned.[1] On Wednesday 10 August, Charles appeared before Gloucester, only to have his summons brusquely rejected. Massey was not in a strong position. He considered that the citizens in general were discontented, and he had only one regiment whose men could be described as regulars. The fortifications were certainly no stronger than those of Bristol, and Rupert, left to his own devices, would undoubtedly have taken the place by storm. Charles, however, deterred by the heavy casualties at Bristol, where 'as gallant men as ever drew sword ... lay upon the ground like rotten sheep',[2] laid siege to the city.

In London, confusion reigned. On 25 July Waller returned to the City, which welcomed him as if Roundway Down had been a Parliamentarian victory. Essex, understandably, was picqued by this, the more so because Waller's many supporters imputed his defeat at Roundway Down to the Earl's inactivity. Essex's vexation was further increased when, on 27 July, Waller was appointed

[1] Clarendon, op. cit., Vol. IV, pp. 175–7.
[2] Atkyns and Gwyn, op. cit., p. 28.

142

to a substantial independent command. Pym, beset on one hand by the extremists, and on the other by the disenchanted moderates who, like the Earl of Holland, sought to persuade Essex to back terms of peace that amounted to capitulation, strove to regain control. His aims were twofold: to strengthen Essex's hand, and to restore the situation in the north by procuring speedy Scottish intervention. News of Massey's firm refusal to surrender Gloucester stiffened Parliamentarian resolve, and Essex, strengthened by five regiments from the London Trained Bands, was sent west to the relief of the besieged city.

Royalist operations before Gloucester were hampered by ill luck and a stout defence. A heavy rainstorm filled the besiegers' mines with water, preventing their firing. Essex reviewed his army at Hounslow on 24 August, and marched, by way of Beaconsfield and Aylesbury, to Brackley Heath, where, on 1 September, he was reinforced, bringing his army to a total of about 15,000 men. Essex was shadowed by Wilmot with a small force of cavalry, and Rupert, with the main body of the Royalist Horse, made an unsuccessful attempt to halt the Earl near Stow-on-the-Wold. On 5 September, Essex's army halted on Prestbury Hill, nearly ten miles from Gloucester. Massey had only three barrels of powder left, but the King had no intention of being trapped between the besieged and Essex, and pulled his men out of their sodden trenches before the city, permitting Essex to relieve Gloucester on 8 September.

The relief accomplished, Essex was now faced with the problem of returning intact to London. Charles's object, quite clearly, was to cut off Essex's retreat. If he could now bring him to battle on ground of his own choosing he might end the war at a blow. Even before the Earl entered Gloucester, the King had posted himself at Sudeley Castle, about twelve miles north-east of the town. On 10 September Essex quitted Gloucester, and marched up the Severn Valley to Tewkesbury. Here he ordered the construction of a bridge of boats over the Severn, probably in an effort to persuade the Royalists that he proposed to march to Hereford or into Wales. Charles was not taken in, and moved to Pershore, blocking the route to London via Evesham and Warwick.

Essex, however, intended to move to the south of the circle of garrisons round Oxford, and, turning south and east, reached Cirencester on the night of 15 September. Charles conformed on the following day, and marched on a roughly parallel route. Essex spent the night of 17 September at Swindon, and Charles at Alvescot, ten miles to the north-east. Essex was now twenty miles from his next objective, Newbury, while the King was a good eight miles farther away. It looked as if Essex would win the race for Newbury, but Rupert checked him in a skirmish at Aldbourne Chase next day, forcing him south, so that the Parliamentarians halted for the night at Hungerford, nine miles short of Newbury. But the Royalists, too, had moved slowly, and were at Wantage, sixteen miles from the vital town. For reasons which remain unexplained, Essex moved at a snail's pace on 19 September. The roads, turned to treacherous quagmires by the constant rain, no doubt slowed him down, but must have had a similar effect on his opponents. As it was, the Parliamentarian quartermasters rode into Newbury in the late afternoon of the 19th, were well received by the citizens, and were engaged in chalking up billets for the damp and dispirited troops, who were as yet several miles off, when they received a rude shock.

With a flurry of hoofbeats and pistol shots, Rupert's Horse swept into the town, drove off the escort and captured several of the unfortunate quarter-masters. Essex, fearing that the Royalist Foot were close behind Rupert, halted, permitting the main body of the Royalist army to enter Newbury, and to bivouac just south of the town. Essex halted for the night near Enborne, two miles to the west of the Royal army, which now lay planted directly on his path to the capital. Charles had won the round decisively; his men retired to rest, tired after four days' march, and soaking from the rain, but exultant.

THE FIRST BATTLE OF NEWBURY, 20 SEPTEMBER

The ground over which the first battle of Newbury was fought has been obscured to some extent by the southward expansion of the town. Nevertheless, the rolling countryside, intersected by lanes, around Enborne gives some idea of what the terrain looked like in 1643. Operations were bounded to the north by the River Kennet, winding through its watermeadows from Hungerford through Newbury. The ground rises from these flat meadows on to a plateau, with two short ridges jutting northwards. The eastern one is marked on the one-inch ordnance survey map by the crossed swords denoting the site of the battle; the western one, when viewed from the low ground to the north, had the appearance of a round hill rather than the edge of a ridge. This fact is of great importance, for it explains much that is otherwise obscure – that is, the position of the 'round hill' to which contemporary writers such as Byron so frequently refer. Byron, from his position to the north-east, would naturally describe it as a round hill, and for convenience we have named it Round Hill. At the present day it is crowned with some trees and a house, which should not be confused with Wash Common Farm, which is 400 yards farther along to the south of the top of the plateau. This plateau, then known as Enborne Heath, is almost dead flat and featureless except for the so-called burial pits (more probably tumuli) to the south-east of Wash Common Farm. Even today there are some signs of heath.

It is curious that while the northern part of the field retains its enclosures, the northern slope of the plateau, which was to form the centre of the battlefield, has lost the many 'closes' of which the chronicles speak. This is exactly the reverse of the usual tendency for ground to be more enclosed today than it was in the seventeenth century.

The exact sizes of the contending armies are unknown. Charles commanded the Royalist force, assisted by Lord Forth. The cavalry, under Rupert, seem to have comprised five brigades, one commanded by the Prince himself, and the others by Lord Wilmot, Sir John Byron, the Earl of Caernarvon and Colonel Charles Gerard. Stout old Sir Jacob Astley commanded the Foot, divided, it seems, into four fairly weak brigades, under Sir Nicholas Byron, Colonel John Belasyse, Sir Gilbert Gerard and Sir William Vavasour. The King had, in all, a little over 14,000 men; his cavalry were up to strength, well-mounted and enthusiastic. The Royalist Foot, though naturally somewhat more numerous than the Horse, were in less prime condition. Essex's army was about the same size, but with a higher proportion of infantry to cavalry. Essex's Horse, some 4,000 in all, were divided into two brigades, under Sir Phillip Stapleton and Colonel John Middleton. The strength of the Parliamentarian Foot lay in the London Trained Bands; three Trained Band regiments, and three of their auxiliary regiments, were present at the battle.[1] Information on the Parliamentarian artillery is obscure. This is not the case for the King's army, however, and the Royalist ordnance papers reveal that at Newbury the King had twenty guns, sixteen of them brass.[2]

The King went to bed in the town of Newbury on the night of 19 September in a cheerful and confident frame of mind. He had won the race. He had obtained ample supplies of food (collected in the town for his opponents), though his powder was dangerously short. The rebels had been outmanoeuvred and cut off from London. To continue in their design of reaching the Capital they must cut their way through. The King was happy to let them attempt this; indeed, it had been his aim throughout the campaign to make Essex fight a battle at a disadvantage. It was principally for that reason that he had abandoned the siege of Gloucester – mistakenly as some thought. Many of his troops were comfortably disposed in billets, whereas the Roundheads were forced to bivouac out in the open on a damp, chilly autumn night.

In the Parliamentarian lines, spirits were far from high. The men were wearied, footsore, homesick, and short of food. Essex rode from bivouac to bivouac in the early morning of 20 September, warning his troops that the Royalists had all the advantages – 'the hill, the town, Hedges, Lane and River...'[3] – but morale was not so low as to stifle the shouts of 'Hey for Robin' with which the popular Earl was customarily greeted. With this, the Earl deployed his forces to break through the King's army and thus regain London safely.

The two armies had faced each other head-on during the night. Essex

[1] See the Hon. H. A. Dillon, 'On a MS. list of Officers of the London Trained Bands in 1643', *Archaeologia*, Vol. 50, 1890.
[2] Demi-cannons, 2; Culverins, 2; 12-pounders, 2; 6-pounders, 5; Sakers, 1; Minions, 2 (Iron); 3-pounders, 4; Bases, 2 (Iron). Burne and Young, op. cit., p. 107. Although the King had the same number of guns as at Edgehill, there was a general increase in calibre, thanks to Edgehill captures and foreign purchase.
[3] Quoted in Walter Money, *The First and Second Battles of Newbury* ... (London 1881), p. 23. Contains much useful material, though Money's interpretation is outdated and many of his details questionable.

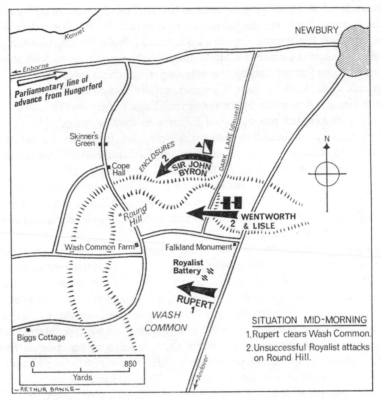

7   FIRST BATTLE OF NEWBURY

approached Newbury via Kintbury and Enborne. He parked his baggage and artillery train at Hampstead Park, just west of the village of Enborne. His army lay in bivouac 1,000 yards farther forward, stretching from the Kennet to the eastern edge of Crockham Heath. Essex himself, so tradition relates, spent the night in Biggs Cottage, at the southern end of his bivouac line.

The Royalists, quartered on the other side of Wash Common, some in bivouacs and some, more fortunate, in billets, had made few defensive preparations. A detachment of Horse was despatched to secure the plateau, and halted in the area of Wash Common Farm, pushing patrols forward. They made, though, what Sir John Byron rightly describes as 'a most gross and absurd' error 'in not viewing the ground, though we had day enough to do it, and not possessing ourselves of those hills above the town by which the enemy was necessarily to march the next day to Reading'.[1] Specifically, the mistake lay in the failure to seize Round Hill, the northern end of the spur pointing towards Skinners Green. The terrain is such that a Parliamentarian advance to this

[1] Ibid., p. 28.

feature from Skinners Green would be invisible from Wash Common Farm, and the enemy could thus gain the hill unobserved. Failure to secure the hill may be attributed to the lateness of the hour at which the Royalist cavalry were posted, or to a casual assumption on the part of their commander that some other unit was to hold it, or merely to sheer laxity and weariness. Whatever the reason, Essex took advantage of this lapse, and during the night, or at dawn, sent a strong detachment under Skippon, with two light field-pieces, up the hill As daylight broke, these guns opened fire on the Royalists in the plain below, thus proclaiming in unmistakable terms that Round Hill was in Parliamentarian hands.

The King's first priority was obviously to dislodge the enemy from Round Hill, his second to secure Wash Common. The latter task was given to Prince Rupert, with the bulk of the Royalist Horse. Rupert successfully secured the common, and guns were brought on to the plateau. A battery was formed not far from where the Falkland Monument now stands, firing north-east at the Parliamentarians on Round Hill.

In an effort to clear Round Hill a party of commanded Foot under Colonel Henry Wentworth and Colonel George Lisle, advanced westwards from the Royalist infantry line along the Andover road. Wentworth was supported by Sir John Byron, with his own and Sir Thomas Aston's regiments of Horse. The Foot ran into a galling fire, and many of them were forced to take cover behind a bank on the edge of Dark Lane, and a cry of 'Horse, Horse' went up. At this, Byron rode forward to reconnoitre. His regiments were probably drawn up just east of Dark Lane, covered from fire by a shoulder of hill. Byron probably conducted his reconnaissance from the flat ground north of the hill, for he makes no mention of hilly ground, but only of closes which were more prevalent in this area. Byron would also naturally have preferred to assault the flanks rather than the front of the Parliamentarians on Round Hill. Sir John saw that his line of advance was blocked by a hedge, with a gap in it wide enough for only one horseman to pass through at a time. Byron ordered the gap to be widened. And as he did so, his horse was wounded. At this, Lord Falkland, whose office of Secretary of State gave him no military rank, and who was riding in Byron's troop as a volunteer '(more gallantly than advisedly) spurred his horse through the gap, where both he and his horse were immediately killed'.[1] Soon after this misfortune,

The passage being then made somewhat wide, and I not having another horse, drew in my own troop first, giving orders for the rest to follow and charged the enemy, who entertained us with a great salvo of musket shot, and discharged their two drakes upon us laden with case shot, which killed some and hurt many of my men, so that we were forced to wheel off and could not meet them at the charge.[2]

[1] Ibid., p. 35.
[2] Loc. cit.

While Byron rallied his troopers, the Parliamentarians withdrew their guns. Sir John then sent in Aston's regiment, which 'beat them to the end of the close, where they faced us again, having the advantage of a hedge at their backs and poured another volley of shot upon us, when Sir Thomas Aston's horse was killed under him, and withal kept us off with their pikes'.[1] The cavalry wheeled off, while the Parliamentarian Foot fell back into another close, and thence into Skinners Green Lane. Here they were stiffened by the London Trained Bands, who checked another charge by the gallant Byron, who had lost 100 men from his regiment alone. Had Sir John's efforts been followed up by the Royalist Foot, Round Hill might yet have been gained. Sir Nicholas Byron's brigade of infantry came forward and consolidated the ground held by the Horse, but seems to have been unwilling to press home its attack. Skippon managed to get more guns[2] forward on to Round Hill, covered by his steady London regiments.

The course of the battle was confused. The fortune of the day swayed to and fro, with the action see-sawing along the armies' southern flanks upon the plateau. Fighting in the enclosed terrain around the northern slopes soon reached deadlock, and reinforcements were pushed farther south by each side. The struggle centred about Round Hill and the Ridge connecting it to Wash Common Farm. Retention of the hill was vital to the Parliamentarians, for without it the field of fire for their artillery would be cripplingly reduced. At one point the Royalist Horse forced their way into the gun position on the hill, and managed to drag off one gun, probably a drake. For the most part, however, the Parliamentarians hung on to the hill, while the Royalists held Wash Common Farm.

Fighting went on until after night had fallen. The Royalist Horse displayed tremendous vigour, but there were dark rumours that their infantry had let them down. Sir John Byron remarked that it was 'generally confessed, that had not our Foot played the poltroons extremely that day, we in all probability had set a period to the war. . . .'[3] On the Parliamentarian side, the London Trained Bands carried off the honours of the day; their rolling musketry and resolute pike-work saved Round Hill from capture in the early stages of the action.

'The casualties of the two armies in this battle,' wrote Walter Money, 'it would be difficult to estimate with anything like exactness.'[4] Numerous Royalist officers were amongst the slain. The Earl of Caernarvon was mortally wounded in the fighting on the plateau, and Lord Sunderland, riding as a volunteer in the lifeguard, was slain by a roundshot. Several other senior officers

---

[1] Ibid., p. 36.
[2] Heavy guns, probably culverins, were brought into action by both sides; several eighteen- and twenty-pound cannon balls have been found on the field.
[3] Money, op. cit., p. 39.
[4] Ibid., p. 42.

were killed or wounded. The Parliamentarians lost no officer of note, though several colonels were among the killed, and the Trained Bands had suffered particularly heavily. Many casualties on both sides were caused by artillery fire; John Gwyn observed 'a whole file of men, six deep, with all their heads struck off by one cannon shot of ours'.[1]

The King held a Council of War after dark. Several of the stouter-hearted officers present wanted the army to remain in position, and to renew the action on the following day. Lord Percy, general of the ordnance, pointed out that powder and shot were running dangerously low. Byron described this as a 'foolish and knavish suggestion'[2] but it persuaded Charles to order a withdrawal. Had he decided to bluff it out the next day, it is by no means certain that Essex would have persevered with the fight. As it was, he completely lost touch with the Royalist army in the night, and next morning fired a single round into what he supposed were the hostile lines, oblivious of the fact that the King was by that time many miles away to the north, on his way to Oxford. Essex then marched on London by way of Reading. Between Aldermaston and Padworth the indefatigable Rupert descended upon his rearguard, drove off its cavalry, and was only checked by the steady firing of musketeers. Little the worse for this, Essex's army returned to London, entering the City to an enthusiastic welcome. Essex had certainly achieved his strategic aim, and the result of the battle was as much of a victory for the Parliamentarians as Edgehill had been for the Royalists.

Although Falkland was not a soldier, his loss was to have a baneful influence on the Royalist cause. George, Lord Digby, brilliant, charming, but thoroughly unreliable, after being wounded at Powick Bridge, Lichfield and Aldbourne Chase, was ready to exchange command of a regiment of Horse for Falkland's office of Secretary of State. For the next two years he had the King's ear, and an influence second only to that of the Queen. The Cavalier who shot Hampden did not strike a more deadly blow than the Roundhead that slew Falkland.

Historians have never tired of condemning Charles for his resolution to besiege Gloucester, proclaiming that this siege was the ruin of his cause. His critics say the King should have pushed forward up the Thames Valley, with Maurice advancing parallel with him through Hampshire and Sussex, and with Newcastle's army pouring southwards through the Eastern Association. But Newcastle was still held up by Hull and had only managed to get as far south as Lincolnshire. The western army, though it had cooperated with the main army at Roundway Down and at Bristol, had still much work to do in its own area. The King's own army was too weak to advance unaided against the Capital. By besieging Gloucester, Charles lured Essex far away from his base and won the opportunity to fight another pitched battle on favourable terms.

The short campaign which ended with the first battle of Newbury is full of

[1] Atkyns and Gwyn, op. cit., p. 53.
[2] Money, op. cit., p. 44.

strategic interest. Everywhere the Royalists had been triumphant; another success now and their cause might be crowned with final victory. Stamford, the Fairfaxes and Waller each in turn had gone down before the conquering advance of the Cavaliers, but Essex still barred the direct route to London. The defeat of Essex in the summer of 1643 might well have changed the whole course of our history.

Ten

THE WAR IN THE NORTH, 1643–2

After his victory at Adwalton Moor, it was to be expected that Newcastle would advance southwards, but he showed no great alacrity in doing so. Indeed, the next blow was struck by the Parliamentarians. On 20 July Lord Willoughby of Parham surprised and captured Gainsborough, where he was soon bottled up by a strong detachment of Newcastle's army, under General Cavendish. Five days later, Parliament ordered Meldrum and Cromwell to march to Lord Willoughby's assistance.

THE BATTLE OF GAINSBOROUGH, 28 JULY

Meldrum, Cromwell and a Lincolnshire detachment met, on 27 July, at North Scarle, about ten miles from Gainsborough. Their combined forces numbered nineteen or twenty troops of Horse, and three or four companies of dragoons, amounting perhaps to 1,200 men. They had wasted no time in coming to the rendezvous, and now they marched to Gainsborough without delay, setting off in the early hours of the 28th. North of the River Lea, about 1½ miles outside Gainsborough, they came upon the forlorn hope of Cavendish's army. The Parliamentarian dragoons, without dismounting, tried to beat back the Cavaliers, who emptied several saddles before being driven off by the Lincolnshire Horse of the Parliamentarian van. The forlorn hope fell back on their main body, drawn up on top of a steep hill just east of Gainsborough, with three regiments in front and Cavendish's own strong regiment in reserve. The Royalist general had altogether thirty troops of Horse and dragoons.

The Parliamentarians continued their advance, still led by the Lincoln men. Behind them came Meldrum with five troops from Nottingham and Northampton, while Cromwell, with six or seven troops of his own regiment, brought up the rear. The going was far from easy, for the ground was pitted with rabbit warrens. The Lincoln men fought their way uphill, and difficult though the tracks proved, they struggled to the summit. By so doing they allowed the main body to deploy just within musket-shot of their opponents.

Before the Parliamentarians were properly drawn up on the uneven ground, the main body of the Royalist Horse advanced, hoping to take them at a disadvantage, but the Roundhead Horse were undismayed. Cromwell gives the best account of what followed:

> ... in such order as we were, we charged their great body, I having the right wing. We came up horse to horse, where we disputed it with our swords and pistols a pretty time, all keeping close order, so that one could not break the other. At last they a little shrinking, our men perceiving it, pressed in upon them, and immediately routed this whole body, some flying on one side, others on the other of the enemy's reserve; and our men pursuing them, had chase and execution about five and six miles.[1]

He goes on to describe how he kept back three of his troops from the chase to oppose General Cavendish, who with his regiment, the reserve, was also facing four of the Lincoln troops.

> At last the General charged the Lincolners, and routed them. I immediately fell on his rear ... which did so astonish him, that he gave over the chase, and would fain have delivered himself from me, but I pressing on forced them down the hill, having good execution of them, and below the hill drove the General with some of his soldiers into a quagmire. ...[2]

Cavendish himself was knocked off his horse by a blow on the head, and as he lay on the ground was stabbed through the chest by Cromwell's captain-lieutenant, Thomas Berry; he died two hours later.

The victory could hardly have been more complete. While credit is due to the Lincoln troops, Cromwell's tactics, and his hold over that part of his regiment which he kept back from the chase, were the deciding factors. There is a tone of decision in Cromwell's account of the fight that was lacking in his description of Grantham. This time there is no question of 'we agreed to charge'; the commander gives the order, the troops obey.

Nothing now prevented the relief of Gainsborough, and the Parliamentarians lost no time in putting powder and provisions into the town. This done, Meldrum and Cromwell received news that a small force of Horse and Foot lay just north of the town. The Roundhead commanders probably assumed this to be a detachment of Cavendish's force; they drew 600 of Lord Willoughby's Foot out of the town, and marched off to try conclusions with this new enemy. Two Royalist troops, operating well ahead of their main body, were driven off, and Cromwell, coming to the top of a nearby hill, received an uncomfortable surprise. He observed 'a regiment of Foot, after that another, after that Newcastle's own regiment, consisting in all of about fifty Foot colours, and a great body of Horse; which indeed was Newcastle's army ...'[3] on its way to besiege Gainsborough.

[1] Carlyle, op. cit., Vol. I, p. 141.
[2] Ibid., p. 142.
[3] Loc. cit.

The Parliamentarians hastily made a plan. Cromwell was sent to order the Foot to return, and to withdraw the Horse. Willoughby's infantry, though they had little more than a mile to go, fell back in disorder, and suffered some casualties when the Royalist Horse got in amongst them. There was initially some disorder in the retirement of the cavalry, partly owing to the large number of hedges which had to be negotiated. After about half a mile, they came to a narrow lane at the end of an open field. Here Cromwell, Major Whalley, and Captain Ayscoghe, the Lincolnshire commander, managed to rally them. As the official report of the Parliamentarian commanders states:

> With these we faced the enemy, stayed their pursuit, and opposed them with about four troops of Cromwell's and four Lincoln troops, the enemy's body in the meantime increasing very much from the army. But such was the goodness of God, giving courage and valour to our men and officers, that whilst Major Whalley and Captain Ayscoghe, sometimes the one with four troops faced the enemy, sometimes the other, to the exceeding glory of God be it spoken, and the great honour of those two gentlemen, they with this handful faced the enemy so and dared them to their teeth in at least eight or nine removes, the enemy following at their heels; and though their horses exceeding tired, retreated in this order, near carbine-shot of the enemy, who thus followed them firing upon them; Colonel Cromwell gathering up the main body and facing them behind those lesser bodies, that, in despite of the enemy we brought off our Horse in this order without the loss of two men.[1]

In this way the Parliamentarians made good their retreat on Lincoln. Gardiner maintains[2] that Cromwell's conduct of the withdrawal showed that he was the most capable cavalry officer in the country. This, though, is open to question and much of the credit must devolve on Meldrum, Whalley and Ayscoghe.

Newcastle laid siege to Gainsborough, and opened a bombardment which set fire to part of the town. Willoughby surrendered on terms three days later, and was soon forced to abandon Lincoln as well, an action for which Cromwell, now governor of the Isle of Ely, was later to censure him. To the north, Lord Fairfax, who, by a Parliamentarian ordinance of 22 July, had been made governor of Hull, and his son Sir Thomas, undismayed by their defeat at Adwalton Moor, were raising troops. They soon assembled a fresh army of 700 Horse and 2,000 to 2,500 Foot. Newcastle, acting perhaps on the advice of General King, but doubtless influenced by Yorkshire Royalists, now decided to lay siege to Hull. At the head of an army of 15,000 men, he drove the Parliamentarians from Beverley, and laid siege to Hull on 2 September. Strong though the

[1] Quoted in several sources. See particularly Lieutenant-Colonel T. S. Baldock, *Cromwell as a Soldier* (London 1899), p. 104. While Baldock's work is rather dated, he offers much useful information.
[2] S. R. Gardiner, *Cromwell's place in History* (London 1897), p. 27.

fortifications were, Lord Fairfax decided to flood the county beyond the walls, cutting the dyke which held back the Humber. This distressed besieged and besiegers alike, for while it swamped Newcastle's works, it made it practically impossible for Fairfax's cavalry to find any fodder for their horses. The Royalists could hardly claim to have done everything in their power to distress the garrison, for on 20 September Willoughby and Cromwell were able to cross the river and enter the besieged city for a conference. The upshot of this was that, on the very same day, Sir Thomas Fairfax was sent with twenty-five troops of Horse across the Humber into Lincolnshire. Sir John Henderson, Governor of Newark, attempted to interfere with this movement, but he was not in sufficient force to prevent it. With 15,000 men at his disposal, however, Newcastle might well have spared 5,000 to occupy Barton and cut off the garrison from their friends in Lincolnshire. Nor did the unenterprising Marquis – he had recently been elevated in the peerage – pay much heed to a message sent direct from the King urging him to advance towards London.

The Earl of Manchester, who in August had been appointed commander of the forces of the Eastern Association, seems to have felt no great alarm for the safety of Hull. He was himself engaged in a siege at Lynn, held for the King by local Royalists. Manchester despatched his Horse, under Cromwell, to aid Willoughby, and after the fall of Lynn on 16 September sent 500 well-armed Foot to reinforce Lord Fairfax in Hull, where they arrived on 5 October.

Having disposed of Lynn, Manchester advanced on Boston, where he was met by Cromwell, with his contingent of Horse and dragoons, and Sir Thomas Fairfax with his detachment. The Foot were reported to be 6,000 strong, and the combined Horse at least 1,500. While this army was assembling, the Royalists were in motion.

Sir William Widdrington, who since the death of General Cavendish was the senior Royalist commander in Lincolnshire, and Henderson, had received orders from Newcastle to take a mounted force to the succour of Bolingbroke Castle, which was now threatened by Manchester. It lay three miles south-east of Spilsby, seven miles south-east of Horncastle and fifteen miles north of Boston. The Cavaliers, by milking the garrisons of Newark, Lincoln and Gainsborough, managed to scrape together a scratch force of between 1,500 and 2,000 Horse and 800 dragoons. Having collected his army at Lincoln, Widdrington set out for Horncastle, some twenty miles to the east.[1]

On 10 October the advanced guard of Manchester's Foot marched from Boston and laid siege to Bolingbroke Castle. Meanwhile Manchester had sent Fairfax forward to throw out a cavalry screen far to the west, for information of the Royalist approach had been received. Fairfax carried out his task well, falling back steadily before the enemy.

[1] Contemporary accounts place Henderson in command. This may well be a mistake, as Widdrington was in fact senior, or it may reflect an agreement between the two officers.

THE BATTLE OF WINCEBY, 11 OCTOBER

By noon on the 11th the whole army was concentrated on Bolingbroke Hill, where Manchester held a Council of War to decide whether to take the offensive and seek a battle. Cromwell advised against it, saying that his horses were exhausted; though so also were those of the Royalists. Manchester, however, overruled him and ordered an immediate advance to meet the enemy.

Thus the two armies met head-on halfway between Horncastle and Bolingbroke, on the southern edge of the Wolds near the tiny village of Winceby, four miles from Horncastle and three from Bolingbroke. On reaching the crest 500 yards beyond the village, Manchester's advanced troops saw the rival army deploying for battle on the next ridge towards Horncastle about 600 yards away. There was a shallow depression between the two ridges, not more than 100 feet in depth. On the right hand the two ridges curved round and joined up; thus the terrain was like a horseshoe lying on its side, the toe being to the Roundhead right. The ground was quite open, except that a few hundred yards away on the left a hedge marked the boundary between the parishes of Winceby and Scradfield.

The Earl of Manchester decided to take up a position on the ridge top, and he formed up his army as follows: in front was the forlorn hope under his quartermaster-general, Colonel Vermuyden. Behind that came the van, consisting of the regiments of Cromwell and Manchester, under the former. In the second line or reserve was Fairfax with his own contingent. Behind that came the Foot, under Colonel Sir Miles Hobart, still some distance in the rear, for the cavalry had advanced at speed. After deploying his mounted troops in the above order Manchester apparently went back to hasten forward the lagging infantry.

The Royalists were drawn up with their dragoons in the van. The main body of Horse was drawn up in three 'divisions' and in the rear were more Horse. Sir William Savile commanded on the right and Sir John Henderson on the left. When both armies were ranged in battle order there was a pause, neither side making any sign of attacking.

The battle seems to have begun at last by the Royalist dragoons advancing across the dip between the two armies. On seeing this Vermuyden conformed with his dragoons and a short sharp contest followed. Contemporary writers stated that he 'charged'. There have been instances of mounted infantry charging, but what is probably meant here is that they advanced to close range, dismounted and opened fire. We know that the Royalist dragoons dismounted. While this skirmish was proceeding the Cavalier first line also crossed the dip. In response to this Cromwell led his two regiments down the hill at a trot. The distance cannot have exceeded 200 yards, and during this short advance the

Royalist dragoons had time to fire two volleys at them, the second being at point-blank range. A bullet from this volley killed Cromwell's horse, and its rider was brought to the ground. While the fight was going on between the two bodies of Horse, Cromwell managed to extricate himself and rose to his feet, but a moment later Sir Ingram Hopton knocked him down, without wounding him, presumably recognising the already well-known Roundhead colonel. Perhaps the Cavalier was anxious to take him prisoner, but Hopton himself was killed in the struggle. Presently a trooper brought up a 'poor horse' which Cromwell mounted, and after that silence descends on his activities in the battle. This silence of the sources has not prevented historians from exercising their imaginative gifts in the matter. A modern biography of Cromwell asserts that he 'rallied his troops and drove home the victory'. Not one of the five writers present at the battle mentions such a thing.[1]

In the confusion of a mounted action where each man is intent on killing and avoiding being killed, it is only natural that detailed and reliable accounts of individuals should not be forthcoming, but it is possible that the expression 'a poor horse' may have some special significance; that the troop horse that was brought up proved rather restive and unmanageable, and that by the time Cromwell was well established in the saddle of his new mount the battle had rolled forward past him. This might account for the sudden silence of the contemporary accounts.

The Royalist first line had recoiled on to the second, creating some disorder as it did so on the right of the line. The action now became general in the bottom of the dip, and lasted for about fifteen minutes. Meanwhile the Roundhead second line was inactive. We can picture Fairfax sitting his horse at the head of his men, looking down on the battle, chewing his moustache and wondering how he could best intervene in the fight. To join directly in the mêlée in that confined space seemed fruitless; a charge into the hostile flank was more in keeping with his nature. But which flank? To attack the enemy's right offered no attractions: it would entail charging uphill, the movement would be visible to the enemy right from its inception and the hedge on his left might constrict his deployment. However, the ground on the other side seemed specially designed for such a manoeuvre. By skirting round the top of the ridge, just out of sight, he could wheel round to his left and crossing the ridge-top charge down into the unsuspecting flank of the enemy on a slope admirably suited for a mounted charge.

Fairfax's decision was made: 'Come, let us fall on,' he cried, and he suited the action to the word, leading his troops round to the right and then wheeling to the left over the crest. Just as the Roundhead Horse came into sight a body of Royalist Horse was also starting to charge, while Henderson had disordered

[1] *See Lords Journals*, VI, pp. 255–6; Ludlow, op. cit., Vol. I, p. 58; Carlyle, op. cit., Vol. I, pp. 163–5; Fairfax Correspondence, IV, pp. 62–5; and the two *True Relations* of the action in Thomason Tracts, E.71 (5) and (22).

the Roundhead's opposite wing. On came Fairfax's men at a rapid pace, making straight for the enemy, but before they could get into them Savile's divisions turned and fled. Their example was followed by the other divisions and soon the whole body disintegrated and took flight – except the dismounted dragoons, whose horses were not at hand and who were consequently killed or made prisoners.

Fairfax pressed his advantage to the full, pursuing relentlessly. Now, owing to the direction of his attack, many, possibly most, of the Royalist Horse were pushed off their direct line of retreat, which was the road towards Horncastle, and forced in a south-westerly direction. This took them along the hedge we have mentioned, and at a sharp salient angle in it there was a gate. The hedge being, presumably, unjumpable, the fleeing horsemen found themselves converging on to this gate in a dense mass. Unfortunately the gate was made to open inwards, and owing to the press and excitement both of man and beast the gate could not be forced open and the fugitives fell easy victims to the Roundhead swords. To this day the spot is known as Slash Hollow.

The battle was over; the victory complete. The bulk of the Royalist troops were either killed, captured or scattered over a wide area of the country without a semblance of cohesion or order. The defeated leaders were quite open about the extent of their disaster. Next day Widdrington wrote a pathetic letter to Newcastle announcing the disintegration of the army and containing this pregnant statement: 'Their Horse are very good, and extraordinarily [well] armed. . . .'[1]

Fairfax continued the pursuit into and beyond Horncastle before drawing rein, and Manchester billeted his infantry in the town for the night. They had not fired a shot. The Royalists now abandoned Gainsborough and lost Lincoln. Before long Newark itself was blockaded.

The importance of the battle of Winceby was out of all proportion to the small numbers engaged in it, and to the brevity of the conflict. At the same time Lord Fairfax made a successful sortie from Hull. Sir Thomas concluded that these two simultaneous reverses induced Newcastle to abandon his march on London, thus bringing to naught the King's strategic plan for 1643; this assessment is in the main correct.

Winceby had two more significant effects. It was the first major victory of the Roundhead Horse over their Royalist opponents, and consequently gave a great boost to the reputation and morale of the Parliamentarian cavalry. Also, it was an important point in the career of Oliver Cromwell. He had now been engaged in three consecutive victories, at a time when Parliamentarian fortunes as a whole were on the wane. However, as Winceby played such an important part in Cromwell's rise, his rôle in the action must be examined in detail. Modern writers are practically unanimous in regarding Winceby as *his* battle

[1] TT E.71 (22).

and *his* victory.[1] Four of them even contrive to describe the battle without mentioning the names of Fairfax or Manchester. Yet the flyleaves of the original tracts describe the battle as Manchester's. Indeed, it is clear from the accounts of eye-witnesses that owing to his accident so early in the day Cromwell could not have had much practical influence over the course of the battle. He can certainly not be given credit for issuing the order that led to victory. The battle was ordered and organised by Manchester; his was the responsibility, and therefore, in general terms, the victory. Of the actual executants, Sir Thomas Fairfax played the dominant part, and his name should be closely associated with the Roundhead victory. Revealing light on this point is afforded by careful reading of Manchester's despatch to the House of Lords announcing his victory. Of Cromwell he wrote somewhat coolly, if not perfunctorily, that he 'behaved himself with honour'. Far different is the tone of his reference to Fairfax: 'Sir Thomas Fairfax (who is a person who exceeds any expressions as a commendation of his resolution and valour) . . . performed what he was commanded with readiness and success.'[2]

11 October 1643 was, then, a memorable day for the Fairfax family, for while Sir Thomas was winning fresh laurels at Winceby, his stout-hearted father was leading a sortie from Hull. Two days earlier a fierce Cavalier assault on the West Jetty Fort had been repulsed and the Parliamentarians, encouraged by this success, determined to take the initiative.

At 7 a.m. the garrison got under arms without beat of drum. The guards on the north side lit many hundred matches and flashed powder in the pans of their muskets to induce the Royalists to expect a sortie there. At 9 a.m. 1,500 Foot, townsmen, soldiers, and seamen, with four troops of Horse, sallied out on the west. They were gallantly received, yet in a quarter of an hour the Royalists were driven out of their first work. Pushing on, the Roundheads got the next position, but a fresh body of Royalists quickly came marching up from their camp a quarter of a mile away in rear of their line. These beat back the Hull men, putting them in disorder, and charging their rear, recaptured all the siege works. The Parliamentarian cavalry meanwhile faced a great body of Cavalier Horse, which dared not advance within range of the guns of the town. Lord Fairfax and Sir John Meldrum rallied their men and persuaded them to charge once more, and after desperate fighting they retook the Royalist forts, turning the guns on the besiegers. Among the ordnance taken was a 36-pounder, probably of Dutch origin, one of the pair called the 'Queen's Pocket Pistols' or 'Gog' and 'Magog', which weighed 5,790 pounds. That night the Marquis broke up the siege.

[1] Maurice Ashley's *The Greatness of Oliver Cromwell* (London 1957), is a notable exception, declaring that Fairfax, rather than Cromwell, 'routed the enemy'.
[2] *Lords Journals*, VI, pp. 255–6.

Eleven

HOPTON AND WALLER

As an immediate result of the first battle of Newbury, the Oxford army – the central prong of the Royalist trident – reoccupied Reading. It was back where it had been in the early spring of the same year. The northern army was held up before Hull, and the old western army, now under Prince Maurice, was fully occupied in Devonshire, where it took Exeter (4 September) and Dartmouth (6 October) only to grind to a halt before Plymouth. The two outer prongs of the trident were thus firmly stuck.

Yet, if regionalism was keeping the Yorkshire and Cornish Cavaliers from the decisive scene of action – the approaches to London – the King's Council of War at Oxford still had their eyes on the main prize. Indeed, they showed an unusual grasp of the essentials of strategy. In the north, they decided to form a new army in Cheshire. This was to be commanded by Sir John Byron, who had recently been made a baron, and who by a dubious intrigue had succeeded in supplanting the gallant Lord Capel, previously the Royalist commander in those parts. Byron was expected to destroy Brereton's forces and to reconquer Lancashire. That done, he could join Newcastle in his struggle with the Fairfaxes and the Eastern Association.

More important still, a new western army was to be formed. For this the obvious commander was Lord Hopton, who was now reasonably well recovered from his wounds. While the Oxford army was operating north of the Thames against Essex himself, Hopton with this new force was to clear Dorset, Wiltshire, and Hampshire, and in his own words 'so point forward as far as he could go towards London'.[1]

On 29 September 1643 there was a Council of War at Oriel College, Oxford, when Hopton was informed of the King's decision, and the composition of this projected army was discussed. Even on paper it was not a very formidable host. The Foot numbered but 2,000; and the 12 regiments of Horse could muster only 1,580 men. Even so there were good regiments among them. Soon after, two old regiments from Munster landed at Bristol. They were

[1] Hopton, op. cit., p. 61. Hopton had been elevated to the peerage on 4 September, as Baron Hopton of Stratton.

about 500 strong in all and well officered, but the soldiers were (as Hopton puts it) 'shrewdly infected with the rebellious humour of England'.[1] When, shortly after, they mutinied, Hopton promptly executed two or three of the ringleaders and the two regiments gave no further trouble.

Money, as usual with the Royalist armies, was the chief difficulty. Hopton was promised £6,000, of which he only received £1,500 from Oxford, but he raised £3,000 in Bristol and was able to take the field at the beginning of November. To improvise an army in just over a month demonstrates his administrative ability.

Once more his adversary was to be Sir William Waller, who had taken the field in mid-October and who on 4 November was formally appointed to command the forces of a new South-Eastern Association – Kent, Surrey, Sussex and Hampshire. While Essex remained strictly on the defensive round St Albans and Newport Pagnell, Waller advanced on 7 November from Farnham, not against Hopton, who was still weak in numbers, but against Basing House, which since the summer had proved a thorn in the side of the Roundheads. Waller made a grave error in not seeking out his opponent's main field army before it could get into its stride, but the Parliamentarian commander, still shaken by Lansdown and Roundway Down, credited Hopton with an army he no longer had.

Waller's army, like Essex's, included a brigade of the London Trained Bands, who were to prove even more mutinous than Hopton's 'Irish'. On 12 November a Westminster regiment refused to obey orders and two days later the Londoners, when ordered to attack, deserted with loud cries of 'Home! Home!' Waller, long the hero of the City, hanged none of them. He fell back to his base at Farnham, having lost fully 300 men in this abortive siege.

Hopton had wished to begin his campaign by reducing the remaining Parliamentary fortresses in Wiltshire and Dorset so as to clear his back area, but Sir William Ogle surprised Winchester at about this time and Hopton was drawn in that direction. During November, Hopton was reinforced by troops from the West Country and by others lent him from the Oxford army, and his field army, not counting those units detached to blockade the Parliamentarian garrisons of Portsmouth, Southampton, Poole and Wardour Castle, rose to some 5,000 men. Hopton concentrated at Odiham, while Waller wrote desperately to London, demanding reinforcements.[2] On 27 November Hopton moved against Farnham, but Waller refused to be drawn from under the guns of the castle, and only stirred in order to harry the eventual Royalist withdrawal.

Following his failure to bring Waller to battle, Hopton, on the advice of his Council of War, sent his army into winter quarters, which, as it transpired, were too widely dispersed. Four brigades, each containing both Horse and Foot, were quartered in Winchester, Alresford, Alton and Petersfield. A strong

[1] Ibid., p. 63.
[2] Portland MSS., Vol. I, p. 154.

detachment from the latter garrison, under Sir Edward Ford and Colonel Joseph Bamfield, descended upon Arundel, but were unable to take the castle until supported by Hopton himself, with a substantial party of Horse and Foot. Ford, High Sheriff of Sussex, had a natural interest in winning over the county; he and Bamfield were left at Arundel with 700 Foot and a good number of Horse. Hopton retired to Petersfield, and thence to Winchester, travelling by way of Alton, where he warned Lord Crawford and Colonel Richard Bolle,[1] commanding the garrison's cavalry and infantry respectively, to observe Waller, and fall back if threatened.[2]

Hopton now suffered three blows in rapid succession. The Royalist regiments of Sir Humphrey Bennet (Horse) and Sir William Courtney (Foot) were quartered at Romsey, so as to threaten the garrison of Southampton. Sir Humphrey was High Sheriff of Hampshire, and unable to devote much time to his regiment, which in consequence became somewhat disorderly. Sir William Courtney rode to Winchester to take up the matter with Sir Humphrey, and during his brief absence, Colonel Richard Norton, governor of Southampton, 'fell suddenly upon that quarter . . . and beat it up, and, in effect, ruined both those regiments'.[3] It must be recalled that Hopton wrote these gloomy words *after* the Royalist defeats of 1645 and 1646, and there is in them a measure of exaggeration. Bennet's regiment did good service at Cheriton and elsewhere.

THE STORM OF ALTON, 13 DECEMBER

Hopton's second misfortune was more serious. Waller's scouts had, for some time, been keeping Alton under observation. In the evening of Tuesday 12 December Waller paraded his Foot in Farnham Park, promising the Londoners that, if they served him well for another week, he would send them home. He then set off down the Basing road, at the head of some 5,000 men, taking with him some of Colonel James Wemyss's[4] leather guns. In the early hours of

---

[1] Bolle's regiment had been part of Sir Jacob Astley's garrison at Reading. Astley himself, with a strong detachment, was sent to reinforce Hopton. Sir Jacob returned to Reading in early December, leaving his troops under Hopton.

[2] Hopton, op. cit., p. 69. These instructions were certainly very wise, and, had they been obeyed, Richard Bolle might have lived longer. Nevertheless, Hopton's army was undeniably overextended.

[3] Hopton, op. cit., p. 70.

[4] James Wemyss (1610?–67). A Scots artillerist of note, Wemyss patented the leather guns believed to have been invented by Colonel Robert Scott. In 1638 he was appointed master-gunner of England, much to the anger of the English candidates for the post. He nevertheless fought for Parliament, and was captured at Cropredy Bridge (24 June 1644). Charles offered to reinstate him as master-gunner, but Wemyss declined. He was soon exchanged, and returned to Scotland in 1648. He became general of ordnance in the Scots army the following year. He escaped from Dunbar (3 September 1650) but was taken prisoner at Worcester (3 September 1651), and imprisoned in Windsor Castle. After the restoration he

13 December, Waller's column turned south, towards Alton, avoiding Crawford's troopers, who were watching the main roads. The alarm was not given until Waller's Foot were dangerously close to the town. Crawford, deciding that his Horse would be of little use in the town, broke out down the Winchester road, leaving Colonel Bolle and his Foot to defend themselves as best they could.

Bolle had posted most of his men around the church, which stood, with several other buildings, at the north-west edge of the town. Waller launched his own regiment of Horse, supported by five companies of Sir Arthur Hesilrige's and five of Kentishmen, against the group of buildings near the church. The Royalists, firing fast from a great brick house, did some damage, but were forced back on the church by the arrival of the leather guns. Meanwhile, the London brigade, with four companies from Farnham Castle, moved in from the west. The red regiment was checked by a hot fire from a crescent-shaped defence work, known as a half-moon, but the green auxilliaries outflanked this obstacle and made their way into the town, under cover of the smoke of a burning thatched house. With this, the defenders of the half-moon retired on the church in some disorder.

The Royalists hung on to the church and a great earthwork on its north side, for two hours more. They had erected scaffolding in the church itself, and kept up a heavy fire from the windows. After a time, the men of the red and yellow London regiments got the better of the fire-fight in the south-east corner of the churchyard. The Parliamentarians could still see muskets sticking over the wall and suspected an ambush, but as no enemy put his head over the wall to fire they eventually concluded that the defenders had fled and – not without misgiving – advanced into the churchyard. Simultaneously, some of the red regiment broke in, driving the Royalists back into the church, following so close on their heels that they prevented the barricading of the door.

A desperate struggle raged around the church, which was full of men 'laying about them stoutly with Halberts, Swords and Musket-stocks, while some threw hand grenades in at the Church windows, others attempting to enter the Church being led in by Sergeant-Major Shambrooke ... who in the entrance received a shot in the thigh. ...'[1] Lieutenant-Colonel John Birch is said to have been the first man to enter. The sight of the enemy waiting to receive him with their pikes and muskets, behind a breastwork of dead horses in the aisles, might well have appalled a fainter heart. Many bullet marks in the church still testify to the severity of that half-forgotten fight.

[1] Elias Archer, *A True Relation of the trained bands of Westminster . . .*, BM 101 b. 64, pp. 11–12. Archer was a lieutenant in the Yellow Regiment of Auxilliaries.

obtained his old office of master-gunner. Wemyss, however, displayed rather more constancy than his compatriot Sir John Urry, who changed sides three times, and ended his colourful career on the scaffold.

Richard Bolle had no thought of surrender. He swore 'God damn his soul if he did not run his sword through the heart of him, which first called for quarter',[1] and slew seven Roundheads before he was struck dead by a blow from the butt of a musket, falling surrounded by a circle of enemies. His death took the heart out of the defence, though a few – 'desperate villains', as a Parliamentarian officer calls them – fought on and were slain in the church. Wildly differing accounts are given of the casualties sustained by the Royalists, but their losses were certainly severe; 700 is perhaps a fair estimate of the number of prisoners alone.

Hopton was greatly depressed by the disaster. The psychological shock to his self-esteem as a commander was very great – indeed, out of all proportion to the realities of the defeat he had sustained. Perhaps he felt a sense of shame at having left his men exposed to such an attack; perhaps he experienced some feeling of guilt at not coming to their rescue in time. Such guilt was hardly justified, for Hopton had set out, at the head of a strong relieving force, as soon as he heard Crawford's ill tidings. The mental shock of Alton, coming as it did so soon after Hopton's injuries at Lansdown, made a changed man of him. Henceforth he lacked something of the old fire and decision which had marked his early battles; he became slower to make up his mind, and more apt to change it, though he was willing as ever to hazard his person. However depressed he may have been by them, his series of reverses can be explained simply enough. Hopton was being invited by the Royalist Council of War at Oxford to carry out a strategic plan for which his army was not strong enough.

Hopton's third defeat was the capture of Arundel Castle, taken by Waller on 6 January. In all, 1,000 Royalists were taken, and about half of these re-enlisted in the Parliamentarian army, following the example of some of the Alton prisoners. Shortly after the fall of Arundel, a change in the weather made further operations impossible. Waller's men belatedly went into winter quarters in west Sussex, where they were joined by two London regiments, replacing Colonel Sir James Harrington's London brigade, which had returned home after Alton.

Snow billowed, too, north of the Thames, where, with veterans at their disposal, the Oxford Cavaliers had done little enough. On 6 October a force under the stalwart Bedfordshire man, Sir Lewis Dyve, seized Newport Pagnell, threatening the Great North Road and jeopardising communications between London and the Eastern Association. Dyve, however, was poorly supported from Oxford, and was forced to relinquish the town at the end of October. Rupert, who had backed Dyve's attempt, made a similar effort to hold and fortify Towcester, but this too had to be abandoned. In Cheshire and the Welsh Marches the situation had worsened; Brereton had seized Wrexham, a useful point from which to intercept Royalist reinforcements from Ireland, who

[1] Loc. cit.

might try to join the King by marching across North Wales. Rupert was sent north to try to restore the situation, and during his absence the Queen, Digby, and the many other courtiers who had no affection for the hot-tempered Prince, worked strenuously at reducing his influence with the King.

The fact that the Oxford army had little to boast of did not prevent its commanders from losing confidence in Hopton. Perhaps they thought he had lost his skill, or that he was making too much of his difficulties. Hopton had asked for 800 or 900 Foot after Alton: 'The return was a very gracious message from his Majesty full of goodness. . . . But the desired supply came not.'[1] Hopton managed to raise some recruits locally, and recovered Romsey, but constantly requested a major reinforcement from Oxford. It was a measure of the Council of War's diminishing confidence in Hopton that, when the reinforcement did at last arrive, it was led by an officer much senior to him – Patrick Ruthven, Earl of Forth.

Forth was loyal, ancient, brave and bibulous, vastly experienced and seriously gouty. Early in March 1644 he joined Hopton with a very handsome body of 1,200 Foot, 800 Horse, and 4 guns. With Hopton's own men, this raised the army to a total of not less than 6,000, of whom nearly 3,000 were cavalry. A good administrator, Hopton had seen to it that his men were well clothed, but it is the spirit that counts, and his new levies and his 'Irish' veterans – even if they were no longer mutinous – were not to be compared with the Cornishmen of Stratton and Lansdown.

Forth was a tactful old gentleman, and, as Hopton tells us, it was only with the utmost difficulty that he 'prevailed with him to honour him with orders'.[2] Clarendon maintains that Forth 'positively refused' to take command, and 'only offered to give him the best assistance he was able, which the Lord Hopton was compelled to be contented with: nor could there be a greater union and consent between two friends; the general [Forth] being ready to give his advice upon all particulars; and the other doing nothing without communication with him, and then conforming to his opinion, and giving orders accordingly'.[3] Yet the ultimate responsibility for command of the army fell upon Lord Forth, though as he was suffering from gout, and could scarcely move from his coach, all the practical work continued to fall upon Hopton, without the actual responsibility being his. This, as we saw at Lansdown, was a vicious system.

Sir William Waller, on the other hand, was in undisputed command of the Parliamentarian army, and had been so for five months. He had 3,000 Horse, 5,000 Foot and 600 dragoons, which, despite the changes among the London regiments, was a firmly welded force. The cavalry were particularly good. Even after Roundway Down, the prestige of Hesilrige's 'Lobsters' remained high. Waller was, furthermore, reinforced with a cavalry brigade from Essex's

[1] Hopton, op. cit., p. 72.
[2] Ibid., pp. 77–8.
[3] Clarendon, op. cit., Vol. IV, p. 459.

army, under the capable Sir William Balfour. The latter's command numbered about 5,000 Horse in all.

Essex, in lending Balfour's brigade to the southern army, had shown a rare flash of strategic insight. The King's Oxford army, holding the passages of the Thames above Reading, and with the river barrier of Thame, Cherwell and Thames covering Oxford itself, was in a much better position to play this game of shifting forces. The King's Council of War failed, however, to support Hopton adequately, and this allowed Essex to tip the scales in Waller's favour.

While Hopton and Waller prepared, with equal confidence, for a decisive clash, events had moved swiftly on the political scene. Negotiations with the Scots had been successfully concluded on 23 November. The Scots were to provide, at English expense, an army of 18,000 Foot and 2,000 Horse, with a suitable train of artillery. Parliament had accepted the covenant two months earlier, undertaking to reform the English Church on the model of the Scottish Kirk. John Pym, architect of the Scottish Alliance, did not live to see the fruits of his labour, dying of cancer on 8 December. His death robbed Parliament of its principal strategist, for few of Pym's colleagues had his broad grasp of political and military problems, his tireless energy or his consummate tact. On Pym's death, the leadership of Parliament fell into the hands of the younger Sir Harry Vane, and Oliver St John. These men were responsible for determining the composition of the new executive, the Committee of Both Kingdoms, appointed by an ordinance on 16 February 1644. They pushed the ordinance through, despite opposition from Essex's supporters, who maintained that the phrase 'order and direct'[1] encroached upon the Lord General's powers. They also excluded Denzil Holles, leader of the peace party from the Committee, but, significantly enough, included Oliver Cromwell.

While Parliament negotiated with the Scots, the King sought aid from Ireland. In September 1643, the Marquis of Ormonde concluded a truce with the Roman Catholic Confederates, this 'Cessation', as it was generally known, releasing the King's troops in Ireland for service in England. The Cessation was denounced, not only by Parliament, but also by the Scots of Ulster, and by several useful professional soldiers serving in Ireland, notably Michael Jones, Lawrence Crawford and George Monck. The Government troops who returned to England – in all, twelve regiments of Foot and one of Horse – found themselves scornfully referred to as 'Irish'; they were accused of having abandoned English settlers to the mercy of the rebels, and retorted with loud murmurings against the Roman Catholic officers in the Royalist army.

It was small wonder that Hopton's army was not altogether happy with its Irish regiments, nor these regiments with their new rôle. But despite this uneasiness in their ranks, Hopton and Forth were eager to engage Waller, and actually went so far as to issue a challenge in the medieval manner, offering to meet him at a prescribed place and time. If Sir William declined the challenge,

[1] Gardiner, *Constitutional Documents*, pp. 271–3, gives the full text of the ordinance.

it was only because, like the good tactician he was, he had resolved to fight wherever he could gain a favourable opportunity.

Having had no success with their challenge, the Royalist generals tried more conventional means of bringing their wily adversary to battle. Waller was threatening Winchester from the east, and had pushed his outposts as far as Warnford and West Meon, in the winding Meon Valley. The Royalist commanders decided to advance rapidly against Waller's forward elements. Forth, suffering from 'a fit of the gout',[1] delegated the command to Hopton. Lord Ralph led the Royalist army eastwards on the afternoon of 26 March, spending the night about three miles from Waller's lines. On the morning of the 27th, Hopton made for Warnford, headquarters of the London brigade, only to find the village deserted, and the Londoners drawn up on the slopes of Westbury Forest, between East and West Meon. The Royalists moved up the rise from Warnford, taking up a position on Old Winchester Hill. Hopton then sent his major-general of the Horse, Sir John Smith, with a strong detachment, 'to seek to draw him [Waller] from his advantage to engage from the woods, and nearer the plain'.[2] Waller refused to be drawn, but instead issued orders for a march on Alresford, 'a reasonable strong quarter, and within five miles of Winchester'.[3] Hopton feared just such a move, and as soon as he discovered what was afoot, marched for Alresford himself, his leading unit, Sir Edward Stawell's brigade, galloping in a neck and neck race for the town with Balfour's vanguard of Horse.

Hopton won the race. Stawell's troopers began erecting barricades in the streets of Alresford, while Hopton summoned reinforcements. Balfour halted, probably on East Down, where he was joined by the Parliamentarian Foot. The Royalists concentrated for the night on Tichborne Down, between Alresford and the little village of Cheriton. That night, and the following day, there was some skirmishing along the front of the rival armies, which resulted in the Royalists seizing a small hill, which gave them a good 'view of the enemy quarters, where they encamped as it is said before in a low field enclosed with a very thick hedge and ditch and their ordnance planted upon the rising of the hill behind them'.[4] Hopton posted Colonel George Lisle, with 1,000 musketeers, on the eminence, with 500 Horse in the lane immediately to Lisle's rear. Both armies spent the night of the 28th in the field. Hopton ordered 'every horseman to rest by his horse, and every footman by his arms, and every officer in his place'.[5] He prevailed upon the gouty Forth to retire to lodgings in Alresford, while he himself slept in his coach, at the head of the army.

[1] Hopton, op. cit., p. 78.
[2] Ibid., p. 79.
[3] Loc. cit.
[4] Ibid., p. 80.
[5] Loc. cit.

THE BATTLE OF CHERITON, 29 MARCH

There is some doubt as to the precise site of the battle of Cheriton.[1] Most accounts of the action place it between Tichborne Down and East Down. Hopton himself stated that 'the enemy . . . had taken their quarters in a low field joining to the Lady Stukeley's house, not a mile and a half from our army so as there was but a little hill and a little vale between us. . . .' Lady Stukeley's house was in Hinton Ampner, and Waller's bivouac line probably ran along the valley towards Bramdean. Captain Jones, a London brigade officer, maintained that 'the Enemy lay in Sutton Down, we lay in Lumborne field, we fought in East Down between Cheriton and Alesford'.[2] Captain Robert Harley, of Waller's Horse, whose letter to Colonel Edward Harley is one of the most useful Parliamentarian accounts of the battle,[3] hints that Waller's left rested on Hinton Ampner rather than on Cheriton. This was probably the case during the early morning when Waller initially deployed, but before the action became general the Parliamentarian left seems to have advanced to the ridge-end just east of Cheriton. There is no doubt that the Parliamentarian right hinged on Cheriton Wood, and a position stretching from this feature to the valley just north of Hinton Ampner would be an improbable one, running across rather than along a ridge, and at an angle to the Royalist line of advance. The authors therefore concur with the traditional location of the action, the shallow depression lying between Cheriton Wood and Cheriton, bordered by ridges to its north and south.

Waller's own quarters were in the Manor House at Hinton Ampner. Here, on the afternoon of 28 March, the Parliamentarian Council of War met to consider what the army should do. Several of those present advised withdrawal, but the meeting eventually decided that a retreat was too hazardous, and resolved to stand, and, if necessary, fight.

29 March 1644 dawned misty. Hopton had suspected a Parliamentarian withdrawal, and rode forward at sunrise to Lisle's position on the hill between the armies. When the mist cleared, some two hours later, Hopton saw that, far from retreating, Waller was forming up for battle, and occupied 'a high woody ground' (Cheriton Wood)[4] on the Royalist left. Hopton at once sent word to Forth, who, on arrival, ordered him to move the whole Royalist army forward into line with Lisle's detachment which, however, had to retire slightly, as its left flank was endangered by the Parliamentarian musketeers in Cheriton

---

[1] We differ here from Dr John Adair's location of the battle, as expressed in his excellent biography of Sir William Waller, *The Roundhead General* (1969).
[2] TT E. 40 (12).
[3] HMC Portland MSS., Vol. 3, pp. 106–10.
[4] Cheriton Wood has undoubtedly changed in shape since the battle. It was certainly smaller and less thick then than it is today.

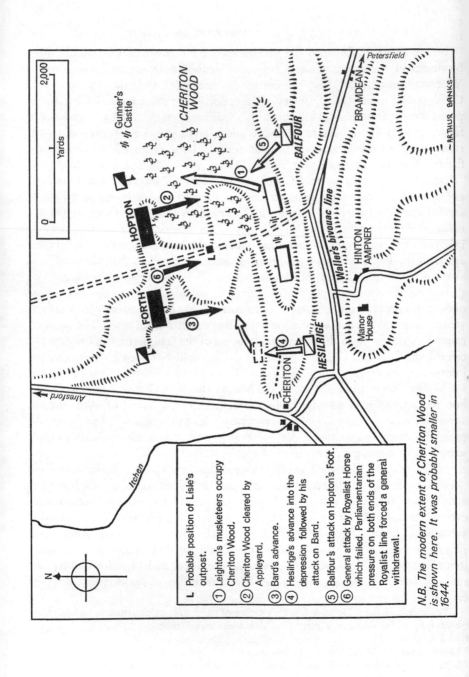

2,000

Yards

0

Petersfield

CHERITON WOOD

Gunner's Castle

BRAMDEAN

BALFOUR

⑤

①

HOPTON

②

FORTH

⑥

③

④

Waller's bivouac line

HINTON AMPNER

HESILRIGE

Manor House

Alresford

CHERITON

Itchen

N

L Probable position of Lisle's outpost.

① Leighton's musketeers occupy Cheriton Wood.

② Cheriton Wood cleared by Appleyard.

③ Bard's advance.

④ Hesilrige's advance into the depression followed by his attack on Bard.

⑤ Balfour's attack on Hopton's Foot.

⑥ General attack by Royalist Horse which failed. Parliamentarian pressure on both ends of the Royalist line forced a general withdrawal.

N.B. The modern extent of Cheriton Wood is shown here. It was probably smaller in 1644.

—ARTHUR BANKS—

Wood. Hopton's own troops took up position north of Cheriton Wood, east of the track from Alresford, and Forth's men swung into line on their right.

Waller was on the move early. Deploying his infantry just north of their bivouac line, he threw 1,000 musketeers, supported by 300 Horse, into Cheriton Wood. Another strong detachment of musketeers lined the hedges east of Cheriton, while the remainder of the Foot moved forward on to the ridge, profiting by the withdrawal of Lisle's detachment. Waller's guns were brought forward on to the ridge, and his cavalry, the left wing under Hesilrige and the right under Balfour, took up position slightly to the rear of their respective flanks, to prevent any encircling movement by the Royalist Horse.

The Royalist army completed its deployment at about 11 a.m. Hopton astutely realised the importance of Cheriton Wood, which threatened his left, and imperilled the Royalist hold on the northern ridge. His Foot were drawn up on the reverse slope of the ridge, within musket shot of Colonel Leighton's men in Cheriton Wood. Hopton ordered Colonel Matthew Appleyard to assemble a body of 1,000 commanded musketeers, divide them into four parties, and assault the wood. Appleyard's men were met with a hot fire as they breasted the rise, and halted to return it. Hopton took in the situation at a glance; he ordered Lieutenant-Colonel Edward Hopton, commander of one of Appleyard's detachments, 'to run with all possible speed into the wood upon the enemy's flank'.[1] This manoeuvre was supported by the fire of the Royalist cannon from the high ground north of the wood, from a spot subsequently known as 'Gunner's Castle'. Lieutenant-Colonel Hopton's musketeers were screened by a 'cross hedge'; they had no sooner given 'one volley from thence but the enemy fell in disorder; and began to run. . . .'[2] Appleyard's men then stormed forward, and threw the Roundheads out of the wood, causing many casualties; they even took a colour from the cavalry supporting Leighton. This success gave the Royalists undisputed command over the whole length of the ridge.

Forth now advised Hopton to remain on the defensive in this strong position, and to leave any further attacking to the Parliamentarians. Hopton 'remained extremely satisfied with that solid advice'.[3] He gave requisite orders to the left wing, and was riding back to the centre to confer with Forth, when he observed that a hot fight was in progress on the Royalist right. The reasons for this turn in the battle are obscure. It is possible that Forth had changed his mind over remaining on the defensive, but more likely than that, as Hopton put it, 'the engagement was by the forwardness of some particular officers, without order'.[4]

[1] Hopton, op. cit., pp. 81–2. Lieutenant-Colonel Hopton's party probably advanced along the eastern fringe of the wood, thus outflanking Leighton's men.
[2] Ibid., p. 82.
[3] Loc. cit.
[4] Loc. cit.

Slingsby attributes the manoeuvre to Colonel Henry Bard, who led his regiment of Foot down the slope, 'with more youthful courage than soldier-like discretion'.[1] Whatever its cause, Bard's advance was to have fatal consequences. Waller, alarmed by the Royalist Horse on the crest of the ridge, had ordered his cavalry forward, 'into a Heath, which stood betwixt the two hills where they did fight . . . the hills being one from another not whole culverin shot'.[2] As Bard's men advanced into the shallow bowl between the two armies, they were thus open to attack by Hesilrige's wing. Sir Arthur formed a commanded party of 300 Horse and sent them against Bard's hapless infantry, who were now completely out of touch with the rest of the Royalist army. Hesilrige's troopers swirled around the isolated regiment and broke it, killing or capturing every man in it.

This success by the cavalry on Waller's left encouraged Balfour to attack the Royalist Foot on his wing. Hopton's own Foot stood here, and were not to be easily dislodged. They fought hard, 'keeping their ground in a close body, not firing till within two pike's length, and then three ranks at a time. . . .'[3] Lord John Stewart, commander of the Royalist cavalry, counter-attacked with the Queen's regiment of Horse, but this unit retired after only one 'unhandsome charge', as Walter Slingsby put it. Waller supported Balfour's Horse with a strong body of infantry, and under their pressure the Royalist left maintained itself with growing difficulty.

On the right, meanwhile, Forth ordered Hopton to select 1,000 Horse with which to dislodge Hesilrige's cavalry. Hopton decided to use Sir Edward Stawell's brigade for this, and, at 2 p.m., ordered Sir Edward to advance. The Royalist Horse were forced to move forward down a lane, which hampered their deployment; nevertheless, Stawell's men fought hard for almost half an hour before being driven off. Sir Edward himself charged home to the Roundhead gunline, where, wounded five times, he was taken prisoner. Forth then decided to support Stawell with almost all the rest of the Horse. Regiment after regiment spurred forward into the battle. Slingsby, not noted for his admiration of the cavalry, was forced to admit that 'our Horse did perform more gallant charges that day than hath been known in any one battle in the war. . . .'[4] The infantry on both sides joined in and the battle in the depression east of Cheriton Wood became a nightmare of musket flashes and sword cuts, lathered horses and sweating men, shrouded in a haze of powder-smoke.

The Royalists came off worse. They had to advance in the teeth of the Parliamentarian guns, and, once in the mêlée, were at a marked disadvantage when fighting Hesilrige's 'Lobsters'. The best cavalry officers in the western army fell

[1] Ibid., pp. 101–2.
[2] Harley, op. cit., p. 108.
[3] Hopton, op. cit., p. 102.
[4] Loc. cit. This contrasts with Clarendon's view that 'the King's Horse never behaved themselves so ill as that day'. (Clarendon, op. cit., Vol. IV, p. 460.)

hat day. Lord John Stewart was killed, and his major-general, Sir John Smith, mortally wounded. Several other officers of note shared their fate. After about two hours the Royalist cavalry were played out. Hopton himself collected 300 troopers and held the Alresford lane, enabling the survivors to retire up and over the slope. Things were going no better on the flanks. The struggle in the entre seems to have denuded the Royalist right of infantry, and those Foot that were there cannot have been cheered by the sight of the retiring Horse. As it was, Colonel Carr's[1] Roundhead infantry pushed up the western end of the ridge while other Parliamentarian Foot fought their way on to its eastern end.

The Royalist army was in danger of total collapse. Its generals managed, however, to fall back in reasonable order, and make a stand on the northern crest of Tichborne Down, just south of Alresford. This respite gave Forth and Hopton the opportunity to consult. Hopton, who knew the ground well, opposed any suggestion of retiring on Winchester. A withdrawal on Basing House was eventually decided on. Hopton first sent off the cannon, under Colonel Richard Feilding, and remained facing the victorious Roundheads for about an hour before falling back, through Alresford, with the main body of the army. The Cavaliers reached Basing House in the early hours of the morning. They rested there for a day, and then marched to Reading. The King, deciding to strengthen his Oxford army and cut his losses in the south, ordered Forth and Hopton to join him. He also took the opportunity to withdraw the Reading garrison to Oxford. Waller declined to pursue, and moved instead on Winchester. The town surrendered on 30 March, though the castle continued to hold out.

The action at Cheriton 'was a very doleful entering into the beginning of the year 1644, and broke all the measures, and altered the whole scheme, of the King's Counsels. . . .'[2] The western prong of the Royalist trident was finally blunted. Important though the results of Cheriton were, it remains an unimpressive battle, distinguished only by a series of command errors on both sides. The Royalist chain of command was tangled and unreliable. Forth's decision to remain on the defensive on the northern edge was questionable; his inability to ensure that this decision was implemented was disastrous. Waller must be censured for accepting defeat in Cheriton Wood, while Forth's failure to exploit Appleyard's seizure of this vital ground is decidedly open to criticism. Waller's victory was due, firstly, to his numerical superiority, especially in Horse, and secondly to his army's greater homogeneity and discipline. Indiscipline – that scourge of the King's armies – was in no small measure responsible for the Royalist defeat. The Royalist cavalry losses, particularly amongst officers, were significantly high. In terms of morale, Cheriton was the Winceby of

Colonel James Carr, another Scots professional, had been appointed major-general of Waller's Foot and dragoons in 1643.
Clarendon, op. cit., Vol. IV, p. 462.

the south; it demonstrated that the Parliamentarian cavalry was able to take on, and beat, the King's Horse. Nevertheless, as Lieutenant-Colonel Birch's secretary, Roe, observed, 'it was indeed a victory, but the worst possible of any I ever saw'.[1]

[1] *The Military Memoir of Colonel John Birch ... written by Roe, his secretary ...* (Camden Society 1873, ed. J. and T. W. Webb).

Twelve

THE SCOTS AND THE 'IRISH'

In the south the war was going badly for the Royalists, though developments in the west, where the Parliamentarians were emphatically on the defensive, were more favourable. It was in the north, however, that the situation was most crucial.

On 19 January 1644 the Scots army began to cross the Tweed. The struggle between the English had become so finely balanced that the intervention of a well-organised army of some 20,000 soldiers was almost bound to tip the scales. Newcastle was in an unenviable position. His field army contained only 8,000 men, and he was threatened from the south by the resurgent Fairfaxes, and from the north by the new Scots menace. Nevertheless, the Marquis moved north to defend Northumberland, and fell back slowly before Scottish pressure. In these inauspicious circumstances Newcastle was visited by James Graham, Marquis of Montrose, the King's lieutenant-general for Scotland, who requested troops for a counter-thrust into that country. Newcastle, himself desperately short of men, could only give Montrose a few troopers and two small guns. He also called out the northern Trained Bands to assist, and, thus supported, the undaunted Montrose set off for Scotland.

There had been little hope since October 1643 that Newcastle's army would play its part in the advance on London envisaged in the Royalist 'Grand Plan'. The Scots intervention destroyed what shreds of hope remained and the Oxford Council of War redoubled its energies in building up a second northern army under Lord Byron. The Cessation negotiated by Ormonde made possible the reinforcement of Byron's army with Irish troops; five regiments of Foot joined Byron in November 1643, and with their aid he made considerable progress against Brereton.

The arrival of Byron and the Irish infused a new and unpleasant element into the war in Cheshire. On 26 December Byron summoned a Parliamentarian detachment in Barthomley church. The Roundheads declined to surrender, whereupon Byron stormed the place. 'I put them all to the sword,' he wrote 'which I find to be the best way to proceed with these kind of people, for mercy to them is cruelty.'[1] Byron's brutal action was strictly in accordance with the usages of war, but, if not a crime, was an atrocious blunder. Such action breeds brutality, and, far from weakening the morale of the victims' friends, often serves to harden it. Nevertheless, Brereton's garrisons collapsed one by one, and before long, 'Nantwich alone remained to contend with a force numbering quite seven thousand fighting men'.[2]

Sir William Brereton was, single-handed, no match for Byron. However, on 20 December Sir Thomas Fairfax had recaptured Gainsborough, and, obedient to the urgings of the Committee for Both Kingdoms, set out on 29 December to march to the relief of his colleague. Newcastle was fully occupied preparing for the Scots, and Fairfax had nothing but his own administrative difficulties, which were, though, very considerable, to hinder his cooperation with Brereton.

Byron, meanwhile, having driven Brereton's men into Nantwich, laid siege to the town on 13 December. The place was poorly fortified, but a general assault, delivered before daybreak on 18 January, was repulsed with loss. Fairfax assembled and reclothed his own troops, numbering about 1,800 Horse and 500 dragoons. He marched through Derbyshire and Staffordshire to Manchester. Here he was joined by his friend, Captain Hodgson, with up to 3,000 Foot, many of them Fairfax's old comrades of Adwalton Moor. These infantry were so tired, ragged and poorly equipped that Fairfax apparently burst into tears when he saw them. He left Manchester on 21 January, and was soon joined by Brereton with a small detachment. The combined force under Fairfax's command numbered 2,500 moderately equipped Foot, with several hundred more 'cudgellers', and twenty-eight troops of Horse. With this ill-assorted army, Black Tom marched to the relief of Nantwich.

The town of Nantwich lies in flat country, on the banks of the River Weaver. In 1644 the town was very small – little more than a large village. It was surrounded by earthworks, and garrisoned by Colonel Sir George Booth with the bulk of Brereton's army. The besiegers were encamped on both sides of the river; Byron's own headquarters were at Acton, about a mile west of Nantwich, on the Chester road. His regiments lay in a broad circle round the town, taking quarter where they could. Relations with the local inhabitants were bad and Byron was able to receive little useful intelligence. The Weaver was about 20 feet wide; it was crossed, in the town itself, by the Chester road. About half a mile north lay Beam Bridge, where a smaller road crossed the river. Byron seems to have constructed a ferry to the north of this, though his reasons for doing so are not clear.

[1] *Mercurius Civicus*, No. 35, p. 374.
[2] J. R. Philips, *Memoirs of the Civil Wars in Wales and the Marches* (London 1874, 2 Volumes) Vol. I, p. 190. Vol. II is particularly useful, containing Lord Byron's letter to Ormonde giving his account of the action at Nantwich, Sir Thomas Fairfax's despatch to Essex, and a clear narrative by Colonel Sir Robert Byron.

THE BATTLE OF NANTWICH, 25 JANUARY

On 24 January Fairfax moved on Nantwich from the north-west. In Delamere Forest 200 Royalists endeavoured to hold the road, but Fairfax dislodged them with his dragoons, and advanced on the town. Byron, poorly informed of Fairfax's real strength, declined to abandon the siege. This rash decision proved particularly unfortunate, for, on the night of 24 to 25 January, there was a sudden thaw. The snow which had lain so thickly on the ground turned into water, swelling the Weaver to torrent-like proportions. The ferry above Beam Bridge was swept away, and the bridge itself wrecked. Byron's army was thus cut in two, and the eastern element, the Horse, under Byron himself, could only join the western part by a six-mile march, crossing by the bridge at Min-hull. Once Byron discovered that Fairfax was threatening to destroy his army in detail, he immediately set off, with his 1,800 Horse, to support his Foot around Acton.

Byron's major-general, Sir Michael Earnley, was sick, and his duties were taken over by Colonel Richard Gibson, who drew up the Royalist infantry about 400 yards north-east of Acton church. Gibson's own regiment was on the Royalist right, and that of Sir Robert Byron on the left. The regiments of Earnley and Colonel Warren stood in the centre, the latter unit being commanded by Colonel George Monck, newly returned from Ireland. Sir Fulk Hunk's regiment covered the Royalist rear against a sortie by the garrison of Nantwich. The Royalist guns were positioned in Acton churchyard, on the left of Gibson's line. The ground was broken up by numerous hedges and ditches, which severely hampered Fairfax's deployment. Nevertheless, Sir Thomas pushed on down the narrow muddy lanes, and along the hedgerows, and shortly after 2 p.m. was approaching Gibson's position.

At this delicate juncture, Fairfax received information that Byron's cavalry were threatening his left rear. Fairfax made a decision with commendable speed. He detailed two regiments of Foot, and his own troop of Horse, under Major Rokeby, to hold Byron, and moved forward to assault Gibson. The Royalist wings fought well, initially forcing the Parliamentarians to give ground. Sir William Fairfax, commanding the Horse, eventually managed to dislodge the Royalist right from the lane on which it rested, while the infantry worked their way forward, from hedge to hedge. The crux of the battle took place in the centre. Warren's regiment soon broke, many of its soldiers going over to the enemy.[1] Earnley's, too, collapsed, leaving the two flanking regiments sadly exposed. While this action was in progress, Colonel Booth, at the head of 600 musketeers, sallied out against Sir Fulk Hunk's regiment. Gibson had failed to ensure that the eastern end of the Chester road bridge was adequately held, and Booth was thus able to drive Hunk's regiment towards Acton, reaching Acton

[1] According to Sir Robert Byron, hardly an impartial witness.

church and throwing the Royalist gun-line and wagon-park into confusion. This probably occurred simultaneously with, or was perhaps the cause of, the flight of Earnley's regiment.

The collapse of the Royalist centre, at about 4.30 p.m., placed Sir Robert Byron's and Colonel Gibson's regiments in a terrible position. The Roundhead centre, Horse and Foot, swept into the gap, and, swinging outwards, assailed the flanks of these unfortunate units. It is greatly to their credit that they managed to stand their ground at all. Nevertheless, outnumbered and out-flanked, they could not hold out for long. Byron's cavalry had proved unable to break through the detachment which Fairfax had thrown into their path; unsupported, the two gallant flank regiments were overwhelmed.

Many of the officers took refuge in Acton church, joining several of their colleagues from the centre regiments. Those of the men who were not killed or captured scattered to all points of the compass. Byron made off to Chester with his Horse. The officers in Acton church soon surrendered on terms, and joined the 1,500 or so soldiers who had become prisoners.[1] All Byron's guns and baggage, together with almost all his colours, fell into Parliamentarian hands, as did 120 Irish women camp-followers.

Fairfax's resounding victory at Nantwich was due primarily to his own excellent generalship, and secondly to the superior morale of his troops. Sir Thomas showed considerable skill in catching his opponents disunited, and in refusing to allow the threat to his rear to deter him from maintaining his true objective. His troops, imbued with anger against 'The Bloody Bragadochio Byron' and his supposedly Papist Irish troops, fought with a determination which most of Byron's Foot could not equal. It is difficult to understand Byron's own conduct in the action, since there is a great degree of confusion amongst contemporary sources,[2] which offer sharply conflicting versions of events.

Byron's account displays a natural reticence in mentioning how large his detachment on the eastern bank of the Weaver was, or even who was in com-mand of it. He explains neither his failure to concentrate against Fairfax while there was still time, nor the lethargy of his cavalry. Although the ground was unsuitable for mounted action, it does not excuse the failure of Byron and his 1,800 horsemen. Fairfax's own cavalry were usefully employed, and even if Byron was unable to make headway against the blocking force, he could have used his superior mobility to skirt this detachment and join up with Gibson's hard-pressed troops.

Nantwich clearly demonstrated to the Oxford Council of War that Byron

[1] Colonel George Monck was amongst those captured. He initially declined proffered employment in the Parliamentarian army, and remained a prisoner for more than two years.
[2] Fairfax's despatch to Essex, and the letters of both Byrons to Ormonde. G. Ormerod *History of the County Palatine*, also contains some interesting source material, including an extract from *Providence Improved*, a tract by Edward Burghall, vicar of Acton. Thomas Malbon's *Memorials of the Civil War in Cheshire* gives the full text of the tract.

was a general of limited capacity. He was certainly not the man to reconquer Cheshire and Lancashire, let alone succour Newcastle or fall upon the Eastern Association. So serious had the situation in the north become that Prince Rupert himself was selected to take over command. He left Oxford on 6 February, and set up his headquarters in Shrewsbury. He brought few troops with him, but he found that the remnants of Byron's army had recently been reinforced by two more infantry regiments from Ireland, under the command of Colonel Henry Tillier, an experienced professional.

Rupert's attention was to be directed, not against the victorious Parliamentarian forces in Cheshire, but towards a new threat to the vital fortress of Newark. This town had been left dangerously isolated by the fall of Lincoln and Gainsborough, following the Royalist defeat at Winceby. Sir Richard Byron had replaced Sir John Henderson as governor. He could expect little help from Newcastle, who was fully committed against the Scots. Though the Marquis was having some success in his struggle, for the Scots were bogged down before the fortifications of Newcastle, and their quarters were successfully raided by Sir Marmaduke Langdale's cavalry, this was cold comfort to Sir Richard Byron. He was threatened by a powerful Parliamentarian force, under Sir John Meldrum. The latter's army, raised for the most part in the surrounding counties, comprised 2,000 Horse and 5,000 Foot, with 11 guns and 2 mortars. Byron had less than 2,000 men in his garrison, including 300 Horse.

On 6 March Meldrum stormed Muskham Bridge, destroying one of Byron's regiments, that of Colonel Gervase Holles, in the process. He established his headquarters in the Spittal, and kept the town tightly invested. An assault on 8 March was repulsed with loss to the besiegers, but on the other hand, an attempted relief by Colonel Gervase Lucas, governor of Belvoir Castle, was beaten off. The King was well aware of the threat, and as early as 18 February had written to Rupert recommending 'the succouring of Newark'.

While the Prince was visiting Chester on 12 March he received positive orders to march to Newark's relief. He was, however, hampered by a great shortage of troops. Acting swiftly, he returned to Shrewsbury, sending Major Will Legge, of his own regiment of Horse, who acted as his chief staff officer, ahead to collect as many musketeers as could be spared from among the Irish regiments in that garrison. Colonel Tillier was sent down the Severn by boat with 1,120 men, to Bridgnorth, where on the 15th he met Rupert and about 800 Horse. On the next day they marched to Wolverhampton, where they were joined by the 300 men of Colonel Thomas Leveson's regiment, the garrison of Dudley Castle. Rupert then set off for Ashby de la Zouch, where Lord Loughborough had concentrated some 2,700 men. The Prince reached Lichfield on the 17th, and made his rendezvous with Loughborough the following day. Meldrum, aware of the danger, had attempted to interpose his cavalry, under Sir Edward Hartop, between Rupert and Loughborough, but this venture had failed miserably.

PRINCE RUPERT'S RELIEF OF NEWARK, 21 MARCH

On 20 March Rupert arrived at Bingham, just over ten miles from Newark, and bivouacked, sending out scouts to observe Meldrum's force. The Prince had with him about 6,420 men, against Meldrum's 7,000. Although Rupert's force had been hastily extemporised, it consisted, in the main, of experienced soldiers, whose morale was excellent. Meldrum's Council of War, meeting on the 20th, decided to make a renewed attempt to intercept Rupert with cavalry, but before such a move could be undertaken, intelligence of Rupert's proximity compelled a change of plan. Sir Miles Hobart advocated a retreat on Lincoln, but Meldrum resolved to concentrate his Foot around the Spittal, and to send his Horse across Muskham Bridge to bring in provisions.

Rupert's spies informed him of Meldrum's concentration, and fearing a Parliamentary withdrawal, he paraded his men at 2 a.m. and led the van of his Horse 'upon the spur' to overtake them. He swung east off the Fosse Way, through Balderton, and saw Meldrum's Horse on Beacon Hill. The Parliamentarian cavalry fell back, under orders from Meldrum, and allowed Rupert to occupy the feature, from which he could see the Roundhead Foot drawn up about the Spittal, and four great bodies of Horse awaiting him on the lower slopes of the hill.

Still fearing that Meldrum intended to retreat, the Prince decided to make a holding attack, although half his cavalry and his Foot were not yet in sight. He drew up his force in two lines, with his own regiment, about 500 strong, on the right and his lifeguard under his own command on the left. Major-General George Porter's regiment was in reserve. The Parliamentarian Horse did not much outnumber the Cavaliers, for Meldrum had sent the Derby Horse into the island to cover a detachment that was building a fort. Colonel Francis Thornhagh commanded the right wing of their Horse and Colonel Edward Rossiter the left.

The battle began about 9 a.m. The fighting was particularly bitter on the Roundhead left where Rossiter, doubling his files so that his men were six deep, charged the flank of the right-hand Royalist squadron. Captain Clement Martin of Rupert's regiment, whose troop was part of the next 'division' or squadron, led his men to the rescue, and by his intervention Rossiter was beaten off, but not before he had driven the Cavaliers back up the hill to their reserves. Charles Gerard's horse fell as he led a counter-charge and he was wounded and taken prisoner. On the other wing the Lincolnshire Horse fled at the outset, leaving the Nottinghamshire men to fight it out.

Prince Rupert himself had pierced deep into the ranks of the Roundheads, his troopers shouting their field-word 'King and Queen', while the Parliamentarians raised the cry of 'Religion'. Set upon by a host of assailants he laid about him with his sword. When a Roundhead trooper laid hold of the Prince's collar,

Sir William Neale sliced the man's hand off. Sir Richard Crane broke clean through the remnants of the Roundhead right wing, pursuing the routed troopers to the works about Spittal. Rossiter, however, managed to fall back to the Spittal in good order. This fierce cavalry action was followed by a lull during which Rupert's infantry came up. While Meldrum's Horse fell back across the bridge of boats into the island, part of the 'Irish' Foot under Tillier made a detour and, supported by detachments of cavalry, fell upon the north-east side of Meldrum's position, trying to capture the bridge of boats. Tillier soon found the Roundheads' position too strong for him and fell back out of range of Meldrum's guns.

Hearing from a prisoner that the Roundheads had only victuals for another two days, the Prince decided to starve rather than storm them. Meldrum was hemmed in, with Tillier to the north-east, Newark itself to the south-west, and Rupert to the south-east, and the Prince now completed his discomfiture by sending part of Byron's garrison into the island to cut the lines of communication between the Spittal and Muskham Fort, whose defenders, after breaking down the bridge, departed without orders. These were not the only Parliamentarian troops to misbehave: the Norfolk Redcoats mutinied, and Meldrum sent a trumpet to sound a parley. The Roundheads were permitted to march away with their drums, colours, horses and swords, baggage and personal belongings, but all guns, ammunition, and firearms remained as a prize for the victor. Over 3,000 muskets, and 11 brass guns and 2 good mortars were among the pieces taken. One of the guns was 'a Basiliske of Hull, four yards long, shooting 32 [pound] ball'. The Roundheads had lost about 200 killed and the Cavaliers less than half that number.

Rupert had surprised his adversaries by the speed and certainty of his movements. Although he had more mounted men than Meldrum, the decisive engagement was won before half of them had come up. The Prince's hastily gathered army obeyed him without question, because of his military reputation and his royal blood. The factious Roundhead commanders, on the other hand, had, by their jealous wranglings, nearly broken the heart of 'the poor old gentleman', as a Parliamentary writer called Meldrum. Newark is not one of the better-known battles of the Civil Wars, but it was a quick and complete victory, and deserves to be rescued from oblivion. Prince Rupert's success enabled the garrison to hold out for another two years.[1]

Newcastle, meanwhile, having fallen back to Durham, contented himself for some time with trying to cut off the invaders' provisions, in which he met with considerable success. On 20 March, however, the Scots took a fort at South

---

[1] See Peter Young, 'The Royalist Army at the relief of Newark', *Journal of the Society for Army Historical Research*, 1952. A. C. Wood, *Nottinghamshire in the Civil War* (Oxford 1937), and R. Thoroton, *Antiquities of Nottinghamshire* (1677), are also useful; the latter contains the best Parliamentarian account, that of Lieutenant-Colonel Bury. *Prince Rupert's Raising of the Siege of Newark* (TT E. 39 (8)) is likewise interesting.

Shields, and surprised a detachment of cavalry at Chester-le-Street. Thus provoked, the Marquis decided to offer battle, and advanced on 23 March to Hilton, near Sunderland.

The Scots came out of their entrenchments around Sunderland, and took up a position on Bedwich Hill. Newcastle, try as he would, could not bring on a general engagement, but at 3 p.m. his Foot attacked the Scots on the hillside. The fight continued until dark, and there was shooting throughout the night. Next day the Scots fell back to Sunderland, and Newcastle drew off towards his own quarters. At this, the Scots attacked the Royalist rearguard with all their Horse. Sir Charles Lucas led his brigade to the support of the hard-pressed rearguard, and charged so well that he forced the entire body, some 3,000 strong, to hasten back to the cover of their artillery. Next day the Marquis again offered battle, but the Scots were not to be drawn, so the Royalists fell back to Durham, having lost some 250 men in the fighting, but having inflicted an estimated 1,000 casualties on the Scots.

Newcastle's efforts to contain the Scots were thus meeting with a measure of success. However, events to the rear gave him less cause for satisfaction. On 11 April the Fairfaxes stormed Selby, capturing John Belasyse and more than 3,000 prisoners. This disaster cut the main road south, and threatened York. Newcastle slipped away from Durham, and entered the stout walls of York on 18 April. He had with him rather less than 6,000 Foot and 5,000 Horse. Realising that cavalry would be of little use to him in a siege, he sent most of his Horse, under Goring[1] and Lucas to Newark, to harass the enemy's rear and join any possible relief attempt. The Scots had followed the Marquis south, linking up with the Fairfaxes at Tadcaster on the 20th, determined to lay siege to York.

[1] Goring, having spent nearly a year in Parliamentarian hands following his capture at Wakefield in May 1643, was exchanged in the spring of 1644.

Thirteen

THE OXFORD CAMPAIGN

At the beginning of April 1644 the Committee of Both Kingdoms had five main armies in the field, besides the local forces of Brereton, Massey and others. In the north, Lord Leven's Scots and Lord Fairfax's English were closing in on York, while the Earl of Manchester was soon to lay siege to Lincoln. In the south, Waller had just won his greatest victory at Cheriton (29 March) while Essex was preparing to take the field. The intervention of the Scots had tipped the scales against the King. In the north the Marquis of Newcastle was hard-pressed by Leven and Fairfax, though Prince Rupert, at Shrewsbury, intended to march to his relief. There was no Royalist army available to make head against Manchester. In the South Midlands Charles still held an extensive position – Oxford, Reading, Abingdon, Banbury, Wallingford, and Faringdon, and a ring of well-fortified garrisons – but in order to form a respectable field army he was compelled, after Cheriton, to absorb Hopton's army into his own.

In the west a small army, 6,000 strong, under Prince Maurice had been besieging Lyme since the middle of March. There was much despondency at the Royalist headquarters, and not without reason. Indeed, had the five Parliamentary armies been directed by a single commander of even ordinary capacity they might well have ended the war in the summer of 1644. But the Committee of Both Kingdoms, although it numbered Essex, Waller, Manchester and Cromwell among its members, was a far less effective instrument than the King's Council of War, which directed Royalist strategy. Its ablest soldiers were almost always absent in the field, and Sir Henry Vane and Oliver St John were thus left the dominant figures. The Cavaliers who discussed strategy at Charles's Council of War also executed its decisions. The Parliamentarian generals regarded the often ambiguous instructions of the Committee of Both Kingdoms as a basis for discussion rather than orders. Quick to complain when pay or recruits were not forthcoming, they were yet more quickly picqued when ordered to carry out operations they had not themselves devised.

On 6 April the Committee ordered Essex and Manchester to rendezvous at Aylesbury on the 19th and to move against the King. Waller would thus be able to advance into the west and deal with Maurice. This promising combination quickly came to grief. Essex, who had no gift for seeing the war as a whole, took a gloomy view of the situation, and on 8 April wrote, not to the Committee, but to the remnants of the House of Lords, saying: 'Newark is not taken, Lincolnshire is lost, Gloucester is unsupplied, and the last week there was but a step between us and death, and – what is worse – slavery.' After protesting his fidelity to the cause he continued in plaintive strain: 'You have been pleased to reduce my army to 7,000 Foot and 3,000 Horse, when my Lord Manchester is allowed an army of 14,000 and receives £34,000 a month for the pay of it – since it is done by you I submit. . . .'[1] But in truth he was far from intending either to submit or cooperate.

Manchester, indeed, was ready to take the field, but with Rupert's recent success at Newark in mind, and with Lincoln still in the hands of the Cavaliers, he felt, not without reason, that it was his duty to guard the Eastern Association. Though Rupert at Shrewsbury had, as it happened, not the least intention of attacking Manchester, the Earl was not to know that.

19 April came and saw no rendezvous at Aylesbury. Nor had Waller been able to follow up his victory at Cheriton, for the City regiments had clamoured to return home and by 12 April Sir William was back with his wife at Farnham. Taking advantage of his withdrawal, the Dorset Cavaliers pounced on Wareham.

While the Parliamentarian senior commanders debated, the Royalist army prepared itself for the coming campaign. On 10 April the Oxford army rendezvoused on Aldbourne Chase, about five miles north-east of Marlborough. Sir Edward Walker, in his invaluable work, *His MAIESTIES Happy Progresse* states that 6,000 Foot and over 4,000 Horse were present. Richard Symonds, of the King's lifeguard of Horse, an eye-witness, puts the infantry at 5,000 and the cavalry at 'full 4,000', a total of 9,000. Charles was at the Aldbourne muster in person, though he returned to Oxford on the following day, in time to declare a recess for the Oxford Parliament, an assembly of Loyalist members of both Houses, which had sat since January. From Oxford, the situation looked bleak. At Lyme, Maurice was still held up by the future Admiral Blake, and with only the army around Oxford at his disposal Charles felt that he himself would be unable to hold his own. The danger seemed so great that he decided to send the Queen, who was expecting a baby, into the West Country, and on 17 April she set out for Exeter. The departure of the 'She-Generalissima', as she had once called herself, however sad for the King who loved and relied upon her, was an excellent thing from a military point of view, for she was a very poor strategist and had certainly used her influence against Rupert. No sooner was she gone than Charles wrote to his nephew summoning him to his side.

The Prince was quick to answer the summons, but he was intent none the less on marching to the relief of York, where Newcastle was now besieged. Rupert was at Oxford from 25 April to 5 May and during that time expounded his

[1] *Lords Journals*, Vol. VI, p. 505.

strategic plan, which was, initially, adopted. Reinforced garrisons were to be retained in Oxford, Wallingford, Abingdon, Reading and Banbury. A good body of Horse was to remain about Oxford, free to manoeuvre in support of the garrisons. The Parliamentarian armies would not be sufficient to overrun this extensive complex of fortresses, nor, it was considered, could they safely push farther west, leaving it to their rear. This would permit Maurice, reinforced by some of the King's cavalry, to complete the conquest of the west, while Rupert himself went to the aid of Newcastle. Such was Rupert's plan.

Charles did not adhere to this excellent scheme for long. Soon after his nephew's return to Shrewsbury, the King decided to abandon Reading, a decision which can probably be attributed to Lord Forth, who, despite Cheriton, was evidently in high favour. The entire army quartered around Reading while the town's fortifications were 'slighted', and, on 18 May the Royalists relinquished the town, which was entered by the Parliamentarian troops on the following day. Without the Foot at Reading, the King would not have had a marching army in 1644. Thus, unless he intended to make another push towards London, he had to give up Reading. From Reading, the Royalist army marched, via Compton, to Wantage, where it remained until the 24th, when the Foot moved to Abingdon, while the Horse quartered around Faringdon.

The Parliamentarians, meanwhile, were on the move. By 17 April Essex's army was at Henley-on-Thames, while on the same day Waller's army marched from its old base at Farnham to Bagshot, where it joined the London brigade under Major-General Harrington. While the army remained at Bagshot for the weekend, Waller rode to Henley, to confer with Essex, whose advanced elements were in progress of occupying Reading. The easy capture of this important town was a useful success for Essex. By withdrawing its garrison, however, the King had added a vital 3,000 men to his army. Nevertheless, the town's abandonment must have had an unhappy effect on Royalist morale, as too did the withdrawal, a week later, of the Abingdon garrison. This consisted of a single regiment, that of Sir Lewis Dyve, too weak to hold the town, yet large enough for its loss in a possible storm to have been a severe blow. The decision to abandon the place was, therefore, quite correct – though the muddled way in which the withdrawal was implemented reflects badly on the Royalist chain of command. Since it was so near Oxford, it may be that the Cavaliers should have made an effort to hold Abingdon, but it must be remembered that, unlike Wallingford, Banbury and Faringdon, it had no medieval castle as a nucleus for its defence.

On other fronts, fortune continued to frown on the Royalists. Manchester had stormed Lincoln on 6 May and Maurice was still held up before Lyme. On the 24th Massey took Malmesbury, and Essex entered Abingdon on the 26th. The same day the King, alarmed for the safety of Bristol, sent Hopton to secure that city. Next day a Council of War at Oxford decided not to give battle against the combined armies of Essex and Waller, but to post the King's army in such a way as to keep the communications of Oxford open on one side. Then, if the two Parliamentary commanders should separate, the Royalists would be strong enough to attack each in turn with a good chance of defeating them in detail. This sound plan was evidently devised by Lord Forth. It can hardly have been coincidence that he was created Earl of Brentford on the very day this Council was held. Accordingly, the Royalist Foot marched through Oxford to quarter in villages to its north, while the Horse crossed the Thames at Newbridge, and quartered around Cassington. Strong patrols watched the Thames and the Cherwell. This did not prevent Essex crossing the Thames at Sandford ferry, and setting up his headquarters at Islip. This done, Essex tried unsuccessfully to force a passage over the Cherwell.

Waller, however, had more luck. His army marched, via Basingstoke, to Abingdon, and, on 1 June, managed to secure a crossing over the Thames at Newbridge. This produced a flurry of alarm in Oxford, and there were even suggestions that the King should surrender. When, on 3 June, there was talk of this in the Council of War, Charles, with praiseworthy resolution, said that 'possibly he might be found in the hands of the Earl of Essex, but he would be dead first'.[1] This firm resolve was backed by determined action. A strong detachment made a 'grimace towards Abingdon',[2] inducing Waller to fall back from Newbridge. On the evening of the 3rd, Charles, at the head of 5,000 Horse and 2,500 musketeers, marched via Port Meadow, Wolvercote and Yarnton, slipping across the Evenlode at Handborough Bridge, to reach Bourton-on-the-Water on the night of 4 June. The rest of the Foot, about 3,500 men, remained in Oxford, together with all the King's heavy guns.

Essex and Waller gave chase, but the King managed to stay ahead of them, and entered Worcester on the 6th to an enthusiastic reception. On the same day, a meeting of some moment occurred. Essex and Waller, whose latent animosity had doubtless not been improved by an unsuccessful pursuit through pouring rain, met, probably at Chipping Norton,[3] and resolved to part company. Essex determined to relieve Lyme, and accordingly left the pursuit of the King to his detested colleague, Waller. By the time the horror-struck Committee of Both Kingdoms issued an order countermanding Essex's about-turn, it was too late. Essex's division, a strategic blunder of the first order, was an unexpected piece of good fortune for the Royalists. One officer observed in retrospect that Royalist victory in the campaign 'would have been a harder for us, had they kept together, as it was admired they did not'.[4]

Though Waller must have been disheartened by Essex's action, he remained determined 'to follow the King wherever an army can march'.[5] On 10 June he

---

[1] Clarendon, op. cit., Vol. IV, p. 485.
[2] Digby to Rupert, 8 June 1644, Warburton, op. cit., Vol. II, pp. 415–16.
[3] See Margaret Toynbee and Peter Young, Cropredy Bridge 1644 (Kineton 1970), p. 49.
[4] Atkyns and Gwyn, op. cit., p. 54.
[5] Calendar of State Papers, Domestic Series chenceforth, CSPD), 1644, p. 214.

took Sudeley Castle, Lord Chandos's seat, and a threat to communications with Gloucester. Charles's army remained in Worcester for six days, recovering from their forced march from Oxford. Waller reached Evesham on 10 June, and the King withdrew to Bewdley two day later, so quartering his army as to make Waller suspect a retirement on Shrewsbury. Instead, Charles doubled back to Worcester on the 15th, and marched through Evesham to Broadway on the following day, taking care to break down the bridges *en route*. Having thus eluded Waller, the King rendezvoused at Witney with the Oxford garrison, and moved on to Buckingham, where he halted for several days, concentrating his army and re-supplying it with ammunition.

Waller, having lost contact with his quarry, arrived at Gloucester on 20 June. Essex, meanwhile, had managed to relieve Lyme, thereby persuading the Committee of Both Kingdoms to sanction his advance into the south-west. The Committee, though, feared that the King would use Buckingham as a springboard for a descent on the Eastern Association, and ordered Waller to intervene. Sir William consequently marched eastwards and by 28 June was at Hanwell, near Banbury. Charles, at Brackley in Northamptonshire, received intelligence of this, and, on the morning of the 28th, set out for Banbury.

Towards mid-morning the Royalists concentrated just north-east of the town, and, when the weather cleared, they could discern Waller's army drawn up near Hanwell Castle, nearly two miles west of the River Cherwell. Waller managed to beat his opponents in a race for Crouch Hill, an imposing feature one mile south-west of Banbury, and took up a position at its foot. The King's army established itself on Grimsbury Hill, and a detachment posted to cover the western side of Banbury successfully repulsed a Parliamentarian probing attack.

THE BATTLE OF CROPREDY BRIDGE, 29 JUNE

The soldiers of neither army got much sleep that night. Charles realised that Waller would not be drawn from his strong position, and, at about 8 a.m., set off northwards towards Daventry, hoping for a better opportunity to bring Waller to battle. The Earl of Brentford led the van. The King was with the main body, while the cavalry brigades of the Earls of Cleveland and Northampton, with 1,000 commanded Foot under Colonel Anthony Thelwall, brought up the rear. No sooner had the King's army set off than Waller, too, began to march north, on a parallel course, along the Banbury–Southam road. The two armies were moving through rolling countryside, initially only a mile apart, and in full view of each other. Waller had a slight numerical advantage for, though his 5,000 or so Horse were equally matched by the King's cavalry, he had well over 4,000 Foot to Charles's 3,500. When Waller reached Bourton Hill, three miles north of Banbury, he halted and surveyed the actions of the Royalists. Waller's eye for the ground had, as usual, not failed him, for on the

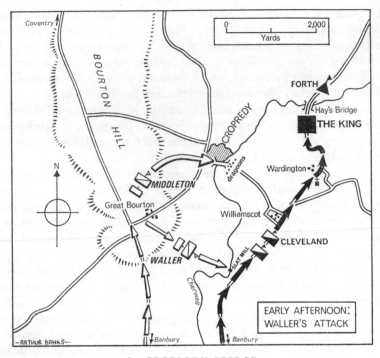

9   CROPREDY BRIDGE

hill he had, as *Mercurius Aulicus* pointed out, 'the advantage of springs and bogs before his front, and both on his flanks and back strong hedges'.[1] From this excellent position the Parliamentarian commander could see the King's army nearing the village of Cropredy.

At Cropredy a small road, linking the Banbury–Southam and Banbury–Daventry roads, crosses the Cherwell by a stone bridge, alongside which was a ford. A good mile south, at Slat Mill, was another ford. North of Cropredy the river swings north-east, and is crossed by the Banbury–Daventry road at Hays Bridge, some two miles from Cropredy.

As the King's army approached Cropredy, a party of dragoons was sent forward to hold the bridge and thus safeguard the army's flank. No sooner had this been done than word was received that 300 Parliamentarian Horse were two miles to the north, intending to join Waller. The Royalist advanced guard was ordered forward towards Hays Bridge to intercept this party, and the King's main body followed as best it could. Unfortunately, this acceleration at the head of the column initially passed unnoticed at the rear, and a gap of about 1½ miles opened between the Royalist centre and the rear-guard. Waller, stationed two miles away on the Royalist flank, was perfectly placed to observe the involun-

[1] *Mercurius Aulicus*, p. 1055.

ary extension of the King's column; moreover, he was not the man to let such an opportunity slip by unexploited.

Waller made a rapid appreciation, and decided to seize the Cherwell crossings and cut off the Royalist rear. He sent Lieutenant-General John Middleton, with two regiments of Horse,[1] and nine companies of Foot, against Cropredy Bridge, while he himself, with 1,000 men, moved across the ford at Slat Mill. Middleton's Horse were immediately successful. They easily drove off the Royalist dragoons covering the bridge, crossed the river, and chased the rear of the Royalist main body as far as Hays Bridge, where some capable Cavalier had turned over a carriage and stationed musketeers behind it, checking their advance.

Waller, meanwhile, had crossed the Cherwell at Slat Mill. Northampton acted quickly, and swung the four regiments of his brigade against the advancing Parliamentarians, driving them back across the ford. Cleveland, commanding the leading brigade of the rear-guard, saw the situation around Cropredy Bridge, realised there was no time to wait for orders from Wilmot, formed up his brigade, and charged, giving his men the Royalist field-word 'Hand and Sword'. Cleveland's onslaught threw Middleton's infantry and part of the Horse into disorder. The Earl then rallied his men, making a stand near a great ash tree beneath which the King had dined not half an hour previously.[2] Charles had by now realised the threat to his rear, and halted his main body north of Hays Bridge, sending back Lord Bernard Stuart and the lifeguard to drive off those of Middleton's Horse who were threatening Cleveland's right flank. Stuart was successful, and this body fell back towards Cropredy, only to find their infantry in disorder and the remainder of their cavalry beaten. Then they in turn were charged by Cleveland, while Wilmot drove into their left flank. There was a brisk mêlée, in which Wilmot was wounded and temporarily captured, but the Parliamentarian Horse were routed and thrown back over Cropredy Bridge. Their artillery, drawn up in the fields just east of the bridge, was overrun by the exultant Royalist troopers. Colonel Wemyss was captured, and with him all his fourteen pieces of ordnance,[3] a loss which Waller found 'extremely wounding'.

With the savage repulse of both prongs of the attack, Waller retired to his position on Bourton Hill, leaving the dragoons and Foot holding Cropredy Bridge and the ford at Slat Mill. Charles had by now marched his main body south, taking up a position at Williamscote, just west of the Banbury–Daventry road, facing Waller's army. The action had commenced at about 11 a.m. and it was now about 3 p.m., leaving ample daylight for renewed fighting. The

Those of Sir Arthur Hesilrige and Colonel Jonas Vandruske.

The 'Wardington Ash' has twice been replaced by new trees, so the historic spot can still be identified.

Walker says that eleven guns were taken, together with '2 Barricadoes of wood drawn with wheels in each 7 small brass and leather guns charged with case shot'. *Mercurius Aulicus* enumerates fourteen captured pieces. Clarendon, op. cit., Vol. IV, p. 503, agrees with Walker.

King consequently threw troops against both Cropredy Bridge and Slat Mill, while his guns thudded out against Waller's lines on Bourton Hill. At Cropredy, a spirited defence by the Tower Hamlets regiment and the Kentish regiment, supported by two drakes, held the Cavaliers at bay, though at Slat Mill the Roundhead dragoons were driven off, and the Royalists seized a foothold on the west bank.

The main bodies of each army remained on the high ground, but towards evening the Royalists drew up below Slat Mill, and opened fire on the Roundhead cavalry on the hill near Bourton, forcing them to fall back in disorder, covered by the fire of Waller's remaining guns. It was probably at this juncture that some shots were deliberately fired at the King himself by cannon planted on the heights beyond the Cherwell, the cannoneers being shown their target 'by several perspective glasses', or so *Aulicus* alleged.

Charles, mindful that his foes were also his subjects, ordered Sir Edward Walker to visit Waller's army with 'a message of grace and pardon'.[1] Walker wisely sent a trumpeter to demand a safe-conduct before delivering the message, and Waller replied that he had no authority to negotiate with the King without Parliamentary consent. Despite this failure Charles had every reason to be satisfied with his day's work. His own losses had been slight, the only officers of distinction to fall being Colonel Sir William Boteler and Colonel Sir William Clerke, who were killed in Cleveland's second charge. Most Royalist accounts assert that no more than fourteen common soldiers were killed, though this seems an improbably low figure. Certainly, several officers and soldiers were wounded, and between sixty and eighty captured. Waller, on the other hand, lost about 700 men, a high proportion of whom were deserters. Most of his hapless gunners were cut down, and casualties in the Horse seem to have been quite heavy. The Parliamentarians had also lost several officer prisoners. Of these Wemyss was the most distinguished. He had previously been made master-gunner of England by Charles, who had the Scot brought before him and rebuked him for his treachery. 'Guid faith,' said Wemyss uneasily, 'my heart was always with your Majesty.' 'So is mine with the *States Committee*,' was *Mercurius*'s malicious comment.[2] Also taken were two lieutenant-colonels, one of whom was James Baker of Waller's own regiment of Foot. Several Parliamentarian colours were also captured.

Both armies remained in position throughout the following day. In the evening Charles received news that Major General Browne, who had left London on the 24th, was at Buckingham with 4,500 men. This persuaded Charles to leave the field, which he did the following morning. Fearing junction between Waller and Brown, the King marched westwards, reaching Evesham on the night of 3 July. After some indecision, worsened by conflicting reports of a major action near York, the Council of War determined to march

[1] Clarendon, op. cit., Vol. IV, p. 505.
[2] *Mercurius Aulicus*, p. 1056.

nto the west, to protect the Queen, who was at Exeter, having given birth to a daughter on 16 June. The army began its westwards march on 12 July; that night the King received Rupert's despatch announcing the disaster of Marston Moor.

As the Royalists marched towards the Earl of Essex in the West Country, Waller was hard put to prevent the total disintegration of his army. On 2 July he joined Browne at Towcester, his march being 'extremely plagued by the mutinies of the City Brigade, who are grown to that height of disorder that I have no help to retain them, being come to their old song of home, home'.[1] Browne's men, furthermore, were in 'no very good temper'.[2] Within a few days the threadbare fabric split completely, and Browne's men mutinied, wounding him in the face during a scuffle. One of the City regiments deserted *en masse*, with its colours and the body of its colonel, who had died of sickness; most of the remaining Trained Band soldiers sloped off home as best they could. Waller had little choice but to retire southwards, and, leaving the wreckage of his army at Abingdon, a mournful Sir William entered London on 26 July. His defeat at Cropredy 'was much greater than it then appeared to be ... it even broke the heart of his army'.[3] It was with some accuracy that Waller wrote to the Committee of Both Kingdoms that 'an army compounded of these men will never go through with their service, and till you have an army merely your own that you may command, it is in a manner impossible to do anything of importance'.[4] His appeal was ultimately to be answered by the creation of the New Model Army, less than a year later.

[1] CSPD 1644, p. 301.
[2] Loc. cit.
[3] Clarendon, op. cit., Vol. IV, p. 506.
[4] CSPD 1644, p. 301.

Fourteen

THE MARSTON MOOR CAMPAIGN

It was on 22 April that the Earl of Leven and Lord Fairfax sat down before York. Prince Rupert knew well that he alone could relieve the Marquis, and he was determined not to be diverted from this object. Summoned to the aid of his uncle he had, as we have seen, laid down the strategy which, with some modification, was successfully followed in the Cropredy campaign. By 8 May he was back at his headquarters.

When on 16 May he set out from Shrewsbury on 'The York March', as the compiler of his *Journal* called it, he did not immediately direct his steps towards that city. He had as yet only 2,000 Horse and 6,000 Foot, including the remains of Byron's Anglo-Irish army, and such a force was not nearly enough for the work in hand. Accordingly the Prince decided to march by way of Lancashire, and to pick up reinforcements as he went.

On 25 May he appeared before Stockport, which was garrisoned by some 3,000 Parliamentarians. The defenders marched out to confront him, but were quickly beaten back by Colonel Henry Washington's dragoons, who drove them into the town in such disorder that the Prince and his Horse pressed in on their heels, and the town speedily fell. Hearing of the disaster, Colonel Alexander Rigby, who for eighteen weeks had been besieging the Countess of Derby in Lathom House, beat a retreat to Bolton, which he reached on the 27th. Bolton was celebrated, if not for the strength of its works, for the strength of its Puritanism. Rigby had little enough time to prepare the unwalled town for defence, for Rupert appeared on the following afternoon. Fighting well, Rigby's men repulsed the first assault, but the Earl of Derby led a break-in, and, in pouring rain, the Royalists surged into the town. They gave little quarter: 1,600 Roundheads fell that day. The town was plundered, and the local feud between Roman Catholic and Puritan made the struggle more than ordinarily bloody. Rigby himself learned the Royalist field-word, and, in the smoky, wet confusion, escaped by posing as a Royalist officer.

Encouraged by Rupert's success, the Lancashire Royalists flocked to join him. On 30 May he was reinforced by Goring and Lucas, with 5,000 Horse and 800 Foot, and with his sizeable army marched to Liverpool, where he arrived on

June. The garrison, under Colonel Moore, made a stout defence, and many of them had escaped by sea by the time Rupert entered the town on 11 June. With Lancashire, for the time being, secured, and his army recruited to some 4,000 men, the Prince was ready to march for York.

Far away in the south the King too was thinking of York. With Digby looking over one shoulder and Wilmot over the other he took up his pen and wrote to his nephew:

If York be lost I shall esteem *my crown little less*; unless supported by your sudden march to me; and a miraculous conquest in the South, before the effects of their Northern power can be found here. But if York be relieved, and you beat the rebels' army of Both Kingdoms, which are before it; then (but not otherwise) I may possibly make a shift (upon the defensive) to spin out time until you come to assist me. Wherefore I command and conjure you, by the duty and affection which I know you bear me, that all new enterprises laid aside, you immediately march, according to your first intention, with all your force to the relief of York.[1]

Charles wrote this fatal order on 14 July, from Tickenhill, having just eluded the armies of Essex and Waller. He was under considerable mental pressure, and his letter was ambiguously phrased and insufficiently thought out. The forthright Lord Culpeper, who was not present when it was written, hearing that it had been sent, said to the King: 'Why, then, before God you are undone, for upon this peremptory order he will fight, whatever comes on't.' Rupert carried this letter about him to his dying day; and well he might.

Behind the walls of beleaguered York, Newcastle held out resolutely. He had got his cavalry away on the night of 22 April, retaining about 300 Horse with his garrison of 4,500 Foot. Leven had 16,000 Scots, and Fairfax 5,000 Foot and Horse, before the city. The Earl of Manchester, having stormed Lincoln on May, joined the Allies before York on 3 June, bringing their numbers up to something like 30,000. Newcastle, no doubt prompted by Eythin, instituted rationing within the city; all staple food was put in a central store, and the garrison and inhabitants were issued with a pint of beans, an ounce of butter and a penny loaf each day.[2] On 8 June Newcastle wrote to Leven, expressing his astonishment that the latter 'hath so near beleaguered the city on all sides, made batteries against it',[3] without summoning it. Leven repaired this breach of military etiquette at once, affirming his intention to reduce the city 'to the obedience due to the King and Parliament'.[4] This was followed by an offer of

Quoted in Peter Young, *Marston Moor* (Kineton 1970), pp. 86–7.
See Peter Wenham, *The Great and Close Siege of York* (Kineton 1970), p. 15.
Letter of Newcastle to Leven, 8 June 1644, in *A Continuation of True Intelligence from the English and Scottish Forces . . .*, TT E. 51.
Loc. cit.

honourable terms, which Newcastle, playing for time, did not reject until th 15th.

There had already been some skirmishing in the suburbs, and on 16 June th first major assault was launched against York. A mine was exploded unde St Mary's Tower, and an attempt made to storm King's Manor. The mine one of three dug, was exploded prematurely, on the orders of Lawrenc Crawford, Manchester's youthful major-general, either because it was in dange of being flooded, or because Crawford wanted the glory of a successful assault Naturally, as Fairfax and Leven had not been informed, the attack was launche without diversion or assistance, and was repulsed with the loss of about 200 men The honours of the day went to Newcastle's men, though they lost Colonc Philip Byron, one of Lord Byron's five martial brothers.

So tight was the Parliamentarian cordon around York that 'a messenge could hardly pass'. To compensate for this, the Cavaliers made fire signal from the Minster, which were answered from Pontefract. The effectiveness c these signals must have been limited indeed, for news of the approach of th relieving force failed to get through to the garrison.[1] Rupert had marched fror Liverpool to Preston, which capitulated without a struggle. He then crosse the Pennines, reaching Skipton Castle on 26 June, where he was joined by strong contingent from Cumberland and Westmorland. Here he halted, t give his men time to put their arms in order, and, no doubt, for the Lancashir levies to catch up with their pike and musket drill, while he sent messengers t York. On 29 June he advanced again, with his usual rapidity, and on the 30t reached Knaresborough, fourteen miles west of the city.

The Parliamentarian commanders were themselves expecting reinforcement in the shape of Sir John Meldrum and the Earl of Denbigh, and hoped, wit their help, to be able to face Rupert without raising the siege. Rupert, howeve easily out-distanced his rivals, and his imminence compelled the Allied genera to lift the siege to meet the threat. Leaving their siege guns and ammunition i the trenches before York, the Allies marched out to a position north-west c Long Marston, covering against an attack from either Knaresborough c Wetherby. On the morning of 1 June a strong body of Royalist cavalr appeared, persuading the Allied generals to form up for battle. But there wa to be no battle that day, for the main body of the relieving force crossed th River Ure at Boroughbridge, and the River Swale at Thornton Bridge, whil the anxious Allies were still drawn up on Marston Moor. From Thornto Bridge, Rupert swung south-west. At Poppleton, some three miles north-we of York, a detachment of Manchester's dragoons, guarding a bridge of boat were surprised, and the bridge was captured intact. Rupert himself did not ente York, but spent the night in the Forest of Galtres. However, Goring, with detachment of Horse, pushed on and relieved the city. The relief march wa by any standards, a remarkable piece of generalship, greatly to the Prince's credi

[1] See *The Diary of Sir Henry Slingsby, Bart*... (London 1836, ed. by D. Parsons), pp. 110–1

With York relieved, Rupert immediately sent out cavalry to reconnoitre the Allied position, with a view to launching an attack next day. Considering that the Allies outnumbered him by perhaps 28,000 to 18,000, Rupert's eagerness is difficult to understand. The King's peremptory letter was not in itself reason for engaging in battle in such unequal terms. It is more probable that Rupert, technically senior to Newcastle, wished to emphasise his rank, and to take command of both armies. The Allies, indeed, took pains to compel Rupert to give battle – as if any such compulsion was necessary. They resolved to march south-west, towards Cawood and Tadcaster, so as to cover Meldrum's approach, and cut off supplies from the East and West Ridings. Consequently, on the morning of Tuesday 2 July, the Allied armies were marching towards Tadcaster, with a strong rear-guard, under Sir Thomas Fairfax, on the ridge above Long Marston.

THE BATTLE OF MARSTON MOOR, 2 JULY

Rupert had some difficulty in persuading Newcastle and Eythin to fall in with his plans. The first consequence of this was that, while Rupert's men were on the move by 4 a.m. on the morning of 2 July, Newcastle did not appear till 9 a.m., and even then without his Foot. This was the first opportunity for personal contact between Rupert and the Marquis and it was far from auspicious. Newcastle very sensibly pointed out that the Royalists had little to gain by an immediate battle, for the Allies might well divide it left to their own devices. He also expected a sizeable reinforcement, under Colonel Sir Robert Clavering, to reach him within the next few days. This force, some 2,000 strong, was in fact on the way. Rupert countered that he had positive instructions from the King ordering him to fight. This seems to have overcome the Marquis's objections, though Rupert was dissuaded from making a sudden descent on the Allied rear-guard.

Indeed, the time for any such manoeuvre was long past. It was now about 10 a.m. and Marston Moor was filling up with troops, as the Allies retraced their steps, abandoning their march on Tadcaster. The returning troops were marshalled just south of the Long Marston–Tockwith road, on rising ground. Rupert's position lay due north, on the low, flat ground on the other side of the road. A 'wide and deep' ditch, running more or less parallel with the road, formed the front of Rupert's position. This ditch can still be traced. It may have been deeper then. Now it is not much of an obstacle and indeed is non-existent at the right of the line of Rupert's Foot. Behind this, the ground was open, and scattered with furze and bushes. Immediately in front of the Allied infantry was a large cornfield, but the ground as a whole was very little enclosed. To the rear of the Royalist centre lay White Sike Close, a small enclosure, and, somewhat farther back, Wilstrop Wood. The tracks on the battlefield were poor apart from the Long Marston–Tockwith road they were narrow, rutted and primitive in the extreme. The soil was, in the main, clay, and the going tended

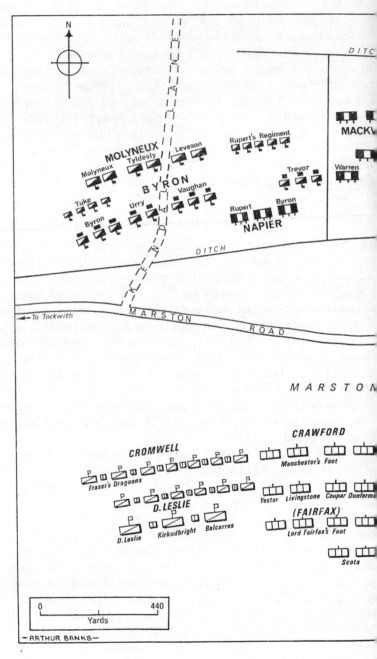

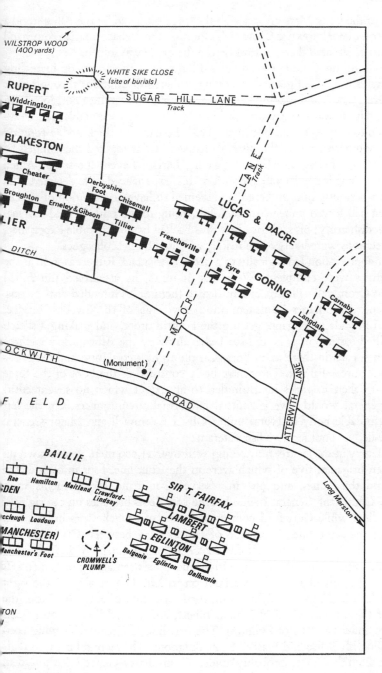

WILSTROP WOOD
(400 yards)

WHITE SIKE CLOSE
(site of burials)

RUPERT

Widdrington

SUGAR HILL LANE
Track

BLAKESTON

Cheater

LANE
Track

Derbyshire
Foot

LUCAS & DACRE

Broughton

Chisemall

Erneley & Gibson

Tillier

LIER

Frescheville

DITCH

Eyre

GORING

Carnaby

Langdale

OCKWITH

M
O
O
R

(Monument)

FIELD

ROAD

ATTERWITH LANE

Long Marston

BAILLIE

Rae   Hamilton   Maitland   Crawford-
Lindsay

SDEN

SIR T. FAIRFAX

ccleugh   Loudoun

LAMBERT

MANCHESTER)

EGLINTON

anchester's Foot

CROMWELL'S
PLUMP

Balgonie   Eglinton   Dalhousie

TON

MIES DEPLOYED

to be soft in the Long Marston area. On the ridge occupied by the Allies stood a group of trees, later known as Cromwell's Plump – the Parliamentarian command post was to be situated there, at least before the battle was joined.

As the morning passed, Cromwell's Plump was the scene of increasing activity, with the Allied generals scanning Rupert's dispositions through their 'perspective glasses', and making haste to get their own men into position along the ridge. The Royalist army cannot have looked very formidable, for Newcastle's Whitecoats were still not in the field. Perhaps the thick hedge running along the southern edge of the ditch to Rupert's front masked the thinness of his array. Nevertheless, as Alexander Leslie, Earl of Leven, the senior Allied general, examined the Royalist position, his experienced eye detected that Rupert was seriously outnumbered, and seemed to have no intention of attacking. Leven had served under Gustav Adolf, rising to the rank of field-marshal in the Swedish army; his seniority was thus backed by considerable experience, and his decisions were likely to be readily accepted by his colleagues.

Leven's appreciation led logically to a decision to attack Rupert as soon as the Allied armies were complete. With this in mind, he assembled the Allied generals at Cromwell's Plump, and informed them of his intended dispositions. Major-General Sir James Lumsden, another veteran of the Swedish service, rode from brigade to brigade, getting the Foot in order, and making a sketch of the Allied formation as he did so. Leven drew up the Allied army in three great bodies, each in three main lines. On the right were Horse and dragoons under Sir Thomas Fairfax. The centre body consisted of the Foot of the three armies with their brigades intermingled to an extent which no seventeenth-century general would have permitted in normal circumstances. On the left was a formidable body of Horse under Oliver Cromwell and Major-General David Leslie, yet another Swedish veteran.

The infantry in the centre, numbering well over 11,000 men, were drawn up in fourteen brigades, five of which were in the front line, four in each of the second and third lines, and one in reserve. Command arrangements were complex. Lieutenant-General Baillie led the two Scots brigades on the right of the front line, while Crawford commanded two of Manchester's brigades on the left of the same line. A brigade of Fairfax's lay between Crawford and Baillie. The second line was entirely Scots, under Lumsden. A Scots brigade formed the centre of the third line, with Manchester's remaining brigade on its right, and two brigades of Fairfax's Foot on its left. The cavalry on the right wing, under Sir Thomas Fairfax, comprised two lines of English Horse, the second of them under Colonel John Lambert, and a third line of three Scots regiments under the Earl of Eglinton. The first line of Cromwell's wing consisted of English Horse and Fraser's Scots dragoons. The second line, two regiments of English Horse, probably under Commissary-General Vermuyden, was supported by a third line of Scots Horse under David Leslie. The guns of the Allied army numbered between thirty and forty, and were probably posiioned between the infantry regiments of the front line.[1] In all, the Allied armies contained something like 28,000 men.

The Allies, summoned by gallopers from their march on Tadcaster, took a considerable time to draw up on the ridge above Marston Moor. Rupert's deployment was, however, far from rapid, for, though the Prince's own army was in the field by early morning, Newcastle's Whitecoats did not appear until mid-afternoon.[2] There may have been something approaching a mutiny within the city, occasioned by the question of arrears of pay, and when the Marquis's foot did at last appear, neither they nor Lord Eythin, who rode at their head, were in particularly good humour. Eythin at once fell out with Rupert. Upon being shown a plan of the latter's intended disposition, he muttered, 'By God, sir, it is very fine in the paper, but there is no such thing in the field'.[3] He followed this sour comment with a tactless reference to Rupert's capture at Lemgo in 1638. 'Sir,' he snapped, 'your forwardness lost us the day in Germany, where yourself was taken prisoner.'[4]

The belated arrival of Newcastle's troops permitted Rupert to put the finishing touches to his deployment. His right wing, under Lord Byron, assisted by Sir John Urry, major-general of Rupert's Horse, comprised 2,000 cavalry and 500 musketeers, drawn up in two lines. The musketeers were split up into platoons of fifty, and placed between the regiments of Horse in the first line. This Swedish practice was adopted by the Allied army as well. Byron's second line contained Prince Rupert's regiment and a brigade under Lord Molyneux, who commanded the line as a whole. In the centre stood the infantry of both armies. Eythin may have been put in command of this body, with the two sergeant-major-generals, Henry Tillier and Sir Francis Mackworth, commanding the infantry of Rupert's and Newcastle's armies respectively. The Royalist foot were drawn up in twenty-two bodies or divisions, whose average strength is unlikely to have exceeded 500.

Detached to the right front, covering the junction of Byron's wing with the centre, perhaps as a 'Forlorn Hope' to break up the enemy's onslaught, and perhaps to guard a point in the ditch where it was not much of an obstacle, was a brigade of two strong regiments,[5] doubtless commanded by Colonel Thomas Napier. The remainder of the Foot were drawn up in two lines, with a

It is, as usual, difficult to establish the exact number of guns present, or to pinpoint their location. The Scots army had sixty-eight pieces of artillery, but not all these were brought into England, and some of the heavier pieces were undoubtedly too cumbersome for field service. Sir Bernard de Gomme's excellent plan, now in the British Museum Library, gives no clue as to the dispositions of the guns on either side.

Prince Rupert's Diary, in the Wiltshire County Record Office, says 2 p.m.; Sir Hugh Cholmley puts it two hours later. The relevant passages of Rupert's Diary are quoted in Peter Young's Marston Moor, pp. 212–14.

Bodleian Library, Clarendon MSS., No. 1805, III, p. 376.

Cholmley's account, in the English Historical Review, Vol. V, 1890, p. 347.

Prince Rupert's Bluecoats and Lord Byron's regiment.

third line to the rear of the right centre. Sir William Blakiston's cavalry brigade perhaps 600 Horse, was posted close behind the centre of the second line, with the four divisions comprising the partial third line to its right rear.

The Royalist left wing consisted of 2,100 northern Horse under their general Lord Goring, and their lieutenant-general, Sir Charles Lucas. Like Byron Goring had 500 musketeers interlined with the cavalry of his front line. Sir Richard Dacre's brigade, 800 strong, formed Goring's second line, probably led by Lucas. Rupert had a reserve of some 700 Horse under his own hand, as well as acting as escort to the Marquis of Newcastle. Part of this reserve was Rupert's lifeguard, leading one to suppose that the Prince wisely considered his post to be in the rear of his centre.[1] Presumably, Rupert's sixteen pieces of ordnance were deployed in the centre.[2] Rupert probably had rather more than 17,000 men under his command, of whom 6,000 or more were mounted Allied numerical superiority, particularly in cavalry, was marked.

While the armies deployed there was some skirmishing, with Rupert' cavalry feeling forward on the Allied left. This move was discouraged by a few roundshot, one of which killed Captain Roger Houghton, the first of the many Royalist casualties that day. Rupert's men, in the field since morning, no doubt ate what provisions were in their knapsacks, and wondered why they had marched out so early. Rupert seems to have decided to remain in the field all night, and to attack the next day. He informed Newcastle of this, and the Marquis thereupon retired to his coach for a quiet pipe of tobacco. The Royalists were thus caught unprepared when, on Leven's signal,[3] the Allied army Horse, Foot and dragoons, began to move swiftly down the gently descending slope towards the hedge.

As the Allies advanced, a sudden rainstorm, one of several that day, swept the field. This must have extinguished many of the matches of the Royalist musketeers lining the ditch, who were presented with the awesome spectacle of the Allied centre coming through the cornfield at a 'running march'. The advancing infantry was received with a volley of musketry and a salvo from the four drakes in the ditch, but, after a brief contest, they crossed the obstacle and engaged the Royalist centre. On the Allied right, however, things went less well. Fairfax' cavalry charged only with difficulty owing to ditches and bushes, and were met by a galling fire from Goring's musketeers before coming to handstroke with the Royalist Horse. Fairfax rallied 400 of his men and managed to defeat the left wing of Goring's front line, which he pursued 'a good way towards York'.

[1] See C. H. Firth, 'Marston Moor', *Transactions of the Royal Historical Society*, Vol. XII 1898, p. 34.

[2] Much of the Royalist artillery had been left in York. See Wenham, op. cit., pp. 81–2.

[3] Probably a signal gun; too few officers possessed watches to enable an attack to be synchronised without some visual or audible signal.

[4] Sir Thomas Fairfax, *A Short Memorial of the Northern Actions* . . ., printed in *Stuart Tracts 1603–1695* (Westminster 1903), pp. 392–7; reprinted in Peter Young, *Marston Moor*, pp. 240–5.

Sir Thomas returned to find that Lambert, who had led the second line forward rather more to the left, was in trouble. Some of the Roundhead troopers, finding the combat too hot for their liking, wheeled about and fled, and Colonel Charles Fairfax, Sir Thomas's brother, was deserted by his men and mortally wounded. Sir Thomas himself had his cheek laid open by a sword cut; the captain of his troop was shot in the arm, and his cornet had both hands cut, maiming him for life. The three Scots regiments which made up Fairfax's third line, fought well but were roughly handled and forced back. Many of Goring's troopers hurtled off after the fugitives, or plundered the baggage, but Lucas managed to keep a good body under his hand, and with these he prepared to assault the right flank of the Allied infantry, laid bare by the defeat of Fairfax's Horse.

On the Allied left, Cromwell managed to get across the ditch, aided by Fraser's dragoons who cleared part of the hedge and ditch of musketeers. He also profited by the discomfiture of Napier's brigade, which Crawford's infantry had driven back. Byron, never the ablest of tacticians, advanced to meet Cromwell rather too early, masking the fire of his own musketeers and losing the advantage of the ground.[1] After a brief struggle, in which Cromwell himself was wounded, Byron's first line[2] was driven from the field.

Prince Rupert had been dismounted, having his supper, when the Allied armies advanced. He mounted in an instant, and surveyed the scene: a swift glance showed that his left wing was victorious and his centre holding well, but the condition of Byron's wing gave reason for serious concern. Consequently, at the head of his lifeguard and Sir Edward Widdrington's cavalry brigade, Rupert set off for the threatened flank. He galloped forward through a cloud of fugitives, including some of his own regiment of Horse. 'Swounds,' he yelled 'do you run, follow me.' With this, he charged Cromwell's Horse. At the time, Cromwell was probably having his wound dressed, and his men were commanded by the fiery Crawford, who had come across from Manchester's Foot. Scoutmaster-General Lionel Watson, whose account of the battle[3] is one of the most valuable, describes how 'Cromwell's own division had a hard pull of it; for they were charged by Rupert's bravest men both in front and flank; they stood at the sword's point a pretty while, hacking one another, but at last (it so

[1] In normal circumstances – a cavalry versus cavalry contest on flat ground – Byron would of course have been perfectly correct in moving forward to meet the oncoming charge. In this instance, however, his action is questionable. Rupert had deliberately posted him behind rough ground, and had interleaved his squadrons with musketeers, intending to compel the enemy to struggle across the difficult terrain, and sustain a volley of musketry, before coming to handstroke. By advancing to meet Cromwell, Byron threw away the advantage of the ground and lost the benefit of his musketeers.
[2] It seems likely that Byron's second line was still intact when Rupert brought up his reserves to counter-attack.
[3] Leonard Watson, *A more Exact Relation of the late Battel Neer York* . . ., TT E. 100 (12). Reprinted in Peter Young, *Marston Moor*, pp. 227–32.

pleased God) he brake through them. . . .' The intervention of David Leslie with his three Scots regiments was decisive, but the Cavaliers put up a stout resistance, 'coming to a close fight with the sword, and standing like an iron wall, so that they were not easily broken. . . .'[1] Rupert, separated from his life-guard, cut down several of the enemy, but was compelled to conceal himself in a beanfield while the rout swept by. Sir John Urry did his best to rally the fugitives, but as dark fell the bulk of Rupert's Horse spurred off towards the walls of York.

While Rupert had been involved in the cavalry combat on the Royalist right, Newcastle, having paid a brief visit to the right, rode forward to the centre, where he met Sir Thomas Metham and his troop of gentleman volunteers, who had escorted him from York. Affairs in the centre were confused. Newcastle's own Whitecoats, fighting with the valour which was to become a watchword before the day was out, held up the infantry brigade belonging to Lord Fair-fax's army, forming the centre of the Allied front line. This presented Sir William Blakiston's cavalry brigade with a remarkable opportunity, and it swept forward, cutting right through the Allied centre and reaching the summit of the ridge. Many of the infantry regiments misbehaved, making off towards the rear to get away from the Royalist troopers. Newcastle may well have ordered Blakiston to charge, and certainly assisted his attack by charging forward at the head of Metham's troop, on Blakiston's left. The gentleman volunteers, led by the Marquis, passed right through a Scots regiment of Foot, and Newcastle himself killed three of the enemy with a 'half-leaden' sword borrowed from his page.[2]

As Newcastle and Blakiston cut a swathe through the Allied centre, Lucas threw his men against the right of this formation. There was a degree of panic, and the Allied line was in danger of collapse. Lord Lindsey's brigade,[3] at the right end of the front line, with both flanks exposed, stood like a rock; Lucas made three charges against this stubborn hedgehog before his horse was killed and he was taken. On the Allied left, meanwhile, Cromwell rallied his men somewhere to Mackworth's right rear. The Royalist Foot had now had time to reorganise, and reformed in a line between White Sike Close and Moor Lane, facing roughly south-south-west. Newcastle's Whitecoats took up a position in White Sike Close itself, keystone of the new Royalist line. The Allied infantry, too, reformed, with Lumsden's Scots closing up the gap in the centre.

By this time the ranks of both armies were thinned, not only by casualties, but also by fugitives. Many of the Allies believed that the attack of Lucas's

[1] Lord Saye, quoted in Firth, 'Marston Moor', p. 42n.

[2] *See* the Duchess of Newcastle's glowing testimonial to her husband in *The Life of William Cavendish Duke of Newcastle* . . . (London 1886, ed. C. H. Firth), pp. 75–81. The relevant passage is reprinted in Peter Young, *Marston Moor*, pp. 218–22. The Duchess's work exhibits considerable bias.

[3] The Fifeshire and Midlothian Regiments, commanded by the Earl of Crawford-Lindsey and Viscount Maitland respectively.

Horse, coming as it did at a time of considerable confusion in the Allied centre, made Royalist victory certain, and had taken to their heels, for 'in all appearance the day was lost'. Arthur Trevor, riding from Skipton with despatches for Rupert, met with 'a shoal of Scots crying *Weys us, we are all undone* . . and anon I met with a ragged troop reduced to four and a cornet; by and by with a little Foot officer without hat, band, sword or indeed anything but feet and so much tongue as would serve to enquire the way to the next garrisons, which (to say the truth) were well filled with the stragglers on both sides within a few hours. . . .'[1] Generals behaved even worse than their men: Leven and Lord Fairfax both left the field in some haste.

The last phase of the battle began with the Royalist Foot more or less intact. Blakiston's Horse, which had supported them at the outset, had shot their bolt, though Goring still had a considerable body of cavalry in the area of Sir Thomas Fairfax's original position. Sir Thomas himself removed the field-sign – a white handkerchief, or piece of paper – from his hat, and made his way through the Royalist army, reaching Cromwell's Horse. Some of Fairfax's horsemen also managed to get through or round the Royalist army, joining up with Cromwell's cavalry. There were few enough Royalist Horse still in the field to meet this threat. The stout-hearted Colonel Sir Phillip Monckton met 2,000 or so broken Horse well to the rear of the Royalist army, but was unable to halt them; he encountered the unpredictable Sir John Urry, who told him that 'broken Horse would not fight, and galloped . . . towards York'.[2]

It is by no means certain that Fairfax and Cromwell conferred in the twilight on Wilstrop Moor. The latter had already lain himself open to accusations of inaction[3] and it is possible that Fairfax, who was senior, ordered him to attack. The Eastern Association cavalry well deserved their nickname of Ironsides. Tightly controlled, they wheeled eastwards and charged. Goring interposed his cavalry; one of his brigade commanders, Sir Richard Dacre, had been mortally wounded, and though the other, the resolute Sir Marmaduke Langdale, fought on, Goring's Horse were scattered. This left the Royalist Foot uncovered to the onslaught of Cromwell's Horse.

Newcastle's Whitecoats, and a brigade of Greencoats – Tillier's or Broughton's – stood firm amidst the flood which surged around them. The former, in White Sike Close, inflicted heavy casualties on the Parliamentarian Horse, 'first peppering them soundly with their shot, [and] when they came to charge stoutly bore them up with their pikes, that they could not enter to break them'.[4]

---

[1] Letter to the Marquis of Ormonde, 10 July 1644, in Thomas Carte, *A Collection of Original Letters and Papers* . . . (London 1739), Vol. I, pp. 55–8. Reprinted in Peter Young, *Marston Moor*, pp. 223–5.

[2] Firth, 'Marston Moor', pp. 52–3n. Reprinted in Peter Young, *Marston Moor*, pp. 222–3.

[3] *See* particularly Crawford's account in Denzil, Lord Holles, *Memoires* . . . (London 1699), p. 16. Cromwell's conduct at Marston Moor remains a bone of contention.

[4] Lieutenant-Colonel James Somervill's account in *Memorie of the Somervilles* (Edinburgh 1815), Vol. II, pp. 343–52. Also Peter Young, *Marston Moor*, pp. 258–63.

A Parliamentarian captain related how they 'would take no quarter, but by mere valour for one whole hour kept the troops of Horse from entering amongst them at near push of pike; when the Horse did enter they would have no quarter, but fought it out till there was not thirty of them living; whose hap it was to be beaten down upon the ground, as the troopers came near them, though they could not rise for their wounds, yet were so desperate as to get either pike or sword or a piece of them, and to gore the troopers' horses as they came over them or passed them by. . . .' It was only after their ammunition was expended, and their ranks were thinned by the fire of Fraser's dragoons, that the Whitecoats were overcome; 'every man fell in the same order and rank wherein he had fought'.[1] Thus passed the immortal Whitecoats, and, as the last hedge of pikes collapsed beneath the harvest moon, so died the last hopes of Rupert's army.

By 9 p.m. the battle was over; it had lasted only two hours. The road to York was littered with dead and dying, and Micklegate Bar was crammed with survivors, many of them wounded. Sir Thomas Glemham, governor of the city, had, quite rightly, shut the gates to prevent any Allied force entering the town on the heels of the fugitives, and there were some ugly scenes as many of the latter were, initially, refused admittance. Rupert himself was among the last to reach York. He had a warm interview with Newcastle, in which each taxed the other with having lost the battle, and then withdrew northwards towards Richmond with his cavalry and as many of his infantry as he could mount.

Newcastle, his fortune depleted and his forces decimated, would not 'endure the laughter of the court';[2] he travelled to Scarborough, and thence took ship to Hamburg. He did not return to England until after the Restoration. The debris of his army was entrusted to Sir Thomas Glemham, as colonel-general of the north. There was little enough for the valiant Sir Thomas to command. Well over 3,000 Royalists, a high proportion of them gentlemen, had been killed; about 1,500 men and a rich booty of arms and colours, as well as Newcastle's coach and papers, had been captured. After Marston Moor, Allied victory in the north could only be a matter of time. York surrendered on terms on 16 July, the garrison marching out with the honours of war. Glemham himself went north, and held Carlisle against the Scots till 2 July 1645. Newcastle's garrisons collapsed one by one, though many of them held out for a considerable time; Newark did not surrender until 8 May 1646, and then only on direct orders from the King, who was by then a prisoner in the hands of the Scots.

Marston Moor was a remarkable battle. For much of the day victory hung in the balance. Had Newcastle fully cooperated with Rupert, a speedy attack on the Allied army while it was still strung out towards Tadcaster might well have succeeded. The late arrival of Newcastle's Foot prevented Rupert from

[1] Loc. cit.
[2] *Prince Rupert's Diary.*

launching a more formal attack on Leven's forces as they trooped back to the ridge. Rupert thus lost these two valuable opportunities, and allowed Leven to seize the initiative. The latter's flight during the battle must not be allowed to obscure the soundness of his initial disposition, and of his decision to attack the Royalists. Of Leven's colleagues, Cromwell and Sir Thomas Fairfax deserve special mention, and whatever Oliver's precise rôle in the action, his Eastern Association cavalry were certainly the chief instrument of Allied victory. Manchester, though no great tactician, had at least remained in the field, and for most of the battle commanded his own regiment of Foot. Crawford, Baillie and Lumsden had also made useful contributions towards victory. On the Royalist side, such laurels as there were must rest with Goring and Lucas. George Goring has suffered at the hands of historians, but at Marston Moor his cavalry managed to rout a force much more numerous than itself.

It was some measure of the disorganisation of the Allies that they remained on the field for almost forty-eight hours after the battle. Leven and Lord Fairfax did not reappear until the 4th, and it was Manchester who rode amongst the exhausted and hungry Allied troops on the night of the battle, thanking them for their efforts but urging them to give credit for the day to God alone. Rupert was equally sure of the identity of the architect of Allied victory – he had been beaten, he remarked, 'because the devil did help his servants'.

Defeated but undismayed, Rupert, with perhaps 6,000 men, marched north, picking up Clavering's force on 3 July, and collecting more stragglers at Richmond. Here he was met by Montrose, yet again in search of troops for a descent on Scotland. Rupert, like Newcastle some months before, had no troops to spare for the fiery Marquis. He crossed the Pennines, and reached Chester on 25 July, where he left Byron in command, continuing to Bristol which he reached a month later. Here he discovered that, disastrous though the northern campaign had been, his uncle was meeting with greater success against Essex in the west.

Fifteen

THE LOSTWITHIEL CAMPAIGN

It was difficult for the King and his advisers to understand the magnitude of Rupert's defeat at Marston Moor. Grim though the news was, it reaffirmed Charles's intention to move against the Earl of Essex in the West Country. One of the Earl's main objectives in invading the west had been the capture of the Queen. Here he was disappointed, for, leaving her baby at Exeter, Henrietta Maria escaped from Falmouth in a Dutch ship, reaching France after a brush with a Parliamentarian man-of-war. Essex, nevertheless, had reinforced Lyme, and occupied Weymouth and Melcombe Regis. From here he pushed on westwards, reaching Tavistock on 23 July, while the King was still in Somerset. He wrote that day to the Committee of Both Kingdoms announcing his intention to adhere to his former resolution of relieving Plymouth, and expressing a hope that Waller would 'take care of the King's army'.

Unfortunately for Essex, Waller was in no position to intervene. The Committee of Both Kingdoms, with a proper appreciation of Essex's danger, voted £20,000 for pay and provisions to be sent to Plymouth for his army, and ordered Waller's lieutenant-general, Middleton, with 2,000 Horse and dragoons to march to his relief. A further £10,000 was voted for Waller, but by 27 August Sir William had got no further than his old quarters at Farnham.

Essex's advance to Tavistock did at least have the effect of relieving Plymouth, for Sir Richard Grenvile raised the siege and fell back across the Tamar to Saltash. Assembling the town's garrison, and those of Mount Stamford and Plympton, he marched north to hold the passage of the Tamar at Horsebridge on the Tavistock road. Essex was now faced with a crucial decision. Should he press on into Cornwall, or turn and attack the King's army? The Earl decided on the former course of action against his better judgement, it would seem, for Lord Robartes, who greatly over-estimated his own influence in Cornwall, pointed out that the King depended on the export of Cornish tin for munitions, and maintained that the Cornishmen would rise for Parliament as soon as Essex's army appeared.

On 26 July Essex moved into Cornwall, brushing aside Grenvile's detachment at Horsebridge. On the same day the King reached Exeter. Essex arrived at Bodmin two days later, and on 2 August received the unwelcome news that the King was at Launceston, only twenty miles away. Thoroughly alarmed, Essex decided to make contact with the fleet, and fell back southwards to Lost-withiel, sending a detachment on to hold the little port of Fowey, where the Earl hoped to contact Warwick's ships. From Lostwithiel, Essex wrote, in some indignation, to the Committee of Both Kingdoms, telling that august body that three armies, under the King, Maurice, and Hopton, were approaching from the east, 'and the country rising unanimously against us, with the exception of a few gentlemen'.[1]

Lord Robartes's cheerful prophesies had proved altogether false. The Cornish, far from rising in favour of Essex, were decidedly hostile. The Earl's plan to raise sufficient Cornish forces to block the King's advance into the county was obviously not feasible. Furthermore, as Essex pointed out to the Committee, 'we must expect another army in the West'.[2] This was Grenvile's force, which had earlier recoiled in some disorder, but was now on its way to Tregony, fifteen miles south-west of Lostwithiel. Essex's army had been reduced to about 10,000 men by leaving garrisons in Dorset, Somerset and Devon; it now began to run short of supplies. The local inhabitants denied the Earl both provisions and intelligence, and the King's army, 16,000 or more Horse and Foot, was dangerously near. Essex's problem was twofold. He had to hold off the King until Waller's army appeared in his rear, and at the same time he had to retain Fowey to await the fleet. Little did the Earl know how slowly Middleton with his relief force was moving, or that Warwick, beset by unfavourable winds, would never arrive.

The King's army, too, was not without its problems. Lord Wilmot, lieutenant-general of the Horse and 'at this time the second officer of the army ...', was 'proud and ambitious, and incapable of being contented ... he drank hard, and had a great power over all who did so, which was a great people'.[3] Wilmot, out of pride and vanity, had been making comments which might be interpreted as seditious, and Digby had reported these in full to the King. The matter came to a head on 8 August. Wilmot, on his horse at the head of his troops, was dismounted and arrested for high treason by the knight marshal and sent under guard to Exeter. Goring, who had just joined the army, was appointed in his place. Wilmot's crony, Henry Percy, the inefficient general of ordnance, was relieved of his command, and replaced by Hopton, obviously an excellent choice. This proved a storm in a teacup, and left the Royalist army more efficient and more resolute than before.

Essex, meanwhile, had decided to hold Lostwithiel in strength. A large detachment of infantry garrisoned Fowey, and the remainder of the Parliamen-tarian Foot were posted on and around Beacon Hill, just east of Lostwithiel,

[1] CSPD 1644, p. 399.
[2] Loc. cit.
[3] Clarendon, op. cit., Vol. IV, p. 526.

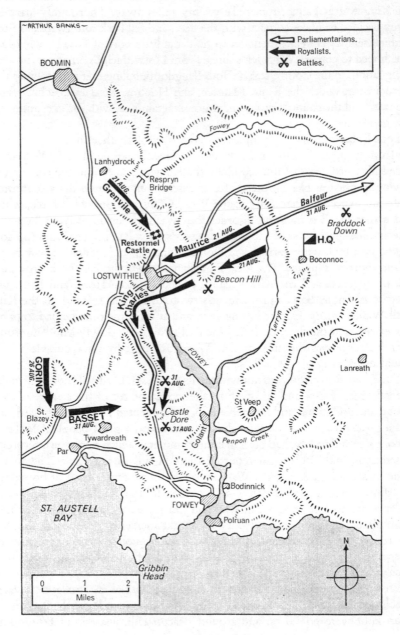

~ARTHUR BANKS~

Parliamentarians.
Royalists.
Battles.

BODMIN

Fowey

Lanhydrock

Respryn
Bridge

21 AUG.
Grenvile

Balfour
31 AUG.

Braddock
Down

Restormel
Castle

Maurice 21 AUG.

21 AUG.

H.Q.

Boconnoc

LOSTWITHIEL

Beacon Hill

King
Charles

FOWEY

Lerryn

Lanreath

GORING
26 AUG.

31
AUG.

St Veep

St.
Blazey

BASSET
31 AUG.

Castle
Dore
31 AUG.

Penpoll Creek

Tywardreath

Golant

Par

Bodinnick

ST. AUSTELL
BAY

FOWEY

Polruan

N

Gribbin
Head

0   1   2
Miles

II LOSTWITHIEL

and Restormel Castle, a mile north of the town, covering Lostwithiel and its bridge, the last over the River Fowey before it reaches the sea. Essex's Horse, and possibly small bodies of Foot, were used to thicken up and cover the flanks of the main positions.

Charles wisely waited for the arrival of Grenvile before moving against the Earl. On 11 August Grenvile, with 2,400 men, threw Essex's cavalry outpost out of Bodmin, and secured Respryn Bridge, 2½ miles north of Lostwithiel, the following day, thus ensuring his communications with the King. He then pushed on to take Lord Robartes's house at Lanhydrock, between Bodmin and Lostwithiel.

On 13 August Goring and Sir Jacob Astley reconnoitred the east bank of the River Fowey southwards to the sea, and the next day posted 200 Foot with two or three guns at Polruan Fort at the mouth of the river and at Hall, Lord Mohun's house by Bodinnick Ferry. Colonel Sir Charles Lloyd's regiment was posted at Cliff, opposite Golant, to guard that ferry. Apart from an inadequate garrison at Polruan Fort, Essex had made no attempt to hold these important positions. Nor did he endeavour to recapture them. Meanwhile, Middleton's relief force, which had penetrated as far as Bridgwater, had been defeated by Sir Francis Doddington, and had fallen back to Sherborne. For about a week nothing of moment took place at Lostwithiel, though on the 17th the King, whose headquarters were at Boconnoc, made a personal reconnaissance of the southern end of Essex's positions from the 'fair walk' which still runs below Hall House. He came under fire, and a fisherman standing near him was killed. He was quite unmoved.

THE BATTLE OF BEACON HILL, 21 AUGUST

On 21 August Charles at last decided to launch a concerted attack. This took the form of a remarkably well-synchronised general advance along the whole front line from Lanhydrock to Boconnoc, a distance of four miles, a very complex operation by the standards of the time. The advance began at 7 a.m. on a mist-shrouded morning. Grenvile on his side took the ruined but still formidable castle of Restormel, held by the men of Colonel John Weare's Devonshire regiment, who retreated without orders. This out-flanked the Roundhead lines on Druid's and Beacon Hills, which fell without serious opposition. Prince Maurice then sent a column, 1,000 strong, to take the hill north-east of Lostwithiel on the north side of the road to Liskeard. Towards nightfall, the main body of the King's Foot penetrated into the fields on the hillside on both sides of the road. Parliamentarian resistance stiffened towards evening, but by nightfall the Royalists were overlooking Lostwithiel. That night they worked hard raising a redoubt twenty yards square to secure the vital ground of Beacon Hill.

On the following day the situation remained unchanged, and there was only sporadic fighting. It seemed that Essex had accepted defeat, and on the 24th so little movement could be detected that the King's entourage suspected a Parliamentarian withdrawal to Fowey. The King planned a general advance for the 25th, and half the cavalry was sent across Respryn Bridge to support Grenvile on the west bank of the Fowey. During the morning, however, reconnaissance disclosed that the Roundheads were not gone; they were merely taking cover from the battery fire on Beacon Hill, and remained ready to oppose any Royalist advance. Seeing this, the King changed his plans, and postponed the projected attack.

Instead, on the next day, the 26th, Charles sent Goring with 2,000 Horse, and Major-General Sir Thomas Bassett, with 1,000 Foot, to march west to St Blazey so as to stop the Parliamentarians landing provisions at Par, four miles west of Fowey, and to prevent foraging. On the same day supplies, including 1,000 barrels of powder, reached the Royalists from Dartmouth and from Pendennis Castle.

Essex's army was now in a desperate plight, bottled up in a narrow tract of land five miles long and two miles wide. There was no sign of Warwick's fleet, and the Parliamentarians, already terribly short of provisions and ammunition, had no means of replenishment. Even so, five days went by before the King had any assurance that this wide dispersal would prove successful. His 16,000 men were strung out on a fifteen-mile front. The country was difficult and badly roaded, and it was all too easy for messengers to lose their way. Even with the wireless and more modern weapons the King would have been taking risks; with seventeenth-century means of communication his dispositions were remarkably bold. At last, on the evening of 30 August, news of a Parliamentarian move reached royal headquarters. Two deserters were brought to Boconnoc, and revealed that Essex intended to fall back on Fowey, while his Horse broke out.

Instantly the King gave orders that both his own army and Prince Maurice's should stand to their arms all night. The two armies were little more than a musket shot apart and in the event of the Roundhead cavalry trying to escape they had orders to fall upon them. A cottage beside the Lostwithiel-Liskeard road half-way between the two main Royalist bodies was fortified and manned by fifty musketeers. All the various detachments of the army were alerted and Sir Edward Waldegrave's regiment of Horse, stationed near Saltash, was ordered to break down the bridges across the Tamar. The lifeguards, quartered at Lanreath, received the information at 1 a.m. and rode into Boconnoc.

At about three o'clock on the morning of 31 August the Roundhead cavalry, led by the redoubtable Sir William Balfour, sallied out of Lostwithiel, and made their way up the Liskeard road. It was a hazardous venture and few of them can have expected to get through. But the musketeers in their cottage were presumably asleep for they did not fire a shot. However, the movement of so great a body – about 2,000 Horse – could not be accomplished in complete silence. The trampling hooves, the clashing armour, the muttered orders – and oaths – roused the Cavalier gunners, who fired a few rounds into the darkness, but they did little damage, and that probably moral rather than physical.

Except for Cleveland's brigade there were few cavalry at hand to deal with this eruption, and they could do little until daylight. Then, with about 500 Horse, Cleveland pursued over Braddock Down and Caradon Down to Saltash, where Balfour managed to beat off Waldegrave, and to ferry his men across into Devonshire, reaching Plymouth with the loss of about 100 men.

The Royalists were mortified by Balfour's escape, and Clarendon laid the blame on Goring, alleging that he was in one of his jovial excesses when the order to pursue reached him,[1] but this is quite untrue, and the accusation must be put down to malice or carelessness. Goring, at St Blazey, could do nothing to stop Balfour. The Royalists, by adopting a cordon system, laid themselves open to an attempt of this kind, but by no other means could they prevent Essex obtaining provisions. Nevertheless, it was a sparkling achievement on the part of Balfour.

A large proportion of the Royalist Foot were by now straggling about the countryside in search of provisions, but the King lost no time in marching on Lostwithiel with what men he had at hand. He could see the colours of the Parliamentarian rear-guard on the hill south of the town, where Major-General Skippon was covering Essex's withdrawal. In his dispatch the Earl reported that the narrow lane leading to Fowey was 'so extreme foul with excessive rain, and the hardness for the draught horses so rotten as that in marching off we lost three demi-culverins and a brass piece . . . thirty horses were put to each of them, but could not move them, the night was so foul and the soldiers so tired that they were hardly to be kept to their colours'.[2] Thus Essex explains his plight, but he does not excuse it. He had been at Lostwithiel for four weeks and he should have known the state of the roads and of the harness of his gun-teams.

While Essex was reeling backwards, the King, who never showed more vigour and ability than now, was moving in for the kill. At 7 a.m. 1,000 Royalist Foot entered Lostwithiel without much opposition, driving off some Parliamentarians who were breaking the bridge. Immediately after this, Charles ordered up two or three guns and planted them 'in the enemies leaguer' to command the hill where Skippon's rear-guard was posted. On this the Round-heads fell back, the Royalist infantry 'following them in chase from field to field in a great pace'.

THE BATTLE OF CASTLE DORE, 31 AUGUST–1 SEPTEMBER

About 8 a.m. the King, at the head of his lifeguard, moved westwards from the redoubt on Beacon Hill and forded the River Fowey south of Lostwithiel, finding everywhere evidence of a disorderly retreat – first a cartload of muskets

[1] Ibid., p. 546.
[2] Rushworth, op. cit., Vol. V, p. 702.

broken down in the mud and then five cannon in different places, 'two of them being very long ones' (probably demi-culverins). The King was in aggressive mood, fully realising that the enemy were on the run. 'With this small force,' Symonds wrote in his diary, 'his Majesty chased them two miles, beating them from hedge to hedge. Being come near that narrow neck of ground between Trewardreth[1] Bay and St Veepe [sic] pass,[2] the rebels made a more forcible resistance . . .' to Grenvile's Foot who were now leading the vanguard.

The Cornish Cavaliers retreated hastily but rallied on a body of infantry commanded by Lieutenant-Colonel William Leighton of the King's lifeguard of Foot. This rearguard action, which occurred between eleven and twelve o'clock, took place in the hedges and fields just west of Trebathevy Farm. Charles now launched his lifeguard to the attack, and, inspired by his personal leadership, they were not to be denied. Major Brett 'led up the Queen's troop, and most gallantly in view of the King charged their Foot and beat them from the hedges, killing many of them, notwithstanding their muskets made abundance of shot at his men: he received a shot in the left arm in the first field . . . yet most gallantly went on and brought his men off. . . .' As the major was riding back to have his wound dressed 'the King called him and took his sword which was drawn in his hand, and knighted Sir Edward Brett on his horse's back',[3] in the very forefront of the battle.

A lull followed, for the Foot had been far outpaced, but by about 2 p.m. the Royalist infantry, advancing fast, came up in force. Sir Thomas Basset from St Blazey fell on the enemy's left flank, and about the same time the King's own infantry, with Colonel Appleyard leading the van, made a frontal attack, gaining ground in the face of heavy musketry. It was probably about 4 p.m. when Essex organised a counter-attack by two or three troops of Horse, which he had retained, and 100 musketeers. Captain Reynolds and the Plymouth Horse charged bravely, driving the Royalist Foot back two or three fields and taking a colour. Lieutenant-Colonel John Boteler of Essex's own Foot regiment supported Reynolds well and took a colour with his own hand. Then, seeing the King's lifeguard approaching, they fell back again. Goring with his cavalry arrived about this time and was ordered by the King to pursue the Roundhead Horse towards Saltash, which he proceeded to do.

At 6 p.m. the Roundheads put in a more serious counter-attack, trying to gain the high ground north of Castle Dore, an Iron Age fort. They drove the Cavaliers back for two fields, but after an hour's fighting, during which Northampton's brigade of Horse came up to support the Royalist Foot, the Roundheads were beaten right back to Castle Dore. Night was falling fast as the Cavaliers charged forward, and although they could see signs of disorder in the Roundhead ranks east of the earthwork, they pursued no farther.

[1] Tywardreath. The Ordnance Survey calls it St Austell Bay.
[2] Golant Ferry.
[3] Sir Edward Walker, *Historical Discourses* (London 1705), pp. 74-5.

Castle Dore, the centre of the Parliamentarian position, is a double entrench-
ment and commands the roads east to Golant, west to Tywardreath and south
to Fowey. Five regiments held this front. Essex's own regiment and that of
Lord Robartes were to the west of Castle Dore, while the remaining three
regiments were to the east of the ancient earthwork. So small a force could not
hope to hold this extensive position indefinitely, even under favourable circumstances. By now the morale of the Parliamentarians was at its lowest. Abandoned
by their cavalry, tired and hungry after a hard day's fighting, the regiments
began to disintegrate in the dusk. Weare's regiment, which had put up so
feeble a resistance at Restormel on the 21st, was one of the first to go. There
was now a great gap in the Roundhead line east of Castle Dore: the Cavaliers
had an open road to Fowey.

To Skippon the position must have seemed hopeless indeed, but he was
determined to save the situation if he could, and sent officers to seek instructions
from the lord-general. His messengers did not reach Essex until about an hour
before dawn, and then they received, not orders, but a few words of ambiguous
advice. The Earl advised Skippon to bring the train to Menabilly, and with the
army to secure that place and Polkerris. If that could not be done he should
draw up the Foot round the train and, by threatening to blow it up, obtain the
best conditions he could. Essex had had enough. 'I thought it fit to look to
myself, it being a greater terror to me to be a slave to their contempts than a
thousand Deaths. . . .'[1] Accompanied by Robartes, the author of the downfall,
he set sail for Plymouth in a fishing boat.

The Earl's motives in escaping were not entirely dishonourable. As a
commander-in-chief of the Parliamentarian forces, it was obviously in the best
interests of his cause if he could avoid capture. He had, on previous occasions,
shown himself a man of considerable personal courage; one suspects, though,
that his hungry and exhausted infantry might have had some hard things to say
about their commander's discreet departure. Skippon, hard old veteran that he
was, disliked the prospect of surrender. Calling a Council of War, he proposed
that the Foot should cut its way out as the Horse had done, but his officers,
who knew better than Skippon how exhausted and demoralised their men
were, considered this impossible.

The King supped and spent the night under a hedge amid his foremost
troops, with the complete absence of ceremony. The night was a stormy one,
but Charles was content, for the wind would make escape for the enemy by
sea out of the question. There was some desultory firing during the night, one
shot falling close to the King, but the next day was a quiet one; the monarch
was biding his time, for he knew that the Parliamentarians were caught like rats
in a trap, and he wished to avoid useless loss of life.

On 1 September, while the Royalists were preparing for a final effort, the
Parliamentarians, still nearly 6,000 strong, asked for a parley. Next day they

[1] Rushworth, op. cit., Vol. V, p. 703.

surrendered, being allowed to march away with their colours – the officers with their swords, and one carriage to each regiment – but a total of 42 guns, a mortar, 100 barrels of powder and 5,000 arms fell into the hands of the victors.

The dejected column of Parliamentarian troops moved off on the afternoon of 2 September. Royalist officers had some difficulty in preventing local inhabitants from attacking the Roundheads.[1] A Royalist force escorted them to Southampton, whence they were shepherded back to Portsmouth, sadly depleted in numbers, and in a pitiful condition. Essex had reached Plymouth safely, and sailed thence to London in one of Warwick's ships. The west wind, which had prevented Warwick from reaching Fowey and evacuating the Earl's army, made for a rapid passage. Balfour's Horse had also reached Plymouth, but quitted it again before Grenvile, having just taken Saltash, reinvested the place.

Thus Essex's invasion of Cornwall ended in disaster. The King had now got the better of both his opponents – Waller at Cropredy Bridge and Essex at Lostwithiel – but Waller's defeat, though it put the army out of action for most of the summer, was not nearly as serious as that suffered by Essex, for the army that surrendered at Fowey was a more homogeneous force than that commanded by Waller. The victory at Cropredy had been, if not a soldiers', a brigadiers' battle. But in Cornwall the King's personal intervention had been decisive in every phase of the fighting. He had been *Generalissimo* in practice as well as in name. From his headquarters at Boconnoc he controlled the whole wide-flung front. His energy and careful arrangements ensured the harmonious cooperation of the various columns – not an easy feat, given the intricate nature of the terrain, the absence of roads and the primitive nature of his intelligence service. For example, the coordinated advance on 21 August could only be achieved by a strict adherence to a prearranged plan, for there was no means of intercommunication save by galloper. And yet Charles's generals managed to carry out a well-synchronised attack.

Essex exhibited none of the skill which he had shown in the relief of Gloucester, nor the dogged courage he had displayed at Newbury. On the contrary, his indecision, infirmity of purpose and finally abrupt abandonment of his army are painful to contemplate even after this lapse of time. In glaring contrast, the King, who had noted the Earl's lack of resolution on the morrow of Edgehill and taken the measure of his man – a mark of a good general – deliberately and rightly decided to take risks. He conducted the campaign with cool confidence in himself, awaiting in patience the day – 21 August – when he judged it was time to strike. And he judged right. The more deeply one examines this little-studied campaign the clearer stands out the firm grip on the situation that Charles possessed. In short, the campaign of Lostwithiel was a triumph for the King and the most striking success obtained by the Royalists in the whole of the war.

[1] Symonds, op. cit., p. 67. The efforts of the King and his officers were not successful; the Roundheads were thoroughly plundered, particularly by the country people.

Sixteen

THE SECOND NEWBURY CAMPAIGN

Great though Charles's victory in the west was, it scarcely counter-balanced Rupert's defeat at Marston Moor. Following the fall of York, the Allied commanders agreed to operate independently. Leven marched north to reduce Newcastle, which threatened his communications with Scotland. Fairfax stayed in Yorkshire to deal with the remaining Royalist garrisons, while Manchester took his battered army back into Lincolnshire. On the way, Manchester was urged by the Committee of Both Kingdoms to attack Rupert's forces in the Chester area. He declined, and continued south, reaching Huntingdon on 8 September. There he received the disquieting news of Lostwithiel, and resumed his southward march, with orders to aid Waller against the King.

If Parliament harboured any vexation with Essex, it was well concealed. He was welcomed as if 'he had not only brought back his own army, but the King himself likewise with him'.[1] The Earl complained of the conduct of Colonel Weare, whose abandonment of Restormel Castle and collapse at Castle Dore had been partially responsible for his defeat, while the Commons, with greater ingenuity, managed to attribute the captain-general's disaster, not to any shortcomings on the part of Essex, but to Middleton's failure to relieve him. Upon this, Sir Arthur Hesilrige burst into peals of laughter, which somewhat upset his Parliamentary colleagues. The Committee at Derby House, while smoothing Essex's ruffled feathers, feared that the King would advance eastwards before the Earl's army could be reconstituted. Waller had been ordered west, and Manchester south, but a rapid advance by the King's victorious army must have been an unpleasant, and very real, prospect in the early weeks of September 1644.

Charles's progress, however, was anything but speedy. On 11 September he summoned Plymouth, hoping that Essex's defeat might have demoralised the garrison, but, being refused, left Sir Richard Grenvile to blockade the town, and marched to Exeter. Some days were consumed in providing for the wants of the army – clothing, pay and shoes – and in settling garrisons to hold the west.

Clarendon, op. cit., Vol. IV, p. 547.

Despite his success during the summer, there is no hint in Sir Edward Walker's narrative, the official Royalist account, that the King ever contemplated an advance on London in the autumn of 1644. His object was simply to relieve the garrisons of Banbury Castle, Basing House and Donnington Castle, before disposing his army in winter quarters. Nevertheless, these relatively pacific intentions were unknown to the Parliamentarians. Waller, writing from Salisbury, warned the Committee that 'if there be not present course taken to oppose the enemy with a strong power, I know of nothing to hinder them from marching to London'.

When this letter was penned the King was still before Plymouth, and it was not until 2 October that his army, 10,000 strong,[1] reached Sherborne, where he remained for several days while a force went south to relieve Portland Castle. By this time Manchester had inched his way to Reading, though he showed a marked disinclination to move any farther, despite the urgings of the Committee. He was not only angry with Cromwell for his claims of having won Marston Moor, but also jealous of Waller. The latter had pushed his infantry into Weymouth, Poole and Lyme, and, on 21 September, posted himself and his cavalry at Shaftesbury. Essex was at Portsmouth, trying to reorganise his tired, dispirited and weaponless Foot. Though the Parliamentarian forces were still widely scattered, the danger to London was past. There remained the possibility, however, that the King might advance and destroy the Parliamentarian armies in detail.

The Royalist command soon became aware that, in order to relieve their beleaguered garrisons, they must risk another battle, and, that being so, consulted as to how they could increase their army. Prince Rupert, who had established his headquarters at Bristol at the end of August, came to Sherborne to take part in their deliberations. It was agreed that he should take the offensive with 2,000 Horse, the remnants of his own and Newcastle's army, who were moving south under Sir Marmaduke Langdale, and 2,000 Foot from South Wales under General Charles Gerard. It was hoped that this body would attract at least one of the Parliamentarian armies, thus reducing the forces that could be brought to bear on the King's main army. If this plan failed to work, Rupert was instructed to rejoin the King. Rupert and Hopton left for Bristol on 5 October in order to organise this operation.

On 15 October the King at last advanced, occupying Salisbury. This jolted even the unwilling Manchester into activity, and the Earl moved into Hampshire to join Essex's Foot. Waller fell back to Andover, afraid that the King would reach Basing House before Essex and Manchester. On the afternoon of the 18th, Goring, with the Royalist advanced guard, drove Waller out of Andover. Manchester, with 4,000 Foot and 3,500 Horse, had reached Basingstoke on the previous day. As Waller's men fell back on the town on the night

[1] This reduction in the size of the King's army was due mainly to the detachment of units to garrison towns and castles, and to blockade Lyme and Plymouth.

of the 18th, Manchester, receiving 'a very hot alarm', ordered up four regiments of the London Trained Bands, about 3,000 men, which, though attached to his command, had been left at Reading. The armies of Waller and Manchester now blocked the way to Basing House, and Essex's Foot, about 3,000 strong, led by the indomitable Skippon, arrived at Alton on 20 October. Balfour's cavalry had already rendezvoused, and it was with some satisfaction that Waller wrote to the Committee that 'you may now look upon the forces as joined. We hope there will be a battle shortly; to our understanding it cannot be avoided.'[1]

As Waller wrote this despatch, the King's army advanced to Whitchurch, seven miles east of Andover, and pushed on to Kingsclere on the following day, the 21st, in the hope of relieving Basing. Donnington was safe enough, for the Roundhead detachment which had been besieging it fell back, on 18 October, to its main body at Basingstoke. Basing, however, was hemmed in by the three Parliamentarian armies, and its relief was thus unlikely. So, on 22 October the King marched to Red Heath, just south of Newbury, establishing his head-quarters in the town, and posting cavalry vedettes well forward. At Newbury Charles received Lieutenant-Colonel John Boys, the gallant defender of Don-nington Castle. Boys was knighted, and promoted colonel. Charles then sent the Earl of Northampton, with 800 Horse, to the relief of Banbury Castle, held by one of the Earl's younger brothers, Sir William Compton. Northampton, reinforced by a body of Foot from the Oxford garrison, successfully raised the siege. Nevertheless, his absence reduced the Royalist army at Newbury to just over 9,000 men. With the hostile forces successfully united, this numerical inferiority was serious enough, even though the King intended to remain on the defensive, hoping that the rigours of a winter campaign would exhaust his opponents and give an opportunity later to relieve Basing. The situation was worsened by the defection of Sir John Urry, who 'in a discontented humour, which was very natural to him',[2] had left the Royalist army on the pretext that he was going overseas, but had instead gone to London, and provided the Parliamentarians with useful intelligence.

As the Royalists quartered in and around Newbury, the Parliamentarian infantry halted for the night at Swallowfield, seventeen miles to the east, with their cavalry at Aldermaston. By the 25th they were at Thatcham, only three miles from Newbury, on the north bank of the Kennet, in contact with Royalist dragoon outposts. Command arrangements were, as usual, obscure. The Com-mittee, on 14 October, had ordered that a council of senior officers, including two civilian deputies sent to represent it, should command the armies 'when they have no particular direction from this committee, or that in ... their judgement ... they have not convenient time to advise with this committee ....' This system of remote control from London was not guaranteed to pro-vide generalship of a high order. Furthermore, Essex, the general with

---

[1] CSPD 1644–5, p. 60.
[2] Clarendon, op. cit., Vol. IV, p. 581.

the best chance of exacting some sort of agreement from his colleagues, had caught a cold while marching through rainy Berkshire, and was bed-ridden in Reading.

THE SECOND BATTLE OF NEWBURY, 27 OCTOBER

By the evening of 26 October the two armies were facing one another just north of Newbury. It looked as if the King had been out-manoeuvred; but there were certain points in his favour which appeared to justify his decision to stand his ground. The first was the natural strength of the position he occupied. His right rear was protected by the River Kennet and the town of Newbury, in which he had placed a garrison. To his left was a small tributary, the Lambourn, while the formidable Donnington Castle, garrisoned by some 200 veterans, its masonry reinforced by earthworks, stood to his left-centre. In the centre stood Shaw House, the property of Sir Thomas Dolman. Round three sides of the garden, forming a sort of arena courtyard, were some ancient embankments,[1] making the house a veritable fortress. To the west the Royalists had thrown up a battery to protect Speen village.

The King had another, intangible, advantage, namely the divided command of his opponents, vested in a council – a notoriously bad method of conducting operations. Moreover, Manchester, the senior general on that council, was a commander of very mediocre capacity. Cromwell ranked lower in the Parliamentary hierarchy than Waller, and merely commanded the cavalry of the Eastern Association. Essex's army had no overall commander, for the Earl was sick: Balfour commanded the Horse, and Skippon the Foot. In addition there was the city brigade under Harrington, apparently an independent formation, answerable only to the Council of War.

However, this peculiar council now nerved itself to a remarkable decision – one that gives this battle its distinctive interest. Not liking the look of the Royalist position from the east front, the council decided – probably on Waller's proposition – to attack it simultaneously from front and rear. To encompass this would entail a wide detour by the outflanking column, owing to the position of Donnington Castle – a site that might have been purposely selected to frustrate such a manoeuvre. The route decided on was as follows: three miles north-east, nearly to Hermitage – west, via Chieveley to North Heath – south to Winterbourne – west to Boxford – south to Wickham Heath – south-east to Speen, a total of thirteen miles. It was a bold decision to take, even though the Royalist army was greatly inferior in numbers. Including a period for rest and sleep, the march, much of it by night, would take the best part of twenty-four hours, and during that time the remainder of the army risked being attacked by the whole force of the Royalists. In fact there was never much prospect of

---

[1] These have often been incorrectly stated to have been thrown up for battle. Money, op. cit., p. 122, makes this error.

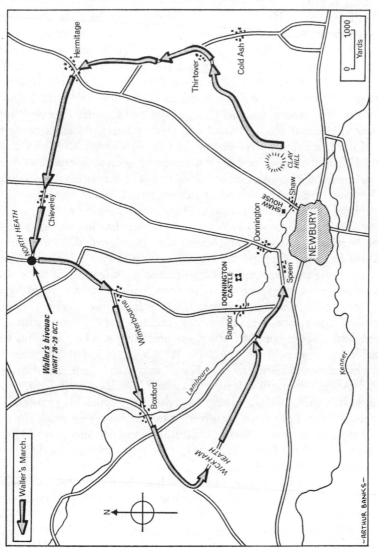

12 SECOND BATTLE OF NEWBURY

the King attacking during this period. By some means he managed to get wind of the flanking move, and in order to counter it he shifted Prince Maurice's troops to occupy a position to the west of Speen.

The Parliamentarian commanders formulated their plan of attack on the evening of 26 October. The day had been spent in skirmishing along the whole front, as the Parliamentarian patrols discovered the full breadth of the Royalist position. There was a half-hearted artillery exchange in the morning, as a Roundhead battery on Clay Hill engaged the Royalist right in Shaw. The Royalists spent the day erecting fortifications. Lord Astley, recently elevated to the peerage, commanded the Foot of the Oxford army. His three brigades, under his son, Sir Bernard, Colonel George Lisle, and Colonel Thomas Blagge, held Shaw village and Shaw House,[1] and were strongly posted to cover the passage of the Lambourn to the west of the village. Maurice, with his Cornish Foot and Horse, took up a position on the rising ground just west of Speen village, and spent the morning of 27 October busily entrenching his position.

The Royalist Horse were formed up in the centre near the train of artillery. Sir Humphrey Bennet's brigade of 600 Horse was posted between Speen and Newbury. To guard against any surprise, a strong detachment watched the south of Newbury, and vedettes guarded the crossings of the Lambourn at Bagnor and Boxford. The King had, in all, some 9,000 men. His weakness in cavalry, following the detachment of Northampton's brigade, was particularly serious. Nevertheless, the Speen–Shaw position, with its front covered by the guns of Donnington, was a strong one. The Royalist failure to seize Clay Hill, overlooking Shaw village, was unfortunate, enabling the Parliamentarian gunners to establish a battery on the feature, and providing attacking columns with a covered line of approach.

Meanwhile the outflanking force – Essex's army, and the London brigade with Waller's and Cromwell's Horse – was steadily plodding on its long, circuitous march. It constituted the greater part of the army – probably two-thirds of it, for, though exact figures are not given, it cannot have been much less than 13,000 strong out of 17,500. Waller commanded the operation, and Skippon took command of all the Foot. The force had set out shortly after midnight and halted to bivouac at North Heath.

The essence of attacks on exterior lines such as the Roundheads planned to make, is that they should be delivered simultaneously – a difficult matter when communications were as primitive as they were in the Civil War. The King had successfully employed this strategy at Lostwithiel, and it may be that this led Balfour and Skippon to suggest it now by way of turning the tables on him. But in spite of the difficulties and hazards inherent in an operation of this nature

---

[1] It is difficult to disentangle the locations of these three brigades. It seems likely that Lisle's brigade was stationed on the right, while Lieutenant-Colonel Richard Page held Shaw House itself. Astley's men covered the left of the Shaw position, with Blagge's brigade in support.

in the seventeenth century, there remained one form of communication common to both ancient and modern times – sound. Manchester sensibly agreed that Skippon should fire his cannon as a signal that he was in position and about to attack; on hearing that signal Manchester would also attack, and thus co-ordination would be achieved in the simplest possible manner. It seemed almost foolproof – but in war few things go so simply.

Waller's force left its bivouac at North Heath in the early morning of 27 October. The Royalist vedette at Boxford was driven in, and Waller's men forded the Lambourn. The garrison at Donnington Castle spotted the marching columns, and Boys sent his twenty-five Horse to harry their flank. By about 3 p.m. Waller was in position on the ridge to the west of Speen, and deployed for the attack. In the centre stood the infantry, under Skippon, with Balfour on the right and Cromwell on the left.

While the flank march was in progress, Manchester, to divert attention from the Royalist left, launched a feint against Shaw. There is a tendency for such attacks either to be recognisably diversionary, or to be pushed too far. Manchester's men erred in the latter direction, and his infantry became seriously committed. They had cunningly constructed a bridge during the night, and at dawn attacked in strength, but were briskly counter-attacked and driven back, disordering a unit which was moving forward to support them. Intermittent skirmishing went on all day, and by the time that Waller's cannon announced that the flanking force was in position, Manchester's troops were seriously dispirited. Royalist attention was, however, focused on the threat from Manchester, rather than on their more seriously menaced left.

Waller's assault went in just after 3 p.m. The exact time is disputed, and even today it is difficult to ascertain exact times in the course of a battle, whilst naturally it was much more difficult then. It is important, though, to fix this moment as precisely as possible in view of what transpired, and it cannot have been far from 3 p.m. There remained two hours of daylight:[1] if Manchester's attack was to prove effective against the strong Shaw House position there was no time to lose. There was no sign, however, that Manchester was moving. Waller, under fire from the guns of Donnington, had no time to wait. 'Their cannon made our ground very hot,' he wrote, 'there was no way left but to fall on with Horse and Foot, and that without delay. . . .'[2]

The Parliamentarians must have been tired after their long march, but eager to revenge themselves on the hated Cornish, they attacked resolutely. Eight hundred musketeers of Essex's army spearheaded the attack, supported by the four regiments of Aldridge's brigade. The redoubt was taken, though not without loss, while the London brigade, on the right, stormed into Speen and became involved in a desperate struggle with Maurice's infantry. After an hour's

---

[1] It was 6 November, New Style; sunset was at 4.26 p.m., and the moon was in its first quarter, setting shortly after midnight.

[2] Waller's *Experiences*, f. 20.

fighting, Speen fell, and the Royalist Foot was sent reeling down Shaw road. Skippon's men took the guns from Maurice's redoubt, clapping their felt hats to the touch-holes to prevent them from being fired. These were, by a strange coincidence, some of Essex's guns from Cornwall, recaptured by the very men who had lost them.

The situation on the Royalist left now looked critical. The King himself, with Prince Maurice, was sitting his horse at the head of the reserve in a large field east of Speen, when some routed Horse from the left came streaming past him. Charles did his best by his own personal efforts to rally them, but they 'very basely forsook him, and ran into Newbury, out of which they were speedily forced by our guards then placed at the bridge'.[1] Balfour pursued the routed western Horse, and a fierce mêlée swirled around the King and his entourage. Charles was in some danger, but was speedily aided by Sir John Campsfield, with two troops of the Queen's regiment, and the omnipresent Lord Bernard Stuart with the lifeguard.

The battle on the left had now reached its crisis. Swift intervention by Cromwell's cavalry on Waller's left would have engaged the last of the King's reserves, and probably brought about the collapse of the position. One of Cromwell's recent biographers maintains, by way of excuse, that his position was on most unfavourable ground, intersected by hedges, and that he came under artillery fire from Donnington Castle. Neither of these excuses is valid. There were hedges all over the battlefield, and there are accounts of bodies of cavalry negotiating them successfully. If all the hedges directly opposite Cromwell's command were impassable, thus rendering his cavalry immobile, why did he not take steps to change position? Waller had done this at Cheriton, and at Nantwich Fairfax had caused his pioneers to make gaps in the hedges through which his cavalry passed. But there is no record of Cromwell attempting either of these steps. There appear to have been four cannon – demi-culverins or sakers – in Donnington Castle. Cromwell's Horse must have been something like 1,000 yards distant, and would have offered a poor target, moving across the garrison's front. Skippon's infantry, who seem to have been fired upon with some success, were a much larger, often stationary, target.

Whatever the cause, Cromwell was slow in intervening, and the initiative was snatched from his hands. Goring placed himself at the head of Cleveland's brigade, only 800 strong, charged Cromwell's leading squadrons, and pushed them back in some confusion. Balfour, having initially beaten Sir Humphrey Bennet's brigade, was held up by Blagge's musketeers, lining the hedges and ditches east of Speen. This allowed Sir Humphrey to rally his troopers, and he counter-attacked successfully, throwing Balfour back to Speen. Skippon's infantry were unable to debouch from the village, and the cavalry on both their flanks had been forced back. Fierce fighting continued until after nightfall, but no major changes took place in this sector.

[1] Walker, op. cit., p. 112.

While the battle raged around Speen, Manchester, with customary drowsiness, did not attack on time. Possibly he was unable to distinguish Waller's signal guns from the artillery which had been in action throughout the day; possibly he doubted whether the attack would take place at all that day, and issued no 'warning order' to his troops, who were depressed by their earlier repulse. Whatever the reason, Manchester's attack was not under way until 4 p.m., less than half an hour before sunset. In the gathering dusk, two columns descended Clay Hill. One advanced against the north-east side of Shaw House, while the other, the larger of the two, wound through Shaw village on the north side of the Lambourn. Both columns were received with a blaze of musketry and cannon fire from the Royalist defences. The right-hand column actually got into the garden of Shaw House, but was speedily evicted; the left-hand column, moving parallel with the river, was counter-attacked and driven back with heavy loss. George Lisle had thrown aside his buff-coat, and, in his shirt-sleeves, inspired the defence. Despite the successful repulse of Manchester's men, it is probable that only the darkness saved the Royalists from the renewed attacks on both flanks; the full weight of the Parliamentarian numbers would then have begun to tell, and the Royalists would have been pressed indeed.

The King was not slow to realise that, although his troops had conducted a successful and spirited defence, a renewal of the action on the following day could only result in disaster. He left his guns, baggage and wounded in the care of Sir John Boys and the garrison of Donnington Castle, and the army marched out through the 1,500-yard gap between Shaw House and Donnington. Charles himself, with an escort of 500 Horse, rode to Bath to confer with Rupert, while the rest of the army slipped away to Wallingford, reaching Oxford next day. The Parliamentarians seem to have been unaware of this retreat until daylight, and, though the cavalry eventually pursued, they were able to accomplish little.

Each side lost perhaps 500 men at the second battle of Newbury, and both, predictably enough, claimed the victory. But although the Parliamentarians occupied the field, their ambitious plan to bring their tremendous superiority to bear had failed completely. This failure may be attributed to the absence of a single commander, with authority to coordinate the attack, and the inherent difficulty of synchronising such an assault. The Royalists appear to have been holding in depth, for, after clearing the defences west of Speen, and then the village itself, the Parliamentarians had to contend with the hedge and ditch positions bordering Speenhamland. Finally, the Parliamentarian plan can have included no provision for blockading the position. A gap was left in the centre through which the King managed to escape. The entire Royalist army must have trooped over the little bridge in Donnington, a line of retreat which could easily have been cut.

If the Roundheads had won a victory, which is questionable, they did little or nothing to prosecute it. On the morning of 28 October a Council of War met at Speen. By now feelings among the Parliamentarian commanders were running high, and a dispute at once broke out as to whether the King should be pursued. Manchester, at length, reluctantly agreed to Waller, Hesilrige and Cromwell taking some Horse after the Royalists. The cavalry reached Blewbury, only to discover that the Royalists had safely crossed the Thames at Wallingford. Waller and Cromwell, realising that further pursuit with the cavalry alone was, owing to the nature of the ground, likely to prove hazardous, rode back to Newbury and tried to persuade Manchester to send up at least part of the Foot.

Manchester's opposition to such a move was supported by the Council of War, and the army, after some fruitless counter-marching, turned its attention instead to Donnington Castle, which, containing as it did the King's train of artillery, was a tempting prize. Sir John Boys was summoned to surrender, and warned that, if he continued to resist, they would not leave one stone of his fortress upon another. Boys characteristically replied that, if they did so, he was not bound to repair it. 'Carry away the Castle walls themselves, if you can,' he said, 'but, with God's help, I am resolved to keep the ground they stand on, till I have orders from the King, my master, to quit it, or will die upon the spot.'[1] The ensuing attempt to storm was repulsed with considerable loss. With this, and being again beset by divided counsels, the Parliamentarians lurched forward to Blewbury, with cavalry outposts at Faringdon and Witney. Patrols from these posts discovered, to their chagrin, that a strong Royalist force was concentrating at Burford.

The King left Bath on 30 October, accompanied by Rupert and a total of about 3,000 Horse and Foot. He marched, *via* Cirencester, to Burford, where he left his detachment to be joined by Northampton's brigade, and a strong force under Gerard and Langdale. Charles himself entered Oxford on 1 November, and five days later he reviewed his assembled army – now not less than 15,000 men – on Bullingdon Green. He also announced an important change in the Royalist command structure: the promotion of Rupert to Brentford's office of general. Brentford had been wounded at Newbury, and was now too old and gouty for further service. Rupert objected to the appointment on the grounds that it gave him seniority over the Prince of Wales; the King compromised by appointing his eldest son commander-in-chief, while Rupert became lieutenant-general of all the King's armies.

Clarendon writes scathingly of this change of command.

The King's army was less united than ever; the old general was set aside, and Prince Rupert put into the command, which was no popular change; for the other was known to be an officer of great experience, and had committed no oversights in his conduct; ... and though he was not of many words, and

[1] Quoted in Money, op. cit., p. 145.

was not quick in hearing, upon any action he was sprightly, and commanded well.[1]

Here Clarendon allows his dislike of Rupert to overshadow the real necessity for the replacement of Brentford, who had shown himself – at Cheriton, for example – too infirm for command in the field. Clarendon likewise condemns Goring, now general of the Horse, as a drunkard, who was 'no more gracious to Prince Rupert than Wilmot had been; had all the other's faults, and wanted his regularity, and preserving his respect with the officers'.[2] But how could such a man have smashed the Allied right at Marston Moor, and led the Royalist Horse with skill and courage on many a bloody field?

Marching south with his reinforced army, the King reached Blewbury on 8 November, and at midday on the 9th appeared at Donnington. On the following day the Royalist army drew up on Speenhamland. The King removed his guns from the castle, and offered battle, but the Parliamentarian Council of War was racked by internal dissension. Manchester, with his usual gloom, warned the Council of the dangers of a fresh attack. 'Gentlemen,' he pleaded 'I beseech you let's consider what we do. The King need not care how oft he fights. . . . If we fight 100 times and beat him 99 he will be King still, but if he beats us but once, or the last time, we shall be hanged, we shall lose our estates, and our posterities be undone.' 'My Lord,' Cromwell replied sourly, 'if this be so, why did we take up arms at first? This is against fighting ever hereafter. If so, let us make peace, be it never so base.'[3] The Council eventually decided against attacking, and the Royalists marched off triumphantly, drums beating and colours flying.

The King reached Lambourn on 10 November, having beaten off a half-hearted attack by the Roundhead Horse. Reaching Marlborough on the 11th, Charles decided to make a new attempt to relieve Basing. He marched back to Hungerford, to attract the attention of the Parliamentarians, and sent Colonel Gage, the energetic deputy governor of Oxford, with 1,000 Horse, each man carrying a bag of corn or other provisions on his saddle bow, to Basing House. Gage, a professional soldier from the Spanish service and a man of considerable ability, arrived at Basing on 19 November to find the siege lifted. It was thus with the three important garrisons of Banbury, Donnington and Basing relieved that the Royalist army, its short-term objectives accomplished, went into winter quarters around Oxford on 23 November.

[1] Clarendon, op. cit., Vol. V, p. 1.
[2] Ibid., p. 2.
[3] CSPD 1644-5, pp. 150-1. *See also Manchester's Quarrel.* Ludlow, whose regiment of Horse had fought on the Parliamentarian left at Newbury, goes as far as to say that 'by this time it was clearly manifest that the nobility had no further quarrel with the King . . .', Ludlow, op. cit., p. 105.

Seventeen

'NEW MODELLING':
RUPERT AND FAIRFAX

Two and a half years of war in which neither side had as yet obtained any decisive advantage had sharpened the temper of every ardent partisan, while inducing a marked degree of war-weariness in the more lukewarm. The majority of the Oxford Parliament, which met during the winter of 1644, was eager for peace – so much so that the King, who valued the members' purses more than their opinions, ungraciously described them in a letter to the Queen as 'our mongrel Parliament. . . .'

A subtle change had been coming over Charles; he had in his earlier years vacillated between one policy and another, but now a fatalistic tenacity began to take hold of him. It may in part be attributed to the execution on 10 January 1645 of Archbishop Laud, long a helpless prisoner of the Parliament, for, since the execution of Strafford, his chief minister, in 1641, the King had been oppressed by a sense of guilt. He now felt that the hand of justice was on his side. But even before Laud's death Charles had expressed his determination not to abandon the episcopacy 'nor that sword which God hath given into my hands'. Negotiations for peace had hitherto achieved little, and Parliament's successes in the north in 1644 made their new proposals, presented to the King at Oxford on 24 November, and subsequently debated in early 1645 as the Treaty of Uxbridge, much sharper than the previous peace terms.[1] So harsh, indeed, were the Uxbridge terms that Gardiner rightly comments that 'it would have been far more reasonable to ask his [the King's] consent to an act of abdication than to such articles as these'.[2]

Neither the King's entourage nor the Parliamentarian war-party had much faith in a negotiated peace. The King had made two attempts in 1644 to offer pardon to his enemies, who strangely failed to avail themselves of his royal clemency. By now, however, he had hardened his heart, expressing to Secretary

[1] The Nineteen Propositions sent to the King at York in June 1642, and the Oxford Propositions of February 1643.
[2] Gardiner, *Constitutional Documents*, p. xlii. For the text of the proposals *see* ibid., pp. 275–86.

Nicholas the view that his enemies 'were arrant rebels, and that their end must be damnation, ruin and infamy. . . .' It was of just such an end that Manchester had warned his colleagues: his speech at the Council of War on 10 November revealed his complete lack of confidence in final victory – an attitude that was shared by all too many of Parliament's soldiers. If the war was to be won, this half-hearted and timorous attitude would have to be eradicated from the army, and a force created with discipline, cohesion and organisational backing.

The campaign of 1644 had ended, in the south, with stalemate. The King had relieved his three beleaguered fortresses, and his army was as strong as ever, although its morale was perhaps not particularly high. The armies of Essex, Manchester and Waller were exhausted, badly equipped and unpaid; desertion was an increasing problem. In the north and midlands, the close of 1644 saw a number of Parliamentarian successes. Sir Thomas Middleton took Montgomery Castle in September, and Lord Byron, attempting to retake it, was defeated by Brereton (18 September), who then returned to assist Meldrum besieging Liverpool. The latter town surrendered on 1 November. The garrison comprised many Irish soldiers, who correctly anticipated that they would get short shrift if the place was stormed. They managed to obtain terms which guaranteed them transport to Ireland if they agreed not to serve again. The English members of the garrison could either go home after giving a similar undertaking, or re-enlist with Meldrum.

The Irish troops in the garrison of Liverpool chose an opportune time to surrender, for Parliament had just passed an ordinance ordering that all Irishmen captured should be executed. This measure was inspired partly by a hatred of Byron's 'Irish' troops, and partly by a fear that mercenaries might be imported from Europe on a large scale for service in the King's armies. If the threat of European mercenaries proved unjustified by events, the threat to Irish prisoners was real enough. Major General Browne hanged five 'Irish' officers following the failure of an assault on Abingdon on 11 January 1645. Thirteen Irishmen were executed at Shrewsbury later in the spring, and the enraged Rupert riposted by stringing up the first thirteen Parliamentarian prisoners who fell into his hands.[1]

The draconian treatment meted out to men who were, after all, legitimate prisoners of war, reflected the hardening of Parliament's attitude. The winter of 1644–5 was spent in an enquiry into Parliamentarian failure at the second battle of Newbury, deepening into a review and reorganisation of Parliament's military forces as a whole. The 'official' version of Newbury, delivered by the martial Hesilrige to a dubious House of Commons, was soon discredited when Cromwell accused Manchester of 'continued backwardness'. A committee was set up to hear the case against Manchester, who endeavoured to defend himself by discrediting his opponents, particularly Cromwell, who, he alleged, hoped

---

[1] An acrimonious correspondence between Rupert and Essex on this subject is to be found in the Bodleian Library, MS. Add D. 114.

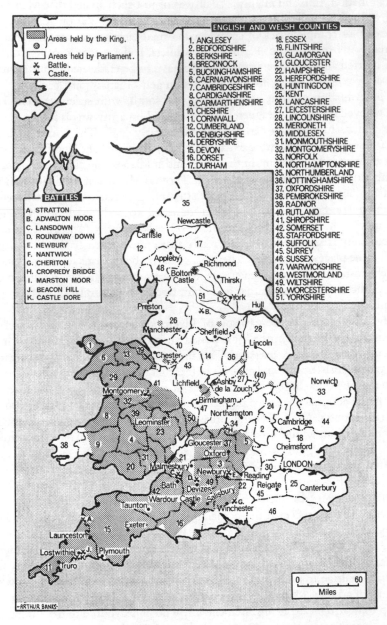

13   ENGLAND AND WALES, NOVEMBER 1644

'to live to see never a nobleman in England'. The Manchester question soon became the focal point of conflict between the Presbyterian Party, with Holles and Essex among them, and the Independents, under the capable leadership of Vane and St John. The evident ill-success of the three armies at Newbury, arguing as it did for some sort of military reorganisation, was a powerful weapon in the hands of the Independents, who were themselves eager to create a single, powerful army.

On 23 November the Commons ordered the Committee of Both Kingdoms 'to consider of a frame or model of the whole militia', and to submit a proposal to the House. On 9 December Cromwell, in an impressive speech, argued that a strict enquiry into Parliamentarian failures was pointless; a better course of action was to set about applying a remedy. Zouch Tate, Member for Northampton, immediately followed by moving the Self-Denying Ordinance, by which all members of either House would be excluded from any military command. An attempt to make an exception in the case of Essex was voted down, and the ordinance was passed by the Commons. The Lords were, as one might expect, less compliant, and threw the measure out on 13 January. A week earlier the Committee of Both Kingdoms had recommended the establishment of an army of 22,000 men – a permanent force under central command. The army was to comprise 11 regiments of Horse, each 600 strong; one regiment of 1,000 dragoons; and 12 regiments of Foot of 1,200 men each.

The Committee's proposal reached the Commons a week before the Lords rejected the first Self-Denying Ordinance, which absolutely excluded members of both Houses from military command. The commander of the newly formed force, to be called the New Model Army, could thus be neither peer nor M.P., and the obvious choice for the post was Sir Thomas Fairfax. Skippon was appointed major-general of the Foot; the post of lieutenant-general was not initially filled, though the Lords' rejection of the Self-Denying Ordinance eventually enabled Cromwell to be appointed. By the time a new ordinance had been pushed through the Lords, on 3 April, Cromwell was already in the field; by a strange irony, the man whose speech had paved the way for Zouch Tate's introduction of the ordinance ultimately managed to get excepted from the final version.

While the debates went on at Westminster, Rupert worked at improving his position in the centre. A garrison was established at Chipping Camden, to block the route between Gloucester and the Cotswold wool upon which its trade so greatly depended. Rupert then turned his attention to Abingdon. On the early morning of 11 January he surprised the town, but was swiftly counter-attacked by Major General Browne and his garrison, and repulsed with casualties, among them the capable Sir Henry Gage, who was mortally wounded. This unhappy state of affairs was paralleled in the west, where the ferocious Grenvile was unable to take Plymouth. Things looked, briefly, brighter, when Goring, with a small field army, pushed rapidly through the southern counties, reaching Farnham, and threatening Portsmouth and Christchurch before retiring on Salisbury. Unsuccessful though this venture was, Goring might have gained some satisfaction from the alarm which his advance caused in the capital.

Goring's proximity jolted the Commons into appointing Waller to command a force of 6,000 cavalry from his own, Essex's and Manchester's armies, to serve in the west. At the beginning of February he was once more in his old haunt at Farnham, and advanced westwards a month later, reinforced by Lieutenant-General Cromwell with some of his own troopers. Waller reached Amesbury on 7 March, and on 12 March destroyed Colonel Sir James Long's regiment of Horse near Trowbridge. Major-General Holbourne had relieved Taunton, held for Parliament by Colonel Robert Blake, defender of Lyme, and Waller sent Cromwell to rendezvous with Holbourne at Cerne Abbas. Sir William himself went towards Bristol, where conspirators within the city planned to let him in, but, in the event, failed to do so. Waller then moved south and ordered Holbourne and Cromwell back to Salisbury; Goring followed up this withdrawal, and once more laid siege to Taunton.

Shortly before Waller's march into the west, Sir Lewis Dyve, whose regiments of Foot and Horse garrisoned Sherborne, descended on Weymouth, capturing one of its forts and part of the town. Goring sent men to reinforce Dyve, but the Royalists proved unable to capture Melcombe, and the harbour remained useless to them. The governor of Melcombe resisted stoutly, and counter-attacked, taking Chapel Fort, which overlooked his defences. The governor's efforts were aided by Captain William Batten, who landed a party of seamen to assist in the defence. Eventually the Royalists drew off and retired on Dorchester.

The Royalist failure before Melcombe, unfortunate though it was, was soon obscured by Waller's march westwards, his retirement, and Goring's pursuit. Waller was short of men and supplies, and his quarters around Salisbury were repeatedly beaten up by Goring's Horse.[1] It was obvious, though, that Goring was incapable of launching a major offensive from the west, and Waller, as a Member of Parliament and bound by the Self-Denying Ordinance, could safely prepare to lay down his commission.

While events in the west died away to stalemate, the Royalists suffered a serious reverse in the midlands. The town of Shrewsbury was a vital link in communications between Oxford and Chester, and also served as a recruiting centre for Wales. However, the governor, Colonel Sir Michael Ernle, one of the colonels from Ireland, had been a sick man for some time, and was unable to exercise much control over the garrison, some of whom were in communication with the enemy. Colonel Thomas Mytton, the local Parliamentarian commander, profiting by the fact that many of the garrison were absent on an expedition, launched a surprise attack on the night of 22 February. A strong detachment crossed the Severn by boat, and opened the gates, letting in the

[1] *See* John Adair, *Roundhead General* (London 1969), p. 183.

remainder of Mytton's 1,200 men, who were seething through the streets before the garrison was aware of what was happening. Sir Michael Ernle, 'rising, upon the alarm, out of his bed, was killed in his shirt; while he behaved himself as well as was possible; and refused quarter. . . .'[1] Sir Michael's bravery availed little, for the garrison, forced back into the castle, surrendered immediately. The English were allowed to march out with their arms, but there was no mercy for the Irish, thirteen of whom were hanged the next day.

The disaster at Shrewsbury was accompanied by a marked deterioration of Royalist fortunes in Wales and the Marches. Gerard's departure from South Wales to assist the King's Oxford army had resulted in a Parliamentarian take-over of the area. Gerard returned at the end of 1644, and eventually managed to recover most of South Wales, though Tenby and Pembroke remained in Parliamentarian hands. In Cheshire, the busy Brereton was besieging Chester and Beeston Castle; he defeated a relief force, under Prince Maurice, at Nant-wich, though the Prince, with Rupert's assistance, managed to relieve Beeston in early March. Rupert then fell back to Oxford, where he was soon visited by an enraged Byron, who threatened to retire unless he was better supported.

Byron's protest was only one of the crises which soon hummed around the hapless Rupert. The King had decided to give the fourteen-year-old Prince of Wales a court of his own, and, duly attended by Richmond, Southampton, Culpeper and others, left Oxford for Bristol on 4 March. On their arrival, the Prince's Council found things in a sorry state. Grenvile had failed to reduce Plymouth, blaming this on the lack of assistance from Sir John Berkeley, governor of Exeter, who in turn claimed to be independent of Grenvile. Neither officer would obey Goring, who was once more battering at Taunton. Discipline was poor; the country people were harried by the troops of all three Royalist commanders, and may, with some justice, have wondered if life could be any worse under Parliamentarian domination.

Prince Charles's presence in Bristol did, however, give the western comman-ders an excellent excuse for non-compliance with Rupert's orders. The Prince was already unpopular in certain quarters; from France, the Queen and New-castle steadily eroded his position, while at home Rupert's tactlessness continued to add to his growing list of enemies. Sir Arthur Aston had lost his leg following a riding accident, and his governorship of Oxford had been conferred on Gage. By the time of Gage's death, Aston was stumping about happily enough on a wooden leg, hoping to take over as governor once more. He was disappointed, for the post went to Will Legge, Rupert's most loyal supporter. This served both to alienate Aston and to add to the dark rumours that Rupert was pushing his friends into high places with some sinister intent. Rupert managed to rout Massey, the energetic governor of Gloucester, in an action at Ledbury on 22 April, and, in the north, Langdale took a party of Horse to relieve Pontefract (1 March 1645), but these two successes were cold comfort to the Royalist

Clarendon, op. cit., Vol. V, p. 67.

commander, faced as he was by growing intrigue, and, worse, by the threat of the new Parliamentarian army.

RAISING THE NEW MODEL ARMY

Rupert, had he known it, might have been comforted by the fact that his adversary, the newly appointed general, Sir Thomas Fairfax, was finding the task of raising the New Model far from easy. It was originally intended to form the New Model from the remnants of the armies of Essex, Waller and Manchester, but the campaign of 1644 had so reduced them that further recruiting proved necessary. Nor was Fairfax able to use the other troops under Parliament's command, for the armies of Massey in the west, and Major-General Poyntz in the north, not to mention Browne's midland levies, were to remain independent. The situation was most serious in the infantry. Just over 7,000 Foot could be gleaned from the armies of Essex, Waller and Manchester, and, of these, Waller's battered army could supply only 600 or so.[1] It was decided to obtain the balance by impressment in London and the south-east. Each county was to provide a fixed quota by a given date; this proved unsatisfactory, for the full quota was rarely sent, and many of those that were impressed contrived to desert. Consequently, when the New Model at last took the field in May 1645, it was 4,000 men short, and a new impressment had to be undertaken in June to fill the gap.

There was less of a problem entailed in raising the cavalry of the New Model. Mounted service was, in any case, more popular, and there were good regiments available which could be taken into the New Model almost *en bloc*. Essex's own regiment, for example, was taken intact into the New Model under the Earl's lieutenant-colonel, Richard Graves. The senior cavalry regiment of the New Model was Fairfax's own; this comprised half of Cromwell's fourteen-troop 'ironsides', and a troop composed of former members of Essex's life-guard. Lieutenant-General Middleton, a Scots Presbyterian, declined a proffered colonelcy, which went instead to John Butler, who had been adjutant-general of Horse to Waller. Colonel Charles Fleetwood, a celebrated – or notorious – Independent, commanded his regiment from Manchester's army, as did Nathaniel Rich and Edward Rossiter. Essex's army provided Colonel James Sheffield's regiment, while most of Colonel Henry Ireton's regiment came from Cromwell's Eastern Association Horse. Colonel Vermuyden commanded a rather mixed regiment, while Cromwell's cousin, Edward Whalley, was given a regiment composed of the remaining half of Oliver's own regiment. In most cases further recruiting was to bring the regiments to their full New Model strength. Such was probably also the case with the New Model's only dragoon regiment, under Colonel John Okey.

The regiments of Foot were rather more mixed. Fairfax and Skippon each

[1] Firth, *Cromwell's Army*, p. 35.

had a regiment; the remaining Foot colonels were men of varying backgrounds, and in most cases of great ability. Sir William Waller's cousin, Sir Hardress Waller, commanded the remnants of Waller's Foot, the command of which had been declined by Holbourne, a Scot. Edward Montague and John Pickering, both Independents, gained colonelcies, though in the face of opposition when Fairfax's list of officers was put before the Lords. Colonels Fortescue, Robert Hammond, Harley, Lloyd, Rainsborough and Weldon led the remaining regiments.

The artillery of the New Model was commanded by the lieutenant-general of the ordnance, Thomas Hammond, whose nephew Robert was a colonel of Foot. Cromwell's brother-in-law, Major John Desborough, led the firelocks, whose task was to defend the guns. Major Leonard Watson, Manchester's scoutmaster-general, held the same office in the New Model.

The ordinance appointing Fairfax to command the New Model had been passed by the Commons on 21 January, and on 4 February by the Lords. It was agreed that all officers should be nominated by Fairfax, subject to Parliamentary approval. The General arrived in London on 18 February, and visited the Commons on the following day; he behaved with his customary modesty, refusing a proffered chair, while Speaker Lenthall expressed Parliament's confidence in him. He set to work at once, organising regiments and, above all, selecting officers. Here he was particularly fortunate, for, unlike the earlier Parliamentarian commanders, he did not have to put up with men who owed their rank to social position or political influence. Among the senior officers of the New Model there were several men whose political views were extreme, or whose backgrounds were humble,[1] but few whose military abilities were in question.

The Lords objected at first to Fairfax being allowed to choose his own officers, and, when overruled on this point, endeavoured to remove two colonels and no less than forty captains from Fairfax's original list. The Lords' objections were as much social as political; they viewed with alarm the inclusion of 'dangerous' Independents like Montague and Pickering. Fairfax's list had a rough passage through the Lords, but eventually scraped through with a majority of one.[2]

MONTROSE, AUGUST 1644–FEBRUARY 1645

The King was undismayed by the prospect of the coming campaign, and continued the negotiations at Uxbridge without any real intention of coming to terms. He was encouraged in this obduracy by a series of dramatic events in

---

[1] Lieutenant-Colonel Thomas Pride of Harley's regiment was a drayman in 1642, and Lieutenant-Colonel John Hewson of Pickering's had been a cobbler. Both had risen from the ranks.

[2] Wedgwood, *The King's War*, p. 432.

Scotland. Montrose's first expedition into the Lowlands in the spring of 1644 had failed, but the Marquis, despite Rupert's failure to provide him with any troops after Marston Moor, moved north again, accompanied by only two companions, but armed with the King's commission as lieutenant-general for Scotland. Charles had previously managed to persuade the Irish Catholic Earl of Antrim to send a force from Ireland. Despite the confused Irish situation, Antrim despatched Alasdair Macdonald with 2,000 battle-hardened Foot to Scotland, where they arrived early in July 1644. Macdonald quickly established control of the Ardnamurchan peninsula in Argyllshire, and recruited some Highlanders, but when he marched inland the expected support failed to materialise.

Montrose fortuitously managed to establish contact with Macdonald, and rendezvoused with him at Blair. After recruiting numbers of local men, Montrose marched towards Perth, and routed a covenanting army under Lord Elcho at Tippermuir on 1 September. He was then threatened by another army under Argyll, and, weakened by the temporary disappearance of his undisciplined Highlanders, moved rapidly to threaten Dundee, and marched thence to Aberdeen, where, on 13 September, he defeated the covenanting Lord Burleigh. Still pursued, though at some distance, by Argyll, Montrose wended his way to Aviemore, where he detached two of his Irish regiments to visit their base on the Ardnamurchan peninsula.

Montrose was incapacitated with fever until 4 October, when, although weak in numbers and dangerously short of ammunition, he marched to the Don, via Blair and Kirriemuir, harrying the covenanting gentry as he went. Argyll lumbered after him, proving no match for his will-o'-the-wisp opponent. As the weather worsened, Montrose took up a defensive position at Fyvie Castle on the River Ythan, and gave the advancing Covenanters a bloody nose before slipping away again into the hills. After a desperate march through the snow, Montrose reached Blair, where he found Alasdair Macdonald with about 1,000 Highlanders from the western clans, many of them Macdonalds who had flocked in to join their Irish kinsmen. The Macdonalds were eager to attack their hereditary enemies, the Campbells, and there was little Montrose could do to dissuade them. He eventually decided to profit by a surprisingly mild December to march straight into Campbell country, heading for Argyll's seat and the Campbells' principal fortress, Inveraray, on the shores of Loch Fyne.

Montrose's little army was upon Inveraray before the Campbells had any idea of his proximity. Argyll escaped by sea, and most of his men fled into the hills or the castle, while Montrose's men looted and destroyed with malicious glee. The attack on Inveraray persuaded the Covenant leaders that stronger measures were needed to deal with Montrose. William Baillie was sent north with a detachment of Leven's army, and, working in uneasy cooperation with Argyll, planned to trap Montrose between their two armies on his withdrawal from Campbell country. Baillie was at Perth and Argyll at Inverlochy; Montrose, after an incredible march across the trackless hills of Lochaber, descended on Inverlochy and, on 2 February, cut Argyll's army to pieces. Sir Duncan Campbell of Auchinbreck, who commanded for Argyll, was mortally wounded, and 1,500 of the Campbells were killed. Argyll hastily took to his galley and escaped down Loch Linnhe while behind him the Macdonalds hunted down his clansmen.

On the following day Montrose, the *Te Deum* of his victorious Irish ringing in his ears, wrote to the King, advising him to have no truck with rebels.

> Forgive me, sacred Sovereign, to tell your Majesty that, in my opinion, it is unworthy of a King to treat with rebel subjects. . . . Through God's blessing I am in the fairest hopes of reducing this Kingdom to your Majesty's obedience, and, if the measures I have concerted with your other loyal subjects fail me not . . . I doubt not before the end of this summer I shall be able to come to your Majesty's assistance with a brave army.[1]

Montrose's tremendous successes strengthened the King's resolve to hold fast to his dangerous course. His most able advisers, who were rash enough to disagree with his Irish policy – Hopton, Capel, Culpeper and Hyde – had been sent to Bristol as Prince Charles's council of the west. Rupert, in between thrusting at Massey and Brereton, advocated a concentration on Worcester, followed by an advance northwards to relieve Chester. Recruits could then be raised in Lancashire and Yorkshire, and it might even be possible to stretch out a hand to Montrose, whose victory at Inverlochy had necessitated the return of many of Leven's soldiers to Scotland. This was one of the few viable courses of action left open to the King, but it depended on the swift concentration of the Oxford army, and the removal of the train of artillery from that city. Charles's chief adviser was now, however, that gifted intriguer Lord Digby, who was a deadly enemy of Rupert's, and the King remained immobile at Oxford.

By the time the decision was taken for Maurice to escort the artillery from Oxford to Rupert at Hereford, the New Model, although not fully formed, was in a position to interfere. Cromwell was ordered to take a brigade of Horse into the Oxford area. He failed to surprise Northampton's regiment at Islip on 23 April, but managed to get his force across the Cherwell, and when Northampton attacked him on the following day with three regiments of Horse he routed them, killing 40, capturing 200 men and 400 horses, and taking a standard from the Queen's regiment. That night Cromwell summoned Bletchingdon House; the governor, Colonel Francis Windebank, had fought bravely at Cheriton, but was unnerved by the presence of his young wife and some of her friends, and 'roused in the small hours, surrounded by frightened girls, he remembered the manners of the drawing-room rather than the camp, and immediately gave up the house to preserve his guests from the horrors of a storm'.[2] He was

---

[1] Quoted ibid., p. 417.
[2] Ibid., p. 440.

condemned to death on his return to Oxford, and even Rupert's intervention could not persuade the King to reprieve him – though Charles, with a characteristic twinge of conscience, later granted the widow a pension, which he had little enough money to pay.

Cromwell moved on westwards. At Bampton-in-the-Bush, eighteen miles west of Oxford, he came upon a body of Royalist Foot, under Sir Richard Vaughan. Two hundred of the infantry were captured, after a stout resistance, and the remainder scattered. Cromwell went on to summon Farringdon Castle, hoping that it too could be bluffed into surrendering to a mounted force. Although threatened with death if he did not instantly capitulate, Lieutenant-Colonel Roger Burges replied briefly: 'You are not now at Bletchingdon', and when Cromwell attempted to storm the place beat him off with loss.

In London there was some indecision as to where the main body of the New Model army should be initially employed. The Scots, despite having taken Newcastle some months previously (19 October 1644), were insecure in the north and demanded Fairfax's assistance against marauding Royalist Horse. In the west, however, Blake's Taunton continued to defy the divided Royalist forces, and it was eventually decided that Fairfax should march to his relief. Goring had already been ordered to Oxford to deal with Cromwell, and, as the latter moved south to join Fairfax for his advance into the west, Goring clashed with a party of his Horse and inflicted numerous casualties.[1] The siege of Taunton was left to the increasingly unpopular Grenvile, who was soon seriously wounded. Sir John Berkeley continued the operation, but was hampered by the continual disobedience of Grenvile's troops.[2]

Goring arrived at Oxford in time to participate in the Council of War which was to decide Royalist strategy for the coming campaign. Rupert advocated a march north, relieving Chester, and then swinging east to attack the Scots army, now very much reduced in size, which was besieging Pontefract Castle. The army rendezvoused at Stow-on-the-Wold on 8 May, and the generals met to discuss Rupert's plan. The Prince's reasoning was sound enough. If Chester fell, then the route for the expected help from Ireland would be closed. Royalist intelligence indicated that 'Fairfax was about Newbury, not in readiness to march; yet reported to be much more unready than he was'.[3] He would, Rupert hoped, be unable to assist the Scots, who were disillusioned and weakened. Sir Marmaduke Langdale, whose northern Horse had a natural disinclination to serve in the south, supported the Prince. The remainder of the Council favoured an advance into the west, to meet Fairfax head-on. Rupert was opposed to this, as the western generals by now had such a tradition of bickering and mutual non-cooperation that he feared they would be of little use.

Rupert averted deadlock by suggesting that Goring should return to the

[1] Clarendon, op. cit., Vol. V, pp. 169–70.
[2] Ibid., p. 149.
[3] Ibid., p. 171.

west, to check Fairfax, while the remainder of the army marched off north. Clarendon maintains that this idea was prompted by Rupert's fear 'that Goring, as a man of ready wit, and an excellent speaker, was like to have most credit with the King in all debates; and was jealous, that, by his friendship with the Lord Digby, he would quickly get such an interest with his Majesty that his own credit would be much eclipsed'.[1] This is probably going too far, but, whatever Rupert's motives for making the suggestion, Goring eagerly fell in with it, as it would give him increased authority, and, at last, a firm precedence over Grenvile and Berkeley.

Fairfax received his orders to march to Taunton on 28 April, and marched from Windsor to Reading on the 30th.[2] By 7 May he had reached Blandford, in Dorset, while Cromwell, scouting well to the north, covered his right flank against a possible threat from the Oxford army. It was not a satisfactory situation, as the Committee of Both Kingdoms were swift to realise; as soon as they heard that Charles was moving north they sent the general an order directing him to send a brigade to the relief of Taunton, but to wheel his main body towards Oxford. Fairfax obediently detached four regiments of Foot and one of Horse under Colonel Weldon to relieve Taunton. Blake was in serious difficulties. On 8 May the Cavaliers stormed the East Gate, and on the following day pressed into the town, but were unable to take the castle. Blake was on the point of collapse when, on 11 May, his attackers, threatened by the advancing Weldon, drew off. The news of Fairfax's change of plan came as a blow to Rupert, though he had every confidence in Will Legge's ability to hold Oxford. He sent a message to Goring, ordering him to join the Central army at Market Harborough. Goring, however, having failed to intercept Fairfax's withdrawal, had no intention of leaving the west, and found some support amongst the Prince's council. Thus, even by this early stage, Royalist strategy for the summer of 1645 had been bent from its original course on to the short road that was to lead to Naseby.

[1] Ibid., pp. 171–2.
[2] Sprigge, op. cit., pp. 331–5, contains a useful table of Fairfax's movements between 30 April 1645 and 24 June 1646.

Eighteen

THE NASEBY CAMPAIGN

Fairfax's army arrived at Newbury on 14 May and rested there for two days before moving on to Oxford, where it arrived on the 19th. Rejoined by Cromwell, Fairfax rapidly invested the city, but was unable to achieve much until the siege train came up from London. The Committee of Both Kingdoms initially hoped that Leven would be able to deal with the King's army, though they sent Colonel Vermuyden with 2,500 Horse to reinforce the Scots.

The King had begun his northward march on 9 May, and on the 11th he was at Droitwich. The news of Fairfax's return from the west was disappointing, but in most other respects the picture was surprisingly rosy. In Wales, Charles Gerard had beaten Laugharne at Newcastle Emlyn, while at Scarborough the active Parliamentarian Sir John Meldrum had been seriously injured – a hurt from which he was to die two months later. The news improved as the King advanced. On 22 May he reached Market Drayton, where he was met by Lord Byron, who reported that Brereton had abandoned the siege of Chester.

Things looked bleak for Leven and his Scots. Far to the north, Montrose had pulled off yet another spectacular victory, this time against the renegade Sir John Urry at Auldearn on 9 May. Leven feared that the King might link up with the seemingly invincible Marquis, and fell back into Westmorland, hampered by his train of artillery, and pursued by protests from old Lord Fairfax, isolated in Yorkshire, who urged the Scots to march south to aid himself and Brereton. Leven had no intention of doing so; from Westmorland he could check a move on Scotland, and offer encouragement, if not support, to Brereton. Digby, somewhat given to excessive enthusiasm, crowed delightedly over the plight of the Allies. 'On my conscience,' he wrote to his crony Goring, 'it will be the last blow in the business.'[1] He was not far from the truth.

While Fairfax, in obedience to the Committee's orders, sat impotently before Oxford, Massey operated with some success against the Royalist lines of communication. Evesham, a vital link between Worcester and Oxford, was attacked on 26 May, and 'stormed and taken for want of men to defend the works'.[2]

[1] HMC Portland MSS., I, pp. 224–5.
[2] Clarendon, op. cit., Vol. V, p. 174.

This was a serious loss, although the garrison were exchanged for Roundheads captured when the King took Hawkesly House in Worcestershire. Fairfax, meanwhile, grumbled, with some justice, that 'we should spend our time unprofitably before a town, whilst the King hath time to strengthen himself and by terror to enforce obedience of all places where he comes. . . .'[1]

Ironically enough, the Royalists were just as eager as Fairfax that the New Model should not remain before Oxford. It had initially seemed useful to have Fairfax tied down by the city, but information had reached the King from Sir Edward Nicholas that the city was not as well provisioned as it should have been. The Royalists therefore decided 'that the best way to draw him from thence, would be to fall upon some place possessed by the Parliament'.[2] Langdale's northern Horse were with the King, and at Ashby-de-la-Zouch Lord Loughborough's local levies further swelled the Royalist army. Thus strengthened, the Royalists advanced on Leicester, where Sir Robert Pye's weak garrison trusted to the strength of the town's medieval walls. Langdale's Horse cut the town off, and Rupert advanced on it on the 29th. On the following day the town was encircled, and the Prince ordered the construction of a battery on the southern side. This work was soon completed, and Rupert summoned the governor to surrender.

> [Sir Robert] returned not such an answer as was required. Thereupon, the battery began to play . . . and made such a breach, that it was thought counsellable, the same night to make a general assault with the whole army, in several places; but principally at the breach; which was defended with great courage and resolution; insomuch that the King's forces were twice repulsed . . . when another party, on the other side of the town . . . entered the town, and made way for their fellows to follow them; so that, by break of day . . . the King's army entered the line . . . and miserably sacked the whole town, without any distinction of persons or places.[3]

The news of the fall of Leicester, embroidered as it was by rumours of a massacre of the garrison, horrified London. The Committee at Derby House, under pressure to recover Leicester and protect the Eastern Association,[4] ordered Fairfax to prepare to march, and warned Sir Samuel Luke, at Newport Pagnell, to levy men to defend the place, and fetch in provisions. The King's Council of War showed no such resolution. Rupert continued to maintain that Oxford could be relieved if the King's army continued to lacerate the midlands, compelling Fairfax to intervene. Cromwell had already been detached to cover the Eastern Association, and a thrust into Yorkshire could not fail, argued the

---

[1] *Fairfax Correspondence*, Vol. III, p. 228.
[2] Clarendon, op. cit., Vol. V, p. 175.
[3] Ibid., p. 176.
[4] See *The Petition of the Lord Maior, Alderman and Commons of London . . .*, 4 June 1645, TT E. 286 (29).

Prince, to draw Fairfax north. Rupert, however, was voted down, and the army lingered about Daventry, collecting supplies for the relief of Oxford. When, on 4 June, the army marched south, Langdale's Yorkshire troopers declined to follow, and the whole move ground to a halt.

Fairfax at last left Oxford on 5 June, and marched north-east to Newport Pagnell. Here he met Vermuyden's brigade, which had failed in its attempt to reinforce Leslie. Vermuyden requested permission to resign his command to go overseas, and Fairfax asked the Committee for Cromwell as his lieutenant-general, if he could be spared from his duties in Parliament. Cromwell's appointment was finally sanctioned on the 10th. Fairfax's Council of War had already decided, on 8 June, to make the King's army their fixed object, and, on the following day, Parliament gave Fairfax a free hand in the conduct of operations.

The King, at Daventry, was in high spirits when he heard that Fairfax had broken up from before Oxford. 'I may without being too much sanguine,' he wrote to the Queen, 'affirm that since this rebellion my affairs were never in so hopeful a way.'[1] Rupert was less cheerful; Goring, beset by contrary orders, had not appeared, and some of the infantry had vanished, sated with loot, following the sack of Leicester. Furthermore, a garrison had been left there. He had a soldier's respect for Fairfax, and found it difficult to join his jolly young swordsmen in their guffaws at the expense of the 'New Noddle'.

Indeed, Fairfax's army exhibited none of the internal conflict which the Royalists eagerly imagined. The King's army was encamped on Burrow Hill, not far from Daventry, and on 12 June Fairfax reached Kislingbury, only five miles to the east. The King was hunting in Fairsley Park when news arrived of this unwelcome turn of events. Leonard Watson, Fairfax's scoutmaster-general, had done his work well. Royalist intelligence had no inkling of Fairfax's presence until it was too late, while Fairfax, for his part, was well informed of the King's strength, and had in his possession an intercepted letter from Goring, announcing his inability to join the King in the midlands. The Royalists were warned of Fairfax's approach when their pickets were driven in; they at once stood-to on Burrow Hill, albeit in some confusion, for many soldiers were foraging, and most of the horses were at grass.

The King had started the campaign with about 5,000 Foot and 6,000 Horse. He had been reinforced by Loughborough and others, but had suffered some casualties, and many soldiers had absented themselves with plunder from Leicester. According to Clarendon, only 3,300 Foot and 4,100 Horse were present at Naseby,[2] though this seems an improbably low figure. Certainly, the infantry were weak in numbers; some of the twenty-six regiments represented fewer than eighty men, and amalgamation of small regiments produced a multi-coloured appearance in several units. The proportion of officers to soldiers was surprisingly high, as many officers whose commands had been amalgamated or

[1] The King's Cabinet Opened . . ., TT E. 292 (27).
[2] Clarendon, op. cit., Vol. V, pp. 181–2.

destroyed continued to serve, as 'reformadoes'. The mounted arm was better off, although, as the previous behaviour of the northern Horse showed, there was some grumbling even amongst the cavalry. Fairfax had under his command some 13,000 men, and was reinforced by Cromwell and a strong party of Horse on the morning of 13 June.

As Cromwell's troopers clattered into Fairfax's lines at Kislingbury, Sir Thomas and his senior officers were discussing the latest report from Watson, whose agents had observed that the King's army was quitting its position on Burrow Hill, and appeared to be falling back. The Council decided to follow the King in an effort to bring him to battle. Consequently, as the King's army withdrew to Market Harborough, Fairfax pursued, and by nightfall had reached Gainsborough, four miles south of Naseby, while his vanguard entered Naseby and captured a Cavalier patrol feasting at a long table in the inn.

The King received this startling news shortly before midnight. He immediately rose, and summoned a Council of War, which met in the early hours of 14 June. There was, as usual, a difference of opinion between the senior officers, some of whom wanted to continue the withdrawal, while others wished to give battle. However, the previous policy of withdrawing was speedily abandoned, 'and a new one as quickly taken, "to fight", to which there was always an immoderate appetite when the enemy was within any distance'.[1] It was decided to turn and face the enemy on the high ground two miles to the south of Market Harborough.

THE BATTLE OF NASEBY, 14 JUNE

To the south of Market Harborough stretches a long, irregular ridge, itself composed of a series of smaller ridges, intersected by the valleys of numerous streams. Several rivers have their source on the ridge: to the north the Welland flows off towards the Wash, while the Avon begins its journey to the Severn from the top of the ridge, near Naseby village. The defensive position selected by the Royalists lay at right angles to the main feature, on a ridge running between the villages of East Farndon and Oxendon, a distance of 1½ miles. This was an excellent position, squarely blocking the route between Fairfax's bivouack area, between Gainsborough and Naseby, and Market Harborough. Should Fairfax attempt to move down the Maidwell–Kelmarsh–Market Harborough road, the modern A508, his left flank would be open to attack from the high ground. An outflanking movement from the west, towards Marston Trussell, incurred similar dangers.

Prince Rupert drew up his army on this well-chosen ground. In the centre, Lord Astley commanded the Foot. He had the support of 800 Horse under Colonel Thomas Howard. On his right were something over 2,000 Horse, under Rupert, while on his left the grim Langdale posted his northern Horse,

[1] Ibid., p. 181.

numbering about 1,600. In reserve were the Foot lifeguard under Lindsey, and Prince Rupert's Bluecoats, together with the lifeguard of Horse under Lord Bernard Stuart, and 800 Newark Horse in two bodies. The Royalists had made an early start, and were in position well before 8 a.m. By that hour, officers were beginning to doubt whether their information as to Fairfax's location was correct, and the Royalist scoutmaster was accordingly despatched to go and search for the enemy.

The men of the New Model, too, had risen early, and were on the move up the Naseby road shortly after 3 a.m. By 5 a.m. Fairfax was concentrated in the Naseby area, striving, like his opponent, to peer through the fog of war, thickened in this instance by the early morning mist. Fairfax knew that the Royalists had quitted Market Harborough, but, initially, did not know whether they had continued their retirement, or had turned to face him. He could not afford to risk stumbling upon the King's army while his own was still in line of march and decided to occupy a position covering Naseby until more accurate information was available.

While Fairfax prepared to reconnoitre a position north of Naseby, Francis Ruse, the Royalist scoutmaster-general, not, it seems, a man of Watson's calibre, though this did not prevent him from being knighted in April 1646, reported to Rupert that he could find no sign of the enemy, although he had, he claimed, been 'three or four miles'. Certainly, had he gone four miles he must have seen Naseby filling with troops; while an advance of three miles should have put him in sight of Fairfax's point elements. Rupert disbelieved this report, and, taking a body of Horse with him, went forward himself. As Rupert and his escort trotted down the road to Clipston, his opposite number, accompanied by his lieutenant-general, was only two miles away, studying the ground.

Fairfax, by this juncture, must have been aware of the Royalist concentration on the East Farndon–Oxendon ridge. He would probably have been informed of it by his scouts, and certainly could have seen his adversaries from the area where the Obelisk now stands, just north of Naseby. He rode forward, crossing the ridge top, and down into the valley crossing the plateau about 1½ miles north of Naseby. The ground was boggy and a little stream crossed the road, about a mile south of Clipston. Fairfax was contemplating occupying this position, covered by the stream and the boggy ground, when Cromwell intervened. The enemy seemed to be strong in cavalry, he observed, but this was no cavalry ground. Rupert, he sensed, would either turn the position or else remain on the defensive on the high ground to the north, declining battle. This would not fit in with the Parliamentarian plans, and it would be better to occupy the ridge in rear, he urged; this would tempt Rupert across the valley and he would be obliged to charge uphill at them. Fairfax saw the force of the contention, and agreed to it. At this moment his army was strung out along the line of march, the rear portion being still in column of route, gradually closing up to the rendezvous near the village. Here the head of the army had halted.

Thus it came about that, at the moment when Rupert with his escort of Horse was approaching Clipston, Fairfax with his escort was withdrawing up the hill to the Naseby ridge. Rupert, seeing this retrograde movement, imagined quite naturally that the enemy were going to occupy the ridge. At the same time he took note of the boggy ground beyond Clipston in front of the hostile position, and decided, as Cromwell had foreseen, that it would not do to commit his cavalry to such ground. From the ridge to the north of Clipston, however, he could see what looked more promising terrain away to the right, by which his Horse might ascend the Naseby ridge. It would be in the nature of a flanking movement, and would give him the windward position, no mean advantage in the days of black powder. Sending back an urgent message to the army to follow in his tracks, Prince Rupert therefore struck off to his right, and hit the Sibbertoft–Naseby road probably near point 571 on the Ordnance Survey map, one mile south of the village.

The Royalist main body, moving down the Clipston road, probably turned right just south of the village, moving towards Sibbertoft. Fairfax at once spotted this flanking move from Naseby ridge, and conformed by edging to his left. After moving just over a mile from the Clipston–Naseby road, Rupert halted and deployed. His formation was the same as it had been on the East Farndon–Oxendon Ridge: on the right, close to Dust Hill, and with some swampy ground to their right front, were the horsemen of Rupert's wing, drawn up in two lines. In the centre, on the edge of the valley of Broad Moor, were Astley's Foot, with the reserve to their rear. Langdale's Horse, on the left, were posted in the area where Long Hold Spinney now stands. The army had been led forward by the King himself, a splendid figure on horseback in full armour, with his drawn sword in his hand. His presence encouraged the troops, and morale was high as the Royalist army swung into line of battle on the edge of Broad Moor.

On the ridge on the southern side of Broad Moor, the New Model deployed for its first major action. Skippon, whose task it was to marshal the Foot, drew them up in the Swedish fashion, with five regiments in the front line – from the right, Fairfax's, Montague's, Pickering's, Hardress Waller's and Skippon's – with a second line of three more, Rainsborough's, Hammond's and Harley's,[1] covering the gaps between the regiments in the front line. A small detachment of Harley's formed a reserve and rear-guard.

To the right of the infantry stood Cromwell's wing, with Oliver's own regiment, part of Pye's, and Whalley's, forming the front line; part of Fiennes's, the remainder of Pye's, and Sheffield's regiments, were in the second line. A partial third line was formed by the remainder of Fiennes's, and some Eastern Association Horse. Rossiter's regiment, which arrived late, had one 'division' on the right rear of the front line, and the other on the right of the third line. The ground upon which Cromwell's men formed up was broken, scattered with

[1] Commanded by its lieutenant-colonel, Thomas Pride.

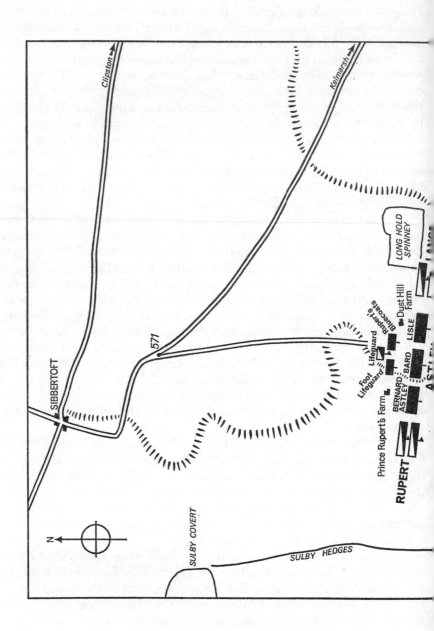

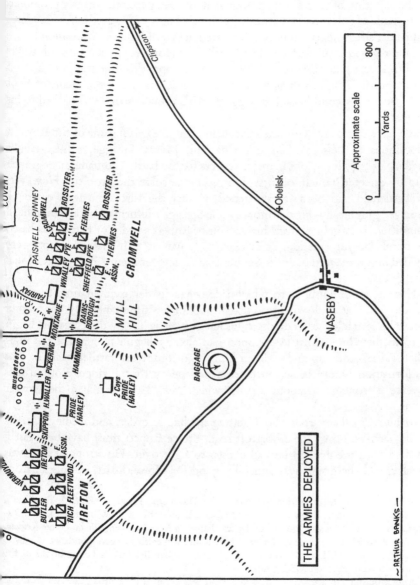

THE ARMIES DEPLOYED

14 NASEBY

~ARTHUR BANKS~

Approximate scale

Yards

0   800

Clipston

+Obelisk

NASEBY

CROMWELL

MILL HILL

PAISNELL SPINNEY

CROMWELL

ROSSITER

FIENNES

WHALLEY PYE

SHEFFIELD PYE

E. FIENNES ASSN.

ROSSITER

FAIRFAX

MONTAGUE

PICKERING

H.WALLER

SKIPPON

musketeers

RAINS-BOROUGH

HAMMOND

PRIDE (HARLEY)

2 Coys PRIDE (HARLEY)

BAGGAGE

BUTLER

IRETON

E. ASSN.

RICH FLEETWOOD

IRETON

VERMUYDEN

furze bushes and riddled with rabbit holes. This forced Cromwell to deploy his men more deeply than usual, to keep off the very difficult ground on his right.

The left wing of Horse was commanded by Henry Ireton, recently promoted to the rank of commissary-general. In his first line were Ireton's, Vermuyden's and Butler's regiments, supported by a second line of Eastern Association Horse and the regiments of Fleetwood and Rich. The Horse regiments on both flanks were formed up in 'divisions', each of three troops; this unit was later known as a squadron. Fairfax's guns were in the intervals between regiments of Foot in the first and second lines. His baggage, with a small escort, was parked to his left rear.

We have one of De Gomme's excellent plans to explain some of the Royalist dispositions at Naseby. Fairfax's Chaplain, Joshua Sprigge, whose *Anglia Rediviva* of 1647 is one of the major sources for the battle,[1] contains an engraved map by Streeter, which, on first sight, seems to solve the problem. However, the battlefield had been foreshortened, so that the forces engaged could be displayed graphically. Furthermore, while Sprigge's information on Roundhead dispositions is largely correct, his version of Rupert's order of battle was based on unreliable information. It is certain, however, that Astley's Foot were divided into three tertias, under Sir Bernard Astley, Sir Henry Bard and Colonel George Lisle.

There is some doubt as to which side began its deployment first. It would seem logical that deployment occurred more or less simultaneously, for Fairfax would be certain to stop edging to his left as soon as he saw the Cavaliers begin to form their line of battle. Skippon had already begun to marshal the Foot when Fairfax rode up and ordered him to go somewhat farther back, so that his formation would be screened from the enemy by the ridge. Both armies covered a frontage of about a mile, which must have stretched the weaker Royalists.[2]

As his staff officers rode about getting the line in order, and feeding in units as they arrived down the Sibbertoft road, Prince Rupert must have been fairly satisfied with the ground he had chosen to fight over. His strongest arm was cavalry, and the going was generally good for Horse, apart, of course, from

---

[1] For other sources *see* crop of pamphlets in the Thomason Tracts, E.288 (25), E.288 (26), E.288 (28), E.288 (27), E.288 (21), E.288 (22) and E.288 (38). Also Walker, *Historical Discourses*, Symonds's *Diary*, 'Journal of Prince Rupert's Marches' (*English Historical Review*, XIII), and Sir Henry Slingsby's *Diary*. There is also a wealth of correspondence in HMC Portland MSS., Vol. I, HMC (Lords MSS.), and Sir Samuel Luke's Letter-Books in the British Museum (Egerton MSS. 786).

[2] Sprigge, op. cit., p. 40, tells us that 'the Field was about a mile broad ... and from the utmost Flank of the right, to the left Wing, took up the whole ground'. As we know that Rupert's right was engaged from Sulby hedges, we can be certain of the east–west boundaries of deployment. It is less easy to be sure of the precise positions of units within these boundaries, though the sources leave much less doubt than in the case of other battles of the war – Cheriton, for example.

the broken terrain on Cromwell's right, and a patch of marshy ground to Rupert's right front. The slope of Dust Hill, on which the Cavalier army stood, was quite gentle, as was the gradient up which Rupert's Horse would have to charge, on the other side of Broad Moor. His right wing brushed the Sulby hedges, marking the boundary between the Manors of Sulby and Naseby; apart from this, the ground was unenclosed, though patches of corn interspersed the bracken and furze. The Royalist Horse would thus not be compelled, as they had been at Edgehill, to jump hedges at the charge. Two things might possibly have vexed the otherwise satisfied Rupert. One was the absence of Goring, but for whose petulance the Royalist Horse would have had a comfortable superiority. As it was, Langdale's men were distressingly thin on the ground; the average strength of his regiments was under 100.[1] A second, less serious, cause for chagrin was the absence of most of his artillery: only a few sakers had been able to keep pace with the advance. This cannot have worried Rupert unduly, as he did not propose to waste time with a preliminary bombardment. Leaving his King and captain-general in a suitable point of vantage, probably near Dust Hill Farm, Rupert rode forward to lead his right wing against the enemy, a task he might well have left for his brother Maurice.

The Roundhead Foot, formed up south of the crest, can have seen little of the Royalist concentration. Not so their commanders, who, a few yards farther forward, were scrutinising the enemy with experienced eyes. The Horse who were probably drawn up without the crest to protect them, would have had a good view of Charles I's last battle array. Cromwell, marshalling the Horse, watched the Royalists advance. 'When I saw the enemy draw up and march in order towards us,' he wrote, 'and we a company of poor ignorant men . . . I could not . . . but smile out to God in praises in assurance of victory.' In between smiles, Cromwell found time to ride to the rear, where John Okey, the vocal, stocky commander of the dragoons, was issuing ammunition to his troopers. Cromwell ordered Okey, whose men were already haggard from continuous outpost duty on the approach march, to line the Sulby hedges, to take a Royalist advance in enfilade. It was a typical dragoon task, but a dangerous one; had Rupert time to spare, he might have 'cleared the hedges' with fatal consequences for the tired dragoons.

Okey had scarcely got his men dismounted behind the hedges and his horseholders told off, when the Royalists, moving in what he described as a 'very stately' formation, began their advance. There was a spatter of musketry along the floor of Broad Moor as the Roundhead forlorn hope fired; on this, Fairfax's whole line moved over the crest. The Parliamentarian guns got off a round apiece, and 'the Foot on either side scarcely saw each other till they were within carbine-shot, and so only gave one volley'.[2] The time was shortly after 10 a.m.,

---

[1] See Peter Young, 'The Northern Horse at Naseby', *Journal of the Society for Army Historical Research*, 1954.
[2] Clarendon, op. cit., Vol. V, p. 183.

and Rupert, though opposed by Astley, who would have preferred to remain on the defensive, had persuaded the King to order a general attack.

The exact sequence of events is difficult to establish, but it seems likely that Rupert on this occasion tried to allow the Foot to come to 'push of pike' at the same time as, if not before, he himself obtained contact. Seated on his horse near the present Prince Rupert's Farm, he could see perfectly the progress of the infantry across the valley and up the gentle slopes to the hedge where the new memorial now stands. A few seconds later he would see the Roundheads streaming forward over the crest beyond it. As the infantry fired their only volley, Rupert's cavalry advanced. Descending the hill and trotting across the valley in two lines, they were abreast of their infantry in a few minutes. At the foot of the slope Rupert momentarily drew rein, either to let his troops pick up their dressing, or to allow the infantry on his left to get farther forward. Opposed to him were Ireton's Horse, almost twice the strength of his own. Rupert's charge went slightly wide of the infantry line, but it kept inside the Sulby hedges, whence it received a ragged fire which neither impeded nor diverted his attack. Sweeping up the gentle slope at an increased pace, his first line crashed into the left of Ireton's line about Redhill Farm. Rupert, accompanied by his brother, led the first line, the Earl of Northampton the second; the clash with Ireton's troops occurred half-way up the hill. The Roundheads seemed undecided as to their course of action; some advanced to meet the enemy head-on, whilst others preferred to halt and give battle in a stationary position. Whichever they did the result was the same – a static sword-fight – for this was no Edgehill charge; these were not raw troops but trained men, and Marston Moor had lowered the reputation of Rupert's troopers.

Ireton's own regiment did well enough, but Butler's, on the left of the front line, was broken, and was saved only by the musketry of Okey's men. The Prince's second line then came up, punching through the smoke and confusion to pierce the Roundhead ranks. Rupert swept Ireton's survivors from the field but then failed to halt his men promptly, in order to hurl them against the exposed flank of Skippon's Foot. Instead, it was stab, shoot and gallop for a mile or so, until the eager troopers came upon Fairfax's baggage-train, leaguered in a hollow near Naseby village. The camp guard, however, put up a sturdy resistance, and valuable time was lost by the Cavalier Horse in attempting to capture the baggage. Mindful of his experience at Edgehill under similar circumstances, Rupert drew rein and exerted himself to collect his troopers and lead them back to the battle. This, as always, was a difficult and lengthy task, and the best part of an hour elapsed before he reappeared on the field at the head of his victorious Horse.

In the centre, the Royalist Foot, although tired and outnumbered, went forward with a will, 'according to their usual custom, falling in with their swords, and the butt ends of their muskets. . . .'[1] In the first exchange Skippon

[1] Loc. cit.

had taken a musket bullet under the ribs, piercing doublet and armour. Swaying in the saddle, he remained in the field, but news of his wounding spread, and morale wavered. The front line wilted and crumpled, though determined knots of men stood around the colours and fell back slowly on to the second line. At this time the cavalry battle was in progress, and Ireton, seeing the peril of the infantry, led his regiment against the right of the Royalist Foot. He imposed some check on Astley's men, but they drove off his troopers with pikes and musketry. Ireton's horse was shot under him; a pikeman ran him through the thigh, a halberd gashed his face, and he was captured. The Parliamentarian Foot gained some respite due to Ireton's action, though it proved but temporary, and soon Skippon's second line was hotly assailed by the eager Royalist Foot.

The battle had been in progress for only half an hour or so, and already the Royalists were victorious on the right, and were winning in the centre. Events on the Royalist left, however, proved crucial. As Langdale's men came on across the eastern end of Broad Moor, Cromwell advanced down the fairly steep slope upon which he was drawn up, so as to meet the Royalist charge while on the move. The difficult ground on Cromwell's right impeded the advance in that quarter, and Whalley's regiment, formerly part of Cromwell's Ironsides, on the left, was first engaged. Langdale's northerners advanced boldly and, 'firing at very close range, they came to the sword'. But the weight of Whalley's men, pressing downhill, proved too much for the two right-hand divisions of Langdale's command, which were thrown back to the shelter of Rupert's Bluecoats, behind which they rallied.

The remainder of the Royalist left wing fared no better. Outflanked on one side by Rossiter, and on the other by Whalley and Sheffield, Langdale's men were 'pressed hard, before they could get to the top of the hill, they gave back, and fled farther and faster than became them'.[1] It was now that Cromwell demonstrated his great ability as a leader of cavalry. He sent four bodies,[2] 'close and in good order', to prevent the northerners from rallying, and threw the remainder of his command against the flank and rear of the Royalist Foot.

As the two regiments from Cromwell's wing chased Langdale off the field, the King, sitting his horse at the head of his lifeguard, prepared to charge them. He was dissuaded from this courageous but rash move by the Earl of Carnwath, who, 'on a sudden, laid his hand on the bridle of the King's horse, and swearing two or three full mouthed Scottish oaths . . . said "Will you go upon your death in an instant?"' With this, he swung the King's horse round; someone shouted that they should march to the right – away from Cromwell's pursuit – and disorder set in, the whole body galloping hard for about 500 yards until they were, with difficulty, halted. Thus, at a critical phase in the battle, the King's mounted reserve was in no condition to assist his hapless Foot.

[1] Ibid., p. 184.
[2] Probably four divisions, that is, two regiments – Cromwell's own and Whalley's would be the most likely.

Astley's infantry, engaged at push of pike with the three regiments of the second line of Roundhead Foot, were in no position to offer an effective resistance to the horsemen who spurred into their ranks with sword and pistol. Okey, reading the battle well, ordered his dragoons to mount as soon as there was no target for their musketry from the Sulby hedges, and led them forward against the right flank of the Foot. Standing like pebbles on a tide-swept beach, Astley's infantry could stand the pressure no longer, and began to throw down their arms and cry out for quarter.

One Royalist brigade, undaunted by the chaos around it, continued to resist. Sprigge indicates that it was one of the three front-line brigades, presumably Lisle's, but it seems likely that it was the reserve of Foot for it looks as if Rupert's Bluecoats took part in this desperate last stand. Fairfax, riding about the field bareheaded, for his helmet had been beaten off, threw his own regiment of Foot, which being unopposed had retained its cohesion, against the Bluecoats, who had already repulsed two cavalry charges. Finally, while the commander of his lifeguard, Captain Charles Doyley, attacked in front, Fairfax led a party of Horse against the rear of the brigade, and at last broke in. Fairfax himself laying about him like a common trooper, cut down an ensign and took his colour

Rupert, meanwhile, having failed to persuade the commander of the Roundhead baggage-train to surrender, and receiving, for his pains, a volley of musketry, rallied his troopers and led them back to the field. A scene of confusion met his horrified gaze. The Foot were laying down their arms, while, well to the rear, the King was trying to rally the flotsam of Langdale's Horse, menaced by the two regiments which Cromwell had detached. Rupert led his men round the flank, past the silent Sulby hedges, and joined the remnants of the King's army. Fairfax had no intention of squandering men in an ill-coordinated attack, and ordered the cavalry not to attack until the Foot were marshalled to support them. Then, with the Foot in the centre and Horse on the wings, he prepared to advance, screened by the musket fire of Okey's dragoons.

It was too much for the Royalist Horse. Even Rupert could not induce his men to charge; heavily outnumbered, and on tired horses, they wheeled about and left the field. Behind them they left the flower of the King's infantry, the men who had fought at Edgehill and First Newbury, who had encircled Essex at Lostwithiel and beaten off the concentric attacks at Second Newbury. It was more than the end of an army: it was, for all practical purposes, the end of a reign.

The Parliamentarian victory at Naseby was due almost entirely to the disciplined and intelligent behaviour of the cavalry on Fairfax's right wing. Clarendon rightly points out the 'difference that was observed all along in the discipline of the King's troops, and of those which marched under the command of Fairfax and Cromwell'.[1] It is tempting to censure Rupert for failing to do precisely what Cromwell achieved, but Cromwell enjoyed sufficient superiority on his

[1] Clarendon, op. cit., Vol. V, p. 184.

flank to be able to retain much of his Horse, uncommitted, under his hand. Rupert, outnumbered, was unable to do this; to break Ireton he had to use the full strength of both his lines. And it is a very difficult matter to reform cavalry once they have charged. Cromwell probably remained at the head of his second and third lines, in an excellent position to lead them against Astley's exposed flank. Had Goring's Horse been there to stiffen Langdale, things might have gone differently.

The most remarkable thing about Naseby is not that the Royalists lost, but that they came so close to winning – and this against a backcloth of fatal strategic errors. First amongst these must be reckoned Goring's initial detachment, and his subsequent failure to rejoin; secondly, the bitter divisions within the Royalist Council of War, coupled with the scornful under-estimation of the New Model, which was so common among the King's over-sanguine advisers, such as Digby and the influential Jack Ashburnham. Finally, in terms of intelligence, the Royalists were fighting blind; while Fairfax had Watson and Luke to supply him with information, Rupert staggered blindly in a world filled with conflicting rumours and malicious gossip. It is small wonder that Royalist strategy, the product of a divided command interlaced with personal vendettas, ended in the greatest disaster incurred by the arms of Charles I.

The fleeing Royalists were given no chance to rally. The Parliamentarian Horse, forbidden, on pain of death, to dismount for plunder, pushed on in an immediate and merciless pursuit. The spoils of the field were left to the Foot. The booty was rich indeed: all the King's guns, a huge quantity of arms and ammunition, and pretty well the entire Royalist baggage-train, were taken. Among the latter was the King's coach, containing his correspondence; this was published as *The King's Cabinet Opened*, and proved very damaging, revealing how Charles had endeavoured to persuade Irish Papists and French mercenaries to assist him. For the soldiers, more welcome was the capture of a good stock of biscuits and cheese, for the New Model had fought its first battle hungry. Many wagons contained plunder from Leicester, still more of which was snatched from the Royalist prisoners.

There were, indeed, many more prisoners than there were dead. Estimates of the number of Royalists captured vary between 4,000[1] and 6,000,[2] though Fiennes, whose task was to herd them into Market Harborough, and thence, by short marches, to London, reckoned the total at 4,500, which seems reasonable. Perhaps 1,000 Royalists were slain, as against fewer than 200 Parliamentarians.[3]

An episode which accrues little to the credit of the New Model occurred during the pursuit. When the Royalist leaguer was overrun, it was found to contain hundreds of women, soldiers' wives or camp-followers with a less defined status.

[1] Sprigge, op. cit., p. 40.
[2] Ludlow, op. cit., p. 120.
[3] Rushworth, who 'viewed the ground where the bodies lay', says 150, though in view of the disintegration of the first line of Fairfax's Foot, this is probably too low.

About 100 of these were killed out of hand, and the rest marked as whores by having their noses slit or their faces slashed. It was averred, by way of excuse, that they were Irish, and armed with long knives, but it seems more likely that they were Welsh, and their knives were to prepare food for the Welsh infantry they followed.[1]

The King halted briefly at Leicester, where he was joined by Rupert and Maurice. With him were the tatters of his Horse, and such of the mounted infantry officers as had managed to get clear. He ordered that the wounded were to be cared for, and Leicester held, but then rode on to Ashby de la Zouch, where he spent the night. He travelled on to Lichfield, and thence to Hereford, where he was soon hard at work trying to raise new infantry around a nucleus of Gerard's Welshmen.

[1] This is Miss Wedgwood's suggestion (op. cit., p. 445); it seems very reasonable.

Nineteen

TAUNTON AND LANGPORT

Naseby had shown that in the New Model, Fairfax had the makings of a formidable army. Moreover, Parliament still had two other armies in the field. These smaller local armies were those of the Western Association, under Major-General Massey, and of the seven associated northern counties under Colonel-General Sydenham Poyntz – a professional soldier who had recently returned to England after serving in Holland and Germany. Besides the three English armies the Committee of Both Kingdoms still had the Scots at their disposal. Leven, realising that Charles no longer threatened to invade Scotland, had marched back from Westmorland and, moving through Yorkshire, had by 20 June got as far south as Mansfield in Nottinghamshire.

Although the King still had about 4,000 cavalry, it was only with the utmost difficulty that he scraped together 3,000 Foot, and these naturally were not to be compared with the homogeneous body destroyed at Naseby. In South Wales, Gerard still commanded a force some 3,000 strong, but that was more than counterbalanced by Massey's army. Byron at Chester was hemmed in by Sir Thomas Middleton and Sir William Brereton, the one commanding in North Wales, the other in Cheshire. Both – like Cromwell – had been allowed to continue in arms despite the Self-Denying Ordinance.

The Royalists had now only one army left to pit against the New Model – namely the western army under Goring. The best course still open to the King was to march into Somerset and build up his field army by combining Goring's men with his own. Only by such a concentration of his remaining strength could he achieve any considerable success. There was little to prevent such a move, for Fairfax, instead of pursuing his beaten foe, sat down before Leicester, which fell to him on 18 June. Next day Charles entered Hereford.

There was now nothing to prevent the King either marching to Goring's assistance, or at the least holding Massey in check. Goring was still stuck fast before Taunton, but it was thought that once that place was captured he could advance to join the King, who would then have an army of 6,000 Horse and perhaps 8,000 Foot. However, this was to reckon without Robert Blake putting up a heroic resistance at Taunton. Goring, indeed, had his hands full.

In London there was popular clamour for the relief of Taunton, and Fairfax now resolved to make the attempt. He had already got as far south as Marlborough when this decision was made. The date was 28 June, and he had done the 113 miles from Leicester in a week.

Fairfax could not be sure how long Taunton would hold out and he decided to take no risks, but to march to its relief with maximum speed. This was all the more necessary inasmuch as the direct route was threatened by several Royalist garrisons – Devizes, Bath, Bristol, Bridgwater. Fairfax therefore elected to approach from the south, at the same time changing his base for supplies to the ports of Lyme and Weymouth.

On Monday 30 June, the forced march began. Twenty miles were covered the first day and the army billeted in Amesbury that night. Next day the army marched out to Stonehenge and then south-west to Bower Chalke (seven miles west of Salisbury). On Wednesday Blandford was reached. On Friday the army was at Beaminster (seven miles south of Crewkerne), having marched *via* Dorchester. This represented a five days' march at seventeen miles per day; moreover, in hot weather. Here totally unexpected news reached Fairfax: Goring had suddenly abandoned the siege of Taunton and marched towards Yeovil.

Unfortunately, nearly all the eye-witness accounts of this campaign come from the Parliamentarian side, and the brilliant but unpredictable Goring has not left us his own version. We are thus reduced to guessing what was in his mind at any given moment, and his movements were on the surface so curious that we are left to conjecture. But the probable reason for abandoning the siege was the news of the approach of Fairfax, for the Roundhead could muster 14,000 men, when General Massey's army in the west had joined him, whilst the Cavaliers had slightly less than half this number.

On retiring from Taunton, Goring fell back behind the rivers Parret and Yeo. This manoeuvre was, no doubt, prompted by a desire to retain communications with Bristol and the King, but it entailed a risky move across Fairfax's front; moreover, the important fortress of Bridgwater was isolated on the extreme right of this position. As Fairfax closed up to Crewkerne, sending Fleetwood ahead to watch Goring, he learnt that the Royalists had now taken up a position behind the Yeo between Langport and Yeovil. Goring's advanced detachments, screening the Parret south of Langport, fell back, though they thoughtfully wrecked the bridge at South Petherton before doing so.

Goring's men now held the line of the Yeo, from Langport to Yeovil, a wide front of twelve miles in a straight line, but much more if measured along the windings of the river. True, the Yeo was fordable only in places, and there were only three bridges in the sector – those at Load Bridge, between Long Load and Long Sutton, and Ilchester and Yeovil – but a long river line is difficult to hold. Goring located his headquarters in Long Sutton, and sent strong detachments to cover the bridges at Load and Ilchester.

On 5 July Fairfax concentrated at Crewkerne, and followed Fleetwood north-wards to make a personal reconnaissance of the hostile position. He also ordered Weldon, whose brigade had broken through to Taunton in May, to rejoin him. The 6th was a Sunday, and Fairfax, who always rested on the Sabbath wherever possible, kept his men in their quarters. On Monday Sir Thomas made yet another reconnaissance, and then called a Council of War. The Council deter-mined to pin Goring by threatening the Load and Ilchester bridges with Horse, while the infantry turned Goring's left at Yeovil, which was weakly guarded.

This plan proved successful; the detachment in Yeovil fell back, and the line was gained without firing a shot. Again, we cannot say what was Goring's intention, and whether Yeovil was given up by his orders or not. Ilchester was also abandoned, and the Royalist army concentrated on Langport. Goring, preoccupied with the need to cover Bridgwater, and to prevent Fairfax cutting him off from Bristol, endeavoured to confuse Fairfax so as to get him to divide his forces. Accordingly, he sent George Porter with a strong detachment of Horse to the south-west, to persuade Fairfax that he was moving on Taunton. This deception plan worked well at first; Fairfax sent Massey, with 4,000 men, towards Taunton, in an effort to check this threat. Unfortunately, Porter's Horse, whose morale and discipline were by now rather frayed, were surprised near Ilminster: 'the enemy were upon them before the men could get upon their horses; they being then feeding in a meadow; so that this body was entirely routed, and very many taken. . . .'[1] Porter was probably the most incompetent general officer on either side during the Civil War, and the blame on this occasion may well be laid squarely on his shoulders.

Angered though he was by Porter's mishap, Goring had every reason to con-gratulate himself; Fairfax now only had 10,000 men with which to oppose his own force of nearly 7,000. With the odds thus weighing less heavily against him, Goring hoped to conduct a safe withdrawal on Bridgwater. On the early morning of 10 July he sent his baggage and guns, with the exception of two small pieces, back to Bridgwater, covering their withdrawal from a strong position on the eastern outskirts of Langport.

THE BATTLE OF LANGPORT, 10 JULY

The little town of Langport lies on slightly rising ground on the north bank of the rivers Parret and Yeo at their point of junction. One thousand yards east of the town is the church of Huish Episcopi with its lofty tower. From its summit a splendid view can be obtained of the battlefield. The Royalist position ran along the west side of a little brook, sometimes called the Wagg Rhyne, that runs through Pibsbury Bottom and crosses the Long Sutton road about 700 yards east of the church. The slope down to the brook is gentle and is equally so up the far (east) side. But farther to the north, it is steeper, and the

[1] Clarendon, op. cit., Vol. V, p. 208.

watercourse runs through a slight ravine, thus making it a fair obstacle to mounted troops. On the day of the battle a good deal of water was coming down, and the ford by which the road crossed the brook was described, with some exaggeration, as 'up to the horses' girths'.

The country beyond the brook was open, but on the near side it was enclosed, and the road was lined with hedges. Royalist musketeers occupied these hedges and others along the line of Pibsbury Bottom, while cavalry were posted on the slight ridge in rear, and the two guns were brought into action at the top of the slope covering the ford (or 'pass' as it was called in all contemporary accounts). The right flank was covered by the deep River Yeo. Thus the position was a fairly strong one. Lord Goring placed himself at the head of the Horse over-looking the 'pass', and awaited events with apparent confidence.

In the Parliamentarian camp, a Council of War had been held in the early morning, the problem being how to bring the Royalists to battle. While the Council was in session, however, news was brought that they were evidently intending to hold their ground. It was thus unnecessary to take steps to bring about a battle; all that had to be decided upon was a plan of attack. The Yeo effectively prevented an outflanking movement from the south. The front of the position was so marshy as to make any attack, save down the lane leading to the ford, impossible. An outflanking movement to the north was possible, but to make it the Parliamentarians would have to wheel across Goring's front; this would have taken some time, and Goring's prime object was to hold the position only long enough to permit his artillery and baggage to reach the safety of Bridgwater.

Fairfax decided to take the bull by the horns, and assault the pass, which both he and Goring realised to be the key to the position. His decision was probably made easier by the fact that Goring had hardly any artillery, and hence could not interdict the narrow lane with a heavy fire. Furthermore, the behaviour of Porter's Horse would have given him an indication that Goring's force was not as formidable as it seemed. Fairfax's first step was to silence the two small guns covering the pass. This was a comparatively easy matter, and the Roundhead guns were deployed in a line along the ridge that runs parallel to Wagg Rhyne, and a few hundred yards from it. From here to the Royalist guns the range was about 700 yards. An overwhelming fire was concentrated on these two unfortunate pieces, 'the cannon playing their part as gallantly as ever I saw gunners in my life', declared the enthusiastic Colonel Lilburne, though it was a one-sided duel. By noon, the Royalist artillery had been battered into silence by sheer weight of metal, and the next part of the Parliamentarian plan unfolded.

Fifteen hundred 'commanded' musketeers, under Colonel Rainsborough, moved forward rapidly, and began to clear the Royalist musketeers from their lodgement in the hedges. Sir Richard Bulstrode, Goring's adjutant-general, maintained that the musketeers – from two fairly new regiments, Wise's and

Slaughter's – behaved badly, some even firing on their own side. However, other accounts indicate that the encounter lasted an hour, until the Royalists were all pushed back from the ford.[1] While Rainsborough's men skirmished among the hedges, Cromwell formed up two forlorn hopes of Horse for Fairfax's masterstroke, which was to be nothing less than a charge across the ford. This must have seemed a hazardous venture, for there was just room for four horses abreast, their riders knee to knee, in the 'pass'. Royalist musketeers still lined the hedges towards the top of the hill, where Goring's Horse stood massed.

Major Bethell, with three troops of Whalley's regiment – Cromwell's Ironsides to a man – was to head the attack, supported by Major Desborough with three troops from Fairfax's regiment. Bethell's squadron galloped forward 'with the greatest gallantry imaginable',[2] down the ridge, across the ford and up the slope beyond. They received a ragged fire from some musketeers in the hedges on the upper part of the slope, but this did not check their progress. Without drawing rein, or even, it seems, deploying,[3] the leading troop crashed straight into the front rank of the waiting Cavaliers, and broke them. The two following troops managed to deploy out of the lane, and overthrew the second line of Royalist Horse. But Goring had more behind; the three Parliamentarian troops were now in the heart of the Royalist position, faced by Goring's lifeguard and his own and Sir Arthur Slingsby's regiments of Horse; once the momentum of the charge was spent, there was no hope of further progress. Bethell's men were gradually overborne by sheer weight of numbers, and began to fall back.

At this critical juncture, Desborough's three troops came forward to their support. On reaching the top Desborough swung his squadron round to the north, and then, wheeling to the left, he fell on the open left flank of the Cavalier Horse, who recoiled from the shock. The Parliamentarian musketeers, moving up the lane, followed by large numbers of fresh infantry, added their fire to the combined assault. There was a confused mêlée on the top of the slope, but the Cavaliers gradually shredded into small bodies and dissolved in flight. Cromwell concentrated his cavalry before embarking upon the pursuit. The retreating Royalists had fired Langport, and the Parliamentarian Horse rode through the town with flames arching overhead. Goring made an unsuccessful attempt to hold the Bridgwater road near the village of Aller, but his shaken troopers would not stand.

Goring rode into Bridgwater that night to find that many of his men had taken shelter within the walls of the fortress. He had left about 300 dead on the

---

[1] There is a good account in Sprigge, op. cit., pp. 64–6. Sir Richard Bulstrode's *Memoirs* . . . (London 1721), and Thomason Tracts E.261 (4), a copy of Fairfax's despatch to Parliament; E.292 (30) Lilburne's account; E.293 (8), E.292 (28) and E.293 (17) are all useful.

[2] Cromwell, in *Good Newes out of the West*, TT E.293 (18).

[3] There is some doubt on this point. It is probable, though, that Bethell's success was due largely to the terrific impact of his squadron, coming on in close column at the gallop. Much of this impact would have been lost had he halted to deploy.

field, and half his army had been captured or had disbanded. Leaving a good garrison in Bridgwater, he fell back, on the following day, into Devonshire. This retreat was accompanied by scenes of growing disorder, for the country people, so long mistreated by both sides, took an ugly revenge on stragglers. For some time war-weariness in the west had manifested itself in the bands of 'clubmen' who announced their intention of defending their homes and property against marauders from either army. In many areas these clubmen were backed, or even led, by the local gentry. Fairfax had reached an agreement with the clubmen as he advanced into the west; moreover, the discipline of the New Model prevented just those abuses which acted as a mainspring for local hostility in the first place.[1] In an effort to buy immunity, Goring had provided some of the clubmen with arms and officers. This expedient produced some success – a detachment of Massey's was sharply attacked by clubmen at Sturminster Newton – but it overlooked the cause of the problem, lack of discipline.

The battle of Langport may not have annihilated Goring's army, but it broke its will to fight. Goring had performed very well strategically; his feint towards Taunton resulted in Massey's 4,000 men being separated from the remainder of Fairfax's army by three rivers: the Isle, the Parret and the Yeo. Tactically, Goring had shown himself less sound, though the Langport position was well chosen and the dispositions for its defence well made. His great failing was that, like so many other Royalist commanders, and particularly his colleagues in the west, he allowed discipline to become eroded and morale to deteriorate; the pivotal defect in the Langport position lay in the morale of the men that held it.

Fairfax had, conversely, shown himself more able to handle the battle than the campaign. Although he succeeded in turning the flank of the Yeo position, he did not endeavour to exploit this manoeuvre until Goring had had ample time to take up a new position on the Wagg Rhyne. Fairfax also fell for Porter's feint towards Taunton, detaching a substantial part of his force to deal with it. Nevertheless, these errors were more than counterbalanced by his ability to assess the relative values of his own and Goring's army, and to plan the battle accordingly. This plan of attack at Langport seems, at first sight, suicidal. Fairfax realised, however, that his men possessed what Goring's brawling troopers lacked – discipline, cohesion and high morale. Particular credit is due to Bethell, whose charge, 'one of the bravest that eyes ever beheld',[2] must rank as one of the most daring, and successful, instances of shock action by the mounted arm.

[1] See Cromwell's interesting letter to Fairfax on the subject of clubmen, written from Shaftesbury on 4 August. Carlyle, op. cit., Vol. I, pp. 209–11.
[2] Lilburne, A more full Relation . . ., TT E.292 (30).

Twenty

TORRINGTON
AND STOW-ON-THE-WOLD

The King was staying at Raglan, in something approaching his old life-style, when he heard of the defeat of his western army at Langport. On 22 July Rupert, working frantically to organise the defence of the Bristol area, slipped across the Bristol Channel to meet his uncle at Crick. It was decided that Bristol would be the King's headquarters for the coming campaign, for while Bridgwater remained Royalist, and Grenvile and Goring had troops in Devonshire, there was still hope in the west. This hope soon dwindled. Although the Self-Denying Ordinance had deprived the capable Warwick of his command, the navy continued to operate efficiently under the command of Batten. Captain Robert Moulton, cruising in the Bristol Channel, captured sixteen ships which were to have been used for ferrying troops from Wales to the West Country.[1]

The next blow came on land. Fairfax's Council of War had, after a prolonged debate, decided to assault the formidable fortress of Bridgwater. The governor, Sir Hugh Wyndham, made a bold defence, but the place fell on 23 July.[2] It was now no longer possible for the King to consider using Bristol as his headquarters. Fairfax continued with the systematic reduction of Royalist strongholds in the west. Bath fell to a surprise attack by Okey's dragoons. Sherborne Castle, held by the seemingly indestructible Sir Lewis Dyve, resisted stoutly, but was taken on 14 August after a ten-day siege.[3] Fairfax then turned his attention to the key to what remained of Royalist power in the west – the city of Bristol, held for the King by Prince Rupert himself.

The tide was running against the Royalists all over England. Glemham had

[1] J. R. Powell, *The Navy in the English Civil War* (London 1962), p. 106.
[2] *See* Fairfax's letter to Parliament, TT E.294 (6). Sprigge, op. cit., pp. 66–74, deals with the siege and surrender of Bridgwater.
[3] Sir Lewis survived the fall of Sherborne. He escaped from the Tower and made his way to France, where, it seems, his tales lost little in the telling. Sprigge, op. cit., pp. 82–7, gives a detailed account of the siege. *See also* Fairfax's letter to Parliament in TT E.297 (3).

at last surrendered Carlisle, but appeared at Oxford, ready to continue the struggle. By now, though, it was apparent to all but the most stout-hearted, like Glemham, or the unrealistic, like Digby, that the game was up. Those Royalists who were professional soldiers saw all too clearly that all was lost; those who came from the landed gentry began to think of saving something from the wreck. The stream of Cavaliers making their way to Westminster to pay their fines and compound for their estates was now becoming a flood. Parliament did not demand the unconditional surrender of the King's supporters; few Royalists were exempted from pardon, and they were denounced by name. Even Rupert had little hope. He wrote to the Duke of Richmond that 'If I were desired to deliver my opinion, which your Lordship may declare to the King, His Majesty hath now no way left to preserve his prosperity, Kingdom and nobility, but by a treaty. I believe it a more prudent way to retain something than to lose all.'[1]

Rupert's letter was shown to Charles, whose reply was unequivocal.

As for your opinion of my business [he wrote] and your counsel thereupon, if I had any other quarrel but the defence of my religion, crown and friends, you had full reason for your advice; for I confess that, speaking either as a mere soldier or statesman, I must say that there is no probability but of my ruin. Yet as a Christian I must tell you that God will not suffer rebels and traitors to prosper, nor this cause to be overthrown. And whatever personal punishment it shall please him to inflict upon me must not make me repine, much less give over this quarrel. . . .[2]

It was in this mood of fatalistic but heroic resignation that the King nerved himself to continue the unequal war.

Digby failed to share the King's fatalism even at this late juncture. He expected imminent aid from Ireland, and maintained that Hopton would raise Cornwall and drive Fairfax into the sea.[3] He was sadly deluded in both instances. The only source of real comfort was Montrose, who cut to pieces a Covenanting army under Baillie at Alford on 2 July. On hearing of this, Charles determined to march north. This decision was not prompted only by a desire to join Montrose, but also by the King's increasing insecurity in Wales. Gerard, a 'passionate and unskilful manager of the affections of the people',[4] had alienated most of the Welsh, and recruiting was going far from well, despite Charles's efforts. At the end of July, Admiral Batten, in a remarkable piece of amphibious cooperation with Major-General Laugharne, enabled the latter to rout Sir Edward Stradling at Colby Moor on 1 August.

On 5 August the King left Cardiff with about 2,500 Horse and Foot. Leven

[1] Warburton, op. cit., Vol. III, p. 149.
[2] Rushworth, op. cit., Vol. VI, p. 132.
[3] Wedgwood, *The King's War*, p. 471.
[4] Clarendon, op. cit., Vol. V, p. 222.

had at last bestirred himself and was besieging Hereford, so the King's party had to tread carefully. At Lichfield, Charles paused long enough to arrest Loughborough, charging him with the premature surrender of Leicester. He reached Doncaster on 18 August, but was soon threatened by Leslie, with 4,000 Scottish Horse, from the west, and by Poyntz from the north. He accordingly fell back into the Eastern Association, reaching Huntingdon on the 24th. By this time the danger from Leslie had evaporated, for on 15 August Montrose defeated Baillie and Balcarres at Kilsyth, and Leslie had swung his cavalry north to assist the hard-pressed Covenanters. Charles's troopers were happily plundering Huntingdon and its environs when the news of Kilsyth arrived. Poyntz, however, blocked the road north, so the King contented himself with marching to Oxford, and thence, by way of Worcester, to Hereford, where Leven raised the siege and retired to Gloucester.

On the same day that Charles entered Hereford, 4 September, Fairfax, having concentrated before Bristol, summoned Rupert to surrender. The Prince had spent some time preparing Bristol for a siege, but there was plague in the city, and the garrison of 1,500 was too small to hold the five-mile circuit of defences. Rupert had some success with cavalry raids on the Parliamentarian quarters before Fairfax closed the ring. Fairfax posted a brigade of Horse on Durdham Down, to prevent either relief or escape. Weldon's brigade was to assault from the south, against the same defences battered by Hopton's Cornishmen in 1643. Four regiments of Foot, under Colonel Rainsborough, were to assault Prior's Hill Fort and the wall between it and the River Frome.

The Parliamentarians attacked on 10 September, supported by a heavy bombardment. Weldon's men made no progress against the southern defences, but Rainsborough's brigade swarmed over the wall on the eastern side, which was not more than five feet high in places. Rupert's cavalry counter-attacked as the Parliamentarian Horse surged in, but this counter-thrust failed. Prior's Hill Fort, assailed from front and rear, held out for two hours, but was eventually stormed and its garrison put to the sword by the infuriated Roundhead infantry. The unfortunate Rupert now found himself in the same situation to which he had condemned Nathaniel Fiennes two years before. Some of the outer forts still held, but the bulk of the garrison had withdrawn to the inner line of defences. Continued resistance could only result in the elimination of the outer defences and the eventual collapse of the citadel. Rupert, with the concurrence of his Council of War, surrendered on terms. His men were to march out with bag and baggage, and swords, though not firearms, and were granted safe conduct to Oxford.

News of the surrender of Bristol came as a shattering blow to Charles, who was at Raglan Castle formulating an unrealistic plan for the relief of the city. His immediate response was to suspect Rupert's loyalty. The continual insinuations of Digby at last bore fruit; Charles wrote his nephew a painful letter, dismissing him from his command:

I must remember you of your letter on 12th of August, whereby you assured me, that, if no mutiny happened, you would keep Bristol for four months. Did you keep it four days? Was there anything like a mutiny ...? My conclusion is, to desire you to seek your subsistence ... somewhere beyond seas, to which end I send you herewith a pass. ...[1]

Things went hard with Rupert's supporters, the clique which, Digby alleged, was involved in a gigantic conspiracy against the King.[2] Will Legge was dismissed from his post as governor of Oxford, and was replaced by Sir Thomas Glemham.

Having thus disposed of Rupert, the unscrupulous Digby continued to spawn a web of impossible plans, which relied upon massive intervention by the Irish, Scots Royalists, or the western generals. Little could be hoped for from the latter, who were once more engaged in their favourite sport, quarrelling amongst themselves. Grenvile recouped his personal fortune by plundering, and paid scant attention to any orders sent him. Goring did nothing to check Fairfax's demolition of the western fortresses; some said he was ill, others, less charitably, maintained that he was permanently drunk. This left the Irish and Montrose. The prospect of assistance from the former, such as it was, depended on the continued Royalist tenure of Chester, besieged, on and off, since July 1643.

Charles's new plan was to make for Scotland, and, marching through Lancashire and Cumberland, to join hands with Montrose. He left Raglan on 18 September, and four days later was at Chirk, about twenty miles south of Chester. Here he received a message from Lord Byron, announcing that Chester was hard pressed, and requesting immediate assistance. Chester lies on the River Dee, which flows from south to north at this point. The Roundheads had been able to invest it only on the east or English side, and it was still open on the west or Welsh side. The King therefore was able, after a rapid and tiring march, to enter the city by the Dee Bridge. He had with him a handful of infantry under Lord Astley, his lifeguards under the Earl of Lichfield and some cavalry under Lord Charles Gerard,[3] perhaps 1,000 in all. Langdale, with the bulk of the cavalry some 3,000 strong, was sent to cross the Dee by a bridge of boats at Holt, eight miles to the south, with orders to swing left-handed and fall upon the besiegers from the rear. It was an admirable plan.

Like so many other admirable plans, the Royalist scheme met with unexpected difficulties. Colonel-General Poyntz, who had failed to engage the King near Worcester, had pursued him from the south with some 3,000 Horse and by

---

[1] Ibid., pp. 252-3.

[2] Several pieces of circumstantial evidence supported Digby's allegations. Rupert and Fairfax behaved with great courtesy towards each other, and, at about the same time that Bristol capitulated, Rupert's elder brother, the Elector Palatine, enjoying Roundhead hospitality at Westminster, was voted £8,000 by Parliament.

[3] Gerard had recently been made a baron, and replaced in the Welsh command by Astley.

dint of a night march he came up with the Cavaliers at about 6 a.m. on 24 September. Langdale, however, had learned of his approach from an intercepted letter. About 9 a.m. he charged Poyntz and drove him back with loss, but the Parliamentarians were not routed. Thus the situation was one of stalemate. Langdale could not march on Chester with Poyntz just behind him, while Poyntz could not join the besiegers while Langdale was on Rowton Heath. Both sides required reinforcements, but while Langdale somehow failed to get news of his predicament to the Royalists in Chester, Poyntz did manage to get in touch with the besiegers and his appeal was promptly answered. About noon 500 Horse and 300 Foot under Colonel Michael Jones marched to meet Poyntz, going round the flank of the Royalists and making contact with Poyntz, who was drawn up on Hatton Heath, two miles south of Rowton.

During the morning the Royalists in Chester had been making preparations for a sally, the citizens clearing away the dung that barricaded the east gate, but it was past 3 p.m. before the King sent orders for a sortie. Then Gerard and Lichfield led their Horse out of Chester and drew them up under the walls. Meanwhile, attacked by Poyntz in front and by Colonel Jones on the flank, Langdale's outnumbered men were, after a short resistance, overpowered; they broke and fled, some making for Farndon bridge and Wales, but the majority galloping towards Chester. Here beneath the city walls they met the rest of the Roundhead besieging force and also their own reinforcements. A terrible fight ensued, friend and foe inextricably mixed and both fired upon from the walls. Gerard's Horse at one time looked like stemming the tide, but a fresh wave of fugitives swept them away, and the unhappy King from his observation post in the Phoenix Tower on the north-east corner of the city wall had the mortification of seeing his troops driven away from the city in a northerly direction and hunted down in the narrow and boggy lanes of Hoole Heath. The young Earl of Lichfield was among the slain.

Charles was profoundly shocked by the defeat of his cavalry on Rowton Heath, and even the normally irrepressible Digby found the death of Lichfield depressing. More serious was the news which percolated south from Scotland. Montrose had been caught by David Leslie at Philiphaugh. His splendid Irish infantry fought desperately against overwhelming odds, and their remnants were persuaded to surrender. Leslie's soldierly honour, however, was no match for the covenanting ministers who accompanied his army. These zealots persuaded the general that he had granted quarter only to the officers who had negotiated the truce, and the weak-willed Leslie consented to the butchering o the Irish, with their camp followers and families; an infamous and unjustifiable act. Montrose wanted to fling himself into the battle and die fighting, but his friends persuaded him to escape, and he cut his way out, accompanied by a few horsemen.

Although Chester remained defensible – Byron, in fact, hung on with dogged courage until 3 February 1646 – it was a poor headquarters for Charles. He decided to go to Newark, prompted largely by Digby, who wished to keep him away from Oxford, where Rupert, who had been permitted to remain in the country, was. On 13 October the King was at Welbeck Abbey, just north of Newark. Here he held a Council of War to decide upon his next step. It was rumoured that Montrose was raising a new army and several members of the Council advocated a new march north. Digby was particularly loud in this, for he had just heard that Rupert and Maurice were on their way to Newark, and a reconciliation between Prince and King could only lead to a diminution of his influence.

The upshot was that Digby, probably with Langdale's connivance, was commissioned as lieutenant-general of all forces north of the Trent, and sent to join Montrose with the northern Horse. The King returned to Newark. Rupert, in an effort to clear his name, had left Oxford accompanied by his lifeguard and a number of his friends. He arrived at Newark on 16 October, undeterred by a message from Charles ordering him to return to Oxford. Rupert managed to have the Bristol question formally raised at the Council of War, which declared that he had held the city as long as possible. The Prince, well pleased with the verdict, recovered much of his former arrogance. The governor of Newark, Sir Richard Willys, was a close friend of Rupert's, as was the recently ennobled but still sour Charles Gerard. The King, irritated by Rupert's disobedience, and disturbed at the hardening of the 'Rupert clique', replaced Willys by Lord John Belasyse, a decision which led to a near-mutiny amongst Rupert's supporters. When the King left Newark for Oxford, his army, already over-officered and under-recruited, was totally dislocated by this last crisis.

Digby, fortified as ever by supreme confidence, had contrived to win, and then lose, a confused action at Sherburn-in-Elmet in Yorkshire on 15 October. He blamed his defeat on the panic of the northern Horse and, accompanied by Langdale and a few hundred troopers, rode north to Scotland, whence, his sanguine temperament still unscarred, he sailed to the Isle of Man, and eventually on to Ireland, to accelerate the arrival of Irish troops. He was to have less success in this venture than he had had as lieutenant-general of the north.

In the west, Royalist fortresses continued to crumble before the artillery of the New Model. Devizes Castle fell to Cromwell with a battering train and a small army of Horse and Foot on 23 September, and Winchester submitted twelve days later. Cromwell then turned his attention to Basing House, which he summoned on 11 October. The old Marquis of Winchester refused to surrender, but Cromwell's powerful artillery knocked his fortifications to pieces about his ears, and on the 14th the Parliamentarians carried Basing by storm. In the heat of the action the exultant soldiery massacred many of the garrison, including six Catholic priests. The daughter of one of these unfortunates was cut down as she tried to protect her father. The house was sacked, but the poor Marquis, standing bareheaded amongst the ruins, was unabashed. 'If the King had no more ground in England but Basing,' he retorted to his taunters, 'I would venture as I did. . . . Basing is called loyalty. I hope,' he added pathetically, 'that the King may have a day again.'

Goring, beset by illness, drink, or both, had departed overseas, and his command had been taken over by Lord Wentworth, who shared his predecessor's liking for the bottle while possessing none of his military talent. The situation in the west was critical, for outside Devon and Cornwall only Dunster Castle, near Minehead, now held a Royalist garrison, and Exeter itself was threatened. Wentworth was not the man to restore so desperate a situation. By the end of December Fairfax had occupied Crediton, and on 9 January 1646, Cromwell, who had returned to the west, surprised Wentworth's cavalry at Bovey Tracey, fourteen miles south-west of Exeter. Wentworth's men were caught in disorder, cut to ribbons, and fled panic-stricken to Tavistock. Internal dispute within the western armies grew to fever pitch; in one instance a fight flared up between Wentworth's Horse, guards and firelocks, and two or three men were killed.[1]

On 15 January the Prince of Wales and his Council at last decided to reorganise the command. Hopton was made general of the remains of the western army; Wentworth was to command the Horse and Grenvile the Foot. Hopton, dependable to the last, told the Prince that 'he could not obey his highness at this time, without resolving to lose his honour, which he knew he must; but since his highness thought it necessary to command him, he was ready to obey him with the loss of his honour'.[2] Troubles began at once, but Hopton faced them with resolution. Grenvile, awkward as ever, refused to take orders from Hopton, and was promptly arrested by the Prince. This was a valuable step towards restoring discipline, and the Cornishmen who liked Grenvile as their fellow countryman would doubtless have recovered from the shock if given time. Wentworth's cavalry, however, seem to have been past hope by now. Clarendon wittily but truly described them as 'Horse whom only their friends feared and their enemies laughed at; being only terrible in plunder, and resolute in running away'.[3] Only the Prince's regiment of lifeguards could be thoroughly depended upon. Nevertheless, Hopton took the offensive in the hope of relieving Exeter. He had less than 2,000 Foot and only a little more than 3,000 Horse when on 10 February 1646 he occupied Torrington.

Fairfax had not been idle in January, for, after relieving Plymouth, he stormed Dartmouth on the 19th. He then laid siege to Exeter, and was before its walls when news of the surrender of Chester arrived. This left Brereton to contain the King's dwindling army; Fairfax was free to deal with Hopton. Leaving a brigade of the New Model to mask Exeter, Fairfax marched to Chumleigh, where he arrived on 14 February. A further advance was delayed by foul

[1] Clarendon, op. cit., Vol. V, pp. 304-5.
[2] Ibid., p. 307.
[3] Ibid., p. 306.

weather until the early morning of the 16th, when Fairfax marched out to Ring Ash, where he drew up his army for an assault on Torrington.

Hopton, as at Devizes in 1643, had thrown up barricades of trees on the approach roads, and had firmly blocked all the streets. The Foot were stationed in small parties at key points, with Horse close by to support them. Stevenstone House, about a mile to the east, contained a strong detachment of dragoons. Fairfax's advancing cavalry bumped these dragoons, and as a party of Horse and Foot covered their withdrawal there was bickering on the high ground which overlooks Torrington from the east. By nightfall the Royalists had all withdrawn into the town, and Fairfax, with the advice of his Council of War, decided to attack next day so as to have an opportunity of reconnoitring the Royalist defences in daylight. It was dark by this time, and Cromwell was sent out to inspect the Parliamentarian outposts. In so doing, he deduced from the noise coming from the town that Hopton was on the point of retirement, and sent forward a patrol of dragoons who drew the fire of the Cornish infantry. At this, a general fire-fight flared up all round the defences, and the Parliamentarians decided to attack without waiting for daylight.

Colonel Hammond assaulted the barricades with three regiments of Foot, backed by the dragoons. For two hours a savage fight raged, the Cornish infantry fighting boldly 'at push of pike, and with the butt-end of their muskets'.[1] Hammond's men at last forced their way into the town, and the defending infantry broke in panic, throwing down their arms and fleeing. Major-General John Digby then counter-attacked with the Cavalier Horse, and there was a general action in the dark streets. In the confusion, the Royalist magazine, which was situated in the church, blew up. Two hundred Parliamentarian prisoners in the church were killed instantly, and Fairfax was narrowly missed by falling debris. Hopton was wounded in the face by a Roundhead pikeman, and his horse was killed under him; nevertheless, he and Lord Capel fought it out with their rear-guard, but, although the attacker's losses had not been light – perhaps 200 men killed, together with the prisoners in the church – few of the Royalists who escaped unwounded could be rallied again.

Fairfax pursued Hopton's remnants westwards. The Prince's Council realised that the end in the west was near, and on 2 March the Prince and his attendants sailed to the Scilly Isles. It proved impossible for Hopton to recruit in Cornwall; the wily Hugh Peters, a Parliamentarian chaplain, had publicised captured letters announcing that 10,000 Irishmen were to be sent to aid Hopton. On 6 March Fairfax offered terms which Hopton found so reasonable that he dare not publish them lest his army should disintegrate. Even Hopton, however, realised that further resistance was impossible; terms were agreed on 12 March, and

---

[1] Fairfax's letter to Speaker Lenthall, printed in Sprigge, op. cit., p. 191. The Royalists fought surprisingly well; Sprigge says that 'the service was very hot, we had many wounded, it was stoutly maintained on both sides for the time' (p. 187). *See also* TT E.325 (2), which gives a list of the Royalist officer prisoners.

the western army disbanded over the following weeks. Stubborn old John Arundel held out in Pendennis Castle, but Berkeley, offered excellent conditions, surrendered Exeter on 9 April.

Charles did not give up hope, even while his western army crumbled. Hoping that his negotiations with the French would produce some assistance, he ordered Lord Astley, who still had 3,000 men in Worcestershire, to cut his way through to Oxford and join him. Thus reinforced, Charles might hold out until one of his fanciful schemes for French, Irish, Scots Royalists, or even Papal, help could materialise. Astley had to wend his way between the garrisons of Gloucester and Evesham, and, although he crossed the Avon safely, he was soon engaged by Brereton's cavalry from the north, while Colonel Morgan, governor of Gloucester, marched to intercept him with infantry. By 20 March Astley was near Stow-on-the-Wold, and that night he took up a defensive position on a hillside below the town. The Parliamentarians came in at dawn the next morning; Astley's levies were overwhelmed, though some of his Horse got off to Oxford, and Astley's lieutenant-general, Sir Charles Lucas, was taken prisoner. Astley himself, confused and surrounded, at last surrendered. The silver-haired old general – he was sixty-seven – sat himself on a drum in the midst of his captors. 'You have done your work, boys,' he said, 'and may go play, unless you will fall out among yourselves.'[1]

The King's last field army had perished at Stow-on-the-Wold. His garrisons still held out at Oxford, Newark, Pendennis, Exeter and Raglan, but elsewhere the Parliamentarians were triumphant. As the first Civil War shuddered to its close, Charles substituted political manoeuvres for military effort. Opportunist as ever, he was quick to note the growing differences between Independents, Presbyterians and Scots. The Presbyterians favoured a church organised on the Genevan pattern which had been introduced into Scotland by John Knox, while the Independents sought a less rigid organisation. The friction between Independents and Presbyterians was as much political as religious, since the former advocated religious toleration which, in Presbyterian eyes, could only result in dangerous gatherings of the lower classes, whose uncontrolled discussion was likely to include social and political questions. Before the war, conflict between the various elements of the Puritan religious spectrum had been averted by united hostility to Laud and the established church. With the war won, social and constitutional issues combined with basic religious differences to produce a rapidly widening gulf between Independent and Presbyterian.

Assisted by the French emissary, Montreuil, the King endeavoured to reach an agreement with the Scots, but this bore as little fruit as did Digby's efforts with the Confederate Irish. Charles's negotiations with the Scots and their English Presbyterian supporters did not, however, prevent his making overtures to Vane and the Independents. Meanwhile, in Rome, Sir Kenelm Digby hoped to procure Papal gold to pay an Irish army, and in France, Holland and

[1] Rushworth, op. cit., Vol. VI, p. 140.

Denmark Royalist agents tried to obtain last-minute aid. Faced with the failure of this web of intrigue, the King tried a desperate move: as Fairfax moved in on Oxford, Charles sought Parliament's permission to return to Westminster. This Parliament refused to grant without certain guarantees, and the Independents in the army declined to negotiate. The perplexed monarch played his last card, and on 27 April, in disguise and accompanied by only two companions, left Oxford for the Scots camp before Newark.

When Charles arrived in the besiegers' lines at Newark, the Scots scarcely knew what to do with him, but were well aware that he remained King in this bizarre game of chess. Nevertheless, he was treated as a prisoner, albeit an honoured one. He was instructed to order the surrender of Newark, though Belasyse made the best terms he could before giving up the fortress on 8 May. With this, the Scots marched north, and had reached Newcastle before they received the horrified protest of an outraged Parliament.

Oxford, defended by Glemham with the determination customarily shown by this steadfast soldier, surrendered on terms on 24 June. This left only three remaining Royalist fortresses – the castles of Pendennis, Raglan and Harlech. The former, bravely defended by Arundel, was besieged on both land and sea, and finally surrendered on 16 August, its provisions exhausted. Raglan, held by the aged Marquis of Worcester, fell at last on the 19th. With the surrender of these two strongholds, the military operations of the first Civil War came to an end, although Harlech held out till 13 March 1647. But though the King's armies had ceased to exist, many of his supporters remained at large. Prince Rupert and his brother had left the country. Montrose, too, had escaped, much to the annoyance of the Scots Committee of Estates, which had granted terms to the outlawed Montrose and his followers, but hoped nevertheless to see the ex-Marquis dangling. Most important, Prince Charles had sailed safely to France and although his father was in enemy hands, the young Prince and his mother would provide a focus for Royalist aspirations.

PART THREE

THE SECOND CIVIL WAR
MARCH–AUGUST 1648

Chronology

1647	30 January	Charles handed over by the Scots.
	31 May	Cornet George Joyce of Fairfax's lifeguard ordered to safeguard the train of artillery at Oxford, and then secure the King at Holmby House.
	4 June	Joyce removes King from Holmby House.
	10	General rendezvous of the army on Triploe Heath.
	14	Declaration of the army.
	6 August	The army enters London.
	October–November	General Council of the army meets in Putney church.
	11 November	General Council breaks up. Charles escapes from Hampton Court and travels to Carisbrooke Castle.
	26 December	Charles signs the Engagement with the Scots.
1648	23 March	Colonel Poyer declares for the King in Wales.
	28 April	Langdale takes Berwick.
	21 May	Revolt breaks out in Kent.
	27	Fleet in the Downs mutinies.
	1 June	Fairfax takes Maidstone.
	14	Fairfax lays siege to Colchester.
	8 July	Hamilton's Scottish army crosses the border.
	11	Pembroke surrenders to Cromwell.
	12 August	Cromwell and Lambert meet at Wetherby.
	17-19	Battle of PRESTON.
	28	Surrender of Colchester.
	6 December	Pride's purge.
1649	30 January	Beheading of King Charles I.

Twenty-one

1648: FAIRFAX'S CAMPAIGN

Charles had surrendered himself to the Scots in the hope that he could negotiate for Scottish support against Parliament. The price for this support, however, was too high, for the Scots insisted that Charles agree to the imposition of Presbyterianism on England, and to this the King could not consent. Charles's obduracy on this point lost him the chance of Scottish and Presbyterian support. He proved equally uncooperative towards a Parliamentarian formula, the Newcastle propositions, submitted to him in mid-July. These proposals, drawn up after two months of debate, and vetted by Argyll, sought to impose the Covenant on Charles and Presbyterianism on England. Over sixty of the King's supporters were specifically exempted from pardon; a sliding scale of confiscation was to be applied to the estates of the King's richer supporters, varying according to their 'treason'.[1] Charles temporised as long as he could, but could never consent to abandon his religion or his friends.

In London, meanwhile, the hostility between Presbyterians and Independents steadily increased. The former party was led, in Parliament, by Denzil Holles, for long well to the fore in the fight against the prerogative, but now, by comparison with Vane and his Independents, somewhat conservative. The Independents were strengthened, qualitatively at least, by elections in 1645–6, in which Henry Ireton, Fleetwood, Blake, Harrison and Hutchinson were all elected, as was the extremist Colonel Rainsborough. The tension between Independent and Presbyterian was not confined to London. The sectaries carried great weight within the army, owing partly to the opinions of senior officers, and partly to the fervent and compelling preaching of Hugh Peters and his associates.

Money, or rather the lack of it, was, as ever, the mainspring of crisis. The Scots at last came to an agreement over their payment for their assistance in the war. The first instalment of this was paid in January 1647, and the Scots, mollified, handed over their intransigent King to his English subjects, and marched off home. Charles was escorted south, and the atrocious weather did

---

[1] For the full text of the Newcastle Propositions *see* Gardiner, *Constitutional Documents*, pp. 290–306.

not prevent his enthusiastic reception in several towns. He was installed at Holmby House in Northamptonshire, in captivity but increasingly hopeful of reaching some workable agreement with one or the other of the contending parties at Westminster. In Ireland, the Cessation had broken down, and on 31 July 1646 Holles had failed in an attempt to send six regiments of the New Model there. It looked suspiciously as if the Presbyterians were eager to dispose of the army, whose Independent opinions and tremendous cost alike represented a threat.

The inevitable economic dislocation produced by the war, together with abysmal harvests and a recession in trade, meant that there was little money available, and Parliament was rash enough to attempt economy by disbanding, without arrears, that portion of the army not required for service in Ireland. This was a serious blunder, for the cavalry were forty-three weeks in arrears, and the infantry eighteen. The effect of this ingratitude roused the army, already suspicious of Holles and his fellows, to open protest. And, though the question of pay was the crucial point of the army's case, it went much further than that. The New Model was a military force of a very peculiar kind. As a pamphlet of August 1647 was to point out,

... We were not merely mercenary soldiers, brought together by the hopes of pay and the fortunes of wars; the peace of our country, our freedom from tyranny, the preservation of due liberty, the administration of judgement and justice, the free course of the laws of the land, the preservation of the King, the privilege of Parliament, and the liberty of the subject, were the main things which brought us together.[1]

A moderate petition, presented to Parliament on 30 March, was pronounced seditious and its chief signatories – including Pride and Lilburne – hauled before the Commons. With this, the situation worsened swiftly; the hold of the officers was imperilled by the election of 'agitators', a word then meaning agents or representatives, first by the cavalry, and later by the infantry too. Fairfax was under pressure not to consent to disbandment until the army's grievances were redressed; he warned Parliament that, owing to the temper of the troops, he would be unable to disband. Instead, he ordered a general muster at Newmarket on 3 June. Cromwell, playing a somewhat equivocal rôle, had authorised Cornet Joyce to proceed to Oxford to safeguard the train of artillery, and then to go on to Holmby to secure the King. Whether Joyce was meant merely to guard the King, or something more, remains unclear. However, he arrived at Holmby to find the Parliamentary commissioners fled – possibly to organise a rescue party – and promptly removed the King.

Cromwell, in some danger of arrest at Westminster, rode into East Anglia to join the army. He assisted Fairfax in setting up the 'General Council of the army', which contained the general officers, and two officers and two agitators

[1] *Vox Militaris; or an apologeticall Declaration concerning the Army . . .*, TT E.401 (24).

from each regiment. Parliamentary commissioners visited the army at Triploe Heath, and found it adamant; it would not disband without full satisfaction – financial and political. On 14 June the Declaration of the Army laid down the army's right to oppose Parliament in defence of its rights. Parliament, perturbed by the army's gradual movement southwards, called out the Trained Bands, but few answered the summons, and Parliament was instead forced to rely for its defence upon a mob of disbanded soldiers and city prentices. These worthies proved more of a danger than a deliverance, for on 26 July, enraged by concessions made towards the army, they flocked into the Commons, and forced the speakers of both Houses, and the leading Independents, to flee to the army.

Fairfax, 'deeply affected with the late carriages towards the Parliament',[1] marched the New Model to Hounslow Heath, and, on 6 August, entered the City. The Heads of Proposals,[2] largely the work of Ireton, were presented to Parliament; they advocated a limited monarchy, biennial Parliaments, and religious toleration. The army's entry into London was followed by an outburst of pamphlets, and growing dissatisfaction amongst the rank and file, who were disgusted at the tortuous negotiations conducted by their officers. Their more extreme views found expression in the pamphlet 'The Case of the Army truly stated',[3] presented to Fairfax on 18 October. This was probably the work of John Wildman, a prominent 'Leveller', and friend of the arch-firebrand Lilburne.

Cromwell and Ireton were hard-pressed by the agitators as the General Council of the army met at Putney church in late October and early November. The Leveller 'Agreement of the people'[4] was presented to the Council on 30 October. The ensuing debates got out of hand, and the agitators were finally ordered to their regiments. The General Council broke up on 11 November; that night Charles escaped from Hampton Court, and made his way to Carisbrooke Castle on the Isle of Wight. The Governor, Colonel Hammond, torn by conflicting loyalties, kept the King in honourable confinement, from which Charles proceeded, as ever, to play both ends against the middle with regard for little except political expediency. Thus, while still negotiating with Parliament, he signed, on 26 December, the 'Engagement'[5] with the Scots, by which he undertook to impose Presbyterianism on England, suppress the sectaries, and confirm the Covenant in Parliament. In return for this, the Scots undertook to restore the King to power, by military means if necessary.

With this devious agreement safely concluded, Charles cheerfully rejected the 'Four Bills', Parliament's reply to his most recent set of proposals. In an

[1] Rushworth, op. cit., Vol. VI, p. 653.
[2] Gardiner, op. cit., pp. 316–26.
[3] TT E.411 (9).
[4] TT E.412 (21).
[5] Gardiner, op. cit., pp. 347–52.

atmosphere of increasing irritation, Parliament passed the Vote of No Addresses,[1] prohibiting further negotiations with a monarch they could no longer bring themselves to trust in any way. Colonel Rainsborough, now translated to the office of vice-admiral, guarded the Channel against foreign incursion, while in London rumour and riot presaged the renewal of hostilities.

The first shots came from Wales, where Colonel Poyer, governor of Pembroke Castle, refused to give up the fortress to his successor, on the grounds that his troops' pay was in arrears – which indeed it was. On 23 March Poyer took the offensive, and declared for the King. The revolt rapidly spread throughout South Wales. In the north, the gaunt Langdale took Berwick on 28 April, and Sir Philip Musgrave surprised Carlisle next day. On 21 May Kent broke into open revolt, and Royalists seized Rochester and other important towns. Dartford and Deptford were taken five days later. On the 27th the fleet in the Downs, whose officers were, in the main, Presbyterian, refused to allow the unpopular Rainsborough to board his flagship, and arrested some of the Independent officers. Parliament tried to cope with this serious mutiny by reappointing Warwick Lord High Admiral, but the sailors, who had by now occupied the Downs forts, refused to obey him.

The military problem facing Fairfax was serious indeed. Following the death of his father on 13 March, he had become Lord Fairfax, but his new status could have been of little comfort to him as he surveyed the revolts which flared up around him. Most military forces apart from the New Model – the armies of Massey and Poyntz, for example – had been disbanded. Some of these troops had been absorbed into the New Model, forming three regiments of Horse, and parts of three new regiments of Foot. Nevertheless, this left Fairfax with a thin enough force to cope with the threat of invasion from Scotland, the revolt in South Wales, the risings in Kent and Essex, and murmurings from the West Country, as well as a discontented and disobedient fleet.

It was, perhaps, fortunate for Fairfax that the revolts did not occur simultaneously; his priorities were, to a great extent, determined for him by the timing of the outbreaks. His first move was to send Cromwell, with one regiment of Horse and three of Foot, to South Wales, where Colonel Horton, who had been sent to supervise the disbandment of Laugharne's army, had one regiment of Horse, part of another, eight companies of Foot and 800 dragoons. Much of Fairfax's strength was already split up in garrisons. The Scottish threat might be checked by the garrison of Newcastle, two regiments of Foot under Sir Arthur Hesilrige, while in the west, Sir Hardress Waller commanded one regiment each of Horse and Foot and 200 dragoons. Half a regiment of Foot held Oxford, while a full regiment garrisoned Gloucester. North Wales, another potential trouble-spot, was covered by Thornhagh's regiment of Horse, which patrolled the area in detachments. A northern field force of three regiments of Horse and one of Foot, under Lambert, watched the Scots and overawed the

[1] Ibid., p. 356.

local Royalists. Lambert was reinforced in early summer by a regiment of Foot and a few Horse; furthermore, two embryo infantry regiments were forming in Yorkshire. The northern force was further strengthened when Sheffield's Horse, sent to Cheshire to guard against a thrust by Langdale, swung across to join it.

These able dispositions were calculated to cover vulnerable or strategically important areas. However, they left Fairfax with a force of only just over 7,000 to hold the Capital, and deal with the outbreaks in Kent and Essex. The Scots, meanwhile, wrote to Parliament, demanding that all Englishmen should take the Covenant, that negotiations should be opened with Charles, and, *inter alia*, that the New Model, which the Scots unkindly termed 'that army of sectaries', should be disbanded. Parliament not unnaturally rejected the Scots' terms; with this, the latter prepared to invade.

It was by no means as easy for the Scots to raise an army in 1648 as it had been in 1643. Firstly, the fact that the newly raised army, under the Duke of Hamilton, would fight in support of Royalists who had not taken the Covenant, meant that the clergy, backed by the powerful Argyll, opposed the war. This opposition had a serious effect on recruiting. Furthermore, David Leslie, who had done so well at Marston Moor, declined the proffered appointment of second-in-command for similar religious reasons. In the light of Leslie's subsequent performance, however, one wonders whether his absence was as great a misfortune as it seemed at the time. Finally, many Scots had had their fill of soldiering, and preferred to stay at home rather than risk a new campaign in an unpromising cause.

Fairfax had successfully quelled a series of outbreaks in London in late March and early April, while in Wales, Horton routed Laugharne at St Fagans, and followed up this success by taking Tenby Castle. Cromwell joined Horton on 11 May, and set about besieging Chepstow and Pembroke Castles. The former, attacked by Colonel Ewer and his regiment of Foot, was stormed on 25 May.

While Cromwell battered Pembroke,[1] Fairfax moved against the Kentish rebels. On 27 May, he assembled his forces on Hounslow Heath, and advanced to Blackheath three days later. The Kentish Royalists were led by the old Earl of Norwich, George Goring's father. Norwich's forces comprised 'for the most part Cavaliers, citizens, seamen and watermen'.[2] There seems to have been little mass support for the Royalists: the population as a whole had no great desire to see a renewal of hostilities.

On the afternoon of 30 May, Fairfax's army marched to Eltham, and on the following day advanced to Gravesend. A party sent forward to reconnoitre Rochester reported that the town was strongly held, and the drawbridge over the Medway had been raised. This persuaded Fairfax to march south, by way

---

[1] He did so with guns borrowed from Captain Crowther's *Lion*, for the vessel carrying his own siege train had sunk in the Severn. *See* Powell, op. cit., p. 151.

[2] *News from Kent*, TTE. 445 (27).

of Malling, towards Maidstone. Norwich's men held Maidstone in some strength. Three thousand of the Earl's best troops were garrisoned in the town, while another 1,000 covered the passage of the Medway at Aylesford. The remainder of the Earl's army, perhaps 7,000 enthusiastic but ill-armed and untrained men, remained outside the town, forming a reserve, albeit an unreliable one. Fairfax reached Malling on 1 June, and advanced on Maidstone, crossing the Medway at the thinly held Farleigh Bridge. His leading regiment, under Colonel Hewson, was briskly received in the outskirts of the town, and the action soon became general, notwithstanding Fairfax's intention to wait until the next day before assaulting.[1]

Despite Clarendon's jests at Norwich's 'very numerous, but likewise very disorderly' troops, the garrison of Maidstone fought desperately, contesting the streets inch by inch. Fierce struggles for the barricades went on until well after dark, and even so, Norwich was able to get away with about 3,000 of the defenders. It was, alas, quite another matter with the 'reserve', who scattered in all directions once Fairfax's soldiery had seized the town. Norwich, hoping to take London by a *coup de main*, reached Blackheath on 3 June, and seized Bow Bridge. Expected support within the City failed to materialise, and the stout old Skippon closed the gates against him. Norwich's situation was perilous, for he was threatened, not only by Skippon's Trained Bands, but also by Whalley, with his own regiment of Horse, and four troops of another.

Faced with this powerful combination, Norwich crossed the Thames into Essex, and made for Colchester, where the Cavaliers had risen on 4 June, led by Colonel Henry Farr of the Trained Bands, who had seized the local County Committee. Sir Charles Lucas immediately assumed command of the Essex insurgents, and was joined by Sir George Lisle, Lord Capel, and, on 9 June, by Norwich's Kentish Cavaliers.

Fairfax had remained in Kent, sending out detachments to deal with various Cavalier strongholds. Ireton entered Canterbury without a fight, while Rich moved farther south to relieve Dover, and reduce the castles of Deal and Walmer. Elsewhere, the Royalists met with mixed success. In the west, Sir Hardress Waller put down local risings, while outbreaks in North Wales, Leicestershire and Northamptonshire were likewise suppressed. In the north, the seizure of Pontefract Castle by one of Langdale's colonels forced Lambert to retain considerable forces in that area. Warwick had managed to retain the allegiance of that part of the fleet at Portsmouth, though Batten escaped to Holland, where he was joined by ten of the mutinous vessels from the Downs.

Fairfax, meanwhile, made for Colchester. He crossed the Thames at Tilbury on 11 June, and his advanced guard was within striking distance of Colchester by the evening of the 12th. On the following day, he was joined by the rest of his Horse, and by an infantry brigade under Colonel Barkstead. Lucas, who held a commission from the Prince of Wales to command Royalist forces in

[1] Fairfax to Speaker Lenthall, 1 June, TT E.445 (37).

Essex, and was an officer of great ability, had speedily thrown Colchester into a state of defence. The Parliamentarian element of the Trained Bands had managed to secure the magazine at Braintree, which greatly reduced the armaments available to Lucas. Nevertheless, he fortified the old castle, placed a battery in St Mary's churchyard, covering the London road as it wound up to Head Gate, and likewise pushed troops into his father's house, a useful bastion for the southern section of the wall.

As Fairfax advanced on the city, Lucas drew up his Foot across the London Road, with Horse on either wing. Fairfax hoped, no doubt, to repeat his success of Maidstone, and threw Barkstead's brigade straight up the road. Barkstead ran into a hot fire from the Royalist musketeers, and three successive attacks were repulsed. Colonel Needham was killed, and Lieutenant-Colonel Shambrook[1] took over command of his regiment. On the Parliamentarian right, the Horse routed their opponents, and attempted to swing in against the open flank of the Royalist Foot, but were checked by musketeers and pikemen holding the well-hedged Maldon road. Barkstead at last managed to penetrate Head Gate, only to be charged by a body of Horse, galloping down the hill leading to the gate, while infantry poured from a lane into his flank. Barkstead was speedily turned out, and Head Gate slammed behind him. Fairfax made renewed attempts to storm the city on the next day, but reluctantly concluded that a formal siege was necessary. One is compelled to conclude that Lucas's force was much better led than Norwich's.

With Fairfax checked before Colchester, the overall situation seemed serious for the Parliamentarians. Cromwell was fully occupied before Pembroke Castle, and Lambert was forced to contend not only with Langdale's rising but with Hamilton's imminent invasion. Fairfax was aware that insurrection could well break out in other parts of the country, and went about his work before Colchester with great haste. He summoned the place on 14 July, only to receive a rude reply, suggesting that a ready cure for his gout was at hand. The general set up his headquarters at Lexden, and threw up batteries to open against the walls of the city.

[1] The officer who had so distinguished himself in the fight for Alton church in December 1643.

Twenty-two

1648: CROMWELL'S CAMPAIGN

The balance now lay, for the second time in four years, with the Scots. Had the Duke of Hamilton been quick off the mark, and struck south in late May or in June, it is difficult to see how the Parliamentarians could have coped. Fairfax, with much of the New Model, was stuck fast at Colchester, while Cromwell was still besieging Pembroke Castle. The unfortunate Lambert had to mask Pontefract, and watch the border, and could have done little more than delay a Scottish offensive.

When, on 8 July, Hamilton did at last lurch across the border, it was with an army that bore all the signs of its troubled origin. Clerical opposition to the expedition had so impeded recruiting that Hamilton had only 3,000 Horse and 6,000 Foot, the latter appallingly raw. The Earl of Callander was Hamilton's second-in-command. The efficiency of this arrangement was limited by the latter's relative inexperience and weakness of will, and the former's vast experience, small ability, and heady temperament, as well as by personal antipathy between the two noblemen. John Middleton, who commanded the Horse, and William Baillie, who led the Foot, were altogether more reliable. The problem of artillery was initially overcome by the unusual expedient of having none at all. Hamilton's ill-assorted army struggled to Carlisle along bad roads worsened by atrocious weather. At Carlisle, Sir Philip Musgrave handed the town over to the Scots, and Langdale arrived with his northern levies. Hamilton remained at Carlisle for six days, and then moved against the wily Lambert, who had withdrawn to Penrith.

Hamilton had held his hand too long. The unsteady Earl of Holland, armed with a commission from the Prince of Wales, but little else, accompanied by the Duke of Buckingham, and his brother Lord Francis Villiers, with about 500 followers, Horse and Foot, rose at Kingston, and marched on Reigate Castle. Fairfax sent Sir Michael Livesey, with a detachment of Horse, in pursuit. Holland fell back, through Dorking, towards Kingston, but Livesey caught the Royalist rear-guard at Ewell, and drove it back, fighting hard, on Kingston, where Holland's men were at last scattered. Villiers was killed, while Holland himself escaped, only to be overtaken and captured at St Neots.

Colchester still held out against the impatient Fairfax, but, on 11 July, Pembroke Castle capitulated, freeing Cromwell for service in the north. His assistance was urgently required, for Lambert, though fighting with considerable skill, was retreating steadily. On 14 July, Hamilton's cavalry had clashed with Lambert's Horse outside Penrith, but the Scottish infantry were too far back to bring about a general engagement. Lambert fell back to Appleby on the following day, and again checked Hamilton's pursuit. Then, frozen by the lack of urgency which so characterised his generalship, Hamilton halted around Kirkby Thore, waiting for reinforcements. He received perhaps 6,000 more Scots, most of them hastily raised Foot. However, he heard that a small veteran force from Ulster, under Sir George Monro, had landed in Scotland, and was on its way to join him.

While Hamilton prepared to resume his advance, Lambert, fearing a descent on Yorkshire, held the Stainmore Pass, with the bulk of his army around Barnard Castle. It was there, on 27 July, that the first elements of Cromwell's force joined him. Oliver himself, having sent most of his cavalry post-haste to Lambert, marched north, by way of Leicester and Nottingham, picking up 1,500 much needed pairs of shoes, and numerous local levies. He, like Lambert, feared that the Scots would cross into Yorkshire, probably in an effort to relieve Pontefract Castle. He sent a message ordering Lambert not to fight until he arrived.

Lambert, whose 3,500 men had been reinforced by Colonel Ashton, with 1,000 Foot and 300 Horse, raised in Lancashire, fought an indecisive engagement on the Stainmore Pass, temporarily giving way before a Scottish reconnaissance in force. Langdale, based at Settle, contemplated thrusting south-east to Pontefract, but, in the event, did nothing. Monro joined the Scots in Kendal in the first week of August, but promptly fell out with Callander; Monro's men were thus left at Kirkby Lonsdale, with some of the northern Foot,[1] to await the arrival of Hamilton's train of artillery. Lambert, meanwhile, had fallen back to Richmond, Ripon and, on 7 August, Knaresborough. He was uncertain as to Hamilton's intention, and was in some doubt as to whether the Duke intended to cross the Pennines through Wensleydale, or to continue into Lancashire, through Preston and Warrington.

If Lambert was puzzled as to the Scottish plan, so too was Hamilton. The Scots reached Hornby on 9 August, and Hamilton's Council of War debated which route the army should take. Sir James Turner, Hamilton's quartermaster-general, reports that Callander was indifferent, Middleton advocated Yorkshire, and Baillie Lancashire. Turner himself was in favour of Yorkshire, 'for this reason only, that I understood Lancashire was a close country, full of ditches and hedges; which was a great advantage the English would have over our raw and undisciplined musketeers ... while, on the other hand, Yorkshire was a more open country and full of heaths, where he might both make better

[1] The regiments of Sir Philip Musgrave and Sir Thomas Tyldesley.

use of our horse, and come sooner to push of pike'. 'My Lord Duke', Turner significantly remarks, 'was for the Lancashire way.' Hamilton's eventual decision was for Lancashire, in the hopes of attracting support from the Lancashire Royalists, and taking Manchester, which 'he thought his own if he came near it'.[1]

Two facts should have deterred Hamilton from this course of action. Firstly, there were many more Royalists in Yorkshire than there were in Lancashire, and secondly, Manchester, defended by the German professional Johan Rosworm, had held for Parliament throughout the first Civil War.

While Hamilton's Council of War arrived at this conclusion, Cromwell was at Doncaster. He received a supply of ammunition from Hull, and launched a brisk attack on Pontefract, forcing the garrison to take refuge in the castle, which he masked with some of his Midland levies. He then marched north, meeting Lambert at Wetherby on 12 August. Cromwell now had at his disposal, by his own account, 2,500 Horse and dragoons, 4,000 Foot, 1,600 Lancashire Foot and 500 Lancashire Horse.[2] These figures seem rather low; the New Model element of Cromwell's force, if up to establishment, would have numbered 10,300 Horse and Foot. It is unlikely that this figure would have been reduced to Cromwell's alleged 6,500 at this stage in the campaign. A total of slightly over 9,000 would seem more reasonable.

Whatever the exact size of Cromwell's force, Hamilton had a comfortable numerical superiority. The Scots element of his army now numbered something around 17,000, with Langdale's 3,000 and Monro's 2,700, the latter well behind him. His army was, though, short of guns and ammunition, and there was a serious lack of food. This, coupled with continuous rain, had reduced morale in Hamilton's army to a low ebb. The Duke's ill-trained infantry, soaked and half-starved, looted mercilessly, and their behaviour served to alienate even those Lancashiremen who might otherwise have been well-disposed to them. Worse still, the food shortage compelled Hamilton to permit a dangerous degree of dispersion, to facilitate foraging. Consequently, on 16 August, the Foot were nearing Preston, while most of the Horse, under Callander and Middleton, were already around Wigan, sixteen miles farther south. Langdale, on the army's left flank, was moving south from Settle, down the valley of the Ribble.

While Hamilton's army was widely dispersed in the Preston area, Cromwell executed a plan that was bold to the point of rashness. He marched straight for Preston – without, of course, knowing that the Scots were there. He hoped either to meet Hamilton as he crossed the Pennines *via* Skipton, or to strike the

---

[1] *Memoirs of Sir James Turner* (Edinburgh), p. 62, and Carlyle, op. cit., Vol. I, p. 327. G. Burnet's *Memoirs of the ... Dukes of Hamilton* maintains that Callander and Langdale favoured Lancashire. But here we agree with Austin Woolrych, who rightly points out that Burnet blames Callander for every wrong decision, while Turner, who was actually present at the Council, is a more reliable source. (*Battles of the English Civil War* (London 1966), p. 165n.)

[2] Cromwell to Speaker, 20 August, Carlyle, op. cit., Vol. I, p. 343.

16 THE PRESTON CAMPAIGN

flank of the Scots if they continued to march through Lancashire. Langdale was at least partly aware of the danger as early as 13 August, but failed to give Hamilton adequate warning of his suspicions. Cromwell reached Gisburn on 15 August, and was joined there by Ashton. On the following day, the Parliamentarian advanced guard clashed with surprised Royalist troopers near Clitheroe. Cromwell then pressed on to Hodder Bridge, some three miles from Clitheroe, where he held a Council of War to discuss his next move.

Two decisions were open to Cromwell. He could remain on the north bank of the Ribble, and march straight on Preston, or he could cross the Ribble, march south to Whalley, cross the Calder there, and place himself on the Scottish line of advance in the Wigan area. The latter move seemed safest, but it offered little opportunity for a decisive engagement, since the Scots, if defeated, would have a clear line of retreat to the north. The most significant factor in Cromwell's decision was probably the information that Monro was moving south to join Hamilton. Cromwell therefore assumed that the Scots would halt to enable Monro to come up. Oddly enough, the news of Monro's movement was false, but Cromwell's plan to move straight on Preston was to prove dramatically successful.

Cromwell's army spent the night of the 16th in the grounds of Stonyhurst Hall. Langdale, whose force lay between Cromwell and Preston, was by now aware of the proximity of the Roundheads. He rode into Preston and warned Hamilton of the imminent danger which threatened his army. Unfortunately, Callander had ridden in from his quarters at Wigan, and belittled Langdale's fears. Hamilton concluded that his left was only threatened by a probing attack which Sir Marmaduke's men should be able to deal with. He declined to reinforce Langdale, and made no effort to get his sprawling host closed up for action.

THE BATTLE OF PRESTON, 17–19 AUGUST

It must have been with a sinking heart that Langdale rode out from Preston on the night of 16 August. He got his detachment under arms early on the morning of the 17th, and retired on Preston. His rear-guard, at Longridge, was caught by the Parliamentarian advanced guard – Horse under Major Smithson, and Foot under Major Pownal and Captain Hodgson. Langdale halted his main body some two miles from Preston, and, while his rear-guard fell back under pressure, Sir Marmaduke spurred off into Preston to inform Hamilton of the worsening situation. When Langdale met him, on Preston Moor, just north of the town, Hamilton had just ordered Baillie and the Foot to cross the Ribble at Preston Bridge, in preparation for a resumption of the march south. Callander's Horse were still sixteen miles away, and Monro's force was far away to the north. Hamilton's army was fatally over-extended, but even at this late stage determined action by the Duke might have saved the day.

Hamilton was not the man to undertake sudden or violent action. We cannot be certain that Langdale knew that he was opposed by the whole of Cromwell's force, though it seems likely that he did. However, Callander, who was still with the main body, disagreed, and prevailed upon Hamilton to send the Foot on over the bridge. Callander may still have argued that Langdale was unnecessarily worried, and was faced only by a small detachment of Parliamentarians.

Whatever Callander's reasoning, his advice to Hamilton was to ensure the defeat of the Scottish army. Langdale rode back to his detachment, and prepared to meet the Parliamentarian attack. Sir Marmaduke's force was strongly posted, blocking the sunken lane leading from Longridge to Preston. About two miles from Preston, the thickly hedged enclosures that flanked the lane met the broad expanse of Ribbleton Moor, which rolled away to the north.[1] The ground was broken up by frequent hedges and ditches, and the going was soft, severely restricting the use of cavalry. Langdale pushed his Foot into the enclosures, his musketeers lining the hedges; outposts watched the moor, and another track on the Royalist right was similarly covered.

Cromwell's forlorn hope, moving rapidly down the lane, soon dislodged Langdale's outposts, and came into contact with the 'stand of pikes, and a great body of colours'[2] marking Langdale's main position. The nature of the ground offered no opportunity for subtle tactics. Cromwell sent the regiments of Bright and Fairfax down the left of the lane, while Reade, Deane and Pride advanced to the right. There was little the Horse could do but thrust straight down the lane; Harrison's and Cromwell's, with another regiment in reserve, went about this difficult task. Two more cavalry regiments, those of Thornhagh and Twistleton, supported the right, while the remainder of the Horse buttressed the left. A detachment of Ashton's Lancashiremen held the bridge over the Calder at Whalley, while the rest, under Ashton himself, were in reserve. It is interesting to note that Cromwell's two right-hand regiments, those of Deane and Pride, overlapped Langdale's left flank, probably because the nature of the ground prevented Cromwell from realising the narrowness of Langdale's position.

The Parliamentarian deployment, impeded as it was by mud and ditches, took some time. Smithson's advanced guard of Horse managed, after a temporary reverse, to repulse some Scottish lancers sent up by Hamilton. It was around 4 p.m. when Cromwell's attack at last went in. Langdale's men fought with incredible valour, and were wrenched back, hedge by hedge, only with the greatest difficulty. The fighting was particularly heavy in the centre, where the regiments of Cromwell, Bright and Reade could make little headway. Only when Ashton's regiment was committed did the tide at last swing against Langdale, who fell back, fighting hard, towards Preston.

[1] A map in the Lancashire County Record Office (DXX 194/28) is invaluable for determining the dispositions for this phase of the action.
[2] The Memoirs of Captain John Hodgson (Edinburgh 1806), p. 116.

Langdale's retreat, initially orderly, soon became a rout once the two armies were clear of the enclosures, and the Parliamentarian Horse could lap around the flanks of Langdale's Foot. Cromwell's cavalry pushed Langdale's remnants into the town, for the lane on Sir Marmaduke's right, leading to Fishwick and Preston Bridge, was already cut.

Hamilton, with his lifeguard on Preston Moor, was soon convinced that Langdale was, in fact, being engaged by the whole of Cromwell's army. He decided to halt the Foot, and give battle on Preston Moor, summoning Middleton to bring the cavalry up as soon as possible. He had already ordered Turner to send some fresh troops and ammunition to Langdale's assistance.[1] Hamilton's plan was viable enough, and might still have worked. At this point, however, Callander once more intervened. Riding up from the bridge, he angrily asked Hamilton why the Foot had halted. To draw up on Preston Moor, stressed the Earl, was to invite disaster. The cavalry could not arrive in time; the ground on the moor was ideal for cavalry, and, denied mounted support, the Scottish Foot would be ridden down by Cromwell's Horse. A far better plan, he argued, was to send all the Foot across the river; they would then have the Ribble between them and the enemy, and could be joined by the Horse. The reunited army would then be capable of offering battle with every chance of success. This scheme, though outwardly plausible, had two major defects. It presupposed the total abandonment of Langdale and his gallant force, and called for well-ordered manoeuvres at a time when cohesion, never the strong point of Hamilton's army, was already lost.

Hamilton, swayed for the second time that day by Callander's fatal advice, weakly assented. Baillie took the Foot over Preston Bridge, leaving two brigades to hold the bridge against Cromwell. Such a precaution was now necessary, for Cromwell's Horse soon burst into Preston, in hot pursuit of Langdale's fugitives. Hamilton had remained on the moor with a rear-guard, consisting of a few Horse in addition to his own lifeguard, and Cromwell's troopers were soon between Hamilton and Preston Bridge; the commander-in-chief was thus cut off from the bulk of his army. Hamilton ordered the rear-guard Horse to escape to the north, and join Monro, while the Duke himself, with the lifeguard and a few officers, tried to cross the Ribble to join the infantry. Showing considerable personal bravery, Hamilton led several charges against some of Cromwell's Horse who attacked his small party, and eventually managed to swim the Ribble.

As Hamilton and his entourage swam their tired horses across the swollen Ribble, Cromwell dealt with those Scots who remained north of the river. A body of Horse pursued those of Hamilton's troopers who were withdrawing towards Monro; Ashton's Foot and three troops watched the Lancaster road in case Monro should appear. Most of Langdale's Foot had by now been killed or captured, though much of his Horse had streamed off to the north.

With Preston cleared of Scots, Cromwell now turned his attention to Preston

[1] Turner, op. cit., p. 64.

Bridge. The two Scots brigades defending it held on for two hours, while Baillie put his infantry in position around Walton Hall, just south of the Darwen, a tributary of the Ribble. The Ribble Bridge eventually fell, though not before it was littered with the dead of both sides. The Parliamentarian Foot carried the Darwen Bridge soon after, dislodging the 600 musketeers that Callander had posted to cover it. It was now becoming so dark as to make further fighting difficult, but some Parliamentarians pressed forward over the bridge, driving in Baillie's outposts, and reaping a rich booty from the Scottish wagons, which lay, abandoned by their civilian drivers, on the slope leading up from the Darwen Bridge.

By nightfall on 17 August Cromwell had won a useful victory. About 4,000 of Hamilton's men had been captured, and something over 1,000 killed. The bulk of the Duke's army was, however, intact, albeit dispirited, and Cromwell's first concern was to ensure that it did not slip round his flank and escape northwards. Some of Ashton's men were at Whalley, and Cromwell reinforced them with Horse from Clitheroe.

The weather, which had been appalling throughout the campaign, continued to make life more than usually unpleasant for the combatants. Some Parliamentarians found dry quarters in Preston, but most soldiers on both sides spent much of the night searching for food and shelter, or trying to coax flame out of soaking wood. Morale in Hamilton's army was low, and the dispirited Scottish Foot passed a night of sodden misery, while their commanders debated their next move. It was, as usual, Callander who worsened an already serious situation. He spoke out in favour of a night withdrawal to meet Middleton, and though Baillie and Turner, two of the leveller heads at Hamilton's Council of War, pointed out the dangers of such a move, the Duke fell in with Callander.

A night withdrawal imposes severe stress on the morale and the staff work of even the best-trained army. For Hamilton's army, the withdrawal, quite predictably, proved a disaster. The infantry, roused from their makeshift bivouacs, poured off down the Standish road to Wigan in damp confusion. The remainder of the train had to be left behind; the powder мas to be blown up, but, with the gloomy inevitability so typical of this terrible night, the order was not passed on, and the powder fell into Parliamentarian hands.

A more serious failure of communication was that Middleton, bringing the cavalry north to the assistance of the Foot, had not been informed down which of the two roads from Preston the infantry were marching. Middleton's Horse thus rode along the Chorley road, while the Foot squelched towards Wigan on the Standish road. The unfortunate Middleton reached the Darwen to find himself in the presence of Cromwell's army. He swung round and made off down the Standish road, but was hotly pursued by young Colonel Francis Thornhagh and three regiments of Horse, while the remainder of Cromwell's command followed as quickly as possible. Middleton conducted a fighting retreat, under very difficult circumstances, with great skill. In one of the many little clashes down the Standish road on the morning of 18 August, Thornhagh, leading with more valour than consideration, galloped into some Scottish lancers and was mortally wounded.[1] He bade his men open to the right and left that he might 'see the rogues run'.

Middleton eventually reached Wigan Moor, where the Foot, thinned by stragglers during the night march, was drawn up. Even at this stage the Scots had a slight numerical superiority, for Cromwell was advancing down the Standish road with about 2,500 mounted men and 3,000 Foot, while the Scots had perhaps 6,000 Foot and several thousand Horse. However, morale, particularly amongst the Foot, was by now fearfully low; such powder as the soldiers carried in their flasks was wet, and the reserve of ammunition had fallen, with the rest of the train, into Cromwell's hands. It was virtually impossible for Hamilton's battered force to make a stand on Wigan Moor, and, covered by Middleton's Horse, the Foot marched off, through Wigan, making for Warrington and the Mersey.

It was by now quite late on the 18th, and darkness fell as the Foot, many of them in the last stages of fatigue, stumbled through Wigan. Just north of the town, Middleton's Horse clashed with Cromwell's advanced guard. Sir James Turner commanded the rear-guard brigade of Foot, and was marching through Wigan when some of Middleton's troopers tore past, and the cry went up that the Horse were routed and the enemy was at hand. Turner at once halted his brigade, and drew it up in the market-place, the men shoulder to shoulder, pikes levelled to repulse any attack. A fleeing regiment of Horse appeared, and Turner ordered his pikemen to form a lane to allow it through.

But now [wrote Sir James] my pikemen, being demented (as I think we were all), would not hear me; and two of them ran full tilt at me. One of their pikes, which was intended for my belly, I gripped with my left hand; the other ran me nearly two inches in the inner side of my right thigh; all of them crying of me and the Horse 'They are Cromwell's men. . . .' I rode to the Horse and desired them to charge through these Foot. They, fearing the hazard of the pikes, stood. I then made a cry come up from behind them, that the enemy was upon them. This encouraged them to charge my Foot so fiercely that the pikemen threw down their pikes, and got into the houses. All the Horse galloped away, and, as I was afterwards told, rode not through, but over, our whole Foot treading them down.[2]

Middleton, however, managed to keep most of the Horse together, and fell back in fair order through Wigan.

Cromwell's troops bivouacked for the night in a field just outside Wigan. Although his men were tired and filthy, he had them on the march again early the next morning. A large body of Scottish Foot, under 'a little spark in a blue

[1] Carlyle, op. cit., Vol. I, p. 340.
[2] Turner, op. cit., pp. 66–7.

bonnet', made a stand near Winwick, three miles from Warrington. They chose an easily defended defile, blocked the road with pikemen, and lined the near-by hedges with musketeers. 'We held them in some dispute,' wrote Cromwell, 'till our Army came up, they maintaining the pass with great resolution for many hours; ours and theirs coming to push of pike and very close charges. . . .'[1] Eventually, the unknown hero in the blue bonnet was killed, and his men, having lost several thousand killed or taken, fell back.[2]

The remainder of Hamilton's army had by now arrived at Warrington, and the Foot set about fortifying the place. Hamilton, however, possibly persuaded by his evil genius Callander, decided to get away with the Horse, and abandon the Foot to their fate. He sent Baillie an order instructing him to make the best terms he could with Cromwell; the unfortunate Baillie, in much the same position as Skippon at Fowey, was shocked. He begged his officers to shoot him through the head and save him from dishonour. Eventually, he was persuaded to write to Cromwell; the latter instructed him to 'surrender himself and all his officers and soldiers prisoners of war, with all his arms and ammunition and horses . . . giving quarter for life, and promising civil usage'.[3] Between 2,500 and 4,000 Scottish Foot fell into Cromwell's hands and he now had more prisoners than soldiers, though the hostility of the country people discouraged the Scots from escaping. 'Ten men,' wrote Cromwell, 'will keep a thousand from running away.'

Hamilton, with the miserable remnants of his army, pursued by Lambert with about 4,000 Horse and Foot, stumbled towards Cheshire, in the hope of joining Lord Byron, who had, unsuccessfully, risen in those parts. Cromwell wrote to his local commanders, urging them to hunt down the Scottish remnants.[4] Middleton was captured near Stone in Staffordshire, and Hamilton at last surrendered at Uttoxeter, only to be executed after trial by the Lords. Langdale had slipped off with a few of his northern Horse, but he too was taken, at Nottingham. Callander, the author of so much misfortune, escaped to London and thence to Holland. Monro, giving little assistance to his English allies, withdrew into Scotland. The northern Royalists fought on, and eventually capitulated on terms at Appleby.

The battle of Preston, and the campaign which led up to it, reveal an interesting contrast in generalship. On the one hand, Hamilton and Callander embarked upon one of the most hopeless of the many Scottish descents on England. They were beset by political problems in Scotland itself, and were cursed with exceptionally bad weather. Moreover, Hamilton failed to act decisively in the early stages of the campaign. His operations were marked by hesitancy, poor

[1] Carlyle, op. cit., Vol. I, p. 341.
[2] Cromwell thought that 1,000 were killed and another 2,000 captured. Carlyle, op. cit., Vol. I, p. 341.
[3] Loc. cit.
[4] Ibid., pp. 345–7.

intelligence, and by staff work which was bad even for the seventeenth century. This is all the more tragic in that the Scottish army, although lacking in training, was capable of giving a good account of itself when a fair opportunity arose. The Foot who held Winwick defile, and the cavalry that covered the retreat, were no cowards, but were defeated by the incapacity and indecision of their senior commanders, and by the rare ability of Parliament's generals.

'Preston,' writes John Buchan, 'was thus far Oliver's most overwhelming victory,' but he adds that 'it is unnecessary to read undue subtleties into his strategy'.[1] The laurels of the early stages of the campaign certainly rest with Lambert, whose strategy of indirect defence, threatening the flanks and communications of the invaders, while at the same time covering Yorkshire against an attack across the Pennines, forced the cautious Hamilton to advance pitifully slowly. Cromwell, when he arrived on the scene, acted with commendable speed. His plan for the flank attack, sketchy as it was, was bold up to, and even beyond, the point of rashness. Nevertheless, he made best use of what little intelligence was available, and managed to defeat his adversaries in detail – the only real way of overcoming their tremendous numerical superiority. Perhaps more remarkable than the battle itself was the pursuit; few pursuits, save perhaps Murat's after Jena, have been so determined or so comprehensively successful.

Preston was the turning-point in the war. Colchester, which had held out with tremendous determination, was surrendered on 28 August. The best terms that the defenders could obtain were that all private soldiers, and officers below the rank of captain, had quarter for their lives, whilst the remainder submitted to the mercy of the Lord General. The harshness of these terms may be attributed partly to the long duration of the siege, but more particularly to a new hardening in the Parliamentarians' attitude. The Royalists were regarded as insurgents rather than soldiers; they had, in the eyes of Fairfax and his colleagues, been responsible for ripping open the scars of the first Civil War. Particularly detested were those who had fought for Parliament in the first war. Cromwell, writing of Major General Laugharne and Colonel Poyer, stressed that he judged 'their iniquity double, because they have sinned against so much light, and against so many evidences of Divine Presence'.[2]

The senior officers from Colchester, who had surrendered at mercy, soon felt the keenness of Fairfax's new temper. Lucas, Lisle and Sir Bernard Gascoigne were sentenced to death, though the latter was reprieved because he was a Florentine. Lucas and Lisle were shot by a file of dragoons in the courtyard of Colchester Castle. Lisle, the last to be shot, died with characteristic bravery. He joked with the dragoons, suggesting that they come closer, remarking 'friends, I have been nearer you, when you have missed me'. The shooting of Lucas and Lisle, draconian though it seems, was in strict accordance with martial

[1] John Buchan, *Oliver Cromwell* (London 1944), p. 283. Although rather old fashioned, Buchan's biography of Cromwell is still useful.
[2] Cromwell to Speaker, 11 July, Carlyle, op. cit., Vol. I, p. 324.

law. They had both surrendered upon mercy, and, furthermore, Lucas had, it appears, broken his parole given in 1646.[1] The execution of these two officers was, though, a grim omen for the future.

If Preston won the war, Colchester virtually ended it. In Scotland, too, events moved rapidly in Parliament's favour. Hamilton's 'Engagement' with Charles had never been popular, and this lingering distrust flared into the brief civil war known as the Wiggamore Raid. The Presbyterians of the west, led by the Earl of Eglinton, descended on Edinburgh. The Earl of Lanark, Hamilton's brother, was unable to assert control; the Committee of Estates sought refuge with Monro's army, and Argyll swept once more into power. Cromwell had followed Monro north, and on 22 September he met Argyll, and agreed to give him military assistance in return for Berwick and Carlisle. He went on to ensure the complete destruction of Hamilton's pro-Royalist party, as well as the disbandment of the armies of Lanark and Monro. With the danger from Scotland satisfactorily overcome, Cromwell re-crossed the border into England, to be confronted by a political problem which was to cause him much soul-searching, and ultimately raise him to a position of unprecedented eminence. He was in no hurry to return south, and seems to have been glad of the opportunity to collect his thoughts while besieging Pontefract Castle. Holles had reopened negotiations with the King, which infuriated Cromwell, but by the time he reached London the exasperated army had already acted against Holles's supporters.

Parliament was largely to blame for its own dismemberment. No sooner had it received news of the victory of Preston than, with a complete disregard for opinion within the army, it repealed the Vote of No Addresses, and sent commissioners to meet the King at Newport, in the Isle of Wight. This was seen by the army to be the work of the Presbyterian element at Westminster, for such negotiations could imperil everything that the army had fought for. Charles, indeed, was in his element. He spun out the talks as long as possible, making concessions he never expected to adhere to, and seeking an opportunity for escape. Charles's flat rejection, on 16 November, of a new treaty which imposed the inevitable checks on the monarchy, infuriated even the moderates, and gave new support to the growing weight of opinion within the army. The Council of Officers failed in a direct approach to the King. Finally, a Remonstrance was drawn up and presented to Parliament. This document, largely the work of Ireton, demanded that the King should be brought to trial.

Parliament took little enough notice of the Remonstrance, forcing the army to more overt action. On 29 November troops of the New Model replaced local units as Charles's guards; on the following day the King was moved to Hurst Castle on the mainland. As Charles was taken into the army's custody, the

[1] For a detailed discussion of this much-debated incident, *see* Clements Markham, *A Life of the Great Lord Fairfax* (London 1870), pp. 327–33, and M. A. Gibb, *The Lord General* (London 1938), pp. 201–4.

officers drew up a new declaration, affirming their intention of marching on London and dissolving Parliament, setting up a new body with the Independent members. The latter objected to this scheme, and suggested instead a purge of the existing Parliament. The Presbyterians precipitated the crisis by declaring, on 5 December, that Charles's answers to their terms constituted a worthwhile basis for further negotiations. On the morning of 6 December, Colonel Pride's regiment of Foot, supported by Colonel Rich's Horse, clattered into Westminster. Pride relieved the Trained Band guards, and posted men around the House of Commons. Pride himself, assisted by Lord Grey of Groby, who could recognise the members, stood at the entrance to the House, denying entrance to all mentioned in a list he held. Over 240 members were barred; of these, thirty-nine who struggled were detained in a nearby tavern called 'Hell'.[1]

Cromwell arrived in London that night. His attitude to the King had by now hardened into ruthless opposition. Charles had shown himself untrustworthy – there was, therefore, no point in further negotiation. Exile or imprisonment were unacceptable; death seemed the only solution. Events now moved with sickening speed. Fairfax, horrified by the intentions of so many of his subordinates, was unable to steer the council of officers from its lethal path. On Christmas day a final attempt to come to terms with Charles failed before the monarch's Stuart obstinacy. On 6 January, the Rump of the Commons set up a 'High Court of Justice' to try the King; the hitherto obscure John Bradshaw was to preside, and Fairfax was one of the 135 commissioners. Fifty-three of these met on 8 January. Fairfax attended, but left the meeting when he finally understood its grim purpose. His dismay was fully justified. Bradshaw's tribunal, its legality highly questionable, duly found Charles guilty of 'High Treason and other high crimes', and ordered that he 'be put to death by the severing of his head from his body'.[2] This sentence was carried out, on a scaffold in Whitehall, in the chilly, grey afternoon of Tuesday 30 January. Charles's failings, as a monarch and a soldier, may have been considerable. By the quiet majesty of his last hours, and his absolute refusal to sacrifice his principles in return for his life, however, he atones for his many faults.

[1] This produced a response from the witty Henry Marten: 'Since Tophet was prepared for Kings, it was fitting their friends should go to Hell.' Quoted in D. Underdown, *Pride's Purge* (Oxford 1971), p. 148n.
[2] *See* the Death-Warrant in Carlyle, op. cit., Vol. I, pp. 405–6.

PART FOUR

THE THIRD CIVIL WAR
JUNE 1650–SEPTEMBER 1651

Chronology

1649	5 February	Charles II proclaimed in Edinburgh.
	15 March	Cromwell appointed lord-lieutenant and commander-in-chief in Ireland.
	May	Leveller mutinies.
	15 August	Cromwell arrives in Dublin.
	12 September	Cromwell storms Drogheda.
	16 October	Cromwell storms Wexford.
1650	27 April	Montrose defeated at Carbisdale by Strachan.
	21 May	Montrose hanged in Edinburgh.
	23 June	Charles takes the Covenant.
	19 July	Cromwell concentrates around Berwick.
	3 September	Battle of DUNBAR.
1651	20 July	Action near Inverkeithing.
	6 August	Charles crosses the border.
	22 August	Charles occupies Worcester.
	25 August	Derby routed at Wigan.
	28 August	Lambert takes Upton Bridge.
	3 September	Battle of WORCESTER.
	13 October	Charles flees to France.

Twenty-three
DUNBAR

The beheading of Charles was followed by the abolition of monarchy and the House of Lords. Executive power was vested in a Council of State of forty-one members, including Cromwell, Fairfax and Bradshaw. Fairfax, whose inclusion was essential if the Council was to have the army's full backing, declined to take the original oath to the new regime, and eventually swore a heavily revised form. As part of the destruction of the monarchy it was declared a treasonable offence for any Englishman to proclaim Prince Charles, or any other man for that matter, King.

The Scots showed no signs of conforming with this radical legislation. Charles I had been King of Scotland as well as England, and though kingship might have been abolished in the latter country, Scotland remained a monarchy. On 5 February Prince Charles was proclaimed King Charles II by the Scottish estates, with the proviso that he was only to be allowed to exercise his office if he agreed to the Covenant. Scottish commissioners visited Charles in the Netherlands and demanded not only that he should accept the Covenant, but that he should impose it throughout his dominions. Charles, who had appointed Montrose lieutenant-governor of Scotland, and captain-general of all his forces in that country, temporised, hoping that Montrose might defeat the Covenanters. He was to be cruelly disappointed.

Charles's position south of the border was weaker still. The judicial axe disposed of Holland, Hamilton and the gallant Capel, and English royalists were chastened by their recent defeat. With few immediate problems on the domestic front, the Council of State and the acquiescent Rump set about dealing with that graveyard of governmental ambitions, Ireland.

The situation in Ireland in 1649 was more than usually complex. In October 1641 the Catholic Irish had risen in revolt, fearing that a strengthening of Parliament's position could only result in an increase of repressive measures against them. The Earl of Ormonde, with few means at his disposal, failed to subdue the revolt, and in the autumn of 1642 an Irish parliament met at Kilkenny and set up the Irish Confederation. Ormonde's continued lack of success gave weight to Parliamentarian allegations that the rebels were in fact supported by the King, allegations which seemed to be given substance by the Cessation, the armistice signed in the autumn of 1643. After an abortive treaty, by which the Confederates were to aid the English Royalists, fighting broke out once more. The Parliamentarian victory in England, however, rapidly convinced the Confederates that little was to be gained by continuing the struggle against Ormonde, who speedily aligned a majority of Irishmen, Catholic and Protestant, behind the imperilled monarchy. With this powerful support Ormonde managed to eject Parliamentarian forces from everywhere but Dublin and Londonderry.

On 15 March the Council of State nominated Cromwell to command in Ireland. He did not formally accept until the 30th, first checking that his logistic support would be adequate. Four regiments each of Horse and Foot, and four companies of dragoons, were selected, by lot, for service in Ireland.[1] Yet not all was well with the army. The early months of 1649 had seen the rapid increase of Levellers, arch-radicals whose most vocal spokesman within their ranks was John Lilburne. The Diggers, agrarian radicals who sought to abolish wage-labour, and Fifth Monarchy, men who believed that God's personal rule on Earth was imminent, were also active, but, whatever their long-term implications, they represented much less of a threat to military discipline than did the doctrines of the Levellers, which, preached by the charismatic Lilburne, found numerous adherents. The Leveller demands were summed up in the 'Agreement of the People' – manhood suffrage, religious toleration, and annual Parliaments. A spate of pamphlets and agitation eventually flared into mutiny. Many of the troops detailed for Ireland refused to march, while at Banbury, Captain Thompson led 200 troopers of Reynolds's regiment in open rebellion. Fairfax and Cromwell dealt swiftly and efficiently with the outbreaks in the London area, while Thompson, after a long chase and sharp resistance, was shot near Wellingborough. His brother, a cornet, who had led a similar revolt in the south-west, shared his fate.

The suppression of the Leveller mutinies enabled the Irish expedition to get under way at last. Cromwell left London on 10 July, riding in a splendidly appointed coach, and escorted by an eighty-man lifeguard, 'the meanest whereof a commander or esquire'. He sailed for Ireland on 13 August, and arrived at Dublin on the 15th.

Cromwell's activities in Ireland fall outside the compass of this book. The Council of State's preoccupation with Ireland cannot, however, have blinded it to new and dangerous developments in the north. Montrose, with a small army of German and Danish mercenaries, landed at Kirkwall in the Orkneys on 23 March 1650. Here he collected about 1,000 Orkney men and sent Sir John Urry, a Royalist once more, to secure the Ord of Caithness, to enable Montrose to march into Sutherland and raise Highlanders. This was successfully accomplished; and Montrose crossed the wild Pentland Firth with his main

[1] Ireton's, Lambert's, Scroop's, and Horton's regiments of Horse, and Ewer's, Cook's, Hewson's, and Deane's regiments of Foot.

body on 12 April, took Thurso and Dunbeath Castle, and marched, *via* the Ord of Caithness, to Dunrobin Castle. This fortress disobligingly failed to surrender; Montrose then swung inland to Lairg, crossed the hills, and marched to the head of the Kyle of Sutherland. Here he halted to await the support which he had been promised. Indeed, Montrose was in desperate need of reinforcements, for he had only 500 or so mercenaries, and his Orkney recruits, though loyal, were untrained.

Leslie acted with considerable speed. He ordered Colonel Strachan, at Inverness, to halt Montrose, while the Scottish army concentrated at Brechin. Montrose, camped at Carbisdale, was lured from his strong position, and his tiny army was cut to ribbons by Strachan, aided by some of the very clansmen on whose support Montrose had relied. He escaped from the field, but was taken soon afterwards. On 21 May, Montrose was hanged in Edinburgh, as was Urry, who had changed sides once too often.

The defeat of Montrose persuaded Charles II that there was little else he could do but accept the Covenant and thus purchase Scottish support. This he did on 23 June 1650, before being allowed to land in Scotland. The Scots then set about raising an army under the command of David Leslie. Scottish military preparations had, in fact, been under way for some time prior to the completion of agreements with Charles, and this gave the Council of State time to prepare to meet the threat. The Leveller mutinies had necessitated the disbandment of some regiments, and others were with Cromwell in Ireland. This left a total of twelve regiments of Horse, eleven regiments of Foot, and six companies of dragoons, for the defence of England against the Scots. Commissions were at once issued for the raising of several new regiments, both Horse and Foot, though it would take some time to recruit, train and equip these units.

By early June, even before Charles II had taken the Covenant, it was obvious at Westminster that the Scots intended to invade. The idea of a pre-emptive attack seemed attractive to Parliament and the Council of State; it would prevent further depredations in the north and midlands, and would, with luck, catch the Scots before their army was fully raised. Cromwell, who returned from his victories in Ireland on 1 June, stressed to Fairfax the need for a rapid mobilisation. Twelve days later, Fairfax and Cromwell were voted to command an army for the war with Scotland, as general and lieutenant-general respectively. On 20 June Parliament declared its intention of invading Scotland. Fairfax was appalled by this apparent aggression, and resisted all efforts to be talked round. He argued that the terms of the Solemn League and Covenant prohibited an attack on the Scots, and, although he was prepared to take command if the Scots invaded, he was unable to do so for an offensive war. There was only one way out of this impasse: on 26 June Fairfax laid down his commission, and Cromwell was appointed general in his place.

It was imperative to leave some troops to secure England against Royalist risings while the main body of the New Model marched against the Scots.

Major-General Harrison was given four regiments of Horse to police the country, while regiments of Foot were quartered in London, Oxford and Newcastle, with a fourth split up between Wallingford, Gloucester and Bristol. Four more regiments of Foot were in the process of formation; the county militias were mobilised, and local cavalry units were raised.

Fleetwood was made Cromwell's lieutenant-general, an appointment which he seems to have owed to his seniority rather than to his military ability. The able Lambert, major-general of the Horse, really executed the office of second-in-command. Colonel George Monck was to command the Foot, though he had no regiment of his own until one was raised for him on the Scottish border,[1] drawing on the garrisons of Berwick and Newcastle. Cromwell's expeditionary force consisted of eight regiments of Horse, and nine of Foot. Two companies of Okey's dragoons were present, aided by some of the newly raised mounted militia units doing the duties of dragoons. All units were almost up to establishment, giving a total of 5,000 Horse and 10,000 Foot. The great majority of soldiers were veterans, serving in regiments with experienced officers and good *esprit de corps*. Expansion to full establishment had naturally involved the inclusion of semi-trained men, but they were in most cases integrated into existing regiments. Only one of the newly raised regiments went north with Cromwell.

Leslie's army, though numerically strong, had two major disadvantages. The first was that none of the 'Engagers' were allowed to serve. Leslie was thus deprived of the services of many able officers and scores of enthusiastic soldiers. Secondly, while Cromwell's recruits could be drafted into existing units, Leslie had to set about raising entirely new regiments. Furthermore, Leslie's officers were not of the same quality as those of the New Model. Sir Edward Walker, whose Cavalier views made him unacceptable in Leslie's army, wrote acidly that most of the Scots officers were ministers' sons, clerks, and the like – men of little military experience.

Cromwell concentrated around Berwick on 19 July. Leslie had taken up a defensive position, stretching from Leith, on the Firth of Forth, to Edinburgh itself, covering the capital, and firmly blocking the coast road. Leslie could be fairly confident that Cromwell would advance by this route. The Scots of the Border area had been ordered to remove all their corn and cattle, so as to leave no supplies for Cromwell to seize on his advance. This meant that the English army would have to be supplied by sea, and was thus restricted to the coast road. Even so, there was only one good harbour between Berwick and Edinburgh – the small port of Dunbar.

On 22 July Cromwell crossed the border. He reached Dunbar four days later, and landed supplies from the fleet. These were necessary, for the Scots had carried off anything that could be of use to the invaders. Cromwell then resumed his advance. At Haddington, he sent Lambert with 1,400 Horse to Musselburgh, to see if the Scots could be surprised. Lambert came into contact

[1] *See* Baldock, op. cit., p. 428. Now the Coldstream Guards.

with Leslie's outposts, and on 29 July Cromwell drew up his army before the Edinburgh–Leith position. It was obvious that Leslie's defences were so strong as to make a frontal attack impossible. The army spent the night in make-shift bivouacs under pouring rain; in the morning, 'the ground being very wet. and our provisions scarce, we resolved to draw back to our quarters at Mussel-burgh, there to refresh and revictual'.[1]

The withdrawal began at about 10 a.m., and speedily became rather ragged. Lambert, with the rear-guard, became separated from the main body of the army, marching rapidly, no doubt, for shelter and provisions. Leslie saw his chance, and sent two bodies of Horse against the rear-guard. Captain Evanson's troop of Whalley's regiment, the rear-most unit, was driven back, but a counter-attack by Cromwell's regiment checked the Scots for a time. A second Scottish charge then dislodged Cromwell's troops, and the rear-guard was hard-pressed. Whalley then brought up an intact troop of his regiment, and Lambert led another regiment forward in person. This new onslaught resulted in a fierce mêlée, in the course of which Lambert was wounded and captured, though he was speedily rescued by Lieutenant Empson of Cromwell's regiment. The Scots were routed, and the retirement went on without further interruption.

Cromwell's men arrived at Musselburgh, 'so tired and wearied for want of sleep, and so dirty by reason of the weather, that we expected the enemy would make an infall upon us. . . .'[2] These suspicions proved correct. Major-General Robert Montgomery, with about 1,000 excellent Horse, fell on Mussel-burgh in the early hours of 31 July. Lilburne's regiment of Horse, on outpost duty, was surprised, owing to the presence of English troopers in Mont-gomery's force, whose familiar accents deceived Lilburne's vedettes into thinking that the Scots were a returning patrol.[3] Despite this initial success, Montgomery was driven off with numerous casualties.[4]

If Cromwell's men expected food at Musselburgh, they were to be dis-appointed, for the rough weather made the landing of supplies impossible. The army consequently fell back on the more sheltered port of Dunbar, where tents were at last issued. The terrible weather, coupled with the scarcity of provisions, had produced an appallingly high rate of sickness.[5] Cromwell must have been sorely tempted to remain in the relative security of Dunbar to allow

---

[1] Cromwell to the President of the Council of State, 30 July 1650, Carlyle, op. cit., Vol. II, p. 74.
[2] Loc. cit.
[3] A familiar *ruse de guerre*. The Englishmen in question had been enlisted despite the Kirk's ban on Cavaliers and Engagers. Obviously not all Scottish colonels were as blind to military reality as were their Ecclesiastical mentors.
[4] *See* Carlyle, op. cit., Vol. II, p. 75. Cromwell, naturally enough, over-emphasised the damage inflicted on the Scots.
[5] Cromwell lost, between crossing the border and defeating Leslie at Dunbar, between 4,000 and 5,000 men, most of them through sickness. *See* Firth, 'The Battle of Dunbar', *Transactions of the Royal Historical Society*, 1900, p. 25.

his men to recover their strength, but he returned to Musselburgh on 12 August. He then resumed his efforts to bring Leslie to battle. His new plan was to circle the Scottish right, reach the Forth, and, with the assistance of the fleet, cut Leslie's communications. Cromwell accordingly occupied Braid Hill on 13 August, threatening the Queensferry road. However, he soon had to return to Musselburgh for supplies, and left some troops to cover the port. He then returned to the Pentland Hills, to find that the wily Leslie had pushed a garrison into Redhall, and seized Corstorphine Hill. Cromwell stormed the former outpost on the 26th, and on the following day marched west, to cut Leslie's communications with Stirling.

Leslie conformed with Cromwell's movements, marching along the high ground near the Forth. The two armies finally came into contact near the village of Gogar. Both sides deployed for action, but Leslie had taken the precaution of drawing up behind a bog, and Cromwell, completely thwarted, fell back to the Pentlands, and thence to Musselburgh. Leslie returned to Edinburgh. He had every reason to feel satisfied, for he had easily foiled Cromwell's outflanking move, and, while the English were exposed to the ferocity of the weather, his own men were comfortably billeted and well supplied. The opening moves of the Dunbar campaign reflect nothing but credit on Leslie; Cromwell had been out-generalled.

Cromwell – his men, in Captain Hodgson's words, 'shattered, hungry, and discouraged' – withdrew from Musselburgh on 31 August, making again for the shelter port of Dunbar. Leslie followed the retirement, but the English reached Dunbar in safety. The town of Dunbar clings to the shore of the North Sea. To the west lies the inlet of Belhaven Bay, while on the south-east a rugged coastline runs on towards the Border. Between Belhaven Bay and Dunbar the ground is relatively flat, but to the south and south-west the Lammermuir Hills glower down on the town and jostle towards the sea. The road to Berwick, known as Cockburnspath, threads through the heights, less than a mile from the sea. Streams empty into the sea on both sides of Dunbar. To the west Biel Water enters the sea at Belhaven, while to the east the Broxburn runs at the foot of the hills. The ground rises sharply on the western bank of the Broxburn, and is crowned with the round eminence of Doon Hill, about two miles from the coast. To the east of the Doon Hill spur flows another stream, Dry Burn.

When Cromwell's exhausted troops entered Dunbar on the evening of 1 September, they were posted in a wide arc around the port, from Belhaven on the west to Broxmouth on the east. This position was well sited to cover Dunbar itself, whose possession was essential if Cromwell's army was to survive. If Dunbar was vital for communications by sea, its land communications were desperately fragile, relying only on Cockburnspath. On the night of 1 September Leslie cut this road, leaving Cromwell with no choice but to fight with his back to the sea, or to rely on the fleet to evacuate his army. The English

17 DUNBAR

stood to arms on the following day, while Leslie marched his army around to the Doon Hill spur, where he drew it up on the east bank of the Broxburn, squarely blocking the Berwick road. Cromwell, in some agitation, wrote to Hesilrige at Newcastle, pointing out that 'we are upon an engagement very difficult. The Enemy has blocked up our way at the Pass at Copperspath [sic], through which we cannot get without almost a miracle.... Our lying here daily consumeth our men, who fall sick beyond imagination.'[1]

2 September dawned dark and stormy. Both armies had spent a wet night, for the gusty wind made it impossible for Cromwell's men to pitch their tents. During the afternoon, Leslie edged his men along from the high ground near Doon Hill towards the less steep slopes near the sea. Most of the Horse were placed on the right, between the Berwick road and the shore. The Foot conformed, closing up between Doon Hill and the road. Leslie's guns were also brought on to the lower slopes of the spur. The Scottish army was thus concentrated into a line rather under two miles long, parallel with the lower reach of the Broxburn. This stream flows, in its upper stretch, through a sharp ravine, which becomes more shallow as the burn nears the sea. Between Broxmouth House and the sea it can be crossed easily, even when swollen with rain.

Leslie's dispositions seem to have been made with a view to launching an attack the following day.[2] Further weight is given to this supposition by a Scottish attack on one of Cromwell's outposts, a farmhouse on the Berwick side of the Broxburn. This building, garrisoned by twenty-four Foot and six Horse, fell to two troops of lancers. One of the Englishmen taken prisoner was led before Leslie, who asked him 'how will you fight, when you have shipped off half your men, and all your great guns?' The prisoner, a stout one-armed veteran, warned Leslie that if he attacked he would 'find both men and great guns too!'[3] This shows that Leslie assumed that Cromwell had already begun an evacuation by sea, and that he was intent on retreating rather than fighting.

THE BATTLE OF DUNBAR, 3 SEPTEMBER

Cromwell and Lambert watched Leslie's manoeuvre from Broxmouth House Cromwell observed how the Scots were crammed on to the hillside between burn and crest, and, though well dispersed to deliver an attack, were not so well placed to receive one. He had heard that Leslie had at least 6,000 Horse and 16,000 Foot, while Cromwell himself had only 7,500 Foot and 3,500 Horse that were fit to fight.[4] Nevertheless, Cromwell resolved to attack the Scots before Leslie was ready to deliver his assault. The experienced Monck was

---

[1] Carlyle, op. cit., Vol. II, p. 75. Cromwell must have intended to send this letter by sea.
[2] There is no real evidence that Leslie was pressured into attacking by the ministers accompanying his army. See Baldock, op. cit., p. 446.
[3] Quoted in Carlyle, op. cit., Vol. II, p. 75.
[4] Cromwell to Speaker, 4 September, in ibid., p. 105.

probably also present at this meeting, and his advice no doubt helped Cromwell arrive at his decision.

The English Council of War, which met at Cromwell's quarters after dark, was far from united behind the general's plan. Several of those present favoured evacuation by sea, and it took Lambert's shrewd logic to convince the Council of the advisability of an attack.[1] The plan of attack was bold and simple. Fleetwood and Lambert, with six regiments of Horse, and Monck, with three and a half regiments of Foot, were to open the assault, crossing the burn in the area of Broxmouth House. The remaining Foot, forming two brigades under Pride and Overton, with two regiments of Horse, were to form the reserve and secure the artillery.

The night of 2 to 3 September was wild and stormy. Cromwell's troop concentrated around the axis of the Berwick road. The Scots, on their rainswept hillside, gained what little shelter they could by lying under the cornstooks. Only the file-leaders were detailed to keep their matches alight, and this must have been difficult enough. Cromwell's deployment, however, took longer than expected, and it was not until between 5 a.m. and 6 a.m. that the attack went in.[2]

Lambert's striking force crossed the Broxburn almost unopposed, and formed up on the east bank. The Scots, having stood to their arms twice earlier in the night, were by now convinced that the weather had made an attack impossible, and many of their officers had retired to take shelter in tents or farmhouses.[3] Lambert's charge consequently caught the cavalry on the Scottish right ill-prepared. Many were entangled in their tents, their guy-ropes cut by the English Horse. Nevertheless, Lambert was outnumbered by between 4,000 and 5,000 to 2,700, and the Scots fought it out manfully, checking his initial charge. Monck now came up on Lambert's right, and charged the infantry on the Scottish right. Lambert and Monck were both temporarily halted by fierce resistance when Cromwell led up his own regiment of Horse and Pride's brigade of Foot. Crossing the burn between Broxmouth House and the sea, Cromwell thrust into the gap between Lambert and Monck. As Pride's men swept forward, Lambert and Monck renewed their attack, while Cromwell's regiment of Horse swung into the Scottish right. At this moment the sun burst through the clouds, its light glinting wetly off the arms and accoutrements of the advancing Foot.

Leslie's right wing, now exposed to the full weight of Cromwell's army from both front and flank, collapsed, with a horde of fugitives making off down the

[1] Captain Hodgson's account (*Memoirs*, pp. 144–6) is useful for details of the Council of War. Cromwell's own version of the battle (Carlyle, op. cit., Vol. II, pp. 102–10) is remarkably reticent on the subject.

[2] The exact time of the attack is open to question. Cromwell, in the letter cited above, says 6 a.m., but Firth's 'Battle of Dunbar' places it two hours earlier. Sunrise was at 5.33 a.m., and all accounts agree that some of the fighting took place in the dark.

[3] Leslie to Argyll, 5 September, quoted in Firth, 'The Battle of Dunbar', p. 42.

Berwick road. This left the main body of Scottish infantry cruelly exposed to a flank attack. Rising in drenched surprise from the dripping shelter of the corn-stooks, Leslie's Foot had no space to form a defensive flank, and little oppor-tunity to light their matches. Most of the infantry could offer no effective resistance to the onslaught of Cromwell's Horse, though two regiments, prob-ably equipped with snaphance muskets, fought on until they were destroyed.[1] The remainder of the Foot, in the centre and on the left, either fled or surren-dered on the spot. Some crossed the upper Broxburn and made off towards Haddington, while others fled eastwards along Cockburnspath.

The major part of the action was over in an hour. 'Their whole army,' wrote Cromwell, 'having been put into confusion, it became a total rout; our men having the chase and execution of them nearly eight miles.'[2] In the battle and in the pursuit that followed, Leslie's own army almost ceased to exist. According to Cromwell, about 3,000 Scots were killed, and almost 10,000 private soldiers were captured, together with perhaps 300 officers. All Leslie's guns, together with a good store of powder, match and small arms, were taken. Cromwell's casualties were light – about 40 killed, including a Major Rooksby and a cornet.[3]

Cromwell's victory at Dunbar is a classic example of the concentration of force at the decisive point. Although some of the detail of the action, particularly the attack of Pride's brigade, is hazy, the excellence of the plan remains clear. By attacking the Scottish right, Cromwell was able to use his superb Horse on the relatively flat ground where their qualitative superiority would be marked. He had also observed the fatal bunching of the infantry in Leslie's centre, and noted that they would be unable to intervene on the right, or resist a flank attack. It is evident that Lambert and Monck supported the plan. But although, according to Hodgson, an officer in Lambert's own regiment, Lambert spoke warmly in its favour in the Council of War, there is no real evidence that the plan was the work of anyone but Cromwell: and, of course, the responsibility was his. Much of the driving force behind the attack itself was also his; he rode about all night, biting his lip till the blood ran down his chin, getting the army in order. Lambert, himself a tactician of the first order, undoubtedly agreed with his general's decision, and his own leadership was certainly instrumental in the victory.

A final point is the iron toughness of the New Model, contrasting as it does with the fragile morale of Leslie's army. Cromwell's men had spent six weeks' fruitless campaigning in hideous conditions, yet their morale remained equal to launching a night attack on a strongly posted enemy. Leslie's army, on the

---

[1] Probably the regiments of Campbell of Lawers and Sir John Haldane of Gleneggies. The former unit was certainly equipped with firelocks rather than matchlocks. *See* Firth, 'The Battle of Dunbar', p. 45.
[2] Carlyle, op. cit., Vol. II, p. 107.
[3] Ibid., pp. 107–8.

other hand, had only recently left its warm, dry billets around Edinburgh. It was in a commanding position, and its general had shown himself Cromwell's equal in manoeuvre. Yet, owing to a mixture of inadequate training, slackness and sheer panic, Leslie's force was routed by an army only half its size.

On 4 September Cromwell sent Lambert, with six regiments of Horse and one of Foot, to Edinburgh. Cromwell himself followed with the rest of the army. Leslie, having collected between 4,000 and 5,000 refugees from Dunbar, had withdrawn to Stirling, and Cromwell speedily marched against him, leaving three regiments of Foot to besiege Edinburgh Castle, and to garrison Edinburgh and Leith. The advance was accompanied by pouring rain, and on 17 September the army was in sight of Stirling. A projected assault was, however, called off owing to the strength of the town's fortifications, and, having fortified and garrisoned Linlithgow, Cromwell returned to Edinburgh.

The political situation in Scotland was, yet again, confused. Colonels Archibald Strachan and Kerr had escaped to Glasgow following Dunbar, and were raising troops among the fanatical Covenanters in those parts. Leslie, in Stirling, had begun to enlist Highlanders, whose military potential was more noteworthy than their affection for the Kirk. Charles was at Perth, in the irksome company of Argyll and his Covenanters. He managed to procure an alliance between Leslie's army and his own Royalist forces, though not before violence had broken out between them. This unholy association infuriated Strachan and his western covenanters, who declined to accept Charles as King, but nevertheless declared their intention of fighting the English.[1]

Cromwell, meanwhile, was plagued by the growing number of 'moss-troopers', bandits who infested the Border area. Lambert and Whalley were ordered to deal with these marauders, while Cromwell strove to catch Kerr and his westerners. Kerr was wounded and captured in an ill-conducted raid on Lambert's quarters, leaving Cromwell free to cannonade Edinburgh Castle, which surrendered on very lenient terms at the end of December.

On 1 January Charles, having publicly confessed not only to his own sins but also those of his unfortunate father, was crowned at Scone. Leslie, secure in his strong position at Stirling, raided Cromwell's outposts, drawing bitter protests from the outraged Oliver. He also recruited hard, and did his best to train his newly raised troops. In early February Cromwell attempted an advance on Stirling, but the weather again forestalled him. He fell ill during the retreat, and was not properly recovered until June. Operations during this period were consequently on a minor scale.

It was by now apparent to the Council of State that the war would continue for some time. Troops were raised to reinforce Cromwell, and Hesilrige sent a regiment of Horse and some Foot north immediately after Dunbar. Colonel Morgan was given command of a new regiment of dragoons, made up from

[1] Strachan, disgusted at the Kirk's alliance with Charles, eventually went over to Cromwell, 'and presently died of religious mania' (1652).

the unregimented companies raised for the 1650 campaign, and Okey's troopers also joined Cromwell in Scotland. Colonel Pye's regiment of Horse marched north, as did two newly raised regiments under Colonels Alured and Lidcott. No less than six regiments of Foot reached Cromwell between Dunbar and June 1651, bringing his total strength up to ten regiments of Horse, fifteen regiments of Foot, and Okey's and Morgan's dragoons.[1]

The new Royal army expanded at a remarkable rate. Paradoxically, Leslie's defeat at Dunbar had strengthened Charles's hand, and his new army included not only Scots, but also English Royalists, hitherto barred from service by the Kirk. Charles himself commanded the army, with Leslie as his lieutenant-general. Middleton commanded the Horse, and Massey the English contingent. The irrepressible James Wemyss was general of the ordnance. Leslie felt confident enough to offer battle at the end of June, and boldly marched from Stirling to Torwood.

Cromwell was by now well enough to take the field, and concentrated his army in his old camp in the Pentlands on 25 June. Five days later he advanced down the Stirling road to Linlithgow, hoping to meet Leslie. The latter declined to move forward from his position at Torwood, which Cromwell reluctantly decided was too strong to attack. Leslie had perhaps 15,000 Foot and 6,000 Horse entrenched behind the Cannon Brook, and skirmishing on 2 July confirmed Cromwell in his view that a direct approach was impossible. He thereupon withdrew to Linlithgow, made a demonstration towards Glasgow, and, on 13 July, returned to Linlithgow. Two days later he made yet another attempt to force Leslie to fight, by storming the outpost of Callander House. Leslie yet again refused to be drawn, forcing Cromwell to adopt a more sophisticated plan. This was to cross the Forth east of Stirling, thereby cutting Leslie's communications with his sources of supply, and particularly with Perth, the seat of Charles's government.

On 16 July Cromwell instructed Colonel Overton, with Daniel's regiment, two companies each from two other regiments, and four troops of Lidcott's Horse, to cross the Forth at Queensferry. Boats had been provided for this purpose, and Overton was ordered to form a firm base on the Northferry peninsula, which he did on the early morning of the 17th. Cromwell, meanwhile, threatened the Torwood position with the remainder of his army, but Leslie, keeping the bulk of his Horse facing Cromwell, sent Major-General Browne with 4,500 men to deal with Overton. The latter was now in a delicate position, but was speedily reinforced by Lambert, with two regiments each of Horse and Foot.[2] Lambert's crossing was completed by mid-morning on

---

[1] A disputed total; some authorities say thirteen Horse and twelve Foot. *See* Baldock, op. cit., p. 479.

[2] Whether Lambert was ordered forward, or attacked on his own initiative, is open to question. Cromwell admitted that Browne 'would probably have beaten our men from the place if he [Lambert] had not come'. (Carlyle, op. cit., Vol. II, p. 203.)

Sunday 20 July, and Browne wisely decided to withdraw. Lambert, however, sent Okey's regiment to follow up the retirement, and Browne was compelled to halt and offer battle. After a long pause, during which each side waited for the other to attack, Lambert at last charged. The action was short but fierce, and nearly 2,000 Scots were killed, a surprisingly large total, probably accounted for by the fact that the Highlanders got 'ill quarter'.

Cromwell at once sent Lambert two more regiments of Horse and two of Foot. Leslie now determined to lead his whole army to Inverkeithing to crush Lambert, but Cromwell followed him too rapidly to permit this, and Leslie slid back into his old position at Stirling. His communications were, however, soon severed, for on 26 July Cromwell wrote that 'we have now in Fife about thirteen or fourteen thousand Horse and Foot'.[1] In the same letter, Cromwell requested a re-supply of arms and equipment, and warned that he was short of money. He crossed the Forth himself on 30 July, and invested Perth on the following day.

Leslie was now in the unenviable position of having the bulk of Cromwell's army squarely across his communications. He could either turn and fight in an effort to reopen his lines of supply, or could march into England, recruiting as he went amongst the old Royalists and disillusioned Presbyterians. Leslie seems to have favoured the former course of action, but Charles, his hopes centred, naturally enough, on England, ordered a march south. Cromwell heard of the Royalist advance on 1 August, but he remained before Perth, which surrendered the following day, until the news was confirmed. He then left a garrison in Perth, and recrossed the Forth. Monck, with 5,000 or 6,000 men, was detached to take Stirling, and Lambert, with about 4,000 Horse, was sent on ahead, to join Harrison and Colonel Rich on the Border, and then to harry the advancing Royalists, much as he had done during Hamilton's invasion in 1648. Cromwell, with the Foot and artillery, followed as quickly as possible.

On 5 August Lambert wrote to Harrison, informing him that he was ready to move, and would advance by way of Jedburgh or Kelso. He told Harrison that he had been ordered to attack the Royalist rear, while Harrison acted against the enemy flank, sending Rich's Horse on ahead. On the following day, Harrison was at Newcastle, with four regiments of Horse. Rich's regiment was at Hexham, and Lambert was on the march with four more regiments. Colonel Fitch's Foot garrisoned Carlisle. Further south, Fleetwood, with his own regiment of Horse and Colonel Gibbon's Foot, was raising troops in the Nottingham area. In London, Fortescue's Foot, which seems to have acted as a depot and training unit, split up to form an extra regiment, under the command of Colonel Corbett. All over the north and the midlands the militia were mobilised to assist the regular forces in halting the King's army. Nevertheless, if Charles moved fast, and if his recruiting proved successful, he had every chance of being able to pose a very serious threat to London.

Ibid., pp. 206–7.

Twenty-four

WORCESTER

Charles crossed the border on 6 August, and reached Penrith two days later. His army seemed much better than that commanded by Hamilton three years previously. However, few recruits appeared, and a latent distrust between English and Scots permeated the force. Major-General Massey, the English Presbyterian who had so resolutely held Gloucester for Parliament during the First Civil War, went ahead of the King's army, striving to raise men. He was hampered in his endeavours by the Committee of Ministers accompanying the army, which prevailed upon Massey to issue a declaration emphasising the King's adherence to the Covenant, thereby alienating many potential recruits.

The Royalist army marched rapidly south. Charles was at Wigan on 15 August; on the same day, Lambert, after a forced march of over two hundred miles in ten days, joined Harrison and Rich. On the next day there was some bickering over the passage of the Mersey, but the Parliamentarians, under orders not to risk a pitched battle, fell back before Charles's advance. At Warrington the Earl of Derby joined the King with a few hundred men brought over from the Isle of Man. He was sent off to raise troops in Lancashire, but met with his customary ill success, and was eventually defeated at Wigan by Colonel Robert Lilburne, with a regiment each of Horse and Foot, detached from Cromwell's army for this purpose (25 August). As the Royalist advance went on, morale declined, particularly in the Scottish contingent. Leslie, gloomy and morose ever since the army left Stirling, was asked by Charles why, marching with such an excellent force, he looked so downcast. Leslie muttered that he 'well knew that the army, how well soever it looked, would not fight'.[1] It seems that his morale had not recovered from Dunbar.

At Warrington, Charles decided to abandon his projected march on the capital, and determined instead to continue southwards in the hope of finding a refuge where his army could rest, refit and recruit. Shrewsbury rejected his summons to surrender, and he marched on to Worcester, the Loyal City, traditionally Royalist, and in some ways an excellent base. The local Parliamentarian commander was unable to offer serious opposition to the Royalist advance, and

[1] Clarendon, op. cit., Vol. VII, p. 498.

on 22 August Charles's royal standard floated over the city. The footsore and weary troops of the Royal army went on to billets in and around Worcester, with the cavalry quartered in the villages on the west bank of the Severn. Some effort was made to repair the city's fortifications, which had been slighted after its capture in the summer of 1646. Despite the indifferent state of its fortifications, Worcester, with the rivers Teme and Severn joining just south of it, was an easily defended base.

The Royalists were given little time to recover from their gruelling march from Scotland. On 25 August Lilburne routed Derby at Wigan. The Earl himself, painfully wounded, made his way to Worcester with a handful of horsemen. The hoped-for recruits failed to flock into the Royalist camp. Gloucester turned a deaf ear to the blandishments of Massey, and those of the local gentry that were inclined to raise men lacked arms, and there were none to be had. There were in all some 2,000 English Royalists at Worcester – not an impressive number. Meanwhile, Cromwell's noose tightened. The general and Lambert, having met at Warwick on 24 August, were at Evesham on the 27th, and Fleetwood marched to Shipston the same day. Cromwell realised the importance of thrusting up both banks of the Severn, and on 28 August he sent Lambert, with a party of Horse and dragoons, to seize the bridge at Upton.

The Royalists were not blind to the importance of Upton Bridge, and Massey had broken down one of its arches some time previously, posting a strong guard at its western end. Lambert reached the bridge at about 9 a.m., and discovered that Massey's men had left it partially intact. The Royalist guard, about 300 men, was comfortably billeted in Upton, and Lambert was able to get some dragoons across the broken portion of the bridge by nothing more complicated than a plank. These dragoons seized Upton church, where they were quickly attacked, but some Horse forded and swam the river, and the bridge-guard soon made off. Massey, trying to rally his fleeing troopers, was wounded. Lambert set his men to repairing the bridge, and sent a messenger back to Fleetwood, who at once rushed troops forward to secure the crossing, and followed rapidly with the rest of his brigade.

With freedom to operate on both sides of the Severn, Cromwell began to invest Worcester. He placed guns on the Perry Wood ridge, and bombarded the reconstructed Fort Royal. Reconnaissance revealed that the Royalists had retired behind the River Teme, and were holding the bridges strongly. Charles's army, its morale now perhaps somewhat brittle, nevertheless held a strong position. The Teme barred an attack up the west bank of the Severn and, while the Royalists were able to cross the Severn at will by Worcester Bridge, Cromwell was tied to the repaired bridge at Upton. The next bridge upstream was at Bewdley, about fifteen miles away. It was obvious that, if Cromwell were to attack, he would first have to solve the problem posed by the rivers.

On 29 August Cromwell held a Council of War within sight of Worcester. For once, he had numerical superiority. His army, swollen by new levies and

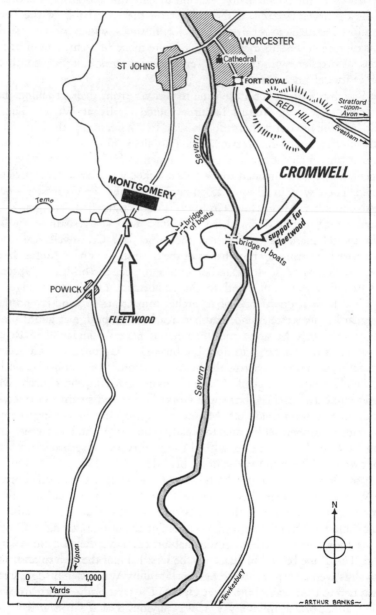

18 WORCESTER

local militia, was between 25,000 and 30,000 strong, while Charles, whose recruits had barely compensated for his stragglers, had something like 12,000 men. The Council decided to launch a two-pronged attack on Worcester. Fleetwood was to advance up the west bank, force a crossing over the Teme, and assault Worcester from the west, while Cromwell attacked the city from the east. To connect the two prongs of the offensive, a bridge of boats was to be thrown across the Severn near its junction with the Teme, and across the Teme 'within pistol-shot' of the Severn Bridge. The attack was to be launched on 3 September, the anniversary of Dunbar.

THE BATTLE OF WORCESTER, 3 SEPTEMBER

There was some skirmishing during the intervening days, while Cromwell collected boats and bridging equipment. Fleetwood advanced at dawn on 3 September, in two columns, one making for Powick Bridge,[1] broken down by the Royalists, and the other heading for the bridging-point near the Teme's confluence with the Severn. The speed of Fleetwood's advance was limited by his need to keep level with the boats, of which the bridges were to be made, which were moving slowly up the Severn, and it was not until mid-afternoon that both columns reached the Teme, exchanging fire with the Royalist musketeers on the north bank. On the east bank of the Severn, Cromwell sent forward a detachment to cover the construction of the bridge, and, as soon as it was finished, led four regiments of Horse and two of Foot across it to support Fleetwood. The latter's pioneers now managed to complete the bridging of the Teme, and Fleetwood crossed the river in strength, over the bridge of boats, and near Powick Bridge, where the river was fordable. The Royalists fought hard, falling back from hedge to hedge, doing considerable execution. Major-General Robert Montgomery, a resolute officer, rode about encouraging his men, giving Cromwell and Fleetwood no easy passage.

While Montgomery's Scots fell back towards the western suburb of St John's, Charles and his staff watched the battle from the tower of Worcester Cathedral. Cromwell appeared to have committed most of his Horse to the fighting on the west bank, and Charles determined to use his Horse, as yet intact and drawn up in the Pitchcroft meadow, north-west of the city, against the troops threatening Worcester from the east. He therefore assembled his cavalry, with what infantry were available, and sallied out of the Sudbury Gate against Cromwell's right wing, covered by the guns of Fort Royal. The Parliamentarian units in this quarter were principally militia from Cheshire and Essex, but they were stiffened by some regular Foot and several regiments of regular Horse.

It was by now late afternoon, for Fleetwood's attack had not gone in until between 2 p.m. and 3 p.m., and the fight on the west bank had been in progress for two hours or so. The Royalists now had an opportunity to make Cromwell

[1] The bridge is still there, and one can easily see the arch that was taken out.

pay dearly for his ambitious plan of attack, and initially it seemed as if Charles's sally might succeed, for the militia were driven back up the slopes of Red Hill. The regular Horse then intervened, and Cromwell pushed reinforcements across from the western bank. Clarendon writes harshly of the conduct of the Royalist army, alleging that many troops threw down their weapons and fled. Cromwell's account of the action contradicts this, saying that Charles's sortie force 'made a very considerable fight with us, for three hours space'.[1] After a hand-to-hand struggle, Royalist Horse would stand no longer, and were not to be rallied. Fort Royal fell to the Essex militia, and the fort's guns were turned against the Royalist fugitives who poured through the town, with Charles and a few other officers making frantic attempts to rally them.

Many of the cavalry got away through the North Gate, but no escape was possible for the vanquished Foot, who surrendered in droves in the gathering darkness. About 6,000 or 7,000 prisoners were taken, including Hamilton, who, mortally wounded, did not live long to enjoy the Dukedom inherited from his executed brother. Still more Royalists were taken as they fled; Leslie, Derby, Massey and Middleton were all captured during the next few days. Harrison pursued the Royalist remnants through Lancashire, sending Colonel Saunders to clear Yorkshire. The country people helped round up the fugitives; those few Scots that returned home were fortunate men.

King Charles managed to free himself from the smoky, bloody chaos of Worcester and eventually escaped to France. His escape was made possible by the old Earl of Cleveland, who led two desperate charges to give him time to get out of his armour and slip away. He left little hope behind him. Three Civil Wars had taken their toll of men who were fitted by military experience or social status to raise armies for him. Conversely, the raw material for Royalist forces no longer existed. The bold troopers and sturdy pikemen of Edgehill, Cropredy and Lostwithiel were long since dead, prisoners, or soldiers of Cromwell's army. The English Royalists had been bled white at Marston Moor and Naseby, and the Scots had suffered cruelly at Preston and Dunbar. Worcester had wrung the last drop of blood from the King's military power; after it any hope of resistance to the New Model could be no more than a wishful illusion. Well might Cromwell term Worcester, his last and finest battle, 'a crowning mercy'.[2]

While Cromwell dealt with Charles's main army, Monck had completed the conquest of Scotland. Stirling Castle surrendered on 14 August, and Dundee was stormed on 1 September. Old Leven had been captured by Colonel Alured while trying to raise troops for Dundee's relief. Monck spent the next year tightening his grip on the Highlands, and once he had accomplished this, Charles was finally deprived of any base for further descents on England.

[1] Carlyle, op. cit., Vol. II, p. 223.
[2] Ibid., p. 236.

PART FIVE

PROTECTORATE AND RESTORATION
SEPTEMBER 1651–MAY 1660

Chronology

1653	20 April	Expulsion of the Rump.
	4 July–12 December	Barebones Parliament.
	16 December	Instrument of Government. Cromwell accepts office of Protector.
1655	March	Penruddock's rising.
	31 October	Rule of the major-generals.
1657	25 March	Humble Petition and Advice passed by Parliament.
	8 May	Cromwell declines Humble Petition and Advice, and with it the kingship.
	26 May	Cromwell, having accepted a revised Petition, is installed as Lord Protector under the new constitution.
1658	14 June	Battle of the Dunes.
	3 September	Death of Cromwell.
1659	August	Booth's rising.
1660	25 February	Monck appointed commander-in-chief by Parliament.
	4 April	Charles II issues Declaration of Breda.
	8 May	Parliament proclaims Charles King.
	25	Charles lands at Dover.

Twenty-five

KEEPING THE PEACE :
THE PROTECTORATE

The Civil War was at last won, but the problem of a settlement remained.
Monarchy and the House of Lords had been abolished; government devolved
upon the Council of State and the Rump of the Long Parliament. Soon after
his return to London, Cromwell attended a conference, held at Speaker Lenthall's house in Chancery Lane, to discuss how the country should in future be
governed. Lenthall urged the necessity of 'improving these mercies to some
settlement'.[1] The question, as seen by Cromwell, was 'whether a Republic, or a
mixed monarchical government will best to be settled? And if anything monarchical, then, in whom that power shall be placed'?[2] He went on to express
himself in favour of a limited monarchy, although he stressed the difficulty of
restoring the Stuarts.

The conference could offer no solution. The Rump was little help, and its
members seemed to have little interest in undertaking the measures of reform
essential in the uneasy situation of post-war dislocation. However, as Underdown points out, internal divisions within the Rump tended to make cohesive
action almost impossible.[3] Cromwell, a harsh man in wartime, was swift to
realise that only clemency could heal the scars of conflict. Yet not until February
1652 did the Rump pass an Act of Indemnity for all the acts of 'treason' committed before Worcester, and even then the act was riddled with exceptions.
The religious question remained unsettled, and the governmental economy was
based on the perilous expedient of living off income produced mainly by fines
on Charles's supporters and confiscations of their property.

The army was the only real power in the nation. Yet even in the New Model,
swollen to the immense total of about 50,000 men, there was little unanimity.
Most senior officers were, at least, determined that the Rump should not devise
some means of perpetuating itself, and should come to terms with the problem

[1] Carlyle, op. cit., Vol. II, p. 242.
[2] Ibid., p. 243.
[3] D. Underdown, *Pride's Purge* (Oxford 1971), pp. 268–96.

of arrears of pay. Agreement went no further than this. Major-General Harrison and a radical clique saw the army as the means of implementing legal and religious reform. A more conservative group, led by Lambert, sought to return to a Parliamentary system based on the 'natural rulers' of the land. A few, like Edmund Ludlow, remained uncompromising republicans.

The Rump sealed its own fate by dawdling over the urgent problems confronting it, and then debating a 'Bill for a New Representative' which was to produce nothing more than a re-fleshed Rump. Cromwell, who held the balance between conservatives and radicals within the army, was under pressure from both extremes to act against the Rump. A conference of officers and Members of Parliament, held at Cromwell's lodgings on 19 April 1653, determined to delay the Bill and to discuss a new provisional government. On the following day, however, the Rump heedlessly ignored this decision, only to be interrupted by a dour Oliver, who strode in and upbraided an astonished House. 'I will put an end to your prattling,' he stormed. 'It is not fit that you should sit here any longer. You have sat here too long for any good you have been doing lately.'[1] With this, he ordered Harrison to 'call them in', and a body of musketeers entered to give weight to their general's argument. Poor Speaker Lenthall, spluttering ineffectually, was hauled down from his chair by Harrison, whilst another officer carried off the mace.

The expulsion of the Rump left the army as the *de facto* government, for the Council of State was dissolved the same afternoon. The task now facing Cromwell was to replace the Rump by some institution more worthy of the name of Parliament. The inevitable compromise between political extremes produced the Barebones Parliament, an appointed assembly, so called after one of its members, a leather-seller named Praise-God Barbon. This 'assembly of saints', having thoughtfully voted itself the title of Parliament, fell to with reforming zeal. So radical were many of its measures that Cromwell, along with the Lambert faction in the army, and much of the gentry and professional classes, was thoroughly alarmed. On 12 December the moderate members contrived to vote the Parliament into dissolution, though some of the more adamant extremists had to be dislodged by Cromwell's usual expedient of a file of musketeers.

While the Barebones Parliament was still in session, Lambert and his adherents in the army produced a document known as the Instrument of Government, which set out a constitution based on a Protector and a single House.[2] Barbon and his fellows took little notice of this scheme, but after the dissolution of the Barebones Parliament Lambert revived his plans, and on 16 December Cromwell accepted the office of Lord Protector, conferred on him by the Instrument of Government. He took over the reins of government at a difficult time. Hostilities had broken out with the Dutch, and, despite the unpopularity of the war, Cromwell was not able to end it until April 1654.

[1] Carlyle, op. cit., Vol. II, p. 264.
[2] Gardiner, *Constitutional Documents*, pp. 405–17.

The Protectorate appealed to conservatives of Lambert's stamp, but it was unpopular with radicals of Harrison's persuasion. Several officers, including Harrison himself, expressed their disapproval by refusing to soldier on. Others protested later: in October the 'petition of the three colonels' attacked the Instrument of Government as giving the Protector greater power than the King had ever possessed, granting as it did absolute control of a standing military force.[1]

The Instrument of Government did not only set up the Protectorate as a cockshy for the radicals. It significantly altered the franchise, giving greater weight to the urban middle class. It also set up a council, the majority of whose members were the army grandees or their supporters, and made provision for an army of 30,000 men. As a result, the first Protectorate Parliament, which met in September 1654, found itself unable to control the executive, and was unwilling to vote money for an army whose usefulness seemed to have long since ceased. It also failed to agree with the wide religious toleration provided for in the Instrument. Such restiveness was to be expected. The Parliament contained at least 100 members of the Long Parliament, amongst them several excluded by Pride's Purge. On one hand, the Republicans regarded the regal Cromwell with loathing, while the other extreme, Wales and the west, had managed to elect a few Royalists, whose attitude to the Protector was scarcely more benign.[2]

Cromwell had opened Parliament with a reminder that its 'great end' was 'Healing and Settling', but the friction that arose over the question of Parliamentary modification of the Instrument made its dissolution, in January 1655, after a session of only five months, predictable. The Protector, meanwhile, had been trying his hand at the hazardous game of diplomacy. He endeavoured, initially, to avoid involvement in the conflict between France and Spain, but sought trading concessions from Spain in the West Indies. When the Spanish refused, Cromwell, in December 1654, sent an expedition under Admiral Penn and General Venables to the West Indies. Penn and Venables took with them only 2,500 soldiers as a leaven to the 4,500 men then raised in the British West Indies; a landing in Hispaniola in April met with a bloody repulse, and when Venables returned to Jamaica his force was ravaged by sickness. So dismal was the failure of the West Indies expedition that both commanders, who had aggravated their incapacity by violent mutual hostility, were clapped in the Tower on their return to England.

The perplexed Protector was faced with more serious problems at home.

[1] See Firth, *Cromwell's Army*, pp. 366–7. The three colonels, Alured, Okey and Saunders, all suffered drastically curtailed military careers as a result.
[2] See Public Record Office SP 18/13, a petition from the inhabitants of the County of Brecknock, objecting to the tactics of the High Sheriff of the county, John Williams, who had rigged the election in favour of Edward Jones, a Royalist. We are grateful to Charles Milner-Williams, a descendant of the said Sheriff, for bringing this document to our notice.

Although the Royalists had little chance of challenging the military power of the Commonwealth, an undercurrent of intrigue persisted. Charles had warned his adherents 'not to enter upon any sudden and rash insurrections, which could only contribute to their own ruin, without the least benefit or advantage to his service'.[1] Several English Royalists hoped, however, to organise a rising not only by the King's supporters, but by the disenchanted Levellers, by Cromwell's opponents within the army, and by the Presbyterians. John Gerard's plot to assassinate the Protector, in May 1654, failed, and numerous arrests followed. Nevertheless, the plan for a general rising gathered momentum during the autumn of 1654 and the spring of 1655.

Cromwell was exceptionally fortunate in having John Thurloe, 'the greatest intelligence officer that ever served an English ruler',[2] as secretary to the Council. Not only did Thurloe provide detailed information of the decisions and intentions of foreign powers, he also amassed a wealth of intelligence on the projected rising. In January 1655 Thurloe's agents uncovered the action party's plans for distributing arms in the midlands, and a wave of arrests followed. Cromwell had already taken the precaution of recalling troops from Ireland to meet the threat, and he went on to ban race meetings, a favourite rendezvous for Royalists, and to confiscate horses and powder from suspects. Despite these signs of vigilance, and their failure fully to involve Levellers and Presbyterians in the planned insurrection, the Royalists persisted in their design.

Charles was at Cologne, and several of his followers, with more courage than good sense, left the security of the Rhine to travel to England to take part in the rising. The Earl of Rochester went into the north, and Sir Joseph Wagstaffe, formerly major-general of Foot in the King's western army, went first to London, and then into the south-west, where he hoped to organise the gentry of Hampshire and Wiltshire. Timing had never been the strong point of Royalist military planning even when the King's armies were at their most successful, and it is not difficult to imagine how, with poor communications and a web of flimsy secrecy, the plotters of 1655 totally failed to synchronise operations.

On 8 March small bodies of Royalists coalesced in various places. In most cases the nervous waiting in the grey dawn proved too much for them, and they disappeared home to see what their friends would do. The south-western Royalists did not rise until 11 March. Wagstaffe had planned a rendezvous for the Wiltshire and Hampshire gentry near Salisbury, but the Hampshire Royalists were so late at their own rendezvous as to be unable to join their Wiltshire brethren. Colonel John Penruddock, 'a gentleman of a fair fortune, and a great zeal and forwardness in the service',[3] led nearly 200 well-armed Horse into Salisbury before dawn, seized all the available horses, opened the jails, and apprehended the High Sheriff and the judges of Assize. Wagstaffe determined

---

[1] Clarendon, op. cit., Vol. VII, p. 129.
[2] Buchan, op. cit., p. 457.
[3] Clarendon, op. cit., Vol. VII, p. 129.

to hang the latter, but was dissuaded by Penruddock. Clarendon maintains that harsh treatment of the sheriff and the judges would have encouraged the numerous Royalists in Salisbury, but it is impossible to agree that their execution would have served any useful purpose.

Having proclaimed Charles II in the market-place, Wagstaffe and Penruddock left Salisbury, without waiting for the 200 or so Hampshire Cavaliers who were riding to join them. Now numbering between 300 and 400, the Royalist force made off westwards, hoping to raise support in the traditional centre of Royalist strength, the West Country. At South Molton, however, they were opposed by a single troop of Horse from Exeter, under Captain Unton Crook, and, after a brief engagement on 14 March, the Royalists broke up. Some, Wagstaffe among them, were hidden in the houses of local people, and later escaped abroad, while others, like Penruddock, surrendered on quarter. If Penruddock had hoped for mercy he was to be disappointed, for he was beheaded at Exeter, while many of his followers were hanged at Salisbury, and the rest shipped off to Barbados.

Rochester had little more luck in the north. The Earl, our old friend Wilmot, newly promoted, 'saw danger at a distance with great courage, and looked upon it less resolutely when it was nearer'.[1] He arrived in Yorkshire only to discover that the date for the rising had been misunderstood; some had already risen, and gone back home to await events. Others raised questions which were 'reasonable rather than seasonable', and the great northern insurrection fizzled out with less sparkle than a damp squib. Rochester himself, making for London, displayed his usual cheery negligence, riding from inn to inn, and even stopping to survey some land owned by his wife. After narrowly escaping capture in Aylesbury, he reached London, and eventually returned thence to Cologne.

The dismal failure of Penruddock's rising, bearing in mind the poor security and lack of coordination which characterised the venture, is scarcely astonishing. Had the Royalists been prepared to submerge their personal disputes, and had they made a serious attempt to enlist Presbyterian aid, the insurrection might have proved more serious, though it is improbable that the Protectorate, backed as it was by the bulk of the New Model, could have been seriously threatened.

The easy suppression of the insurrection enabled Cromwell to disband about 10,000 men, for the army was still well over the 30,000 permitted by the Instrument of Government, and the Commonwealth was in financial difficulties. Cromwell's next scheme was an attempt to solve the problem of internal security and to minimise the drain on the exchequer. On 31 October it was announced that the country was to be divided into twelve districts, 'over each of which he placed a Bashaw under the title of Major-General . . . with orders to seize the estates and persons of such as should be refracting, and to put in execution such further directions as they should receive from him [Cromwell]'.[2]

[1] Ibid., p. 145.
[2] Ludlow, op. cit., Vol. I, p. 406.

The major-generals enforced their decisions with troops of Horse, backed by the local militia. The expense entailed in these measures was covered by an iniquitous Decimation Tax, which confiscated one tenth of all the property of all Royalists, even if they had not participated in Penruddock's rising. Numerous Royalists objected, on the grounds that they had already compounded for their estates and the Act of Oblivion had granted them pardon for their earlier 'treasons'. Such men received short shrift from the major-generals. Whalley quartered 50 men on one objector, threatening to send 500 more if he did not pay up forthwith.

The major-generals rammed Puritanism down the nation's throat with the butt-end of a musket. Horse-racing was already forbidden; they added bear-baiting, cock-fighting – cruel but traditional sports – to the growing list of prohibitions. Royalists had to give security for their peaceable behaviour and that of their servants; the major-generals often fixed these bonds at an impossibly high level. It was perhaps ironic that objections were raised to this new tyranny, founded on the same arguments used by the opposition to Charles I in the years before the war. Cony, a London merchant, refused to pay a tax, on the grounds that the ordinance imposing it was invalid. His counsel were imprisoned until they repented of their folly, and Cony paid, albeit with a bad grace. Some lawyers went on to mumble of Magna Carta – one of the lynchpins of the pre-war opposition – only to be roundly castigated by the Protector.

Blake, a capable soldier turned brilliant Admiral, was sent, in March, to attack the Spanish treasure fleet – another of the Protector's attempts to boost governmental revenue. Cromwell's diplomacy, alas, tended to meet the same fate as Charles's, for the Spaniards, goaded by English attacks on their colonies, declared war. The Protector was thus reduced to call a Parliament in an effort to raise money for the Spanish War, and, on 17 September 1656, the Second Protectorate Parliament met. The major-generals had promised Cromwell that they would ensure that only those well-disposed to the government were elected, but they miscalculated, and over 100 members had to be excluded from the first sitting. News of a useful naval success, in which Captain Stayer captured a treasure ship with £600,000, encouraged the Parliament to vote £400,000 towards the war, but, apart from this, its compliance with the Protector's wishes was limited indeed.

Cromwell's speech opening the Parliament expressed the hope that a wide measure of religious toleration would be granted.[1] Parliament, however, seized James Naylor, a Quaker, and fined, mutilated, and imprisoned him. It also proceeded to throw out the Militia Bill, which included a continuation of the Decimation Tax, and in the course of the debate the major-generals were hotly assailed. Cromwell too came under attack, though from a different quarter. Charles II was offering a knighthood and a pension of £500 a year to anyone who would kill the usurper, while disillusioned radicals, at the other end of the

[1] Carlyle, op. cit., Vol. II, p. 537.

political spectrum, also conspired against him. Miles Sindercombe, a former quartermaster, and an adherent of the Leveller Sexby, constructed an 'infernal machine' to destroy the chapel at Whitehall and the Protector with it. Sindercombe was betrayed, arrested and sentenced to a traitor's death, though he managed to cheat rope and knife by taking poison.

Parliament may have been prepared to oppose the Protector over the questions of religion and military rule, but its address of congratulation presented to Cromwell on his escape from Sindercombe's plot has the ring of sincerity. A Presbyterian M.P., John Ashe, proposed an addition to the address, suggesting that Cromwell 'take upon him the government according to the ancient constitution'. This could only be interpreted as a request for the Protector to call himself King. It was by no means a new suggestion, for the title of King had been mentioned in the first draft of the Instrument of Government. Ashe's proposal was soon followed by a new constitutional scheme, the Humble Petition and Advice.

This document[1] was introduced into Parliament by Sir Christopher Pack on 23 February. It had no easy passage, for, although the lawyers and civilians in Parliament and the Council were in favour of it, the major-generals, backed by opinion within the army, and, of course, the Levellers, were bitterly hostile. On 25 March the measure was passed, nevertheless, by a comfortable majority, and was presented to Cromwell six days later.

The Protector was undecided. The constitution propounded in the Humble Petition and Advice certainly pleased him. He was to be permitted to choose his own successor, and to appoint members to a new Upper House. The position of Parliament was also to be strengthened: members could be excluded only with the consent of the House, and, though a permanent revenue of £1,300,000 per year was granted to the Protector, Parliament was to decide how this sum was to be raised. Cromwell found all this reasonable enough, and thought it likely to produce a more lasting settlement than the Instrument of Government. The rub lay, though, in the title of King. Oliver hovered for some days, but at last refused, saying 'I have not been able to find it my duty to God and you to undertake this charge under that Title'.[2] The Humble Petition and Advice, now suitably amended to avoid mention of the royal title, was passed on 25 May, and was accepted by Cromwell. A month later, the Additional Petition and Advice modified some details of the former document. On 26 June Cromwell, in a ceremony reminiscent of the coronation of a monarch, was installed as Protector under the new constitution.

The Protector's foreign policy began, at last, to bear fruit. His hope of an alliance with Sweden, leading perhaps to the formation of a Protestant league, had come to little, for too much of the fleet was engaged in the West Indies to permit the risk of war in the Baltic. In July 1656, however, a commercial treaty

---

[1] Gardiner, *Constitutional Documents*, pp. 447–59.
[2] Carlyle, op. cit., Vol. III, p. 32.

was signed between England and Sweden, though this must have disillusioned those who had taken Cromwell's talk of 'a Protestant Alliance' seriously. After the defeat of the Penn-Venables expedition, the Spanish War went well, but in April 1656 Charles II signed a treaty with Philip IV of Spain, permitting him to maintain a small army in the Spanish Netherlands. Charles speedily raised four regiments. Lord Wentworth commanded a regiment of Foot guards, while Ormonde held the colonelcy of an Irish regiment, to encourage Irishmen to join the King. Rochester commanded an English regiment, and Lord Newburgh a Scots unit. These regiments were soon recruited to full strength. There were several English, Scots or Irish regiments in the French service at this time. Many of their soldiers deserted to join Charles, and one colonel, Lord Muskerry, brought over 800 men of his regiment.[1]

Charles's growing army in Flanders was an unacceptable threat to the Commonwealth's security and prestige. Consequently, on 23 March 1657, Cromwell signed an unlikely alliance with Catholic France, agreeing to send 6,000 men, backed by a fleet, to fight the Spaniards in the Low Countries. In return for this assistance, Cromwell was to receive Dunkirk and Mardyck when they were eventually wrested from the Spaniards. Mardyck was besieged in September 1657, surrendered on 3 October, and was occupied by Colonel Sir John Reynolds's Englishmen the following day. Reynolds was lost at sea not long afterwards, and Sir William Lockhart took over the command of Cromwell's troops in Flanders. On 14 June 1658, Turenne, his French army strengthened by the English contingent, attacked the Spaniards near Dunkirk. The future James II was present with the Spanish army at this action, known as the Battle of the Dunes. James observed 'Lockhart's own regiment . . . commanded by Lieutenant-Colonel Fenwick; who so soon as he came to the bottom of the hill, seeing that it was exceeding steep, and difficult to ascend, commanded his men to halt and take breath for two or three minutes . . . as soon as the body were in a condition to climb, they began their ascent with a great shout, which was general from all their Foot.' Fenwick was shot down, but his major led the regiment on, 'who stopped not till they came to push of pike; where notwithstanding the great resistance which was made by the Spaniards, and the advantage they had of the higher ground . . . the English gained the hill and drove them off from it. . . .'[2] The Spaniards were roundly beaten, and Dunkirk surrendered ten days later.

Before this great victory, however, the second Protectorate Parliament, after a recess of six months, had met again in January 1658. Cromwell had by now nominated the Upper House, whose members included his two sons, three sons-in-law, and two brothers-in-law, as well as seventeen regimental colonels. The new House was singularly empty of the old nobility, only two of the

---

[1] See Clarendon, op. cit., Vol. VII, pp. 227–8, and The Memoirs of James II (Bloomington, Indiana, 1962), trans. and ed. A. Lytton Sells, p. 223.
[2] James II, op. cit., p. 264.

hereditary lords summoned obeyed the writ. Unfortunately for the Protector, the election of several Members of Parliament enabled the opposition to gain strength in the Lower House. Those Members previously excluded were allowed to return, having first sworn a mild oath not to conspire against the lawful authority of the Protector. Hesilrige and his friends were well experienced in Parliamentary obstruction, and at once commenced to attack the Upper House. So serious was the rift that on 25 January Cromwell warned both Houses of the danger of a total breakdown, but the opposition continued to rant, and agitated for support in the City and within the army. On 4 February the Protector addressed Lords and Commons, remarking upon his disappointment in them, and closing with the stern injunction 'I do dissolve this Parliament! And let God be judge between you and me.'[1]

Cromwell's only real basis of power had been, and indeed remained, the army. Yet even this tempered instrument had its flaws; Leveller and Fifth Monarchy propaganda continued to find ready ears. In February 1657 a massive petition had begged Cromwell not to take the title of King. His refusal to assume the hated title had quelled much hostility, but the Parliamentary opposition had had some success in aggravating the discontent in some sections of the army. Cromwell could not afford to have the source of his power eroded, and his dissolution of Parliament was promoted largely by its interference with the army. On 6 February, the Protector addressed 200 officers from units in the London area, and the meeting ended in a reaffirmation of military support for Cromwell. The day was not, though, without its worries. Cromwell's own regiment of Horse had become seriously infected with extreme republicanism, and the Protector felt compelled to cashier its commanding officer, Major William Packer, and five troop commanders.[2] This must have pained Cromwell, for he had jettisoned Harrison in 1654, and Lambert in 1657, and now his own regiment was contaminated.

It was as well that the Protector once more had the army securely behind him, for the spring of 1658 witnessed a renewed Royalist outburst. The tireless Sir Henry Slingsby had tried to infiltrate the garrison of Hull, and was betrayed and arrested. While he was awaiting trial, there was a new spate of arrests, and rumours of a planned insurrection in the City. Slingsby was beheaded on 8 June, and was followed by Dr John Hewet, another Royalist. Other conspirators suffered more harshly, being 'hanged, drawn and quartered, with the utmost rigour, in several great streets in the city'.[3]

Cromwell did not long survive the steadfast Slingsby. The summer of 1658 was a sickly one: disease was rife, and the weather strangely unseasonable. On 6 August, Cromwell's favourite daughter, Elizabeth Claypole, died. The Protector felt the loss keenly, and took to his bed for some days. His health had

---

[1] Carlyle, op. cit., Vol. III, p. 192.
[2] Firth, *Cromwell's Army*, p. 370.
[3] Clarendon, op. cit., Vol. VII, p. 253.

been weakened by the physical strain of campaigning, and by the mental pressures of his office. He was up and about again by 17 August, but within a few days he was sick once more, of a 'bastard tertian ague'. He struggled like the soldier he was, but, on the morning of 3 September, the anniversary of Dunbar and Worcester, the Lord Protector died.

Cromwell had nominated his eldest son Richard as his successor, and 'Tumbledown Dick' was accepted by the Council and the army. However, Richard Cromwell altogether lacked his father's firm hand. When Parliament met once more, the republican element within it attacked the Petition and Advice, root of the Protectorate; even the moderates, while supporting Richard and his government, assailed the army, which counter-attacked by petitioning the Protector for arrears of pay. The army went on to signify its readiness to act against the 'wicked' elements of Parliament, and eventually Fleetwood, by a show of force, compelled the helpless Protector to dissolve Parliament on 22 April 1659.

Safely rid of its enemies in Parliament, the Council of Officers, the *de facto* government, cast about for a new constitution. This resulted in the exhumation, in early May, of the mouldered skeleton of the Long Parliament, which creaked once again into Westminster Hall. This reassembled body endeavoured to reduce the army to subservience to the civil power, by appointing Fleetwood general, but with limited tenure of command, and by declaring that officers' commissions should be signed by the Speaker. The army was alarmed at this, but its friction with Parliament was temporarily checked by yet another Royalist outbreak.

The rising in the summer of 1659 was, like its ill-fated predecessor, intended to be nationwide. Lord Willoughby of Parham was to seize Lynn, and Massey hoped to bring over his old charge, Gloucester. Several Shropshire gentlemen planned to take Shrewsbury, while the Cornwall and Devon Royalists prepared to raise the west. Sir George Booth, with large estates in Cheshire, hoped to seize Chester. As usual, Thurloe's agents got wind of the Royalist designs. 'The affairs in England had no prosperous aspect;' writes Clarendon with unusual understatement, 'every post brought news of many persons of honour and quality committed to several prisons, throughout the Kingdom, before the day appointed [for the rising].'[1] Massey was captured, but managed to escape, though his plan to take Gloucester was exposed. Only Booth had any real success. He seized Chester, with the help of Sir Thomas Middleton, and issued a proclamation stating that they had taken up arms not specifically for the King, but rather 'in vindication of the freedom of Parliaments, of the known laws, liberty and property....'[2] Parliament sent Lambert against Chester. Booth and his officers were divided; Sir George lacked military experience, and, instead of standing a siege in Chester, he marched out to meet Lambert and

[1] Ibid., p. 331.
[2] Sir George Booth, quoted ibid., p. 333.

was routed after a short engagement at Winnington Bridge. .Chester fell next day; Booth was captured as he fled in disguise, and was imprisoned in the Tower.

The news of Booth's defeat and the total collapse of the rising came as a grave blow to Charles II and James, Duke of York, who were making preparations for a landing on the English coast. In England, meanwhile, the disappearance of the military threat produced renewed conflict between army and Parliament. The crisis centred upon the command of the army. Parliament cancelled Fleetwood's commission as commander-in-chief, and placed command in the hands of seven commissioners. Lambert and eight other officers were cashiered. Predictably enraged, the army acted rapidly; Lambert marched to Westminster, and placed his musketeers at the entrances to the House, effectively ending the session.

The Council of Officers returned to its task of constitution-making. A Committee of Safety was set up to administer the country until a new Parliament should meet, in the following February. A new constitution was devised, but was never implemented, for by now opinion within the nation at large ran strongly against the Council of Officers. Even the army was no longer united behind the Council. 'Is England's dear-bought freedom come to this?' lamented a petition signed by five colonels.[1] A far more serious protest came from Monck, who warned the Council that he intended to march south with his army unless the Long Parliament was restored. Monck's soldiers were not required to strike a blow, for unanimity within the army vanished in the latter months of 1659; garrison after garrison went over to the Parliament, and Fleetwood was compelled to reinstate the Long Parliament on 26 December.

Monck entered London, and was appointed commander-in-chief by Parliament on 25 February 1660. He complied with Parliament's instructions to demolish some of London's defences, and to carry out numerous arrests, but retorted by requesting Parliament to dissolve after readmitting those members excluded in 1648. The reinforced Long Parliament made provisions for new elections, and, on 16 March, dissolved itself. A new Parliament, containing a majority of moderate Presbyterians and Royalists, was elected, and met on 25 April. The old House of Lords, though without the Royalist peers, returned once more to Westminster.

By this time there was widespread, and by no means unfounded, suspicion that Monck favoured a restoration of the Stuarts. Opinion within the army was generally hostile to this, but Monck correctly appreciated that the army was too haggard and disunited to offer any serious opposition. Lambert, a skilful general, and popular with his soldiers, had tried to block Monck's march southwards, but his army had collapsed owing to lack of pay, and its leader had been lodged in the Tower. Lambert managed to escape, and in April collected a small force in Northamptonshire. Most of his adherents, however,

[1] Quoted in Firth, *Cromwell's Army*, p. 379.

deserted to a loyal detachment under Colonel Ingoldsby, and a rueful Lambert was returned to the Tower.

The new Parliament, with Monck's backing, entered into negotiations with Charles, now at Breda. A deputation from both houses visited the King and requested him to return. On 4 April Charles had issued the Declaration of Breda, offering an indemnity to all not excepted by Parliament, 'liberty to tender consciences', a settlement of the land question, and payment of army arrears. Parliament accepted this Declaration, and on 8 May Charles was proclaimed King. On 25 May he landed at Dover, and travelled to London amidst scenes of wild rejoicing.

Charles, with technical exactitude, dated his reign from 30 January 1649. However, he went through a lavish coronation ceremony, riding, strangely enough, a horse from the stables of Lord Fairfax, the man whose military skill had brought his father's régime to the ground. This was only one of the ironies of the Restoration. After eighteen years of Civil War and Commonwealth a Stuart sat once more in Whitehall, and there can be little doubt that the nation as a whole approved. The wheel had come full circle.

CONCLUSION

The political results of the Civil Wars were, in the short term, clear-cut and decisive: the abolition of the monarchy and the establishment of the Protectorate. The long-term consequences of the conflict are less easy to discern, but are none the less of the greatest importance.

The wheel of State had spun full circle, from monarchy, through republicanism, to Protectorate, and it is not strange that it should come to rest with a restored monarchy. Yet if the commonwealth ended in a Stuart Restoration, it ended also in the repossession of political power by the 'natural rulers' of the country. In terms of social position and wealth the Convention Parliament of 1660 contained much the same sort of men as the Long Parliament twenty years earlier. The status of the House of Lords had certainly suffered as a result of changes in membership, ill-determined political attitude and sheer aristocratic obtuseness over the past quarter-century. The Commons, however, had made several useful gains. Charles II accepted the Acts of the Long Parliament up to the final breakdown between it and his father. The Restoration Parliament went on to emphasise its control of supply, and deprived the Lords of its power to tamper with financial Bills.

While Charles II might claim the broad prerogative of his father, its practical application was drastically curtailed, even though no specific limitations were placed upon it by the Restoration settlement. The prerogative courts had fallen victim to the zeal of the Long Parliament, and no attempt was made to revive them, and without their legal sanctions, the prerogative was effectively emasculated.

In purely constitutional terms, the Restoration settlement represented a compromise that the moderates of 1640-2, men like Falkland or Hopton, would have found attractive. The political results of the war, however, went deeper than the constitutional fabric. The execution of Charles I was of profound psychological effect. The last English monarch to meet a violent end had been Richard III, killed on Bosworth Field in 1485. Since then, the monarchy had acquired new prestige, particularly during the reign of Elizabeth, and with this went a strange inviolability, felt rather than expressed. The beheading of the King broke the spell, and whatever Charles II might say about absolutism, he could never forget that his father's head had been hacked off on a scaffold in Whitehall. The prestige of the monarchy had been, if not lessened, transformed by the tragedy of 30 January 1649.

If the 1640s proved that revolution in England was feasible, then, conversely, the 1650s showed that the practical effects of the revolution were indecision, insecurity and possible anarchy. The spectre of the Levellers chilled the hearts of the 'natural rulers', and in 1661 the Act against Tumultuous Petitioning struck directly at Leveller propaganda techniques by forbidding the petitioning of King or Parliament without the prior consent of Justices or Grand Jury. Another important legacy of the commonwealth was dislike of military rule. The iron puritanism of the major-generals was long remembered. The militia acts of 1661–2, while placing the militia under the control of the King, ensured that he had to act through the lords-lieutenant, in whose hands lay the appointment of officers. The militia was thus built around the 'natural rulers': service in it was dependent upon a property qualification, and it was officered by the local gentry. Thurloe's description, 'the fortress of liberty', was indeed an apt one.

The Civil Wars and the Commonwealth witnessed a redistribution of land on a scale equal to the Dissolution of the Monasteries.[1] Much confiscated land was, naturally, bought by Parliamentarians. However, the Royalists were themselves not slow in repurchasing their estates whenever possible. The Marquis of Winchester 'bought all but two of his fifteen estates in Hampshire and Berkshire, and all his houses in the City of London'.[2] Some of the lesser gentry, unable to raise money to repurchase their estates, undoubtedly disappeared, but it would be quite wrong to see the confiscations of Royalist land as having an immediate and catastrophic effect upon the Royalist gentry as a whole. Repurchase was not without its long-term effects, though, and many Royalists were, long after the Restoration, forced to sell all or part of their estates to pay off debts which were themselves often the result of loans raised for repurchase. Thus, while confiscations did not, in the short term, separate the bulk of the Royalist gentry from their land, the financial strain of recovering land, by repurchase before the Restoration or by legal action after it, left many families impoverished. No longer could such families remain blind to the importance of agricultural improvements; nor could they afford not to raise rents.

The Declaration of Breda promised a satisfactory solution to the land question. It was eventually decided that Church, Crown and confiscated Royalist lands would be returned to their original owners. Land sold by Royalists – even if the proceeds were used to buy arms, raise troops or to pay fines for delinquency – was not restored. In fact, it proved impolitic for the Crown to repossess all its

[1] J. Thirsk, 'The Sale of Royalist Land during the Interregnum', *Economic History Review*, 1952, p. 188.
[2] Ibid., p. 193.

land. Much of this was left in the hands of its purchasers, often on a long lease, and royal revenue from land consequently fell somewhat.[1]

Generalisations on the effects of the war on industry and trade are dangerous. Certainly, the increased demand for arms gave a powerful stimulus to the metal industry, while the large numbers of demobilised soldiers who thronged the land in the late 1650s and early 1660s provided at once a cheap source of labour, and, so it was believed, a source of political disorder. In 1662 the Act of Settlement endeavoured to restrict the movement of such persons, but was unable to prevent a general drift to the towns. The old pre-war grievance, monopolies, had almost disappeared, owing largely to the abolition of the Star Chamber, the prerogative court which had upheld them. In the case of trade, governmental policy after 1660 was remarkably similar to that under the Protectorate. The Navigation Act of 1660 endeavoured to restrict trade with England to English vessels and English merchants. It was aimed primarily at the Dutch carrying trade, and was the prime cause of the Second and Third Dutch Wars. Nevertheless, it resulted in a tremendous increase in English merchant shipping, and played an important part in the growth of colonial trade.

Although the military consequences of the war are of less general significance than its political and economic results, they are none the less noteworthy. The Civil Wars may justly be regarded as the cradle of the British Regular Army, for, while most of the New Model was disbanded immediately after the Restoration, some regiments were retained, and became the basis of the standing army. The Lifeguards and the Royal Horse Guards[2] trace their descent from Charles's lifeguard and from Colonel Crooke's regiment of Horse respectively. Charles's Royal regiment of guards, which had been with him in Flanders, continued in service, and was to become the Grenadier Guards, while General Monck's regiment was retained as 'the Coldstream Regiment of Footguards'.[3] Between 1660 and 1680 four regiments of Foot were formed,[4] often around a nucleus of regiments originally in foreign service. Some of the units were soon to be sent to Tangier, which was part of the dowry of Charles's Queen, Catherine of Braganza, and 'Tangier' is the earliest battle honour borne on the colours of British regiments.

The Civil Wars may have contributed nothing entirely new to the military art, but they set the seal on several current developments. They witnessed the disappearance of the caracoling pistoleer, and demonstrated that shock action was the true task of the cavalryman. Cromwell went one step further, and

---

[1] See S. J. Madge, *The Doomsday of Crown Lands* (London 1938).

[2] Now amalgamated with the 1st Royal Dragoons to form the Blues and Royals.

[3] So called because it was raised around the village of Coldstream on the Border. Now the Coldstream Guards.

[4] Later known as The Royal Scots; The Queen's Royal Regiment (West Surrey); The Buffs (The Royal East Kent Regiment); The King's Own Royal Regiment (Lancaster). The Queen's and the Buffs now form part of the Queen's Regiment. The King's Own has been amalgamated with the Border Regiment to form The King's Own Royal Border Regiment.

showed what thoroughly trained, well-disciplined cavalry could achieve, providing their commander kept them well under his hand. The battles of the Thirty Years War contain few charges as brilliantly led or as completely successful as the Parliamentarian onslaughts at Naseby or Dunbar. The infantry of the Civil Wars, following as they did the continental trend towards more flexible units than the unwieldy Spanish *tercio*, combined fire and shock in almost equal proportions. Furthermore, their commanders realised the vital importance of following lead with steel, and there was little of the ineffectual long-range volleying so frequent on the continent.

The paucity of accurate information on artillery during the Civil Wars makes it difficult to assess trends in that field. Nevertheless, there seems to have been a marked tendency for artillery to become lighter and more mobile; the Swedish 'battalion gun' was in constant use between 1642 and 1651. James Wemyss's leather guns, very similar weapons, were likewise widely used. Prince Rupert's galloping guns were a genuine form of horse artillery.

The Civil Wars displayed generalship of a widely varying quality. They produced at least two first-rate military commanders: Sir Thomas Fairfax and Oliver Cromwell. The former was a tactician of considerable ability. He was personally brave, quick-witted and decisive. His actions were almost uniformly successful, but in his skilful conduct of the retreat after Adwalton Moor Fairfax showed the resolution in adversity which is the *sine qua non* of generalship. Strategically, Fairfax was not his own master until the eve of Naseby, but, when at last released from the apron-string of Parliament, the result was dramatic. Thrusting first at his nearest opponent, the King, he struck him a fatal blow; then, swinging round to face the only other major Royalist army in the field, he lunged at Goring. It was swift and decisive. For all practical purposes he had won the war in six weeks.

Cromwell is altogether a more puzzling – and in many ways a less sympathetic – character than Fairfax. His indecisive behaviour in his earlier engagements is doubtless due to his prior lack of military experience, while his action at Marston Moor remains very much open to question. In this period his chief importance lies in his ability to raise and train cavalry, rather than in any astounding tactical mastery. Cromwell's tactics did not reach maturity until Naseby, and until the Preston campaign he had had no opportunity for the free exercise of his strategic skill. Cromwell's hagiographers imply that he was vested with all the attributes of generalship from the moment when he first clapped hand to sword. Yet few great captains have not taken time to learn their trade, and 1642–4 was Cromwell's military apprenticeship.

Cromwell's handling of the Preston campaign, his first major independent command, vividly illustrates his tactical flair and decisive approach to strategy. His march to join Lambert in the north was unusually rapid. Once in Yorkshire, he spent the minimum time concentrating, and then struck at Preston and the Scottish flank. An infinitely less risky, though potentially less decisive, manoeuvre would have been to interpose his army between the Scots and London, and fight a holding action. This desire for a conclusive battle is typical of Cromwell's approach to war; his emphasis on pursuing the fleeing enemy, as exemplified after Preston and Worcester, further illustrates his preoccupation with decisive victory.

A third great commander to emerge from the war was Prince Rupert. He was, though, less a product of the war than were Fairfax or Cromwell, for he came to England with considerable experience and an enviable reputation. Close study of his career shows how little justified is his popular image as a mere swashbuckling *sabreur*. His fiery, temperamental pride and tactlessness should not be allowed to obscure his broad mastery of generalship. As a leader of cavalry he had few equals; he was perhaps less good at training and disciplining his Horse, but here he was hampered by the independence and parochialism of his subordinates. These same factors hindered him as an army commander. At Marston Moor, Newcastle and Eythin gave only grudging cooperation, and at Naseby he was hamstrung by the King and his Council of War. Rupert was as unpopular with the Royalist generals as he was popular with the rank and file of the army. His youth, foreign upbringing, and favour with the King provoked jealousy and suspicion amongst the high command, while his courage and dash won him the confidence of the regimental officers and soldiers.

The generals of Parliament lie in a wide spectrum, ranging from sound ability to woeful incapacity. The Earl of Essex owed his position as captain-general to his rank in the nobility as much as to his military experience. He was no strategist; in the Edgehill and First Newbury campaigns he contrived to let the King get astride his lines of communication. In the Cropredy Bridge campaign, his parting with Waller when almost in the presence of the enemy, and when their combined armies might have crushed the King, was the act of an imbecile – paralleled only by the folly of the Committee of Both Kingdoms in sending the New Model to relieve Taunton, thus leaving the capital open to attack by the main Royalist Oxford army. Before Lostwithiel the Earl was, admittedly, badly misled by Robartes, but it is difficult to excuse the way in which he allowed his army to be bottled up around Fowey. He was, though, not without his good points. He remained popular with the troops, and showed considerable powers of man-management. His relief of Gloucester is the brightest spot in an otherwise undistinguished military career.

Sir William Waller, an altogether more capable officer, was skilful but unlucky. He was almost always plagued with internal dissension in his army, and constantly lacked money and recruits. His eye for the ground sometimes betrayed him, for his superb position at Lansdown was not proof against the valour of the Cornishmen, and at Cropredy Bridge he allowed himself to be drawn from a safe position into a hazardous engagement. Cheriton was his most important victory, yet he hovered on the brink of losing it until saved by the impetuosity of Sir Henry Bard. Philip Skippon displayed Waller's reliability but lacked both his bad luck and his disunited army. A soldier of proven ability and ready appeal, Skippon is the epitome of the infantry divisional commander: brave, experienced and unflappable, with a charisma that flashes clearly across three centuries. His opposite number on the Royalist side, Sir Jacob Astley, deserves the same tribute.

The senior officers of the New Model army were, in the main, able men, for they were selected on a more national basis than the commanders of the armies that the New Model replaced. Fleetwood, Ireton, Whalley and Monck were all excellent officers, though they would have done better to confine their energies to soldiering and leave the murky fields of politics to others. Of the New Model's generals, Lambert deserves special mention. His strategy in the Preston campaign was masterly; by holding Yorkshire by grimacing across the Pennines he inflicted fatal delay on the already lethargic Hamilton, and was in no small measure responsible for the ultimate defeat of that luckless nobleman. He displayed similar ability in the march south before Worcester.

Like their Parliamentarian opponents, the Royalist generals were a mixed bag. In many ways, the most remarkable commander was Charles I himself. He was involved in the war much against his will, and suffered from a total lack of military experience. Despite this, he soon acquired enough practical knowledge to play an active part in operations. In 1644 he commanded the Oxford army in fact as well as in name, soundly beating Waller and Essex at Cropredy Bridge and Lostwithiel respectively. His overall strategy was initially for a three-pronged advance on London and, when this became impossible following Cheriton and the Scottish invasion, an effort to meet the enemy's main armies in battle with concentrated forces. This plan was impeded by dispersion and regionalism, but much of this, given the importance of ports and strategic points such as Oxford, Bristol, Chester, York and Newark, was inevitable and indeed justifiable. Charles's character, though, contained flaws which had a detrimental effect upon his generalship. He was a bad judge of men, the readiness with which he listened to the accusations against Rupert is ample evidence of this. He compounded this weakness with a habit of agreeing with whoever last spoke to him – a fatal tendency, bearing in mind the poor quality of many of his advisers. Charles's faltering is shown most clearly in the Naseby campaign, when he placed his nephew in an impossible position by a lively stream of order and counter-order. Despite his imperfections, Charles showed a praiseworthy determination – some might call it unrealistic obstinacy – and never abandoned hope, even when his army was collapsing about him and his kingdom was lost.

Newcastle, who commanded the northern thrust of the Royalist strategic plan, was a brave man but, alas, no soldier. His tremendous value to the Royalist cause was due to his ability to use his wealth and influence to raise, equip and train an excellent army. He was a sensible administrator but his military decisions were those of his professional advisers. Hopton, commander of the western prong of the trident, is in many ways Newcastle's antithesis. He was a good tactician, and a determined and compelling leader. He lacked, however, Newcastle's vast fortune, and was always pitifully short of money and equipment. His victory at Lansdown must be reckoned a remarkable feat of arms by any standards. Even when badly burnt and temporarily blinded as a result of the gunpowder accident, he remained lucid enough to solve the problem of the match shortage at Devizes, and retained enough determination to press his Council of War to march out against Waller on Roundway Down.

Enough has been said of Goring, whose fondness for the bottle, pride and hot temper cannot conceal his very real talent. Lord Byron exhibited many of Goring's faults, but was altogether more limited as a commander. Lord Astley is a more pleasant character than either of the former; his solid, unpretentious professionalism was a useful antidote to the heady air of the King's headquarters.

The ability of so many of Charles I's generals, and the valour and self-sacrifice of his armies, could not prevent the utter ruin of the Royalist cause. It is interesting to speculate upon what might have happened if only things had gone a little differently. If Charles had pursued after Edgehill, or had remained on the field of First Newbury, then the war might well have ended as a Royalist victory. But the hard facts remain, and it is from these that the historian must draw his conclusions. The essence of the military problem was, as Firth points out, the evolution of an efficient army out of chaos. The first side to field a unified, well-organised and soundly equipped force was, given moderately competent generalship, sure of victory. Parliament's possession of London, with the Tower armouries, and most of the major ports in the Kingdom gave it an overwhelming advantage in terms of resources. The intervention of the Scots tipped the scales of manpower firmly in favour of Parliament; the formation of the New Model, which linked manpower with resources, made Parliamentarian victory inevitable after 1645.

The New Model was undoubtedly the decisive instrument of Parliament's success in the First Civil War. It was no less important in the Second and Third Civil Wars. The Alliance between Scots and Royalists was never a happy one; the Allied army was plagued by internal dissension, and could in no way compare with the well-oiled military machine which opposed it. The New Model marked a turning-point in English military organisation; it made the extemporised armies of 1648 and 1650 totally anachronistic.

It is possible to argue that the defeat of Charles I was due primarily to the very nature of his support. Generalisations are, as ever, perilous, but in broad terms, the King's supporters were rural rather than urban, landowning rather than manufacturing. Their geographical location and particularist attitude largely determined Royalist strategy, and at the same time conspired to obstruct the smooth working of the King's plans. Parliament was, to be sure, beset by similar problems, but never to the same degree as its opponents. It could, moreover, afford to enact a thoroughgoing military reorganisation; Charles hedged about with localism and hamstrung by a feudal hierarchy, had neither the opportunity nor the inclination to reform the 'rabble of gentility' which marched beneath his banner. He championed the old order with a weapon flawed by the essence of the cause for which it fought.

GLOSSARY
NOTE ON SOURCES
BIBLIOGRAPHY

Glossary

It should be noted that, in their descriptions of pieces of artillery, the authors adopt the scale of weight and calibre given in William Eldred, *The Gunner's Glasse* (London 1646). Several other scales exist, and on occasion differ substantially.

BASILISK or BASILISKE: Piece of artillery firing a shot weighing approximately thirty pounds. The gun itself was usually deemed too heavy for field service by the time of the Civil War.

BUFF-COAT: A heavy leather coat, long-skirted and often sleeved, worn by cavalry.

CALIVER: Matchlock weapon of musket bore, midway in size between musket and carbine.

CARACOLE: Cavalry manoeuvre whereby the front rank fired its pistols, trotted to the rear to reload, and was followed by the second and successive ranks. First used by the German *Reiters* in the sixteenth century, but outmoded by the 1640s.

CESSATION: Temporary truce signed in the autumn of 1643 between Ormonde and the Irish Confederates.

CLUBMEN: (i) Hastily-levied infantry armed only with clubs; (ii) Bands of countrymen who endeavoured to protect their areas from the depredations of either army. Particularly important in the West Country towards the close of the First Civil War.

COMMISSION OF ARRAY: Commission issued by the King to the lords-lieutenant, ordering them to summon the militia. The legality of this process was contested by Parliament.

COMMITTEE OF BOTH KINGDOMS: Created by Parliamentary Ordinances of 16 February and 22 May 1644, to ensure cooperation between English Parliamentarians and the Scots. Sitting at Derby House, the committee had both an advisory and an executive function. Its members included Essex, Warwick, Manchester, Waller and Cromwell. John, Lord Maitland, was the most significant of the Scottish Commissioners.

COMMITTEE OF PUBLIC SAFETY: Committee of both Houses of Parliament, set up on 4 July 1642, for the prosecution of the war. Dominated by John Pym, the committee nevertheless included Denzil Holles and other moderates.

CORSELET or CORSLET: In the 1640s this usually referred to pikemen's armour, consisting of breast- and backplate, with tassets to cover the thighs.

CUIRASSIER: Heavy cavalry, equipped, in the 1640s, with three-quarter armour. Seldom seen in the Civil War – with the notable exception of Sir Arthur Hesilrige's 'Lobsters'. Their disappearance was partly due to the difficulty of finding horses strong enough to bear their weight, and partly to the cumbrousness of fighting in armour.

CULVERIN: A piece of artillery weighing 4,000 pounds and firing a 15-pound shot.

DEMI-CULVERIN: A piece of artillery weight 3,600 pounds and firing a 9-pound shot.

DRAGON: Short matchlock weapon of musket bore.

DRAGOON: Probably deriving their name from the weapon they originally carried, dragoons were mounted infantry who rode to battle and fought on foot, although they were, on occasion, required to fight on horseback.

DRAKE: Light field-piece.

ENGAGEMENT: The Agreement between Charles I and the Scots, signed on 26 December 1647, by which Charles undertook to establish Presbyterianism in England for three years in return for Scottish military assistance.

FLINTLOCK: System of firearm ignition. A piece of flint was held in the jaws of the cock when the trigger was pressed, the flint was struck against a steel plate, the frizzen, and a shower of sparks ignited the priming powder, firing the weapon.

FUSIL: Light snaphaunce or flintlock gun, carried by the escort to the artillery, who later acquired the name fusiliers.

GUIDON: (i) The standard of a troop of horse or a company of dragoons; (ii) Officer who carried a dragoon standard, equivalent in rank to an ensign in the infantry.

HALBERD, HALBERT, HALBARD: Staff weapon with an axe blade tipped with a spike. Carried by sergeants as a badge of rank.

HARQUEBUSIER: By the 1640s this term had come to mean a cavalryman equipped with harquebus or carbine. He also usually carried a sword and a pair of pistols. The majority of cavalry on both sides in the Civil War could have been called harquebusiers, though the term itself fell rapidly out of use.

IRONSIDES: Nickname of Oliver Cromwell's regiment of Horse, later applied to the cavalry of the Eastern Association, and sometimes to the cavalry of the New Model as a whole.

LEAGUER: Camp. Usually used of the encampment of a besieging army.

LOBSTER-TAIL HELMET: Cavalry helmet owing its name to its neck-guard of overlapping steel plates. Several types of this helmet were used during the Civil War, the most common being the 'English pot', with a three-bar guard covering the face, and the 'Dutch pot', with a single sliding noseguard.

MATCHLOCK: The most common system of firearm ignition at the time of the Civil War. An S-shaped lever, the serpentine, held the match, a length of glowing cord. When the trigger was pressed, the serpentine descended, bringing the match into contact with the priming powder and firing the weapon. Although inefficient, the matchlock had the advantage of cheapness, costing less than a wheel-lock or snaphaunce.

MINION: Four-pounder field-piece.

MONTERO: Cap sometimes worn with military dress. Its exact appearance is unknown, but it may have resembled a modern riding hat.

MORION: Open helmet with a high comb and a brim rising to peaks at front and rear. Sometimes provided with earpieces. Often worn by pikemen.

MUSKET or MUSQUET: Smooth-bore infantry weapon. Most muskets in use in the Civil War were matchlock, and were usually fired from a rest.

PARTISAN or PARTIZAN: Staff weapon with a broad, symmetrical blade. Carried by infantry officers during the Civil War.

PIKE: Staff weapon, usually between twelve and eighteen feet in length. The head was usually small, either leaf- or diamond-shaped. The half-pike was a short version, similar to the partisan, and sometimes carried by infantry officers.

PISTOLEER: Cavalryman equipped with a pair of pistols as his main offensive weapon. Obsolete by the time of the Civil War.

POLE-AXE or POLL-AXE: Weapon similar to a small battle-axe, usually with an axe blade on one side and a hammer or spike on the other. Useful for piercing armour or helmet, and very popular with the Royalist cavalry.

POSSE COMITATUS: The able-bodied private citizens of a county, raised and commanded by the sheriff.

RAPIER: Straight-bladed sword, usually with an elaborate hilt. The rapier was designed for thrusting rather than cutting. It was a civil, not a military weapon, though numerous rapiers saw service in the Civil War.

AKER: Field-piece firing a 5¼-pound shot.

NAPHANCE or SNAPHAUNCE: Early form of flintlock. Invented towards the end of the ixteenth century. More efficient than the matchlock, and less expensive than the wheel-lock.

PONTOON: Staff weapon similar to partisan and half-pike.

TAFF WEAPON: A cutting or thrusting weapon mounted on a long handle. Pikes, hal-berds, partisans and spontoons are all staff weapons. Sometimes known as pole arms.

WINE-FEATHER or SWEDISH FEATHER: Metal-tipped stake, usually about 4½ feet long, arried by musketeers to make an improvised palisade against cavalry.

WHEEL-LOCK: System of firearm ignition. A piece of iron pyrites was held against a oothed wheel, which was wound up against a spring. Pressure on the trigger caused the wheel to spin, and sparks flew into the priming-pan, firing the weapon. Infinitely preferable o the matchlock, but its expense restricted its availability. Normally used on cavalry istols and carbines.

Note on Sources

There is a wealth of material, both primary and secondary, on the Civil War, its background and consequences. No bibliography can hope to deal with all this without itself attaining book-like proportions.

The period produced a flood of pamphlets and tracts, most of which were collected by the London bookseller George Thomason, and are to be found in the British Museum. The Thomason Tracts are particularly useful, reflecting as they do a wide range of opinion, but the accuracy of many of the pamphlets, which were often little more than propaganda, makes them unreliable for detail. Of the manuscript sources, Prince Rupert's Correspondence, in the British Museum, is particularly valuable.

No study of the war should be unaccompanied by reference to some of the contemporary military manuals and drill books, which give an excellent idea of the state of the military art at the time, though it must be remembered that few units in the Civil War can have attained the excellence envisaged by the drill-masters.

Rushworth's *Historical Collections* and Clarendon's often unreliable but nevertheless remarkable *History of the Rebellion* are both essential reading, as is Firth's *Letters and Speeches of Oliver Cromwell*.

S. R. Gardiner's *History of the Great Civil War* and C. V. Wedgwood's *The King's War* are classic accounts, and, although sometimes questionable on points of military detail, remain indispensable.

There are numerous local histories dealing with the Civil War in a specified area or county. The best of these are very good indeed, while the worst all too often employ local tradition as a substitute for fact.

Many of the leading figures of the war have attracted biographers; Cromwell in particular has suffered in this respect, for few of his biographers have provided a balanced assessment of his generalship, which was, after all, his prime claim to power.

Bibliography

Place of publication London unless otherwise stated. The publication date given is that of the edition consulted, not necessarily the first edition. Space prevents a detailed examination of manuscript sources.

PRIMARY SOURCES: DOCUMENTS

Acts and Ordinances of the Interregnum, 1642–60, 3 vols, ed. C. H. Firth and R. S. Rait (1911).
The Army Lists of the Roundheads and Cavaliers, ed. Edward Peacock (1874).
Calendar of the Proceedings of the Committee for Advance of Money, 1642–56, 3 vols, ed. M. A. E. Green (1888).
Calendar of the Proceedings of the Committee for Compounding, etc., 1643–60, 5 vols, ed. M. A. E. Green (1889–92).
Calendar of State Papers, Domestic Series.
Calendar of State Papers, Venetian Series.
Commons Journals, 1625–60.
Constitutional Documents of the Puritan Revolution, 1625–60, ed. S. R. Gardiner (1962).
Constitutional Documents of the Reign of James I, 1603–25, ed. J. R. Tanner (1960).
Documents relating to the Civil War, ed. J. R. Powell and E. K. Timings (1963).
English Army Lists and Commission Registers, 1661–1714, Vol. I (1661–87), ed. Charles Dalton (1892).
Historical Manuscripts Commission, Portland, Marlborough, Ormonde and Lords MSS.
Lords Journals, 1625–60.
Papers Relating to the Army of the Solemn League and Covenant, 2 vols, ed. C. S. Terry (Edinburgh 1917).
Tudor and Stuart Proclamations, 2 vols, ed. R. Steele (Oxford 1910).
Yorkshire Royalist Composition Papers, 3 vols, ed. J. W. Clay (Yorkshire Archaeological Society 1893–6).

PRIMARY SOURCES: MANUSCRIPTS

Bodleian Library:
  Clarendon MSS.
  Additional MSS.
British Museum:
  Harleian MSS.
  Egerton MSS.
  Additional MSS.
Public Record Office:
  Commonwealth Exchequer Papers
  Uncalendared State Papers

Royal Library, Windsor Castle:
  De Gomme's 'Plan of the Battle of Etch Hill 1642'
South Kensington Museum:
  Letters of Sir Bevil Grenvile
Wadham College Library, Oxford:
  The experiences of Sir William Waller
Wiltshire County Records Office:
  Prince Rupert's Diary

MILITARY MANUALS

George Monck, Duke of Albemarle, *Observations upon Military and Political Affairs* (1796). Written when Monck was a prisoner in the Tower in 1644, and first published in 1671.

William Barriffe, *Military Discipline: Or The Young Artillery-Man* (3rd edn, 1643). First published in 1635, and reprinted six times between then and 1661. Barriffe was major to John Hampden's regiment of Foot in 1642, and was a colonel by 1661. His book was in constant use throughout the war, and is a most valuable guide to the formations and tactics in use.

John Cruso, *Militarie Instructions for the Cavallerie* (Cambridge 1635). Cruso was a Fellow of Caius College from 1639 until his ejection by the Parliamentarians in 1644. His work ran into several editions, and was doubtless used by both sides, but, since it was published at Cambridge it seems likely that it was used by Cromwell and the cavalry of the Eastern Association. Barriffe, in his first edition of *Militarie Discipline*, praised Cruso's book which, he said, made it unnecessary for him to write on the subject. By 1661, however, Barriffe seems to have considered it out of date, for he added *Some Brief Instructions For The Exercising of the Cavalry . . .* to his 1661 edition.

William Eldred, *The Gunner's Glasse* (1646), in the Thomason Tracts E.371 (10), 19 January 1647. Eldred had served as master-gunner of Dover Castle.

Richard Elton, *The Compleat Body Of The Art Military . . .* (1650). The author had been a member of the Military Garden; he was major when he wrote the *Compleat Body* and rose to the rank of lieutenant-colonel. His book was very widely used in the New Model.

Gervase Markham, *The Souldier's Grammar* (1626). Markham was a veteran of the Dutch Service. His *The Souldier's Exercise* (1643) is more likely to have been of use to combatants in the Civil War.

Roger Boyle, Earl of Orrery, *A Treatise of the Art of War* (1677). Orrery's work reflects his experience of Irish warfare.

Sir James Turner, *Pallas Armata . . .* (1683). Turner was an officer of great experience; he had served under Gustav Adolf, was a major to Lord Leven's regiment of Foot in 1644, and had a regiment of his own in the Preston campaign.

Thomas Venn, *Military Discipline* (1672). The author was the son of the regicide John Venn.

Robert Ward, *Animadversions of Warre. . . .* Ward's was probably the most comprehensive work on the Art of War available in England at the time of the First Civil War. Drawing upon the best classical and modern authors, as well as upon his own extensive experience, he covered many aspects of strategy, tactics and training. This must have been a valuable work of reference to Royalist and Parliamentarian alike.

CONTEMPORARY HISTORIES, MEMOIRS, CORRESPONDENCE AND TRACTS

A List of (Indigent) Officers: *A List of Officers Claiming to the Sixty Thousand Pounds &c. Granted by His Sacred Majesty (King Charles II) for the Relief of his Truly-Loyal and Indigent Party* (1663).

ANON (Sir William Dugdale?), *A Relation of the Battel fought between Keynton and Edgehill* (Oxford 1642).

ANON (Sir Bernard de Gomme?), *His Highnesse Prince Rupert's late beating up the Rebels quarters at Postcomb and Chinnor* (Oxford 1643).

ANON (Sir Bernard de Gomme?), *His Highnesse Prince Rupert's raising of the siege at Newarke* (Oxford 1644).

Captain Richard Atkyns, *Vindication*, in *Military Memoirs: The Civil War*, Richard Atkyns (ed. Peter Young) and John Gwyn (ed. Norman Tucker) (1967).

Colonel Joseph Bamfield, *Apologie . . .* (The Hague 1685).

Colonel John Birch, *Military Memoir . . . written by Roe, his Secretary*, ed. J. and T. W. Webb (Camden Society, 1873).

T(homas) B(lount), *The Art of Making devises . . .*, from the French of Henri Estienne (1646).

Sir Richard Bulstrode, *Memoirs . . .* (1721).

Edward Burghall, *Providence Improved* (1644), in Thomas Malbon, *Memorials of the Civil War in Cheshire* (1855).

A. H. Burne, ed., *The Battle of Hopton Heath, 1643*, transcribed from the Sutherland Papers, Vol. 2, f. 29, preserved in Dunrobin Castle Library. (Staffordshire Record Society, 1936.)

G. Burnet, *Memoirs of . . . the Dukes of Hamilton . . .* (1747).

Thomas Carlyle, *The Letters and Speeches of Oliver Cromwell*, 3 vols, ed. S. C. Lomas (1904).

T. Carte, *Original Letters and Papers . . .*, 2 vols (1739).

Edward Hyde, Earl of Clarendon, *The History of the Rebellion . . .*, 8 vols (Oxford 1826).

Sir William Dugdale, *The Life, Diary, and Correspondence of Sir William Dugdale, Knight . . .*, ed. William Hamper (1827).

Sir Henry Ellis, *Original Letters Illustrative of English History*, 11 vols (1825–46).

Thomas Lord Fairfax, *Fairfax Correspondence*, Vols I and II, ed. G. W. Johnson (London 1848); Vols II and III, ed. R. Bell (London 1849).

Short Memorials . . ., ed. B. Fairfax (1699).

A Short Memorial of the Northern Actions . . ., in *Stuart Tracts 1603–95* (Westminster 1903).

Denzil Lord Holles, *Memoirs . . .* (1699).

Robert Monro, *His Expedition with the worthy Scots Regiment . . . to which is annexed the abridgement of exercise and divers practical observations, for the youngest officer his consideration* (1637).

Margaret Duchess of Newcastle, *The Life of . . . William Cavendish, Duke of Newcastle*, ed. C. H. Firth (1886).

Sir Francis Ottley, *Original Letters and Papers . . .*, ed. William Philips, *Transactions of the Shropshire Archaeological Society* (1893).

John Rushworth, *Historical Collections . . .*, 7 vols (1659–1701).

Perfect Passages of every daies intelligence from the Parliament's Army (news-sheet).

Sir William Sanderson, *A Compleat History of the Life and Raigne of King Charles from his Cradle to his Grave* (1658).

Sir Henry Slingsby, *Diary . . .*, ed. D. Parsons (1936).

Speciall Passages (news-sheet).

John Baron Somers, *State Tracts*, 16 vols, ed. Sir W. Scott (1748–52).

James Lord Somerville, *Memoire of the Somervilles*, ed. Sir W. Scott (Edinburgh 1815).

Ralph Lord Hopton, *Bellum Civile . . .*, ed. C. E. H. Chadwyck-Healey (Somerset Records Society 1902).

Captain John Hodgson, *Memoirs* (Edinburgh 1806).

Lucy Hutchinson, *Memoirs of the Life of Colonel Hutchinson*, 2 vols, ed. C. H. Firth (1885).

King James II, *Life of James II . . . collected out of memoirs writ of his own hand . . .*, ed. J. S. Clarke (1816).

——, *The Memoirs of James II; His Campaigns as Duke of York 1652–60*, trans. and ed. A. Lytton Sells (Bloomington, Indiana 1962).

Lieutenant-General Edmund Ludlow, *Memoirs* . . ., 2 vols, ed. C. H. Firth (Oxford 1894).

Sir Samuel Luke, *Journal* . . ., 3 vols, ed. I. G. Phillip (Oxfordshire Record Society 1947, 1950 and 1952–3).

——, *Letter Books, 1644–45*, ed. H. G. Tibbutt (Historical Manuscripts Commission and Bedfordshire Historical Record Society). The originals are in the British Museum, Egerton MSS.

Manchester's Quarrel; Documents relating to the quarrel between the Earl of Manchester and Oliver Cromwell, ed. J. B. Bruce and D. Masson (Camden Society 1875).

F. Maseres, *Select Tracts*, 2 vols (1815).

Mercurius Aulicus. The Royalist 'weekly' ed. Sir John Berkenhead (Oxford 1643–5).

Joshua Sprigge, *Anglia Rediviva* (1647).

Captain Henry Stevens, *Papers* . . ., ed. Dr Margaret Toynbee (Oxfordshire Record Society 1961).

The Swedish Intelligencer, 8 parts (1632–5).

Richard Symonds, *Diary* . . ., ed. C. E. Long (Camden Society 1859).

The Kingdome's Weekly Intelligencer.

Thomason Tracts: pamphlets, books, newspapers and manuscripts collected by George Thomason (1640–61).

R. Thoroton, *Antiquities of Nottinghampshire* (1677).

Verney Memoirs, 4 vols, ed. Lady Francis and Lady Margaret Verney (1892).

Verney Papers, ed. J. Bruce (Camden Society 1853).

John Vicars, *England's Parliamentarie Chronicle*, 3 vols (1643–6).

Sir Edward Walker, *Historical Discourses upon Several Occasions* . . . (1705).

Sir William Waller, *Vindication of the Character and conduct of* . . . (1793).

Edward Walsingham, *Brittannicae Virtutis Imago or . . . life . . . of . . . Major-General Smith* (Oxford 1644), Thomason Tracts E.53 (10).

Eliot Warburton, *Memoirs of Prince Rupert and the Cavaliers*, 3 vols (1849).

Sir Philip Warwick, *Memoires of the Reign of King Charles I* (1702).

J. Washbourne, *Bibliotheca Gloucestrensis; a collection of . . . Tracts relating to the County and City of Gloucester during the Civil War* (London 1823).

Sergeant Nehemiah Wharton, *Letters* . . ., ed. Sir Henry Ellis in *Archaeologia* (1853).

Bulstrode Whitelocke, *Memorials of the English Affairs* (1682 and Oxford 1853).

Anthony Wood, *Survey of the Antiquities of the City of Oxford, 1661–66*, 3 vols, ed. Andrew Clark (Oxford 1891).

——, *The Life and Times of Antony Wood* . . ., ed. Andrew Clark (Oxford 1891).

SECONDARY SOURCES: BOOKS

H. Abell, *Kent and the Great Civil War* (Ashford 1901).

John Adair, *Roundhead General: A Military Biography of Sir William Waller* (1969).

J. W. Allen, *English Political Thought, 1603–44* (1938).

J. J. Alexander and W. R. Hooper, *The History of Great Torrington in the County of Devon* (Sutton, Surrey, 1948).

Maurice Ashley, *The Greatness of Oliver Cromwell* (1957).

Lieutenant-Colonel T. S. Baldock, *Cromwell as a Soldier* (1899).

A. R. Bayley, *The Great Civil War in Dorset* (1901).

Ian Beckwith, *Gainsborough during the Civil War* (Gainsborough 1969).

N. H. Brailsford, *The Levellers* (1961).

E. Broxap, *The Great Civil War in Lancashire, 1642–51* (Manchester 1910).

D. Brunton and D. H. Pennington, *Members of the Long Parliament* (1953).

John Buchan, *Oliver Cromwell* (1944).

Lieutenant-Colonel A. H. Burne, *Battlefields of England* (1951).

——, *More Battlefields of England* (1952).

Lieutenant-Colonel A. H. Burne and Brigadier Peter Young, *The Great Civil War* (1959).

W. Y. Carman, *A History of Firearms* (1955).

Sir George Clarke, *War and Society in the Seventeenth Century* (Cambridge 1958).

C. M. Clode, *London during the Great Rebellion* (1892).

Mary Coate, *Cornwall in the Great Civil War and Interregnum, 1642–60* (Truro 1963).

Leonard Cooper, *British Regular Cavalry 1644–1914* (1965).

The Dictionary of National Biography; entries for all the major figures of the period. The articles by C. H. Firth are particularly useful.

F. T. R. Edgar, *Sir Ralph Hopton* (Oxford 1968).

Sir Charles H. Firth, *Cromwell's Army* (1962).

——, *Oliver Cromwell* (New York 1901).

Sir Charles H. Firth and G. Davies, *The Regimental History of Cromwell's Army*, 2 vols (Oxford 1940).

S. R. Gardiner, *History of the Great Civil War, 1642–48*, 4 vols (1901).

——, *History of England . . . 1603–42*, 10 vols (1883–4).

——, *Oliver Cromwell* (1899).

M. A. Gibb, *The Lord General: A Life of Thomas Fairfax* (1938).

G. N. Godwin, *The Civil War in Hampshire, 1642–45, and the story of Basing House* (1904).

G. P. Gooch and H. J. Laski, *The History of English Democratic Ideas in the Seventeenth Century* (Cambridge 1927).

J. H. Hexter, *The Reign of King Pym* (Harvard 1941).

Christopher Hill, *The Century of Revolution* (Edinburgh 1961).

——, *The Intellectual Origins of the English Revolution* (Oxford 1965).

Prince Kraft von Höhenlohe-Ingelfingen, *Letters on Artillery*, trans. (1888).

D. A. Johnson and D. G. Vaisey, eds, *Staffordshire and the Great Rebellion* (Staffordshire County Council Records Committee).

M. F. Keeler, *The Long Parliament, 1640–41* (Philadelphia 1954).

A. Kingston, *Hertfordshire during the Civil War* (1894).

A. D. H. Leadman, *Battles fought in Yorkshire . . .* (1891).

S. J. Madge, *The Doomsday of Crown Lands* (1938).

Sir Clements Markham, *A Life of the Great Lord Fairfax* (1870).

G. Miller, *Rambles Round the Edgehills* (1900).

Walter Money, *The First and Second Battles of Newbury and the Siege of Donnington Castle, 1643–46* (1881).

Canon R. H. Morris, *The Siege of Chester, 1643–46* (Chester 1924).

A. L. Morton, *The English Utopia* (1952).

Newark on Trent: The Civil War Siegeworks (The Royal Commission on Historical Monuments 1964).

Wallace Notestein, *The Winning of the Initiative by the House of Commons* (Ralegh Lecture 1924).

Sir Charles Oman, *A History of the Art of War in the Sixteenth Century* (1937).

G. Ormerod, *History of the County Palatine* (1882).

R. H. Parry, ed., *The English Civil War and After, 1642–58* (1970).

D. H. Pennington and I. A. Roots, *The Committee at Stafford, 1642–45* (Manchester 1957).

J. R. Phillips, *Memoirs of the Civil War in Wales and the Marches*, 2 vols (1874).

J. R. Powell, *The Navy in the English Civil War* (1962).

Basil N. Reckitt, *Charles the First and Hull, 1639–45* (1952).

Michael Roberts, *Essays in Swedish History* (1967). Essay 3, 'Gustav Adolf and the Art of

War'; Essay 6, 'Cromwell and the Baltic'; and Essay 7, 'The Military Revolution, 1560–1660'.

Colonel H. C. B. Rogers, *Battles and Generals of the Civil Wars* (1968).

D. M. Ross, *Langport and its Church* (Langport 1911).

Ian Roy, *The Royalist Army in the First Civil War*, unpublished Oxford D.Phil. thesis (1963).

——, *The Royalist Ordnance Papers, 1642–46*, Part I (Oxfordshire Record Society 1964).

J. R. Tanner, *English Constitutional Conflicts of the Seventeenth Century* (1928).

C. Thomas-Stanford, *Sussex in the Great Civil War and the Interregnum, 1642–60* (1910).

H. G. Tibbutt, *The Life and Letters of Sir Lewis Dyve* (Bedfordshire Historical Records Society 1948).

Margaret Toynbee and Brigadier Peter Young, *Cropredy Bridge, 1644* (Kineton 1970).

H. R. Trevor-Roper, *Historical Essays* (1957).

John Tucker and Lewis S. Winstock, eds, *The English Civil War* (1972).

Norman Tucker, *Royalist Officers of North Wales, 1642–60* (Colwyn Bay 1961).

Major G. Tylden, *Horses and Saddelry* (1965).

D. Underdown, *Royalist Conspiracy in England, 1649–60* (New Haven 1960).

——, *Pride's Purge* (Oxford 1971).

E. A. Walford, *Edgehill: the Battle and the Battlefield* . . . (Banbury 1886).

John Webb, *The Siege of Portsmouth in the Civil War*, The Portsmouth Papers (Portsmouth 1969).

C. V. Wedgwood, *The Thirty Years War* (1962).

——, *The Great Rebellion: The King's Peace* (1955).

——, *The Great Rebellion: The King's War* (1958).

Peter Wenham, *The Great and Close Siege of York, 1644* (Kineton 1970).

A. C. Wood, *Nottinghamshire and the Civil War* (Oxford 1937).

Austin Woolrych, *Battles of the English Civil War* (1961).

——, *Penruddock's Rising* (Historical Association Pamphlet 1955).

Brigadier Peter Young, *Oliver Cromwell* (1962).

——, *Edgehill 1642* (Kineton 1967).

——, *Marston Moor 1644* (Kineton 1970).

Brigadier Peter Young and John Adair, *Hastings to Culloden* (1964).

P. Zagorin, *A History of Political Thought in the English Revolution* (1954).

SECONDARY SOURCES: ARTICLES

Abbreviations:

EHR   *English Historical Review*
TRHS   *Transactions of the Royal Historical Society*
JSAHR *Journal of the Society for Army Historical Research*
P&P   *Past and Present*

John Adair, 'The Court Martial Papers of Sir William Waller's Army, 1644', *JSAHR*, 1966.

T. Arnold, 'Notes on the Battle of Edgehill', *EHR*, 1887.

The Rev. E. J. Bodington, 'The Battle of Roundway Down', *The Wiltshire Archaeological and Natural History Magazine*, 1912.

Godfrey Davies, 'The Parliamentary Army Under the Earl of Essex', *EHR*, 1934.

——, 'The Army of the Eastern Association', *EHR*, 1931.

The Hon. H. A. Dillon, 'On a MS. list of Officers of the London Trained Bands in 1643', *Archaeologia*, 1890.

Sir Charles H. Firth, 'Marston Moor', *TRHS*, 1898.

——, 'The Journal of Prince Rupert's Marches, 5 September 1642 to 4 July 1646', *EHR*, 1898.

——, 'Raising of the Ironsides', *TRHS*, 1899.

——, 'Dunbar', *TRHS*, 1900.

——, Introduction to De Gomme's 'Bristoll taken by Prince Rupert . . .', *JSAHR*, 1925.

P. Geyl, 'Frederick Henry of Orange and King Charles I', *EHR*, vol. 38.

E. Green, 'On the Civil War in Somerset', *Proceedings of the Somerset Archaeological and Natural History Society*, 1867.

H. J. Habakkuk, 'Public Finance and the Sale of confiscated property during the Interregnum', *Economic History Review*, 1962.

F. A. Hyett, 'The Civil War in the Forest of Dean', *Transactions of the Bristol and Gloucestershire Archaeological Society*, 1893–4.

J. R. Jones, 'Booth's Rising', *Bulletin of the John Rylands Library*, 1956–7.

Brian Manning, 'The Nobles, The People and the Constitution', P&P, No. 9, 1956.

Wallace Notestein, 'The Establishment of the Committee of Both Kingdoms', *American Historical Review*, 1911–12.

Colonel W. G. Ross, 'Notes on the Battle of Edgehill', *EHR*, 1887.

Ian Roy, 'The Royalist Council of War', *Bulletin of the Institute of Historical Research*, 1962.

Laurence Stone, 'The Inflation of Honours', *P&P*, No. 14, 1958.

C. S. Terry, 'The Scottish Campaign in Northumberland and Durham', *Archaeologia Aeliana*, 1899.

Joan Thirsk, 'The Sale of Royalist Land during the Interregnum', *Economic History Review*, 1952.

M. Toynbee and J. Leening, 'Cropredy Bridge', *Oxoniensia*, 1938.

H. R. Trevor-Roper, 'The General Crisis of the Seventeenth Century', *P&P*, No. 16, 1959.

——, 'Oliver Cromwell and his Parliaments', *Essays presented to Sir Lewis Namier*, ed. R. Pares and A. J. P. Taylor (1956).

——, *et al*, 'General Symposium', *P&P*, No. 18, 1960.

Norman Tucker, 'Lord Byron's Final Fling', *Transactions of the Anglesey Antiquarian Society and Field Club*, 1968.

Brigadier Peter Young, 'King Charles I's Army of 1642', *JSAHR*, 1938.

——, 'King Charles I's Army of 1643–5', *JSAHR*, 1939.

——, 'The Prince of Wales's Regiment of Horse, 1642–6', 3 parts, *JSAHR*, 1945–6, 1953.

——, 'The Royalist Army at the relief of Newark', *JSAHR*, 1952.

——, 'The Royalist Artillery at Edgehill', *JSAHR*, 1953.

——, 'The Royalist Army at the Battle of Roundway Down', *JSAHR*, 1953.

——, 'The Northern Horse at Naseby', *JSAHR*, 1954.

——, 'The Royalist Army at Edgehill', *JSAHR*, 1955.

INDEX

INDEX